Sociology Unlocked

Sara Cumming

OXFORD
UNIVERSITY PRESS

OXFORD
UNIVERSITY PRESS

Oxford University Press is a department of the University of Oxford.
It furthers the University's objective of excellence in research, scholarship,
and education by publishing worldwide. Oxford is a registered trade mark of
Oxford University Press in the UK and in certain other countries.

Published in Canada by
Oxford University Press
8 Sampson Mews, Suite 204,
Don Mills, Ontario M3C 0H5 Canada

www.oupcanada.com

Library and Archives Canada Cataloguing in Publication
Title: Sociology unlocked / Sara Cumming.
Names: Cumming, Sara, author.
Description: Includes bibliographical references and index.
Identifiers: Canadiana (print) 20190168021 | Canadiana (ebook) 20190168064 | ISBN 9780199031016
(softcover) | ISBN 9780199038664 (loose-leaf) | ISBN 9780199031078 (EPUB)
Subjects: LCSH: Sociology—Textbooks. | LCGFT: Textbooks.
Classification: LCC HM586 .C86 2020 | DDC 301—dc23

Cover image: rubberball/Getty Images
Cover and interior design: Laurie McGregor

Photo of Harriet Martineau, page xxii © Georgios Kollidas | Dreamstime.com
Photo of Harold Innis, page xxii University of Toronto Archives/ B72-0003/Box 034, file 056 © Public Domain nlc-12491
Photo of Kimberlé Williams Crenshaw, page 29 by Mike Coppola/Getty Images for Busboys and Poets

"Bad Guy" words and music by Billie Eilish O'Connell and Finneas O'Connell.
Copyright (c) 2019 UNIVERSAL MUSIC CORP., DRUP and LAST FRONTIER.
All Rights for DRUP Administered by UNIVERSAL MUSIC CORP.
All Rights for LAST FRONTIER Administered Worldwide by KOBALT SONGS MUSIC PUBLISHING.
All Rights Reserved. Used by Permission.
Reprinted by Permission of Hal Leonard LLC

Oxford University Press is committed to our environment.
Wherever possible, our books are printed on paper which comes from
responsible sources.

Printed and bound in the United States of America

1 2 3 4 — 23 22 21 20

Contents

Chapter 1

What Is Sociology?   1

Chapter 2

What Do Sociologists Do?   19

Chapter 3 *Culture* **43**

Chapter 4 *Socialization* **63**

Chapter 5 · *Social Interaction, Groups, and Social Structure 87*

Chapter 6 · *Class Inequality 105*

Chapter 9

"Race" and Racialization   **167**

Chapter 10 *Deviance and Crime 191*

Chapter 11 *Population and Environment 213*

Chapter 12   *Health and Illness*   **235**

Guided Tour of . . . Sociology Unlocked

Sociological forces shape almost everything in our lives, and we in turn affect those forces. It takes a well-developed sociological imagination in order to see and understand how this interaction happens. It is our hope that *Sociology Unlocked* will not only unlock your sociological imagination, but will also help you understand why this skill is so important.

In preparing this new book, we had one paramount goal: to produce the most authentic, applied, and accessible introduction to sociology available to Canadian students. We hope that as you browse through the pages that follow, you will see why *Sociology Unlocked* is the most practical and relatable textbook available to Canadian sociology students today.

What Makes This a One-of-a-Kind Textbook

A Canadian Textbook for Twenty-first Century Canadian Students

While people raised in Canada may find it difficult to understand why female circumcision is allowed to continue, many girls and women allegedly choose to have the procedure, and women have resisted and even opposed changing these practices in some countries (Althaus, 1997). Research reveals that, often, in the cultures in which female circumcision occurs, if a woman has not been circumcised she will not be viewed as marriageable and thus will live a life of poverty (Althaus, 1997). Additionally, attempts by England, the United States, Canada, or the United Nations to impose change are often seen by citizens of these countries where it is practised as patronizing and just another attempt at colonialism—the practice of acquiring control over another country and then exploiting it economically (Althaus, 1997).

Another explosive topic is the treatment of animals. Bullfighting is a traditional spectacle in Spain, parts of southern France, and some Latin American countries in which humans (called matadors) fight one or more bulls in a bullring. Although in North America this practice is seen as cruel and unnecessary, within the areas where it is practised, bullfighting is considered a highly ritualized cultural event and art form, which some see as deeply tied to Spanish culture and identity. Dogfighting is also commonly practised for revenue in many places. Traditionally, the dogs fight until one dies and the owner of the winning dog earns all of the money. While this is illegal in many countries, it is common practice in some cultures.

An extension of cultural relativism is xenocentrism, whereby rather than merely attempting to assess another culture based on its own merit, people assume that everything about another culture is superior to their own. For example, even though the Niagara Region in Ontario and the Okanagan Valley in British Columbia are known for their wine, many Canadians assume French or Italian wines are superior (whether they drink wine themselves or not). Japanese electronics, German cars, and Swiss chocolate are also perceived to be superior to domestic-made products.

xenocentrism The preference for a culture other than one's own.

Canadian Culture

Is there a Canadian culture that distinguishes us from, for example, Americans—our nearest neighbours? Where researchers do find cultural differences between Canadians and Americans, they find Canadians to be less traditional and elitist. Both in our social policies, such as medicare, and in our attitudes toward the disadvantaged, Canadians are much more egalitarian than Americans. Other likely differences in preferences are between liberty (Americans prefer more) and order (Canadians prefer more).

The Tragically Hip are Canadian icons although they reached only minimal fame globally. Arguably, this is because their lyrics often focus on Canadian history and events, and challenge elements of Canadian identity. After frontman Gord Downie was diagnosed with terminal brain cancer, the band went on tour, ending in the band's hometown of Kingston, Ontario, in 2016. CBC televised the sold-out venue across Canada, and almost 12 million viewers tuned in. During the show, Downie begged Prime Minister Justin Trudeau to address the deplorable conditions under which Indigenous people are forced to live in Canada. Downie passed away in October 2017.

58   Sociology Unlocked

Written by Canadians for Canadians, *Sociology Unlocked* uses recent major events relevant to Canadians— such as Gord Downie's final tour, the Humboldt crash, the opioid crisis, the National Inquiry into the Missing and Murdered Indigenous Women and Girls' Final Report, the body positivity movement, and many more—to illustrate sociological concepts.

An Accessible yet Academic Approach

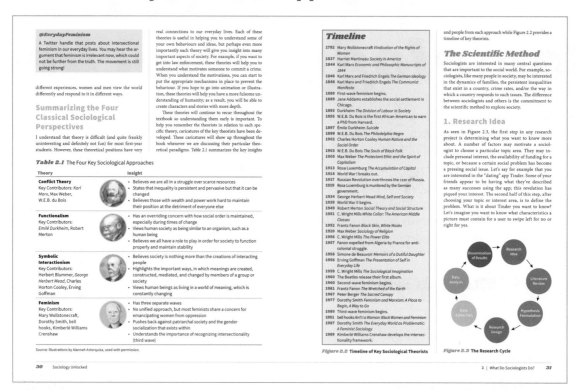

Author Sara Cumming's unique and authentic narrative voice presents complex topics—including key theories in every chapter—in easy-to-understand, relatable language that helps to unlock students' sociological imaginations.

Practical Application in Every Chapter

In addition to the engaging examples and clear explanations throughout, every chapter includes a Practicing Sociology box, which is an interactive activity that helps students apply what they have learned. These activities can be done alone or assigned in class in order to help students immediately see how sociology interacts with their everyday lives.

A Student-Friendly Visual Presentation

Chapter 4

Socialization

Do you love or hate to read? Do you think your feelings about reading are purely related to your personal interests or to your intellectual abilities? If you love reading, can you trace where and when this love began? Researchers have found that reading to children every day improves their understanding of words and concepts at young ages and also improves their memories throughout their lives (Hutton, Horowitz-Kraus, Mendelsohn, DeWitt, & Holland, 2015). In addition to these positive developmental effects, spending this one-on-one time with a child helps to foster the parental bond, transmitting different types of knowledge such as how to parent and how to develop a routine. In this chapter you will learn how your interactions with different social agents, such as your parents, friends, school, and the media, have helped shape who you are today. You will begin to see how your relationships with people and your interests (such as reading) have been socialized into you from a young age.

▲ Michael Berman/Getty Images

Learning Outcomes

1. Understand the role of socialization
2. Critique the nature versus nurture debate as it relates to sociology
3. Summarize the different theoretical approaches to socialization
4. Outline the agents of socialization
5. Describe how resocialization can be voluntary or involuntary

Key Terms

agents of socialization
biological determinism
cognitive theory of development
degradation ceremony
feral children
gender socialization
looking-glass self
peer group
primary socialization
resocialization
secondary socialization
social integration
socialization
total institutions

Introduction

Socialization is one of the most important forces acting on us throughout our lives. Like culture, socialization is also essential for the survival and stability of a society. And as members of society, we must learn how to be active members of our communities to maintain the social structure. We need to learn how to follow rules and to develop a work ethic, and we also learn to purchase products to maintain capitalism. We also need to learn how to reproduce—not simply the act of having children, but the process of passing down our cultures from one generation to the next.

The Role of Socialization

Socialization is often defined as the social learning a person goes through to become a capable member of society. The learning is "social" because we learn through interactions with other people. These interactions teach us a society's language, skills, likes and dislikes, norms, values, and beliefs.

> **socialization** The learning process through which an individual becomes a capable member of society.

Although the techniques used to teach beliefs, values, and norms are somewhat similar in many societies, the content of socialization differs greatly from society to society. Our body language, way of speaking (including language, accent, and slang), food preferences, music tastes, and expected lifestyle are all functions of the culture in which we are raised. We are also, at the same time, influenced by other social influences, such as the class in which we are raised, our ethnicity, whether or not we are racialized by those around us, the religion in which we are raised, our

When it comes to Halloween, many women are expected to wear revealing costumes that emphasize physical attractiveness: maid, "sexy nurse," etcetera. Men, on the other hand, are expected to choose costumes that emphasize strength and competitiveness: superhero, policeman, doctor, and so forth. What does this tell us about how men and women are socialized differently? What are the consequences?

© Banxpix | Dreamstime.com

64   Sociology Unlocked

---

consistent with a sociological view, as it takes environmental factors into consideration and recognizes the systemic discrimination that exists within society when considering an individual's circumstances.

world and provides the character reminders of their economic positi amines the cycle of poverty that is coping skills that children develop t social position.

Top 10 Takeaways

1 Social stratification is the hierarchical arrangement of individuals based on wealth, power, and prestige.
pp. 107–112

2 Most assume Canada to be a meritocracy—a system whereby if you work hard you have equal chances for success.
pp. 107–108

3 There are four systems of stratification: slavery, caste, clan, and class.
pp. 110–112

4 The four theoretical approaches look at different elements of inequality. Functionalists use the Davis-Moore hypothesis to argue that inequality is functional and necessary for the well-being of society. Conflict theorists argue that inequality is a result of the bourgeoisie exerting their power over the proletariat. Feminist theorists are concerned with the gendered patterns of inequality apparent both in the home and in the workplace. Symbolic interactionists highlight the ways in which people display their wealth through conspicuous consumption.
pp. 112–113

5 Most of the elites in Canada were born into their wealth and continue to pass it down generationally.
pp. 114–116

6 The middle class is slowly disappearing in Canada.
p. 116

7 Poverty is a term used to describe situations in which people lack opportunities available to the average citizen. Absolute poverty refers to the inability to afford particular goods, while relative poverty refers to the perceived difference between your own circumstances and those around you.
pp. 116–117

8 The most common measures of poverty are the LICO (an absolute measure based on the percentage of income spent on necessities), LIM (a relative measure that is calculated based on 50 per cent of the median income, adjusted for household sizes), and MBM (an absolute measure based on the cost of a set of goods representing a modest standard of living).
p. 117

9 The five most disadvantaged groups in Canada are women, single adults, Indigenous people, visible minority and recent immigrants, and disabled people.
pp. 117–119

10 There are two prominent explanations for poverty. One blames the victim, stating that individuals are responsible for their life situations. The second blames the system, which takes environmental factors into consideration.
pp. 119–120, 122

122   Sociology Unlocked

Student learning is scaffolded throughout the text, with each chapter starting with clear learning objectives and key terms, and ending with a list of top ten takeaways for each chapter, questions for critical thought, and additional resources. Key sociological theories within the chapter are accompanied by icons that visually signal to students when and which theory is being discussed, and helps them draw connections between theories introduced elsewhere in the book.

Icons that Appear Throughout the Book

Image	Name	Signifier
	Sara Cumming	Personal reflections of the author
	Émile Durkheim	Functionalism
	Charles H. Cooley	Symbolic interactionism
	Karl Marx	Conflict theory
	Dorothy Smith	Feminist theory
	W. E. B. Du Bois	Critical race theory
	bell hooks	Intersectional theory

Sources: Illustration of Sara Cumming provided by David Bragdon; Illustrations of Durkheim, Cooley, Marx, Smith, Du Bois and hooks provided by Alannah Astorquiza; used with permission

Media Recommendations Throughout

Pop culture examples are integrated into the chapters and appear as media recommendations that provide suggested videos, websites, television, films, and podcasts related to the topics under discussion, encouraging students to apply concepts in the chapter beyond the book. Note: Some of these recommendations are available for free streaming as part of our Sociology Streaming Video Collection (see below).

Because of the abundance of resources in Canada, and the time scales at which resource depletion is occurring, it can be difficult to see that we are running out of precious resources, such as water, when we look around our environment. And keep in mind that over 100 Indigenous communities in Canada do not have access to clean water (see Chapter 9). Inequality can also hide the scarcity of certain resources.

energy, industrial uses, and human consumption. Most agricultural production is water intensive, and "agriculture alone accounts for 70% of all water withdrawn by the combined agriculture, municipal and industrial (including energy) sectors" (ENESCO, 2017). Thus, as the global population continues to grow, and the demand for food continues to grow, the demand for water will grow accordingly.

Like water, most of the natural resources we need are non-renewable: there is only so much petroleum, aluminum, iron, etc., on (or in) the earth. Once we have used it all . . . well, no one knows how to finish that sentence yet. One strategy is recycling these materials to get more use out of them. Another is to invent alternatives (for example, synthetic rubber to replace rubber extracted from a rubber tree) or find natural alternatives (for example, wind or solar power to replace petroleum). A third strategy is to look for new resources in currently inaccessible places (for instance, under the sea, at the centre of the earth, or on asteroids). A fourth is to reduce the rate at which we use these resources; however, this is only a short-term answer as it only slows down the inevitable disappearance of these finite resources.

Cowspiracy: The Sustainability Secret

Dir. Kip Andersen and Keegan Kuhn (2014). A documentary exploring the effects on the planet of large-scale farming. This documentary argues that these large-scale farming operations are the leading cause of global warming, water depletion, species extinction, deforestation, and ocean dead zones.

Before the Flood

Dir. Fisher Stevens (2016). A documentary featuring actor and environmental activist Leonardo DiCaprio. The film discusses all of the opposition to climate change. DiCaprio critiques the level of fossil fuels emitted by the US.

Theoretical Approaches to the Environment

With global temperatures and sea levels rising, we have begun to see new issues developing that we may not be entirely prepared for. While sociology has generally kept its distance from natural sciences, the effects of climate change are generating problems that need to be understood from a sociological perspective as much as a scientific one. We need to not only understand the effects of climate change on the population but also the causes that can be traced back to how our society is organized, functions, and is reproduced. Furthermore, each of the sociological theories has a part to play in understanding these issues.

Functionalism

Functionalists, concerned especially with the proper and effective functioning of society and how that can be reproduced, are concerned with how climate change will disrupt our social systems and infrastructure. For example, higher than average summer temperatures mean there is more demand on power systems as people try to shelter themselves from the heat, while more intense and frequent storms can cause damage resulting in even more outages (Dominianni et al., 2018). This can

11 | Population and Environment **227**

Contemporary Cases and Compelling Viewpoints

In addition to the Practicing Sociology boxes, *Sociology Unlocked* features five other types of boxes that illustrate sociological concepts by highlighting how contemporary issues, events, and ideas relate to the topics at hand.

#Sociology

#CommitSociology

In 2013 and again in 2014, then prime minister Stephen Harper urged Canadians not to "commit sociology." His 2013 comments were in reference to an alleged terrorist plot against VIA Rail, where he proclaimed that Canada was facing a serious threat and thus it was not a time to "commit sociology." His comments in 2014 were in reference to a national inquiry into missing and murdered Indigenous women. He urged Canadians to stop viewing the tragedy of missing and murdered Indigenous women as a "sociological phenomenon" and instead "view it as a crime."

In response, critical thinkers from many disciplines fought back with articles and information on why these issues were precisely sociological phenomenon. Crime is a social phenomenon that is most often shaped by powerful historical social forces, and so it needs to be understood and examined more deeply than as someone's simply choosing to "break the law." Treating these "crimes" as standalone cases erases the colonial history of Canada as well as the current disadvantages experienced by Indigenous people in this country that put them at higher risk of violence. Such disadvantages include infrastructure issues, poverty and lack of access to employment, and lack of social services (Amnesty International Canada, 2018). The oppression of Indigenous people, who were removed from their homes, stripped of their culture and language, and far too often physically and sexually abused, has led to a society that too often dehumanizes Indigenous peoples and ignores their demands for justice. As you will learn in this chapter, there is a strong link between what happens to individual people and the broader social forces at work in society. A Twitter feed was started, #commitsociology, to keep sociological inquiry at the forefront of a variety of events and issues.

Look up *#sociology* on your social media platform of choice: What kinds of social issues are being discussed?

#Sociology boxes describe online social phenomena related to chapter content in order to help students relate chapter content to their everyday experiences on social media.

In the News

The Burden of Proof in Rape and Sexual Assault Cases

Jian Ghomeshi, centre left, with his lawyer, arriving to court in 2016.

Prior to being charged with sexual assault, Jian Ghomeshi was a household name across Canada among those 40 years of age and older. Throughout the 1990s, he was a member of the band Moxy Früvous, and he became a television and radio broadcaster in the early 2000s. He held many positions at CBC, with his most prominent being Q, a talk show that featured interviews with prominent entertainment and cultural figures. The show, which ran from 2007 until his dismissal in 2014, was the highest rated show in CBC history (Zekas, 2010).

In 2014, an ex-girlfriend of Ghomeshi's made accusations that he had engaged in non-consensual rough sex—an accusation he denied. A few months later, CBC terminated Ghomeshi, stating that evidence had come to light that required CBC to discontinue its relationship with him. The evidence included private pictures and videos related to his sexual life. Less than a month later, Ghomeshi was charged with four counts of sexual assault and one count of overcoming resistance by choking. The charges were in relation to three separate women (CBC News, 2014). Three months later, Ghomeshi was charged with three additional counts of sexual assault related to three more women (Donovan & Hasham, 2015).

Ghomeshi's trial began on 1 February 2016 and lasted eight days. Despite six women sharing very similar stories of non-consensual sexual violence, Ghomeshi was found not guilty. In a number of the cases the women had engaged in what could be considered amicable, or even flirtatious, behaviour with Ghomeshi after the alleged attack occurred. The judge ruled that this behaviour problematized their accusations and went against what he deemed to be appropriate behaviour by a victim. Experts on victimization, however, argue that putting the victims' post-incident behaviour on trial is unfair as there is often much confusion following an assault, with some women at least partially blaming themselves for the incident (Donovan, 2016).

The Ghomeshi case draws our attention to the intersections of class, gender, and power in the criminal justice system—Ghomeshi was a well-known, wealthy man—but also to the difficulties associated with the burden of proof being on the female accuser. The criminal justice system's understanding of sexual assaults and the responses of (mostly) female victims is still gravely misunderstood.

In the News boxes tie chapter content to contemporary news stories, helping students understand sociology in the real world.

World Events

Where Does Our Technology Go?

Companies such as Apple (as an example) are always competing to release a newer and faster model. During the writing of this textbook, for example, Apple released the iPhone X, the iPhone XR, and the iPhone XS, with an expectation that the iPhone 11 would be released before this book publishes. Apple sold an estimated 30 million of these new iPhones in the first few months. What happened to those phones that most of those 30 million people already had prior to obtaining the newest release?

According to a recent United Nations report, China is the largest e-waste—electronic waste consisting of computers and cellphones, among other items—dumping site in the world (Watson, 2013). Many of these products were initially manufactured in China and are returned to China when no longer in use. Indeed, the United Nations data suggests that about 70 per cent of global electronic waste ends up there (Watson, 2013).

For the past decade, Guiyu, a town located in China's main manufacturing zone, has been the largest hub for disposal of e-waste (Watson, 2013). The United Nations report indicates that Guiyu is experiencing an "environmental calamity" as a result of this disposal industry. Toxic pollutions are released during the recycling processes, contaminating workers and the environment with heavy metals—such as lead, beryllium, and cadmium—while simultaneously releasing hydrocarbon ashes into the air, water, and soil (Wason, 2013). In 2018, however, Beijing officially stopped accepting garbage from other countries and China has embarked on a mission to rid the country of toxic waste (Petric, 2018).

Canada produces more solid waste per capita than any other country in the world, and recently our attempts to dump this waste in other countries (such as the Philippines and Malaysia) have been denied (Ferreras & Drolet, 2019). We will need to find new strategies for processing our own waste (and, ideally, producing less of it in the first place) if we want to avoid further international incidents.

How many smart phones have you gone through in your lifetime? Have you ever thought about the environmental impact of discarding your old smart phone for a new model?

World Events boxes bring global content into each chapter, ensuring that students understand how topics connect not just to their lives in Canada, but to the rest of the world as well.

From My Perspective

Katie and Jess

Unlike the majority of couples we know, we are high school sweethearts! We were both known as jocks in high school and quickly became inseparable friends at the age of 14. Feelings developed on both sides just as they would in any other typical young romance. For us it was quite simple—we met, we dated, we fell in love—just like we see all couples falling in love in the media. It was, however, not that simple for society.

Being a same-sex couple meant that we had to "come out of the closet." Such a ridiculous concept when you don't feel as though you were ever *in* a closet to begin with! Our "coming out" story is a lot less terrible and dramatic than many others we know of; however, it was still accompanied by the loss of some friendships and the loss of communication with some family members. There were feelings of exclusion and people stumbling over words because they seemed to no longer know how to speak to us, as if the fact that we were gay changed the people we had been our entire lives. Some people overcompensate while trying to be careful to not offend, and others just throw out offensive remarks freely.

Katie and Jess, a 33-year-old married couple currently living and working in Yellowknife, Canada.

As the stages of life progressed, we watched siblings and cousins enter heterosexual relationships and new partners were welcomed into the family fold with no questions asked. There was an almost immediate banter about marriage and babies with these couples, but nobody ever jokes or speaks about these things with us. Most people likely do not even realize they are doing this.

Society says that the next step in a relationship is marriage, so that is what we did. Please don't get us wrong—we loved each other and were very committed to one another, but the internal desire to follow the norm was an influencing factor in the decision to legally marry. Contrary to popular belief, lesbian relationships go through all the same kinds of difficulties as straight relationships. Life happens, people change, we forget to put each other first, we don't equally share the household responsibilities, partners are taken for granted, and marriages struggle. We ended up needing to go see a counsellor, which should have been a simple process of looking up local practitioners, phoning, and making an appointment. However, for gay couples, the process is a little more complex as we must first find out which counsellors are open to working with same-sex couples.

After a lot of work and self-reflection, reconnecting, and refocusing on what is truly important, we have decided to start a family! We are surrounded by nieces and nephews and have known for a long time that we wanted our own child. We want nothing more than to welcome a little bundle of joy into our lives that will eventually become a teenager and make us question every life decision we have ever made (we have watched our siblings struggle through their children's teen years with half their sanity intact). For most heterosexual couples starting a family, it is as simple as no longer using your method of birth control. As a same sex couple we had far more decision making ahead of us: Would we adopt or carry? Which one of us would carry? Would we both carry? Where and how would we get the semen? How do we choose the donor? How do we pay for the insemination? If we adopt, which agencies support gay adoptions? How long are the lists? How much money will it cost?

We are still on this journey and can tell you that it is very difficult to continuously be jumping over hurdle after hurdle in our quest to be a family.

Source: Provided by Jess Collins, used by permission.

From My Perspective boxes incorporate diverse voices from contributors who relate their experiences to the chapter topic, modelling the sociological imagination for students.

Current Research

The Relationship between Housing and Health

Housing and income are two of the most important social determinants of health (SDOH). Research shows that being unhoused can lead to poor mental and physical health. Conversely, experiences of poor mental and physical health place people at greater risk of experiencing housing loss. Most people who experience homelessness in Canada do so on a short-term basis. However, health outcomes are much worse for the small proportion of individuals who are homeless for long periods of time.

A recent study conducted by Julia Woodhall-Melnik et al. (Woodhall-Melnik, Dunn, Svenson, Patterson, & Matheson, 2018) investigated the journeys of 25 men into chronic or long-term homelessness. Dr Woodhall-Melnik and her team conducted a thematic analysis of transcripts from semi-structured interviews with men who had been homeless for 30 days or longer in 2014. They found that all of the men interviewed had experienced trauma or adversity in youth. Examples of this trauma or adversity included living in severe poverty; having interactions with the youth justice and child protection systems; experiencing physical injury; having early onset mental illness; experiencing early substance use; witnessing parental or caregiver substance use; being abandoned by a caregiver; and undergoing physical, sexual, or emotional abuse.

Woodhall-Melnik et al. (2018) theorize that the men who experienced youth trauma and long-term homelessness followed one of three paths:

1. *Entry into homelessness during youth.* The men in this pathway described leaving their caregivers' homes, couch surfing, and living in other unstable conditions before the age of 18. They left high school and ultimately ending up on the streets or in emergency shelters.

2. *Entry into homelessness during adulthood.* The men in this pathway lived with their caregivers until they were able to move into rented accommodations. This was often done with friends or romantic partners. These men held jobs and many experienced layoffs, job loss, or workplace injuries, which were followed by problematic substance use and relationship loss. For many of these men, their entry into homelessness corresponded with the loss of their relationships.

3. *Entry into homelessness during later adulthood.* The men in this pathway experienced mental illness or developmental delays and remained with their parents or caregivers until they passed away. These men were then left without the means to care for themselves and subsequently entered homelessness.

These pathways indicate a need to provide youth who experience trauma or adversity with targeted services to improve health, housing, and social outcomes in later life.

Source: Provided by Dr Julia Woodhall-Melnik.

Current Research boxes describe contemporary social research on the topic, helping students to understand how sociological research is done.

Online Resources

Sociology Unlocked is part of a comprehensive package of learning and teaching tools that includes resources for both students and instructors.

Dashboard: OUP's Learning Management System platform

Dashboard is a text-specific integrated learning system that offers quality content and tools to track student progress in an intuitive, web-based learning environment. It features a streamlined interface that connects students and lecturers with the functions used most frequently, simplifying the learning experience to save time and put student progress first.

In addition to the functionality of Dashboard as a platform, Dashboard for *Sociology Unlocked* includes the following content:

- Integrated ebook
- Interactive Flash Cards
- Student sociological survey with viewable results
- Self-grading quizzes for students. Each chapter has:
- 25 multiple choice questions
- 10 true/false questions
- Integrated test bank

Dashboard for *Sociology Unlocked* is available through your OUP sales representative, or visit dashboard.oup.com.

OUP Canada's Sociology Streaming Video Library

Sociology Video Collection

Click on the link to download the Video Viewing Guide for all 23 videos of the Sociology Collection (PDF).

Over 20 award-winning feature films and documentaries of various lengths (feature-length, short films, and clips) are available online as streaming video for instructors to either show in the classroom or assign to students to watch at home. An accompanying video guide contains summaries, suggested clips, discussion questions, and related activities so that instructors can easily integrate videos into their course lectures, assignments, and class discussions. Access to this collection is free for instructors who have assigned this book for their course. The ebook version of *Sociology Unlocked* offers links to relevant videos integrated throughout, with no additional login required. For access when using the print version of this book, speak to your OUP sales representative, or visit www.oupcanada.com/SocVideos.

 Ancillary Resource Center

Student and Instructor Supplements to the Text

OUP Canada offers a wide range of supplementary online items for students and instructors alike, all designed to enhance and complete the learning and teaching experience. These resources are available at www.oup.com/he/Cumming

For Students

A comprehensive Student Study Guide includes lists of learning objectives and key terms, critical thinking questions, recommended readings, recommended online resources, and self-grading quizzes to help you review the textbook and classroom material and to take concepts further.

For Instructors

The following resources are free to qualified adopters of the textbook. Please contact your OUP sales representative for more information:

- An extensive Test Generator enables instructors to sort, edit, import, and distribute a bank of questions in multiple-choice, true–false, and short-answer formats.
- A comprehensive instructor's manual provides an extensive set of pedagogical tools and suggestions for every chapter, including a sample syllabus, lecture outlines, suggested in-class or assigned activities, suggested teaching aids, cumulative assignments, and cumulative essay questions.
- Classroom-ready PowerPoint slides summarize key points from each chapter and incorporate graphics and tables drawn straight from the text.

About the Author

Leah Burton

Sara Cumming is a professor of sociology at Sheridan College and is the chair of Applied Sociology in Canada, a research cluster under the Canadian Sociological Association. Her primary research interest is in the area of gender and social inequality, focusing particularly on social assistance, subsidized housing, subsidized child care, and student loan programs. Dr Cumming's most recent research grant is a collaboration with Dr Michael McNamara, which relies on qualitative research and creative problem solving to help community partners produce new, creative, and fundable projects aimed at ameliorating hardships for Halton's vulnerable populations. She has also taken on the role of executive director for the non-profit Home Suite Hope, a program offering wrap-around services to move lone mother–led families from homelessness to self-sufficiency.

Acknowledgements

Although I remain solely responsible for the content of this textbook, it reflects the collective input and support of numerous people, only a handful of whom are named in the paragraphs that follow. Whether they are named or not, my heartfelt thanks go out to them all.

I would like to send a special thank you to Lorne Tepperman, who first introduced me to the idea of writing this introductory text for the college classroom and who acted as a mentor throughout the process. Lorne's talent to write quickly and effectively is remarkable, as is his ability to bring his students into the process. Thank you for checking up on me throughout the process and for continuing to cheer me on in the final stages.

I would like to acknowledge two promising former students with whom I have had the pleasure to work: Mark Omiencinski and Tierney Kobryn-Dietrich provided invaluable assistance in the editing phases of the text and ensured that the examples used were current and would resonate with the student body. In addition, I would like to thank the team of animation and illustration students from Sheridan College, who provided much material for the text: Alannah Astorquiza, David Bragdon, Kayden Chan, Zach Gray, and Alexandria Phillips. In addition, I would like to thank all of the people who contributed to the "In My Perspective" boxes. I am grateful that you were willing to share pieces of your life with the readers in hopes of offering a new lens through which they might view a social issue.

Throughout my academic journey I have been very fortunate to find myself surrounded by a strong group of mentors who continue to inspire and motivate me. I will be forever thankful to Michelle Webber, Viola Shuart, Kate Bezanson, June Corman, Ann Duffy, and Lea Caragata for first believing in me and then convincing me to believe in myself. I would also like to thank three colleagues, Jessica Pulis, Morgan Dennis, and Michael McNamara, who have provided me with countless hours of intellectual discussion, feedback, and support in every project that I take on and, in the process, have become important friends. Lastly, I would like to thank Augie Fleras, a man of few words in face-to-face interactions but a prolific researcher and writer. I never had the pleasure of working under Augie during my doctorate at the University of Waterloo, yet I count him as one of the most influential people in that experience. Augie's love and dedication to the writing process is beyond admirable as is his advice on getting it done: "Stop whining, sit down and do it. End of discussion."

To my family by birth and by choice, thank you for always encouraging me to reach higher, even when that requires an unbelievable amount of patience and tolerance on all of your parts. Tom, you always offer me incredible patience and support—even when you are visibly exhausted by my never-ending list of projects. Talor, Maddy, Ryleigh, and Kennedy: thank you first for providing me with many of the anecdotes throughout this text; and second, for always accepting that I share our trials and tribulations in my classrooms and now in text. Watching the four of you grow into adulthood has been the most rewarding experience of my life (although scary and exhausting, too). I can't wait to see where all your paths take you next and to see what kind of material it provides me for future use.

I would like to thank the team at Oxford University Press, particularly Ian Nussbaum, who convinced me to take on this endeavour and believed in my vision for something less formal and more practical for the college classroom. Amy Gordon, my developmental editor, is also deserving of the sincerest thank you for patiently guiding me to the version of the text that is presented here. In writing anything of this magnitude, I experienced many tough days where I couldn't clearly see the vision or how to move forward. Amy's kindness and incredible knowledge helped me to keep moving forward, strengthening difficult sections and bringing fresh ideas to the project. I would also like to thank copy editor Colleen Ste. Marie.

Finally, I would like to thank the following reviewers, as well as the anonymous reviewers, who spent many hours reading the manuscript in rough form and offering constructive criticisms and insightful suggestions for the new edition:

- Angela Aujla, Georgian College
- Alexa Carson, Humber College
- Joel Casséus, Vanier College
- Erin Dolmage, Seneca College
- Kathleen Flynn, Durham College
- Tara Gauld, Confederation College
- Cindy Gervais, Fleming College
- Melanie Greene, Memorial University of Newfoundland and College of the North Atlantic
- Thomas Groulx, St Clair College
- Monique Harvison, Humber Institute of Technology and Advanced Learning
- Anthony Iafrate, Lambton College
- Lise Kozlinski, Durham College
- Peter Laurie, Fleming College
- Mikhael Missakabo, George Brown College
- Monireh Mohammadi, University of Guelph-Humber
- John Patterson, Canadore College
- Krista Robson, Red Deer College
- Marlene Santin, Sheridan College

Sara Cumming, Professor of Sociology
Department of Social and Life Sciences
Sheridan Institute of Technology and Advanced Learning
Oakville, Ontario
e-mail: sara.cumming@sheridancollege.ca

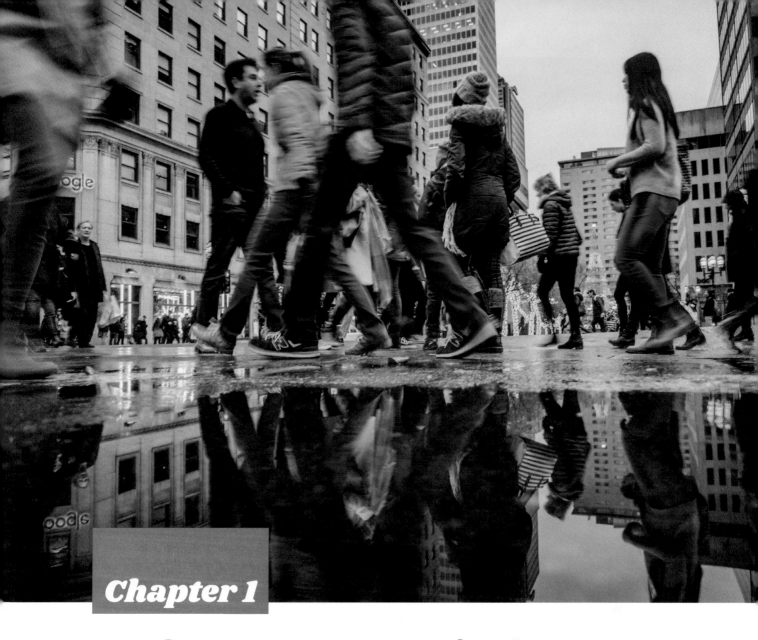

Chapter 1

What Is Sociology?

We all like to believe that we are individuals who make our own decisions and choices about most of the aspects of our lives. Think about a simple choice you made this morning: You woke up and chose a particular pair of shoes to wear. You might say that those shoes were the ones that you felt best matched your outfit or were the most comfortable. However, look around the room at your classmates' shoes. You will most likely see that many people made choices similar to yours.

There is, in fact, much more going on here than simply personal choice. Personal choice is shaped by many factors external to you, including your financial circumstances, your family, your peers, and the media. Examining these factors and how they have influenced you is an example of sociological inquiry. A sociological analysis requires us to look beyond your personal circumstances to the larger social, economic, and cultural environment in which you reside.

Introduction

Prior to becoming a student in post-secondary school, I used to think that professors had such different lives than I did—in my mind, they definitely had a higher socio-economic status, had their lives together, and were brilliant people who got through school with ease. My life, on the other hand, was far from "together," and I was extremely poor. My circumstances felt unique, much like how your choice of what to wear today felt like a reflection of your own personal taste. I did not feel like college or university was a place where I would belong.

I was born to a 16-year-old mother and a 20-year-old father in the mid-1970s when children out of wedlock were less common. Just prior to my birth, my parents were forced to marry and to become financially independent of their parents. Eighteen months later, my mother gave birth to a second child, my brother. Within one year of my brother's birth, my parents separated, and my brother and I moved into a tiny two-bedroom apartment with my then 19-year-old mother. For the next decade, we survived on social assistance (welfare) in a rural community in the Niagara Region of Ontario with no mode of transportation. (There were no city buses and Uber did not yet exist.)

Being poor shapes your life in many ways. Not only is it difficult to obtain the basic necessities of life, it is almost impossible to keep up with your peer group in social settings. We didn't have the "right" clothing and couldn't purchase the hot lunches or book orders at school; nor could we regularly attend any of our classmates' birthday parties as we couldn't purchase the necessary gifts or get to the party location. Being poor meant that we were generally isolated, with the exception of those who lived within walking distance of our house (which was difficult considering we lived in a rural area).

Being poor also meant something else, though—it meant that in my home there was little focus on education after high school. When you were poor in the 1980s and 1990s, you generally finished high school and then worked full-time at a low-wage job immediately following graduation. Thus, despite having strong grades in school, my work life began quite young and by the age of 17 I was living on my own and working full-time. (Also, because my mom had remarried when I was 12 and I "knew everything," I had rebelled against my parents). I had my first child, unmarried, at 22 years old, and, because of my low-income status, I had to return to work almost immediately after her birth. About a year later, a family member suggested that I go to school. I qualified for an Ontario Student Assistance Program (OSAP) loan and, as a result, was able to attend the local university. The student loan allowed me to concentrate on my studies and to be home in the evenings to put my daughter to bed rather than continuing my evening bartending job. Thus, my foray into post-secondary education began.

It was September of 1999 and I was sitting in a large lecture hall at the local university with my one-year-old daughter safely at the daycare on campus. This was my first sociology class. It was in this class that I started to make the connections between my own experiences and larger social factors. I learned that the decisions I had made in my life up until that point were really an accumulation of my experiences with my parents, extended family, and peers and of the lessons they had taught me, rather than my personal free choice. Poverty, gender, race, sexuality, and a whole host of other factors had all influenced my decisions. I also learned that for most of my life I had lived in a bubble of sorts, where only those who lived in the same situation had influenced my thinking. I attribute my drastically changing my life to my discovery of sociology as a discipline.

My life has changed in many ways since that first sociology class. I had a second daughter in my third year of university and left their father the first year of my master's degree. I went on to do a doctorate and raised my children as a single mom for a large portion of their lives. I later married a man who also had two daughters from a previous relationship. We have raised our four children together. I have also accomplished many of the things academics aspire to: I have written theses and dissertations, published journal articles, conferenced nationally and internationally, and served on too many academic and non-academic committees to list.

The thing that I have remained most passionate about, however, has been teaching Introduction to Sociology. More than anything, I enjoy finding ways to relate the material to my students' lives. I am not naive enough to believe that all the students who encounter this material will have the same sort of light bulb moment or find a deep connection to the material the way that I did. I do, however, aspire to give individuals the capacity to use their sociological toolkit to help them navigate their relationships and understand the world around them. The skills you learn in sociology are transferable to all different types of employment and will inform your work whether it is in the arts, the health sector, the humanities, or the sciences.

In the many trials and tribulations of teaching introductory courses, I have learned that sharing my life and the lives of my immediate family members in lectures helps students to better grasp the concepts. (This is the most common comment on my course evaluations.) At times, this also has allowed students to see that while our social positions at birth structure many aspects of our lives, we do have some control in the direction our lives take. My social position at birth as the daughter of a teenager receiving welfare is quite different from my current position as a professor of sociology in a post-secondary institution—the two are, however, deeply entwined. Thus, I endeavour to keep my voice in this text and to bring in personal anecdotes where they are relevant

Your introductory sociology course, and this book, will hopefully help you to understand how external forces that are outside your control have influenced your life so far, as well as the lives of those around you.

and may enhance your comprehension. In what follows, you should already be able to start making connections between my introduction and the sociological concepts.

An introductory course in sociology will give you some insight into the different topics that sociologists explore: culture, socialization, social inequality, gender, race, and crime, for example. This chapter will help provide you with an introduction to sociology and the sociological perspective. By using the sociological perspective, you will begin to understand how our lives have been shaped through each one of the above factors (culture, race, gender, socio-economic status, etc.). Through learning about the historical development of sociology, you will be able to see the shifts in thinking that have occurred (and continue to occur) as society evolves—as well as the parts of society that have stayed eerily similar throughout history. Our starting point is a formal definition of *sociology* and the way sociologists connect personal problems and public issues—or the individual to society.

What Is Sociology?
Defining *Sociology*

Sociology is the scientific study of human **society** and social behaviour. Sociologists attempt to capture and explain the complexity of human social life by examining our social relationships, social interactions, and culture. We humans spend most of our waking hours with other people, creating social groups that sociologists study. These groups range in size from groups of two to large companies and even whole societies. But whatever the size of the grouping, sociologists want to know what factors influence the ability of people to co-operate, understand one another, and achieve group goals. Beyond that, they want to know how belonging to a group affects a person's self-perception.

Most of what sociologists look at, and most sociological ways of looking, fall into one of two distinct subfields: macrosociology and microsociology. **Macrosociology** is sociological study on a large scale. It is the study of **social institutions**, such as religious institutions, marriage, and sports, as well as the study of large social groups, such as visible minorities or college students. Macrosociology also includes the study of whole societies—in particular, the study of social arrangements and patterns

sociology The systematic study of human and social behaviour; including culture, social structures, relationships, social interactions, and the study of society as a whole.

society The largest-scale social **structure**, whose members interact with one another, share a common geographic territory, and share common institutions.

structure The identifiable elements of society that produce relatively stable opportunities and constraints in people's lives.

macrosociology The study of society, social institutions, and large social groups.

social institution A social structure made up of two or more relationships (i.e., stable patterns of meaningful orientations to one another.

microsociology The study of small social groups and individual social interaction.

within these societies (for example, marriage rate patterns in a country over a certain period of time). In contrast, **microsociology** is sociological study on a small scale—the study of small groups, such as your class or your peer group. Microsociology also zooms in on groups to study the individual people within them, and how they interact. These interactions create the bigger social patterns that macrosociologists like to study in "sociologically imaginative" ways.

Charles Wright Mills and the Sociological Imagination

Today, every sociologist knows the importance of a "sociological imagination." The American sociologist C. Wright Mills (1955) defines *sociological imagination* as a "vivid awareness of the relationship between personal experience and the wider society." Sociological imagination is not a theory but an outlook of society that tries to steer us away from thinking routinely about our everyday lives so that we can look at our lives in fresh ways.

C. Wright Mills recognizes that the individual and society are intricately linked and that we cannot fully understand one without the other. When exploring the link between the individual and society, Mills underlines the difference between the way we understand what he calls "personal troubles" and "public issues." *Personal troubles* result from individual challenges while *public issues* are caused by larger social factors. For instance, if you struggle with your weight, you may consider it to be a personal trouble—it is your body, and your decisions have led to your body shape. In fact, society in general is full of negative imagery surrounding obesity, and many people take part in fat-shaming. The underlying shared belief is that if you eat well and work out you should be able to maintain a healthy weight. Clearly, then, many would view your weight as a personal trouble. However, what if a large percentage of people in your neighbourhood are also overweight? Do you then just live in a particularly lazy or undisciplined part of town? This is highly unlikely. Instead, high obesity rates tend to suggest that there is more—a public issue—going on. For instance, low-income areas tend to lack green space for outdoor activity. Moreover, healthy food is expensive. It is cheaper to buy a combo meal at most fast-food restaurants than it is to purchase a head of lettuce and a cauliflower

#*Sociology*

#CommitSociology

In 2013 and again in 2014, then prime minister Stephen Harper urged Canadians not to "commit sociology." His 2013 comments were in reference to an alleged terrorist plot against VIA Rail, where he proclaimed that Canada was facing a serious threat and thus it was not a time to "commit sociology." His comments in 2014 were in reference to a national inquiry into missing and murdered Indigenous women. He urged Canadians to stop viewing the tragedy of missing and murdered Indigenous women as a "sociological phenomenon" and instead "view it as a crime."

In response, critical thinkers from many disciplines fought back with articles and information on why these issues were precisely sociological phenomenon. Crime is a social phenomenon that is most often shaped by powerful historical social forces, and so it needs to be understood and examined more deeply than as someone's simply choosing to "break the law." Treating these "crimes" as stand-alone cases erases the colonial history of Canada as well as the current disadvantages experienced by Indigenous people in this country that put them at higher risk of violence. Such disadvantages include infrastructure issues, poverty and lack of access to employment, and lack of social services (Amnesty International Canada, 2018). The oppression of Indigenous people, who were removed from their homes, stripped of their culture and language, and far too often physically and sexually abused, has led to a society that too often dehumanizes Indigenous peoples and ignores their demands for justice. As you will learn in this chapter, there is a strong link between what happens to individual people and the broader social forces at work in society. A Twitter feed was started, #*commitsociology,* to keep sociological inquiry at the forefront of a variety of events and issues.

Look up #*sociology* on your social media platform of choice: What kinds of social issues are being discussed?

Documentaries on Missing and Murdered Indigenous Women and Girls

Kairos Canada. Several documentaries on missing and murdered Indigenous women in Canada. https://www.kairoscanada.org/missing-murdered-indigenous-women-girls/films

at the grocery store (also one of the primary reasons for the "freshmen 15" phenomenon). Preparing healthy food also takes longer. A person who is considered obese might think this is his or her personal trouble, and to some extent it is; however, once people understand that there is a link between widespread poverty and obesity, it becomes clear that it is also a public issue. Furthermore, that we even have measures that decide if someone's body shape is within an

---

Current Research

The Poor Sociological Imagination of the Rich

Daniel Edmiston (2018) conducted a qualitative research study of 50 individuals in the United Kingdom and New Zealand to attempt to understand how lived experiences of inequality would affect individuals' ideas about and attitudes toward welfare use. He used scenario-driven stories to motivate a discussion of the principles pertaining to welfare use and inequality in society. Edmiston (2018) found that affluent individuals are less likely to recognize systemic features that shape individuals' socio-economic life. As a result, Edmiston (2018) argued that wealthy individuals tend to have a poor sociological imagination that is used to make sense of and, at times, justify economic policies that disadvantage the poor. Conversely, those living with a lower socio-economic status were more likely to acknowledge the systemic features of both advantages and disadvantages.

"acceptable" range is a direct link to larger social structures that predetermine norms (see, for example, Etilé, 2007).

When we are able to see this connection between individuals and social forces we are using our **sociological imagination**. Doing so allows us to step outside our own circumstances to see how those circumstances are products of our family, friends, income level, race, gender, and sexuality, to list just a few influences. It was not just a coincidence that I became a young mom living in poverty without an education. Almost everyone who influenced my life up until the point I entered school had lived eerily similar lives. Sociology, then, is applying the sociological imagination to the systematic study of society and social interaction. Sociology helps us gain a better understanding of our social world and ourselves. It helps us to see how the groups to which we belong shape our behaviour. Even our mundane choices, such as what we eat at a particular time of the day or what we choose to wear to school, have rich social significance and can reveal a lot about who our influences are. Thus, the essence of sociology is understanding this connection between the *micro* level and *macro* level—the individual and society.

Peter Berger and Seeing the Strange in the Familiar

In 1963, Peter Berger, an Austrian-born American sociologist, defined the **sociological perspective** as an ability to view the world from two distinct perspectives: seeing the general in the particular and seeing the strange in the

> **sociological imagination** The ability to place and understand the personal experiences of individuals within the societal context in which these experiences occur.
>
> **sociological perspective** The ability to see the general in the particular and the strange in the familiar.

familiar. Seeing *the general in the particular* is similar to the sociological imagination. Being able to move from the general to the particular is having the ability to look at seemingly unique circumstances and recognize the common features involved. While we are all individuals, society is organized into various constructed or made-up categories (women and men, wealthy and poor, young and old, children and adults) that shape the lives of people very differently. For example, we may think that marriage is the result of personal feelings of love and desire. Yet the sociological perspective shows us that factors such as age, sex, social class, and race guide our desire for and selection of a life partner. According to Berger, sociologists also need to hone their sociological perspective by *seeing the strange in the familiar*, which is the ability to look at things that appear normal and familiar and see the peculiar and strange elements in behaviours and situations.

Let's think about breakfast, for example. If we started class by asking each of you what your very favourite thing to eat is, we would get a variety of answers—from pasta, steak, and pizza to pho, seafood, sushi, tandoori masala, jerk chicken, and so on. If we were then to do a survey and we asked the class members what they ate for breakfast, it is highly likely that we would find that the class choices fall into a few specific categories: bread, protein, fruit, dairy, and caffeine. Very few of the favourite foods would be likely to be found on the list. Why do we all eat the same types of food in the morning (with variance dependent upon culture) despite our own food preferences and, furthermore, without any scientific evidence that those particular foods are better digested in the morning? We have been trained throughout our lives to eat very specific foods at breakfast time—a process that is taught through our parents and reinforced through social structures. A favourite among my children is when I say that we are having bacon and eggs (and, if I am feeling very generous, pancakes) for dinner. My children are delighted to have "breakfast for dinner." This is familiar to all of us, and chain restaurants are now advertising themselves based on their offering of breakfast for dinner. However, if we take a moment to reflect on this, it is quite strange. Do you ever have dinner for breakfast? (Note: nursing a hangover by eating pizza left over from the night before does not count).

Research also continues to explore these ideas. Sociologists in 2010 using qualitative research techniques at three elementary schools in the Midwestern United States found that the lives and identities of working class African-American students were shaped by what seemed like strange practices to an outside observer

Is this a picture of breakfast or dinner? It may depend on where in the world you are! Soup, fish, vegetables, and rice are common breakfast items in Japan but would more likely be seen on a dinner menu in Canada. What dictates when a particular food "should" or "shouldn't" be eaten? Sometimes the rules of society are so ingrained they can be difficult to see, although once you do see them, they can seem arbitrary!

"Body Ritual among the Nacirema"

By Horace Miner (1956). An article published in *American Anthropologist* that at first appears to be describing a newly found tribe discovered by an anthropologist named Professor Linton. A closer reading, however, reveals that in fact the article is taking everyday American (Nacirema spelled backwards) familiar rituals and detailing the "strangeness" of such activities. The article can easily be accessed through an Internet search or your local library: Miner, H. (1956), Body ritual among the Nacirema, *American Anthropologist*, 58(3), 503–507.

Practising Sociology

Seeing the Familiar as Strange

	First, look around the classroom and then outside the classroom. Look at the familiar and try to describe it as though this is the first time you have witnessed it.
Classroom	e.g., A person is standing at the front of the room and appears to be dictating for transcription as 40 people are staring intently at the person and frantically writing down everything the person says. That person is the only one allowed to speak—the rest of the attendees are sitting in quiet reverence. (a professor and students)
Outside	e.g., Several young people are clustered together near the entrance of a door. All of them are dressed in some type of uniform with fitted pants and baggy hooded cloaks, and are all holding a mysterious silver wand. Each person quickly puts the silver wand to his or her mouth, and then a cloud appears over each person's head. This must be some type of exclusive ritual witchcraft. (students vaping outside the school doors)
	Reflection: While at first this appears to be a rather silly exercise, reflect on the actual process of seeing something familiar as strange. Did you find the process easy? If not, why do you think it was difficult? How do we learn what is familiar and what is strange?

but that to them were familiar (Brown, Souto-Manning, & Laman, 2010). A reward points system was used for tracking reading in which only books by white authors were included, and black students fell behind. The schools held a fundraiser where children had to sell candy but many could not because their parents were working and couldn't take them door to door. Since their sales were low, these children saw themselves as being less "good" than others. These "familiar" experiences are shot through with classism and racism and become exposed by researchers as "strange" when understood in a sociological context. It is the hope of the researchers that others can see the strange in the familiar (in this case) educational practices, in order to begin a process of change to improve them.

Thus, using your sociological imagination requires that you step back from your taken for granted assumptions and attempt to see the "strange" nature of things that are completely "familiar" to you. Next time you hold the door open for someone else, ride the bus, or even sit in class, look around and see how such familiar activities are actually composed of strange, or perhaps even bizarre, rituals

> **agency** The ability of individuals to make free, independent decisions.
>
> **social structure** Any enduring, predictable pattern of social relations among people in society.

and expectations. At least, they would seem strange to people born into another culture. So, what we really mean by "strange" is culturally specific: the job of the sociologist is to remind us that our ways of doing things are far from universal, necessary, inherently correct, or even "sensible."

A Predestined Life?

Contrary to what we might think, sociology shows us that, often, we are not in control of our own lives. However, recognizing the ways in which our activities, choices, and circumstances are embedded in the larger social environment in which we live does not mean believing that our lives are predestined. Sociologists think that to some extent each one of us has what sociologists refer to as agency—the capacity to make choices that can alter our life paths as well as the paths of those around us. The concept of agency allows us to acknowledge how we have the capacity for choice and free will while still being affected by our social and physical environment. This means that sociologists also stress the important role that structure plays in each of our lives. Social structure

Social structures that make things easier for only some tend to be invisible, particularly to those who experience the inherent benefits built in to society for them. For example, the Ontario government proposed making some high school credits mandatory e-learning credits in 2019 (a decision being protested in this photograph), putting students who do not have a home computer or who have no or poor home Internet access at a disadvantage. Sociology works to make these invisible benefits and their sources visible.

is the organized pattern of social relationships and social institutions that together compose society. Structure is not something that necessarily restricts agency—it can enable some while restricting others based on a number of factors. Social class, for example, is a structure that shapes the access that different groups have to resources in society.

In the introduction to this chapter, we learned that I grew up poor (structure). While I made the choice to go to school (agency) to change my life circumstance, I had to take a large student loan (structure) to do so. I could only attend the school in my hometown as I could not afford, even with the loan, to move away (structure). When I graduated and got my full-time position, my life was still constrained by the amount of money that I owed the government for school (well over $100,000 at the end of the doctorate degree) (structure). Let's say that in my full-time position my colleagues and I had a starting wage of $65,000. The majority of my colleagues went through school without debt (structure). Some quickly bought homes after obtaining their full-time positions, and then purchased new vehicles. Many were able to exert their agency to choose what they liked. I, on the other hand, was paying half my income back to my student loan. Thus, structure still deeply affected my agency. I had to "choose" a less expensive car and home in order to be able to continue to pay back my student loan. While this is a very simplistic explanation of the structure versus agency debate that continues in sociology, it should help to illustrate that our choices (agency) are often confined by life circumstances that are beyond our control (structure).

Our attempt to explain people's everyday experiences raises important questions: Why do some people get more choice in their lives than others? Why are some people hurt and harmed more than other people? Where do the ideas contained in "common sense" come from? Are these ideas likely to benefit some groups (e.g., rich, white, cis-gender men) more than others (e.g., poor, black women)? By the end of this book, you will have a beginner's answer to these questions.

Is Sociology a Science?

Sociology is, at its best, a "science of society," meaning that sociologists study society scientifically. Sociology is a way of explaining our lives to ourselves and, more

broadly, is a search for meanings, accounts, and explanations. Every day in society we see how relying on common sense notions can have disastrous consequences. For example, common sense might tell you that the way most people get a good job is by answering a job advertisement or seeking help from a close relative. Yet sociological research has shown that, under many conditions, information about the best jobs travels through networks of acquaintances (Granovetter, 1974; Cumming, 2014). It's not what you know, or who you are, but whom you know. Interestingly, you are more likely to hear about a great job through a distant friend than a close friend (Granovetter, 1974; Cumming, 2014). When we don't understand the factors that result in an increased likelihood of securing a job, we might make uninformed judgments around why an individual is unable to find work, believing for example that he or she is not trying hard enough. Furthermore, we might miss opportunities to build social networks when we are solely focused on building resumé-worthy skills. Understanding our society through science allows us to make informed decisions in our own lives. Perhaps more importantly, a science of society helps us to build strong policies and practices that can make the world better for everyone in it.

What Is Science?

Science is the discovery, explanation, and prediction of events in our experience, and the accounting of relations between these events. Science needs *research*—the application of logical, systematic methods to produce verifiable evidence. The scientific method forces us to follow a systematic, organized series of steps that ensures as much objectivity as possible in researching a problem. Objectivity is the use of reason and the best evidence possible to interpret an event. Seen another way, objectivity means looking beyond the impressions of a single view. To study something objectively means to avoid personal bias and prejudice as much as possible.

The social sciences tend to study the social world subjectively as well as objectively. Subjectivity is the opposite of objectivity: a tendency to interpret reality through our own experiences, opinions, values, and beliefs. Social sciences see the validity in understanding subjective experience as a portal into generalizing about the social world. Individuals live through and experience the events,

scientific method
An investigative process that involves the creation and testing of hypotheses through systematic observation and measurement.

objectivity A lack of bias, prejudice, or judgment.

social science A major category of academic discipline, concerned with society and the relationships among individuals within a society—included in this are sociology, anthropology, political science, and social geography, among others.

subjectivity
An interpretation of reality through our own experiences, opinions, values, feelings, and beliefs.

struggles, and circumstances that we as social scientists are most interested in studying. Whether we are studying someone's (in)ability to locate employment or someone's transition from surviving on social assistance to obtaining a successful career, sociologists believe that understanding the lived experience is important for a more nuanced and in-depth understanding of the social world.

The scientific method helps us construct theories, collect evidence, test predictions against careful observations, and accurately record our findings. If our predictions fail, we must change or reject our original theory. What is the best explanation for a problem we are studying, and how would we go about testing our answer? These kinds of questions go through a scientist's mind whenever someone raises a problem. As you can see, good science depends on imagination and insight.

How Does Sociology Differ from Other Sciences?

Perhaps you are wondering if sociology can really be scientific. Like any scientific research, sociological research tests hypotheses and strives to discover new information. So, like other scientists, sociologists collect, organize, and interpret data. There are many ways to carry out research. Some fields that study human behaviour—for example, psychology—use experiments. Other fields that study human behaviour—for example, history, economics, and anthropology—use other methods, such as secondary sources and observation. While many disciplines

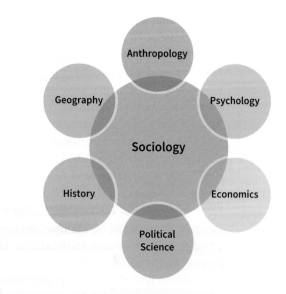

Figure 1.1 **Sociology and the (Overlapping) Social Sciences**

use the same methods to carry out their research, it is often the focus of the research that differs slightly. The social sciences include anthropology, economics, history, psychology, political science, and sociology. They are similar in their focus on human behaviour; however, while each of the other disciplines focuses primarily on one aspect (for example, anthropology focuses on culture while economics focuses on the ways in which people produce and exchange goods and services), sociology overlaps with the other social science disciplines as it studies the influence that all of these separate components of society have on people's behaviours and attitudes (see Figure 1.1). In Chapter 2, we will learn how sociologists do their research.

Well-informed and well-intentioned people may disagree about the causes of social problems and about their solutions. What's more, data collection and experimentation can help clarify these debates, but fully objective research may be impossible. When you study sociology, you must be alert to the hidden assumptions that shape your argument. An awareness of our biases is as important to good research as carefully collected facts and powerful statistical techniques. Public issues are all complex, emotionally charged topics in which sociologists must struggle to find the most compelling explanation, despite their personal limits. Sociology, then, pushes you to question all your taken-for-granted assumptions—a fact that makes some students feel a little uncomfortable from time to time. Just remember that growth often happens through discomfort.

The Origins of Sociology

The sociological approach as it is studied in Canada today emerged in the eighteenth and nineteenth centuries and grew out of philosophy, economics, history, psychology, and law. It was not until the twentieth century that distinct boundaries were constructed around bodies of knowledge and the subject matter of specific disciplines (Delanty, 2007). However, people have been discussing their place in the universe and their relationship with each other for thousands of years. Philosophers such as Confucius (551–479 BCE), Socrates (469–399 BCE), and Plato (427–347 BCE) engaged in writings and elaborate discussions about society, the meaning of life, and the human condition. Thus, the ideas that form the foundation of sociology have been around for a long time. It was not until 1838, however, that the term *sociology* was coined by Auguste Comte—who has since been referred to as the father of sociology (Ravelli & Webber, 2016).

The nineteenth century was a chaotic time in France, with the overthrow of the monarchy and the subsequent defeat of Napoleon. During this unsettling time, philosophers tried to reason out how society might be improved. Comte (1798–1857) considered himself a scientist and believed that the techniques used in the sciences could be applied to the social world. He also believed that a systematic investigation of human behaviour was required to improve society. Comte thought that this could lead to more rational interactions between humans.

The English-speaking world was able to learn of Comte's work largely through the English translations of Harriet Martineau (1802–1876). Martineau is also known as a trailblazing sociologist who studied the customs and social practices of both Britain and North America. Her work emphasized the effect that the economy, law, trade, and population could have on the social problems of contemporary society. She also advocated for the rights of women, the emancipation of slaves, and religious tolerance. Martineau put forth the argument that intellectuals and scholars should not simply offer observations of social conditions, but that they should act on their beliefs in a way that will benefit society.

Harriet Martineau

Another important contributor to the discipline was Herbert Spencer (1820–1903), an English philosopher and sociologist. Spencer was a major figure in the intellectual life of the Victorian era. Unlike Martineau, Spencer did not find it necessary to attempt to change or improve society—rather, his goal was simply to understand it better. He believed that societies would naturally change over time. He applied the concept of evolution of the species to societies. In 1852 he published an article called "A Theory of Population, Deduced from the General Law of Animal Fertility," where he presented the evolutionary view of the "survival of the fittest." The phrase "survival of the fittest" was later adopted by Charles Darwin to describe the struggle between competing life forms. Darwin differed from Comte and Martineau as well, as he suggested that societies would eventually naturally evolve and that, therefore, there was no need to be highly critical of social arrangements or to work to actively change them.

European Influences

Three key European figures arose in the late nineteenth and early twentieth centuries whose insights helped to firmly shape sociology as a discipline: Karl Marx, Émile Durkheim, and Max Weber. These three theorists witnessed the effects of the Industrial Revolution across Europe.

The Industrial Revolution began in Britain before spreading across Europe, and then through those countries to their global colonies. There was a shift from predominantly agricultural production as people's way of sustaining themselves and their families to industrialization, where people work for a corporation and are paid for their labour. During this time, many moved from rural settings into cities. This shift was largely the result of major technological advancements (steam power, coal, electricity) and the invention of new machines, such as the cotton gin. These changes also resulted in a new way of organizing work, called the factory. Marx, Durkheim, and Weber (pronounced Vayber) were macro-theorists who wrote extensively about the effects of these changes in society. The contributions that these three have made to our understanding of the social world are so significant that their names will reappear in many chapters of this text, and they will be discussed in depth in Chapter 2. For now, it is important to know that they were influenced by the circumstances they witnessed and that they were key figures in shaping the discipline of sociology.

American Influences

Early American sociology was derived mainly from W.E.B. Du Bois (1868–1963) and the University of Chicago (which became known as the Chicago school of thought). Du Bois was a theorist who brought the understanding of structural racism as a significant social constraint to the discipline of sociology. We will discuss him in more depth in Chapter 2.

The Chicago school, founded in 1892, promoted a microsociological rather than a macrosociological perspective (Denzin, 1992). There was a realization that human beings are not fixed objects to be studied—they are rational beings who act with intention and who are capable of changing their behaviour. Humans, for example, interact with each other based upon their own interpretation of social circumstances. To illustrate this idea, think about how you interact differently with your parents, professors, and friends. This is because you have interpreted shared meanings and understandings of the forms that these interactions may take. Rolling your eyes at a comment your friend might say would not be interpreted the same as rolling your eyes at your mother or at your professor. The Chicago school highlighted the importance of understanding individuals and their relationships in particular contexts—thus, a microsociological perspective. The theorists from this school of thought became known as symbolic interactionists and will also be discussed throughout this text.

Early Sociology in Canada

Sociology began to make its way into Canada in 1924 as an established department at McGill University in Montreal. One of the areas that differentiated Canadian sociology from its American counterpart was its early interest in political economy, which studies the relationships between individuals and society, and between markets and the state (Clement, 2001). Scholar Harold A. Innis (1894–1952) was arguably the first Canadian sociologist to focus on political economy with works such as *A History of the Canadian Pacific Railway* (1923), *The Fur Trade in Canada: An Introduction to Canadian Economic History* (1930), and *Political Economy in the Modern State* (1946). His work focused on the important relationships between communication and transportation to the development of our political and economic systems.

Harold Innis
University of Toronto Archives/
B72-0003/Box 034, file 056
© Public Domain nlc-12491

Over the years Canadian sociology has developed to include many varied areas of study; however, some of our most notable scholars have focused on the enduring nature of inequality. John Porter (1921–1979) conducted one of the most well-known studies of the relationship of race, ethnicity, gender, and social class with inequality in Canada. In *The Vertical Mosaic* (1965), he relied on Canadian census data to examine inequality among ethnic groups. Porter argued that Canada was far from the classless society with easy

social mobility (the ability to rise in social class) that people seemed to think it was; rather, there existed a hierarchy where French and British people occupied the top socio-economic positions, while visible minority groups, such as Chinese, black, and Indigenous people, were at the bottom. His study opened up the field to studies of elites and power, social mobility, immigration and integration, and ethnic inequality (Wanner, 1998).

Contemporary sociology in Canada and around the world has been deeply influenced by the contributions of these early thinkers (see Figure 1.2). As we approach topics such as culture, socialization, inequality, gender, race, and crime, as well as others, we will be able to see the influences of these theoretical insights that influence today's research and understanding of the social world.

How Does Sociology Relate to Your Future Career?

Many students love their sociology courses but are concerned with what kind of job they may obtain with a degree in sociology (see Figure 1.3). An accounting degree can lead to someone's becoming an accountant; a human resources certificate will allow someone to work in a human resource department at any organization. There are no sociology departments outside of post-secondary schools; indeed, most sociology students do not become sociologists. Sociology, however, imparts important skill sets, including critical thinking and analytical skills that are easily transferable to the workplace.

Moving Forward

This textbook has been designed to help you navigate the discipline with plenty of personal anecdotes, humour, and current research. As well, news items, music, television, and social media are used to illustrate that the discipline is indeed relevant to your everyday lives. The chapters that follow will explore the theoretical and methodological underpinnings of the discipline (Chapter 2), culture (Chapter 3), socialization

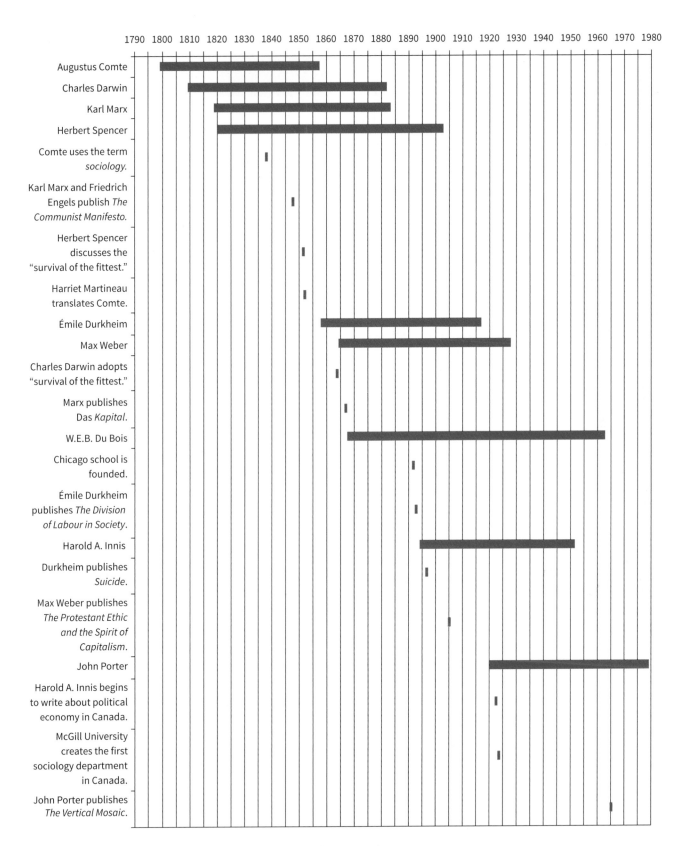

Figure 1.2 Timeline of Select Major Sociological Figures and Events

Current Research

Contemporary Canadian Sociologists

Jim Curtis

James (Jim) Curtis is one of the most respected and well-known Canadian sociologists. From the beginning of his career in 1970 to his death in 2005, Dr Curtis was a professor at the University of Waterloo in Ontario, Canada. His work covered a variety of topics, including religion, social inequality, gender, aging, social values, and sport. He authored numerous sociology textbooks that were used to educate hundreds of thousands of sociology students over the duration of his career—and some of those books are still used in classrooms today. In 2004, Curtis was inducted as a Fellow of the Royal Society of Canada, which is the highest academic honour in Canada.

Weizhen Dong

Weizhen Dong is a professor of Sociology at the University of Waterloo in Ontario. Dr Dong's research interests include healthcare systems, social policy, and the social determinants of health. Her work has primarily focused on the impacts of gender, class, race, and age on health outcomes and their policy implications. She is a commissioner on The Commission on the Accreditation of Programs in Applied and Clinical Sociology, and the Chair of the Canadian Sociology Association's Social Policy and Social Equality Research Cluster. She has also edited books, including *Social Policy in China: From State-Led to Market-Led Economy* (Rock's Mills Press, 2019).

Rinaldo Walcott

Rinaldo Walcott is a professor in the Department of Sociology and Equity Studies at the Ontario Institute for Studies in Education (OISE) in Toronto, ON. Dr Walcott's research interests are in the area of black diaspora cultural studies, gender, and sexuality. He is the current director of the Women and Gender Studies Institute at OISIE. He wrote the book *Black Like Who? Writing Black Canada* (1997), which explored the use of rap music as an important social and political force. He also edited *Rude: Contemporary Black Canadian Cultural Criticism* (2000), which critically engages with black Canadian expressive cultures in a Canadian context.

Kate Bezason

Kate Bezanson is an associate professor at Brock University in St Catharines, Ontario. As a feminist scholar, Dr Bezanson specializes in political economy and social/family/labour market policy. She currently holds a collaborative Social Sciences and Humanities Research Council (SSHRC) funded project on Canadian social policy and care theory. Her current research and advisory work involve assessments of law, gender, budgeting and taxation, federalism, social reproduction, parental leave, and child care. She has a long-standing interest in equality issues related to the Canadian Charter of Rights and Freedoms and Indigenous legal theory, and is currently pursuing a part-time masters of law in constitutional law.

(Chapter 4), families (Chapter 8), and social structure and interactions (Chapter 5). We will also explore different forms of inequality, including class (Chapter 6), gender (Chapter 7), and race (Chapter 9). Lastly, we will examine how the tools of sociology can be used to help us understand larger social forces, such as crime and deviance (Chapter 10), population and the environment (Chapter 11), and health and illness (Chapter 12).

Courtesy of UWaterloo

Courtesy of Weizhen Dong

Courtesy of Rinaldo Walcot

Courtesy of Kate Bezanson

Business	Community Services	Health Services
Marketing	Non-profit	Substance abuse education
Human resources	Urban planning	Rehabilitation counselling
Training	Community development	Hospital admission
Entreneurship	Environmental groups	
Public relations	Advocacy	
Consumer research		

Higher Education	Law	Publishing
Professor/instructor	Law enforcement	Professional writing
Admissions	Investigations	Research
Advising	Probation and parole	Editing
Development	Criminal justice	Journalism
	Paralegal	
	Lawyer	

Social Services
- Rehabilitation
- Case management
- Recreation
- Government agencies

Figure 1.3 **Employment Sectors for Sociology Majors**

Sociology also helps those in film, animation, illustration, and design as it allows for deeper understanding of human behaviour.

Source: Adapted from http://www.asanet.org/career-center/careers-sociology

Top 10 Takeaways

1 Sociology relates to your everyday life. — pp. 3–4, 12–14

2 Sociology helps you to build strong skill sets for a number of careers. — p. 12

3 Sociology is the scientific study of human society and social behaviour. — p. 4

4 Macrosociology is sociological study on a large scale (large groups and societies as a whole). Microsociology is sociological study on a small scale (individual and small group behaviour). — p. 4

5 Charles Wright Mills coined the term "sociological imagination"—a term used to explain one's ability to link the personal to the public. — p. 4

6 Peter Berger defined the sociological perspective as the ability to view the world from two distinct perspectives—seeing the *general in the particular* and seeing the *strange in the familiar.* — pp. 6–8

7 Sociology is a social science that employs a variety of research methods to better understand the workings of the social world. — pp. 9–10

Questions for Critical Thinking

1. How can you relate sociology to your everyday life?

2. What kind of skills can sociology help you build for a career in animation or illustration, or in human resources?

3. Give an example of a problem in your life that would be better understood by a sociologist than by a psychologist, or by common sense knowledge.

4. Provide examples of the type of research macrosociologists might do in comparison to microsociologists.

5. Brainstorm and describe ways in which you could build your sociological imagination.

6. Explain the "strangeness" of one familiar activity that you take part in daily.

7. Provide an example in your life where structure has deeply influenced your agency.

8. Compare and contrast the European, American, and Canadian developments in the discipline of sociology discussed in this chapter.

Recommended Readings

- **Allan, K. (2007). *The social lens: An invitation to social and sociological theory.* Thousand Oaks, CA: Pine Forge Press.** The goal of this book is to provide a comprehensive discussion of both classical and contemporary social theory. It outlines different approaches to sociology and describes the scholars behind these approaches. Each perspective is intended as a starting point for students, an introduction to its ideas, and a base for future exploration.

- **Bicchieri, C. (2006). *The grammar of society: The nature and dynamics of social norms.* Cambridge, UK: Cambridge University Press.** The goal of this text is to explain social norms. It considers how and why social norms emerge, evolve, and survive. It provides an extensive account of how and why people follow social norms.

- **Mills, C.W. (1959). *The sociological imagination.* Oxford, UK: Oxford University Press.** This text outlines Mills's conception of the sociological imagination, arguing for a connection between the social, personal, and historical dimensions of our lives. C. Wright Mills provides readers with a way of looking at the world that examines links between private issues of individuals to larger social issues.

Recommended Websites

Canadian Sociological Association (CSA)
https://www.csa-scs.ca/
- The CSA is a professional association that promotes research, publication, and teaching in sociology in Canada.

Centre for Social Justice (CSJ)
http://www.socialjustice.org
- CSJ is a group that focuses on research, education, and advocacy in hopes of reducing inequalities related to income, wealth, and power while improving security

and peace. This website provides a brief overview of key issues impacting a variety of groups, such as Indigenous people and racial minorities, links to publications, as well as information about getting involved.

Parliament of Canada
http://www.parl.gc.ca/HousePublications/ Publication.aspx?DocId=6079428&Mode= 1&Parl=41&Ses=1&Language=E
• This website provides links to a variety of publications related to inequalities in Canada, including ones related to policy alternatives, services available, income inequalities, support for working parents, and employment services in Canada.

Broadbent Institute
https://www.broadbentinstitute.ca
• The Broadbent Institute is a group that speaks for progressive change, democracy, equality, and the training of Canada's future leaders. The organization addresses a wide range of issues, including those related to economic development, social progress, intercultural equality, and gender equality, as well as inequalities among Indigenous communities.

Chapter 2

What Do Sociologists Do?

In 2010, the Canadian government declared that the 2011 census was no longer going to be mandatory as it had been for decades (Ramp & Harrison, 2012). Supporters of the change argued that this protected privacy rights while others were concerned that this would inadvertently eliminate a large portion of Canadians from the data pool, especially those who rely on social programs, which in turn are informed by census data (Raywat, 2011). This change drew immediate criticisms from a variety of sociological and professional sources for being both methodologically and constitutionally questionable (Ramp & Harrison, 2012), particularly since long-term research that depends on mandatory census data could be irreparably disrupted by the change in data-collection methodology (i.e., who is and is not included in research). The decision was reversed for the 2016 census, which had the best response rate in Canadian history (Sanderson, 2017).

▲ Owen Richards/Getty Images

Learning Outcomes

1. Understand the difference between common sense and sociological research
2. Outline the major theoretical perspectives in sociology
3. Explain the difference between qualitative and quantitative research methods
4. Identify the different types of research that fall under each of the methods
5. Understand the importance of undertaking ethical research

Key Terms

anomie

backstage interactions

bourgeoisie

class consciousness

common sense

conflict theory

content analysis

convenience sampling

dependent variable

double-consciousness

dysfunction

experiment

fake news

feminist theory

front stage interactions

functionalist theory

hypothesis

I

independent variable

intersectionality

latent functions

manifest functions

Me

mixed methods

mode of production

Introduction

At some point in your life, and perhaps without even realizing you were doing it, you have theorized about the social world. You may have a roommate who was rather grumpy one morning and you came up with guesses as to why this was the case. Perhaps you knew that your roommate had a big test that day, and you theorized that he or she must have stayed up late studying and so was just overly tired and nervous. Or perhaps your girlfriend was being very short with you yesterday and was upset with you for something you perceived to be silly. Rather than contemplating what you may have done wrong, your first (very risky) thought might have been that she was suffering from PMS (hopefully you were smart enough to keep that thought to yourself). These are examples of theories that were derived from "common sense."

Common sense is the knowledge we get from our lived experiences, through conversations with others and from what we have heard our parents say, what we read, what we see on television, and what we hear on streaming services. While sometimes common sense is accurate, it is not always reliable. Sociologists do not accept something as "fact" just because "everyone knows it." Rather, each piece of information must be examined, tested, recorded, and then analyzed in relation to other data. In this era of fake news—misinformation that is presented as being authentic—the need for scientific research becomes exceedingly important. Thus, sociologists engage in scientific research to explore the social world and avoid taking common sense knowledge to be factual. In this chapter, we will explore both the ways in which research is done and the theoretical underpinnings that guide sociological insights. We will first begin by examining sociological theory.

Theoretical Positions in Sociology

A theory is a set of propositions (or system of ideas) intended to explain a fact or social phenomenon. In order to undertake research, sociologists develop a theory that offers a general explanation of a phenomenon. A theory may explain something about the social world and may have explanatory power, predictive power, or both. A theory may help us to see the relationships between two variables, as well as to understand changes over time. In sociology, many different theoretical paradigms are used to explain the social world. The four most commonly taught in an introductory class are functionalism, conflict theory, symbolic interactionism, and feminism (see Figure 2.1). There are many other theories that you will learn if you choose to take future sociology

---

common sense
The knowledge we get from our life experiences, through conversations with others and from what we have heard our parents say, what we read, what we see on television, and what we hear on streaming services.

fake news Misinformation that is presented as being authentic.

theory A set of propositions intended to explain a fact or social phenomenon.

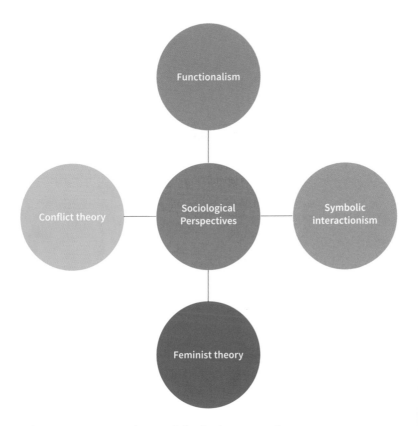

Figure 2.1 The Major Sociological Perspectives

moral order
participant observation
patriarchy
population
proletariat
qualitative research
quantitative research
questionnaires
reliability
research ethics
response bias
sample
secondary data analysis
significant others
snowball sampling
social reproduction
standpoint theory
structured interview
symbolic interactionism
systematic random sampling
theory
unobtrusive measures
unstructured interview
validity
variable

classes, such as anticolonial theory, postcolonial theory, critical race theory, queer theory, and postmodernism.

Functionalism

Functionalist theory views society as a set of interconnected parts that work together to preserve the stability and efficiency of social life. In this model, the various parts that make up society are likened to the parts of a human body that work together for the whole organism to survive.

Functionalists think that if we are to understand society, we must look at how the parts of society fit together to make a whole and how each part contributes to this survival of society. Families, for instance, reproduce and nurture members of society while the economy regulates the production, distribution, and consumption of goods and services. Both parts—families and economies—are different, but both are necessary and the two affect each other to reproduce society.

How does this "social reproduction" work? (**Social reproduction** is a term that sociologists use to encompass all that goes into reproducing society: having children and teaching them the rules, roles, and norms of

functionalist theory
A sociological approach that assumes social behaviour is best understood in terms of parts working together to maintain the larger society as a whole.

social reproduction
The process by which a society reproduces itself from one generation to another and also within generations.

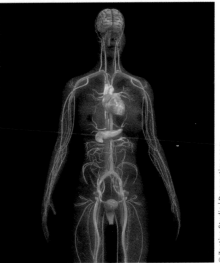

Much as the human body depends on cells, organs, and systems all working together, functionalists see society as dependent on different institutions.

#Sociology

Social Media "Truths" versus Research Facts

This meme has been circulated around social media sites like Facebook, Twitter, and Instagram hundreds of thousands of times. The use of mathematical "facts" appears to lend strength by illustrating in "real" dollar amounts the way in which the Canadian government is (mis)treating its seniors in an effort to help (undeserving) refugees. Psychologist and professor of creativity and creative thinking Nathaniel Barr (2015) refers to this type of information as "quantifiable bullshit," information designed to impress but lacking a direct concern for the truth.

Research reveals that in fact some refugees are only entitled to financial assistance for *one* year upon arrival in Canada at a rate of $800 per month, while low-income seniors are entitled to over $1300 per month for as long as they live (Mehler Paperny, 2015). In addition, while some refugees may also be entitled to a one-time payment of $900 to help set up a home in Canada, asylum seekers and privately sponsored refugees are not entitled to any assistance at all (Mehler Paperny, 2015). Research also shows that within two years of being in Canada most refugees reported income from paid employment and that refugees only represent just over 3 per cent of all social assistance recipients (Statistics Canada, 2015).

Have you seen this meme, or something similar, reposted by members of your family or your circle of friends? Have you ever thought to do research to find out if what was being claimed was actually true? How does the presentation of statistics in this meme advocate certain values and assumptions to its readers?

Only in Canada

* It is interesting to know that the federal Government of Canada allows:

A monthly pension of : $1,890.00 to a simple refugee
plus : 580.00 in social aid

=========

A grand total of : $2,470.00 monthly

X 12 months
=========
$28,920.00 annual income

By comparison, the Old Age Pension of a senior citizen who has contributed to the development of Our Beautiful Big Country during 40 or 50 years, CANNOT receive more than :

Amount/month $1,012.00 in Old Age Pension and Guaranteed Income Supplement
X 12 months
===========
$12,144.00 annual income
A difference of : $16,776.00 per year

* Perhaps our senior citizens should ask for the Status of Refugees instead of applying for Old Age Pension.

* Let us send this message to as many Canadians as possible, and maybe the allowance of refugee could then be reduced to $1,012.00, and that of our Canadian pensioners raised to $2,470.00 per month. (who actually deserve it) the money that they have been paying in income taxes for 40 or 50 years,
AN INCREDIBLE NONSENSE !!!
OUR CANADIAN SENIORS CITIZENS, DESERVE BETTER

Please circulate this text to see the reaction of your contacts !

https://twitter.com/caroledodd/status/667365973356343296

---

society so that they become good employees and consumers, etc.) To make this clear, let us take one social status: mother. Because of the pressure of societal norms, a mother is taught that her primary role is to take care of her children and her house. She will enact this role by spending more time at home and less time at work or at building her career. Of course, her decision (along with similar decisions of many other mothers) will have broader impacts on the economy. This is how the two social institutions of the economy and the family are interconnected. The same holds true for fathers—however, in the reverse.

Functionalists think that any social institutions that persist for a long time likely serve a purpose and help the society to survive. Sociologist Talcott Parsons (1951) viewed society as being in a natural state of equilibrium—meaning that society tends toward stability or balance. As changes occur in one part of society, there must be adjustments in other parts; otherwise, equilibrium will be endangered. Sociologist Robert Merton offered a refinement to this theory, pointing out that some of these functions are obvious to all and are clearly stated. We call these **manifest functions**. Other functions are unintended or less visible and are called **latent functions**. When a system does not function properly, it experiences **dysfunctions**.

Consider marriage as a social institution. Historically, the manifest function—the intended outcome—was the reproduction of children within a family. There are, however, many latent functions of marriage—the unintended consequences or less visible results—such as tax breaks, a dual income, extended family networks, and, theoretically, sex. The institution of marriage also experiences many dysfunctions, such as divorce and domestic violence. Think about other social institutions, such as school, work, or the church. Can you list some of the manifest and latent functions of these institutions?

What happens when rapid social changes rob people of certainty and stability? As we saw in the introductory chapter, French sociologist Émile Durkheim (1858–1917), an early functionalist thinker, lived through the Industrial Revolution, which influenced his understanding of the world. Durkheim highlighted social order and the consequences of a loss of solidarity within society in his classic work, *Suicide*. Durkheim noted that in modern societies, the traditional bases of solidarity are weakened. People are no longer working toward a common goal of farming and providing for their families; rather, they find themselves in competition for wages. People have fewer common experiences, ideas, and values; and social cohesion suffers. According to Durkheim, with industrialization and modernization, the **moral order** of earlier societies decays, and people are at a greater risk of experiencing **anomie** (normlessness). A new sense of anomie causes personal and social problems, even leading to suicide.

Some present-day researchers still incorporate this perspective into their work. Consider recent functionalist

manifest functions
The intended and easily recognized ways in which an institution or social phenomenon operates.

latent functions
The unintended and often hidden ways in which an institution or social phenomenon operates.

dysfunction An element or a process of society that may lead to a decrease in stability.

moral order Unwritten social norms and conventions that serve to maintain societal order.

anomie Instability resulting from a breakdown of standards and values or from a lack of purpose or ideals.

conflict theory
A sociological approach that assumes that social behaviour is best understood in terms of conflict between competing groups over scarce resources.

mode of production
A way of producing the material things we need to survive.

research on families. Joan Patterson's (2002) work on family resilience explores why some families are better able to survive risk and adversity than other families. Some families deal better with adversity (hard times) because they are more cohesive and more flexible than others. Patterson (2002) found that healthy family routines, such as sharing meals and activities together, contribute to cohesion and flexibility. They protect their members from anomie in the face of misfortune.

Conflict Theory

Conflict theory gained prominence in the late 1960s as a reaction against functionalism's overemphasis on consensus and stability. Conflict theorists felt that functionalists had wrongly ignored the importance of conflict and change, as well as the conditions (such as inequality and exploitation) that produce them. In short, while functionalists are likely to stress stability and consensus, conflict theorists see social life as a continuing struggle for fairness, security, and respect.

Conflict theorists propose that society is organized around inequalities that produce conflict between social groups. Money and power are inextricably linked in society, and elite groups want to preserve and extend their wealth and power. Disadvantaged groups want to gain more wealth and power of their own. Conflict theorists do not simply feel compassion for the disadvantaged; they also view them as social actors with agency who could change the world by challenging the power structures that oppress them. This happens, for example, when workers organize unions, when people of colour challenge systemic racism, when women build movements against gendered violence, or when transgender people lobby to be treated equally.

Karl Marx (1818–1883), a philosopher, social scientist, historian, and revolutionary, was the most influential socialist thinker to emerge in the nineteenth century. Although many social thinkers ignored Marx during his own lifetime, Marx's social, economic, and political ideas gained wide acceptance and political influence after his death. His writings focus on the workings of capitalism as a **mode of production**, a

way of producing the material things we need to survive. Other modes of production—for example, hunting and gathering or feudalism—produce other kinds of social orders, with different kinds of exploitation.

At the top of the industrial capitalist hierarchy are the capitalists, or **bourgeoisie**, who own the means of industrial production: the factories, equipment, and raw materials, for example. At the bottom are the **proletariat**, the people who work for the capitalists for a wage and who produce profits for their employers. Marx proposed that conflict between these two classes is inevitable because their interests are directly opposed. For one class to rise economically, the other class must decline.

Marx thought the proletariat could free themselves from this exploitation and oppression only by recognizing

> ***bourgeoisie*** The owners of the means of production; the capitalists.
>
> ***proletariat*** The workers; those who produce for the bourgeoisie.
>
> ***class consciousness*** Occurs when members of an oppressed group come together in recognition of their domination and oppression and collectively act to change it.

their disadvantage and acting together to change society. He believed that since the proletariat far outnumbered the bourgeoisie, **class consciousness** could bring about a successful revolt against the unfair wage–labour relationship that underlies capitalism. In simple terms, Marx believed that since there are far more workers than owners of businesses in society, workers hold an immense amount of power. If the workers could recognize this power and join together, they could overthrow the business owners and change their living conditions.

Contrary to Marx's expectations, today, a large percentage of the world continues to live under capitalism. Yet Marx's theorizing was instrumental in promoting labour rights and demands for what we today call the "welfare state"—universal measures to deliver health, education, and welfare to everyone, regardless of their social origins.

Photo by Mohamed Kadri/Imagespic/Sipa USA (Sipa via AP Images)

Marx's theories are still influential today. In this photo, police shoot gas canisters at anti-capitalist protesters in Montreal, 2016. The red stickers on the police helmets read "Libre Négo" in reference to their own labour dispute over pensions.

Symbolic Interactionism

Symbolic interactionism, given its name by sociologist Herbert Blumer (1900–1987), is largely based on the early-twentieth-century writings of George Herbert Mead and Charles Horton Cooley.

Symbolic interactionists focus on the "glue" that holds people together in social relationships: the shared meanings, definitions, and interpretations that make interactions among individuals possible. They ask this: How do we humans come to share the understandings that are necessary for relationships and institutions to exist? To answer this question, researchers study how certain behaviours come to be defined or framed, and how people learn to engage in everyday activities. In this sense, symbolic interactionism is the close study of everyday life.

All social interaction involves what sociologist Erving Goffman (1922–1982) called "backstage interactions" and "front stage interactions." Backstage interactions would include sitting at home in your pyjamas while binge-watching Netflix. You are relaxed, uninhibited, and your real self shows through. In front stage interactions, we perform the way other people expect us to behave. We display those parts of ourselves that we want other people to see, and we hide those parts we don't want people to see. Have you ever worked in the service industry? Working in a restaurant is an excellent example of a place where you can have both front stage and backstage interactions. Imagine having a table that just received their meal and one of the members of the party does not look happy. When you go to the table, the customer complains about her meat being under-cooked so you apologize profusely and take it back to the kitchen. A few minutes later you bring back the meat and the customer complains that it is over-done. In your front stage interactions with the customer you are most likely very understanding and polite. However, when you walk into

symbolic interactionism
A sociological perspective asserting that people create meaning through interactions.

backstage interactions
Interactions where people are free of the expectations and norms that dictate front stage behaviour.

front stage interactions
Interactions where people's behaviour reflects internalized norms and expectations.

Our sense of self is affected by our stage, our audience, and our co-actors.

the kitchen, your response to the customer in the presence of only your co-workers may differ drastically—as this is your backstage in this scenario.

According to George Herbert Mead (1863–1931) in his famous work *Mind, Self and Society* (1934), through social interaction we gradually develop a sense of who we really are. We do this mainly by observing the ways other people treat us and react to us. The people Mead called **significant others** are especially important. These people—including family members and close friends—play a major role in shaping a person's self. Through these interactions, people come to have somewhat different senses of self—also, different expectations about their lives, their families, their work, and so on.

George Herbert Mead (1863–1931) is widely viewed as the founder of the interactionist approach. Mead focused on one-to-one interactions and small groups. According to him, our self has two parts. The **I** is our unsocialized self that is impulsive, creative, and craves spontaneity. The **Me**, socialized by significant others, reflects the values and attitudes of society that people have acquired through social interaction. The *Me* monitors the actions of the *I* and tries to control it.

> **significant others** Those people who play a major role in shaping a person's self.
>
> **I** Mead's term for the element of the self that is spontaneous, creative, and impulsive.
>
> **Me** Mead's term for the socialized element of the self.
>
> **double-consciousness** Feeling as though your identity is divided into several parts, making it impossible to have one unified identity.

More Diverse Sources

You may have noticed that, up to this point, there has been a lack of diversity in the sociologists we've discussed. The founders of functionalism (Durkheim), conflict theory (Marx), and symbolic interactionism (Mead and Cooley) were all white men, of European and American descent. This is largely because white men held the most power in society during the nineteenth and early twentieth centuries. However, women, visible minorities, and non-Western scholars contributed to social theory even during this time, as we will see.

Black Voices

One important figure was William Edward Burghardt Du Bois, known as W.E.B Du Bois (1868–1963), who was arguably a key founder of American sociology (though until recently has

not received credit for this; see Morris, 2015). He was a civil rights leader and social scientist, as well as the first black person to receive a PhD from Harvard University. In addition, he was the founder of the National Association for the Advancement of Colored People (NAACP). In 1899 Du Bois published *The Philadelphia Negro* based on research into the black communities of Philadelphia ("W.E.B. Du Bois," 2017). In 1903 Du Bois published his most famous work, *The Souls of Black Folk* ("W.E.B. Du Bois," 2017), where he introduced his concept of **double-consciousness**—the experience of looking at one's self through the eyes of a racist white society. This term helped Du Bois to capture the discomfort of having multiple senses of who you are—both your own sense and how others, particularly racist others, see you—and how this tension can prevent a person (specifically a black person in America, though his work applies to black people in Canada as well) from having a unified sense of self.

Another key black voice in sociology was Frantz Fanon (1925–1961), who produced work that was significant in the push for independence from colonial powers. In his book *The Wretched of the Earth* (1961), Fanon voiced his support for the resistance to French colonialism in Algeria. He also defended the right of the colonized to use violence to gain independence from colonizers. Fanon proposed that people who are not deemed human by the colonizer should not be limited in their response to colonizers by the principles that normally apply to humanity. Not surprisingly, the French government censored Fanon's book (Kidder & Oppenheim, 2010, p. 324).

Women's Contributions

Harriet Martineau (1802–1876) is one of many women who made historically unrecognized contributions to classical theory (she was discussed in Chapter 1). Others included Florence Nightingale (1820–1910), Jane Addams (1860–1935), Rosa Luxemburg (1871–1919), Annie Marion MacLean (1870–1934), and Mary Wollstonecraft (1759–1797). All these women promoted social equality long before women received any real recognition as social thinkers. Wollstonecraft is now recognized as one of history's first feminists (which will be discussed later in the chapter). She wrote *A Vindication of the Rights of Women* ([1792] 1972), a book that challenged the subjugation of women in marriage, contending that present-day marriage was a form of legal prostitution. A century later,

Annie Marion MacLean became the first Canadian woman to receive a PhD in sociology and was an active member of the Chicago school. She wrote extensively on the lives of working women.

That these able women and men of colour were marginalized while they were alive speaks to many of the issues we will discuss in this book: sexism, racism, xenophobia, and ethnocentrism. Some of their influence can be seen in the following discussion on feminism. Unlike the earlier

> **feminist theory**
> A sociological approach that attempts to understand, explain, and change the ways in which the construction of gender creates inequality.

The Color of Fear

Dir. Lee Mun Wah (1994). An emotionally charged film. Eight North American males of different races: two African Americans, two Latinos, two Asian Americans, and two Caucasians discuss their viewpoints and experiences with race, prejudice, and discrimination in North America.

approaches we discussed, this approach is especially concerned with issues of sexism and racism.

Feminism

Not surprisingly, **feminist theory** is an approach that focuses on gender inequality: what causes and maintains it, and how it affects women's lives, making them different from men's lives in important ways. As we will see in this book, women's lives are different from men's lives at home, school, and work, and in public places. That said, the differences have shifted as gender inequality diminishes, through legislation, education, and public protest.

The first wave of the feminist movement, roughly between 1880 and 1920, culminated in (some) women gaining the right to vote in Canada and many other Western countries. Second-wave feminism began in the 1960s and manifested itself in social movements demanding wider

© Angela Ostafichuk | Dreamstime.com

The Slutwalk is a feminist phenomenon and movement that originated in response to Toronto Police comments urging sexual assault victims to not "dress like sluts" in order to protect themselves from unwanted male attention (Tyszkiewicz, 2017). Pictured are attendees of a Slutwalk in Edmonton, AB.

social equality for women. Feminists began to discuss women as a cohesive group who shared a common experience of gender oppression. The second-wave brought women together for consciousness-raising, to better understand the patriarchal organization of society and its resulting oppression of women. **Patriarchy** is a cultural system that promotes the idea that men must play the dominant roles in society.

Think about just one way that the legacy of patriarchy persists in Canada. In a Western-style wedding—the kind depicted in most romantic comedies—we watch the bride walk down the aisle, most often accompanied by her father, to her waiting groom or bride. When the bride gets to the front, the officiant of the ceremony asks, "Who gives this bride away?" to which the father replies, "I do." This is because historically children are the property of their fathers. When a female married she then became the "property" of her husband, which is also evident in the woman's giving up her father's name to take on her husband's last name (except in Quebec).

> **patriarchy** The cultural system in which men hold power and authority; the father is the authority in the family and descent is reckoned in the male line.
>
> **standpoint theory** A feminist political position that argues that knowledge stems from social position.

Although Dorothy Smith (1926–) was born in England and completed her degrees at the London School of Economics and the University of California, Berkeley, she lived most of her life in Canada and is the most famous Canadian feminist. In the 1960s, Smith started to develop her now well-known understanding of **standpoint theory**. During this time, she was a mother, wife, student, and then single mother and professor. She recognized that she lived two lives that did not understand each other—one at home with her children and one at the university with her (mostly male) colleagues. Smith came to the realization that living within these two unrelated worlds simultaneously resulted in her having her own, unique standpoint—a view of the world from a marginalized status (woman, single mother). Smith, among others, shed light on the fact that sociology was missing (or had intentionally left out, as in

The father of the bride still traditionally "gives this bride away" to the awaiting spouse.

Yunhyok Choi/Shutterstock

Kimberlé Williams Crenshaw, the scholar and activist who coined the term "intersectionality."

the case of Du Bois and Martineau, as just two examples) the voices of marginalized groups as it had been formed in a white male–dominated world.

Third-wave feminists (1980–present day) differ substantially from second-wave feminists in their understanding of "women's experiences." Rather than thinking that women speak with a single voice, they give attention to the multiplicity of women's voices. In their view, by talking about "all women," second-wave theorizing was mainly concerned with the problems and desires of white, middle-class, heterosexual, educated cisgender women. To avoid this, third-wave feminists use the analytical framework of intersectionality (a term coined by critical race theory scholar Kimberlé Williams Crenshaw), which argues that a woman's experience of oppression is unique to her particular circumstances. Thus, for example, third-wave feminists are interested in ideas such as the intersection of sexism and racism and the ways that racialized women's problems are different from white women's problems. Think for example of the issues that a racialized woman who is a newcomer to Canada from India may experience in her day-to-day life in comparison to a white low-income woman who was

intersectionality
The interrelationships among various systems of discrimination and disadvantage as they apply to an individual or a group, resulting in unique experiences of inequality based on the individual or group's overlapping circumstances (e.g., race, class, gender, and ability).

born here. Both face disadvantage in a number of ways; however, their experiences of disadvantage will be very different. Understanding these differences, and capturing the experience of both women, is of utmost importance for a third-wave feminist.

One such third-wave feminist is bell hooks, who is a critical figure in anti-racist feminism. *bell hooks* is a pen name purposely kept in lower-case letters to emphasize her ideas rather than herself ("bell hooks Biography," 2017). She proposed that both race and gender determine a woman's destiny. Frustrated by the failure of the 1960s civil rights and women's movements to pay attention to the realities of black women's lives, hooks focused her attention on black women as distinct from black men and from white women (hooks, 1981).

Despite the differences in the waves of feminist thought, one central feature is common to all feminist thinking: namely, the assumption that gendered inequality is a result of social practice, not biological differences between men and women. From this, it follows that the sociological imagination must be carefully attuned to gender differences. We must always be on the lookout for differences in male and female experience, since women's experiences routinely differ from men's experiences in every domain of life. In particular, we must always be on the lookout for social patterns or institutions that support patriarchy. We must also recognize that, because of their

Are the "common sense" differences between men and women (such as the ability to have close, meaningful conversations with your friends) biological or sociological? Is this difference imagined, or does it actually exist? How might you figure out the answers to these questions?

different experiences, women and men view the world differently and respond to it in different ways.

Summarizing the Four Classical Sociological Perspectives

I understand that theory is difficult (and quite frankly uninteresting and definitely not fun) for most first-year students. However, these theoretical positions have very real connections to our everyday lives. Each of these theories is useful in helping you to understand some of your own behaviours and ideas, but perhaps even more importantly each theory will give you insight into many important aspects of society. For example, if you want to get into law enforcement, these theories will help you to understand what motivates someone to commit a crime. When you understand the motivations, you can start to put the appropriate mechanisms in place to prevent the behaviour. If you hope to go into animation or illustration, these theories will help you have a more fulsome understanding of humanity; as a result, you will be able to create characters and stories with more depth.

These theories will continue to recur throughout the textbook so understanding them early is important. To help you remember the theorists in relation to each specific theory, caricatures of the key theorists have been developed. These caricatures will show up throughout the book whenever we are discussing their particular theoretical paradigms. Table 2.1 summarizes the key insights

Table 2.1 The Four Key Sociological Approaches

Theory		Insight
Conflict Theory Key Contributors: *Karl Marx*, Max Weber, W.E.B. du Bois		• Believes we are all in a struggle over scarce resources • States that inequality is persistent and pervasive but that it can be changed • Believes those with wealth and power work hard to maintain their position at the detriment of everyone else
Functionalism Key Contributors: *Emilé Durkheim*, Robert Merton		• Has an overriding concern with how social order is maintained, especially during times of change • Views human society as being similar to an organism, such as a human being • Believes we all have a role to play in order for society to function properly and maintain stability
Symbolic Interactionism Key Contributors: Herbert Blummer, *George Herbert Mead*, Charles Horton Cooley, Erving Goffman		• Believes society is nothing more than the creations of interacting people • Highlights the important ways, in which meanings are created, constructed, mediated, and changed by members of a group or society • Views human beings as living in a world of meaning, which is constantly changing
Feminism Key Contributors: Mary Wollstonecraft, Dorothy Smith, bell hooks, Kimberlé Williams Crenshaw		• Has three separate waves • No unified approach, but most feminists share a concern for emancipating women from oppression • Pushes back against patriarchal society and the gender socialization that exists within • Understands the importance of recognizing intersectionality (third wave)

Source: Illustrations by Alannah Astorquiza, used with permission.

Timeline

1792 Mary Wollstonecraft *Vindication of the Rights of Women*

1837 Harriet Martineau *Society in America*

1844 Karl Marx *Economic and Philosophic Manuscripts of 1844*

1846 Karl Marx and Friedrich Engels *The German Ideology*

1848 Karl Marx and Friedrich Engels *The Communist Manifesto*

1880 First-wave feminism begins.

1889 Jane Addams establishes the social settlement in Chicago.

1893 Durkheim *The Division of Labour in Society*

1895 W.E.B. Du Bois is the first African-American to earn a PhD from Harvard.

1897 Émile Durkheim *Suicide*

1899 W.E.B. Du Bois *The Philadelphia Negro*

1902 Charles Horton Cooley *Human Nature and the Social Order*

1903 W.E.B. Du Bois *The Souls of Black Folk*

1905 Max Weber *The Protestant Ethic and the Spirit of Capitalism*

1913 Rosa Luxemburg *The Accumulation of Capital*

1914 World War I breaks out.

1917 Russian Revolution overthrows the czar of Russia.

1919 Rosa Luxemburg is murdered by the German government.

1934 George Herbert Mead *Mind, Self and Society*

1939 World War II begins.

1949 Robert Merton *Social Theory and Social Structure*

1951 C. Wright Mills *White Collar: The American Middle Classes*

1952 Frantz Fanon *Black Skin, White Masks*

1920 Max Weber *Sociology of Religion*

1956 C. Wright Mills *The Power Elite*

1957 Fanon expelled from Algeria by France for anti-colonial struggle.

1958 Simone de Beauvoir *Memoirs of a Dutiful Daughter*

1956 Erving Goffman *The Presentation of Self in Everyday Life*

1959 C. Wright Mills *The Sociological Imagination*

1960 The Beatles release their first album.

1960 Second-wave feminism begins.

1961 Frantz Fanon *The Wretched of the Earth*

1967 Peter Berger *The Sacred Canopy*

1977 Dorothy Smith *Feminism and Marxism: A Place to Begin, A Way to Go*

1980 Third-wave feminism begins.

1981 bell hooks *Ain't I a Woman: Black Women and Feminism*

1987 Dorothy Smith *The Everyday World as Problematic: A Feminist Sociology*

1989 Kimberlé Williams Crenshaw develops the intersectionality framework.

Figure 2.2 **Timeline of Key Sociological Theorists**

and people from each approach while Figure 2.2 provides a timeline of key theorists.

The Scientific Method

Sociologists are interested in many central questions that are important to the social world. For example, sociologists, like many people in society, may be interested in the dynamics of families, the persistent inequalities that exist in a country, crime rates, and/or the way in which a country responds to such issues. The difference between sociologists and others is the commitment to the scientific method to explore society.

1. Research Idea

As seen in Figure 2.3, the first step in any research project is determining what you want to know more about. A number of factors may motivate a sociologist to choose a particular topic area. They may include personal interest, the availability of funding for a topic, or because a certain social problem has become a pressing social issue. Let's say for example that you are interested in the "dating" app Tinder. Some of your friends appear to be having what they've described as many successes using the app; this revelation has piqued your interest. The second half of this step, after choosing your topic or interest area, is to define the problem. What is it about Tinder you want to know? Let's imagine you want to know what characteristics a picture must contain for a user to swipe left for no or right for yes.

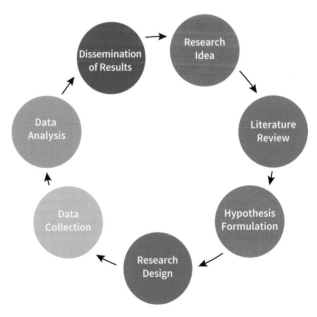

Figure 2.3 **The Research Cycle**

2. Literature Review

The second step is to review existing literature/research to learn what has already been written on the topic. Reading published research helps you narrow down your topic and pinpoint areas for study. You should not limit your research to search engines like Google because they don't reveal all of the scholarly research that has been done. Instead, you should search for published articles on databases like Google Scholar or Sociological Abstracts. Your professor or school librarian can provide you with access to these and other sources.

3. Hypothesis Formulation

To explain something, we start with some hunches or guesses, usually called hypotheses. A **hypothesis** is a proposition or tentative statement about the relationship between variables that we can test with research. Once we have our hypotheses, we can then test them.

A **variable** is any trait, quality, or social characteristic that can vary in size or amount over time, across individuals and groups. In every case, the variable we are trying to predict and explain is the **dependent variable**. The variables that we think will change or influence the dependent variable are called the **independent variables**. Let's go back to our interest in researching Tinder. We hypothesize that Tinder users are more likely to swipe right (say yes) to "dates" who have active pictures (participating in activities such as playing sports, hiking, yoga). In this case, our dependent variable is swiping right (because we expect it to change depending on the photo presented), and our independent variable is active profile pictures.

There are multiple reasons that lead a person to swipe right (i.e., choose someone for a date) on Tinder. These reasons may include active photos but also gender, race, physical appearance, body shape, or eye colour. All these factors combine to increase (or decrease) the likelihood that a person will swipe right. And many of them may be correlated with one another. This is called a multi-causal relationship.

In some situations, one particular factor will lead to swiping right under some conditions but not others. For example, a picture in which a person reveals a lot of skin may result in a person swiping right only when that person has consumed alcohol. This is called a conditional relationship. Our explanation of tinder behaviour might, in that case, run as follows: "People are more likely to swipe right when they see a lot of skin *if* they have consumed a lot of alcohol than if they have not consumed a lot of alcohol." This finding might suggest that alcohol consumption reduces inhibition and increases sexual interest in a potential partner—something you may have already noticed in other contexts.

4. Research Design

Sociologists collect and analyze their data following one or another research method. There are two main approaches to social research: quantitative and qualitative. Simply put, **quantitative research** refers to numerical data and **qualitative research** refers to non-numerical data. Some researchers may use a combination of these two methods simultaneously—referred to as **mixed methods**; however, most will fall within one of these camps.

Quantitative researchers conduct and analyze research by converting aspects of social life into numbers. For example, if you have ever filled out a questionnaire or survey, you likely were asked to give your opinion as a number ("Rate your satisfaction from 1 to 5"), which can then be analyzed and compared with the answers others gave. Quantitative researchers are interested in questions about behaviour and trends over time.

Qualitative researchers are much more interested in individual people's experiences, motivations, and understanding of their own social worlds. Moreover, qualitative studies tend to have smaller samples than quantitative studies and are more focused on collecting rich detail. Rather than asking "How many?" or "How has this changed?" qualitative researchers focus on how and why people make and act upon decisions in their lives. For example, if you have ever been interviewed, you have taken part in a form of qualitative information gathering.

---

hypothesis A proposition or tentative statement about the relationship between two or more variables that we can test through research.

variable Any trait, quality, or characteristic that can vary in size over time or across individuals or groups.

dependent variable The variable that is being tested and measured in a scientific experiment.

independent variable The variable that is changed or controlled in a scientific experiment to test the effects of the dependent variable.

quantitative research Using the scientific method to gather numerical data; usually used for larger sample sizes, quantitative research is interested in broader analysis of behaviours and trends that can be applied to populations as a whole.

qualitative research Using the scientific method to gather non-numerical data; usually uses smaller sample sizes and is interested in detailed analysis of motivations and personal interpretations.

mixed methods A way of conducting research that involves both quantitative and qualitative data.

Current Research

Using Mix Methods

As an example of mixed methods work, consider research by Deborah Harrison and Patrizia Albanese (2017) designed to find out how children in Canadian military families deal with the emotionally wrenching deployment of a parent to fight in the Middle East.

To do this, the researchers carried out surveys and semi-structured in-depth interviews with students at a high school near a military base. Armyville High School (a pseudonym to disguise the real name of the school) is one of the largest schools in the province, with nearly 1300 students.

The first phase of the project was a survey administered to a majority of the students attending Armyville High School (AHS). The survey collected quantitative data on the well-being, family functioning, attitudes toward school, and peer relationships of adolescents from Canadian Armed Forces (CAF) families with those of their non-military peers at AHS. Then, it compared these data to data produced by same-aged young people in Cycle 7 (2006–7) of the National Longitudinal Survey of Children and Youth, which asked comparable questions.

Next, to get a deeper understanding of the results, the researchers conducted two-hour semi-structured interviews (a qualitative method) with 35 girls and 26 boys, who, taken together, had 69 parents who were present

or recently retired CAF members. These interviews covered a range of topics related to military life, including geographical relocations, deployments, post-traumatic stress disorder (PTSD), and family functioning.

Because of the mixed methods approach, this research was able to offer great insight regarding the mindset of the children of military men and women and their ability to deal with their own, as well as their parent's, stress.

Chad Hipolito for The Globe and Mail

5. Data Collection

When designing a research project, the researcher must decide how to obtain the information needed. Popular data collection strategies include the experiment, the survey, and participant observation.

An **experiment** is a method designed to study a possible cause-and-effect relationship under well-controlled, carefully regulated laboratory conditions. Unlike psychologists, however, few sociologists use the experimental method for their research. They see experiments as artificial and unlike real life. Sociologists are more likely to prefer so-called "unobtrusive measures."

Unobtrusive Measures

People know when researchers are studying them and, often, play a role when they

are aware of being studied. On one hand, they may give answers that they think the researcher wants to hear. On the other hand, they may give the exact opposite of expected answers to shake up the researcher a bit. Often, when questioned, people being studied think about things they have never considered before and are transformed by the research process. The respondent, then, is rarely just a passive object of study.

This is where **unobtrusive measures** come in, which are measures that are unaffected by respondent participation. In their classic work on the topic, *Unobtrusive Measures*, Webb, Campbell, Schwartz, and Sechrest (1966) discuss the strengths and weaknesses of several types of unobtrusive measure. These can include the observation of external physical signs (beards, tattoos, clothing, expressive movements), the ways people cluster or space themselves

> **experiment** A method designed to study a possible cause-and-effect relationship under well-controlled, carefully regulated laboratory conditions.
>
> **unobtrusive measures** Measures that don't require the researcher to intrude in the research context.

Twitter: Fuelling Movements?

Beginning in December of 2010, a number of Arabic countries saw a dramatic rise in protests, riots, and both violent and non-violent demonstrations. These rallies became known as Arab Spring and were widely believed to have been the result of growing youth dissatisfaction with poorly run governments and frustration with extreme and growing gaps in income levels.

Researchers Ogan and Varal (2017) used content analysis of Twitter to explore the role it played in fuelling the Arab Spring. By examining Tweets and Retweets on Twitter the researchers discovered that information sharing was the most common use of this social media source. Leadership of the movement constituted only a small percentage of the overall Tweets (Ogan & Varal, 2017).

in a room, and the sampling of overheard conversation. Another unobtrusive measure is using archival records or personal documents (such as diaries or letters). A present-day example of an unobtrusive measure is the study of the most commonly asked questions on Google ("The Most Asked Questions on Google," 2017). The questions people ask anonymously on Google reflect the concerns, worries, and preoccupations of millions. In order to make sense of all this information, researchers use content analysis.

Content analysis involves analyzing the content of public communications, including books, websites, speeches, TV scripts, comic books, magazine articles, and popular songs. Using this method, the researcher picks out the main themes and classifies them according to a predetermined set of categories. The beauty of this approach is that it is unobtrusive and uses material that is easily available, then carefully and systematically looks for patterns.

Current scholars have used content analysis to explore social media use. For example, Humphreys, Gill, Krishnamurthy, and Newbury (2013) used content analysis to explore the kinds of personally identifiable information that can be found on public Twitter messages. Their study found that while many users share similar kinds of personal information on Twitter to what they do in public spaces, identifiable information such as phone numbers, email, and home addresses are in fact rare. Another current example of a content analysis of social media can be read in the World Events box.

Participant Observation

Sometimes unobtrusive observation cannot get you answers to the specific questions you may be interested in. Sociologists use **participant observation** to gain first-hand information about a group, an organization, or a community. This is a method of gathering data that requires the sociologist to participate in the social unit being studied. Because the researcher takes part in the group's activities, he or she gains insight into the activities and attitudes of the group members. The participant observer also gains their trust, for example by playing online video games with gamers, going to synagogue with orthodox Jews, smoking marijuana with musicians, playing basketball with local kids, or working in the cafeteria of a prison or mental hospital.

In participant observation, the sociologist acts as both a participant and an observer of the research process. This double role sometimes confuses the new researcher and also runs a risk of distorting the research. On one hand, by taking part in the group, a researcher risks taking on the world view of that group and losing an objective sense of what the group is doing. On the other hand, by watching the group while participating in it, the researcher risks changing the processes he or she has set out to study.

So, participant observation is hard, but it has produced a significant legacy of excellent research. This research style was popularized among sociologists at the University of Chicago in the 1920s and came to be the method of choice for microsociologists, such as symbolic interactionists. Erving Goffman (discussed above) produced such provocative and insightful research reports from his observations that some of his books—including *Asylums* (1961), *Stigma* (1963), and *The Presentation of Self in Everyday Life* (1956)—remain among the widest-read and bestselling sociology books to date.

Surveys

Surveys are excellent for reaching a lot of people in a relatively short amount of time. However, to design a survey, you first have to figure out who you are studying and how you will select them.

---

content analysis
A research method for studying documents and communications, which might be texts of various formats, pictures, audio, or video.

participant observation
A method for gathering information by participating in the social group being studied.

A **population** is the set of all people who share a specific characteristic of interest to the researcher: for example, the population may be all Canadians or only Canadians who are over age 45, all people who speak Chinese at home, or who are gamers, or who drive sports cars. It would be expensive and time-consuming to collect data from every member of a population, so we study a **sample** of that population. Yet even with a sample that contains only a small percentage of the total population, accuracy is possible if the sample is drawn randomly and systematically (called **systematic random sampling**). The least accurate sample methods are so-called snowball samples and convenience samples. **Convenience sampling** studies people who just happen to pass by the researcher when data are being collected. **Snowball sampling** refers to samples in which people selected for study suggest the names of other people to study.

With the sample selected, we are ready to begin the survey. Typically, researchers design **questionnaires** for use in their surveys. These are sets of questions given to respondents, who are asked to record their own answers. Questionnaires may be sent out by mail or online, to be filled out by the respondent without the help of an interviewer. The longer a questionnaire is, the less willing a respondent is to complete it or even begin filling it out.

Some people are less willing to fill out a questionnaire than others. Even in a well-planned questionnaire survey, the response rate may fall well below 50 per cent, meaning that half of the people who have been approached refuse to take part. Indeed, public opinion polling on political issues currently falls far below this—perhaps closer to 10 per cent than to 50 per cent (Cassino, 2016). Consider the changes to the census discussed at the beginning of the chapter—research on the results of making the census non-mandatory showed that minority, low-income, Indigenous, low-education, and mobile student groups were most affected and counted less (Wilson et al., 2017).

Another problem with questionnaires is **response bias**, which can seriously damage a study's validity. Response bias occurs when respondents answer untruthfully or misleadingly. Perhaps they do so because they want to be seen as socially desirable. For example, they may lie and say they own a car even if they don't. The questionnaire may also be designed in such way as to provoke certain answers and not others. So, for example, a survey commissioned by a political party may ask respondents to name all of the things they like about the party but not ask them what they dislike. This then produces a misleading set of quotes that may lead the public to think that people are generally satisfied with that party and its candidates.

Interviews

In an interview, an interviewer asks subjects questions in a face-to-face encounter or over the telephone. An interview may collect qualitative or quantitative data, and it may ask structured or unstructured questions. The interviewer, not the subject or respondent, records the answers.

A **structured interview** asks each respondent a standard set of questions in the same form and the same order. This type of interview at times forces the respondent to choose from among specific answers. But when questions are open-ended, they allow the respondent to answer in his or her own preferred way. An **unstructured interview** is even more flexible; most questions are open-ended ones that the interviewee can answer freely, and the interviewer is free to change the order or ask other questions based on the respondent's responses. Whether the interview

---

population In research, the set of all individuals who share some specific characteristic of interest to the researcher.

sample A relatively small number of people drawn from the population of interest.

systematic random sampling A method of narrowing down potential respondents in a population by taking a complete list of all members of the population, choosing a random starting point, and selecting people on a set interval.

convenience sampling A method of narrowing down potential respondents in a population by asking only those people who pass a particular place.

snowball sampling A method of narrowing down potential respondents in a population by starting with one respondent and asking that person to recommend the next person to talk to.

questionnaires A set of questions with a choice of predetermined answers devised for the purpose of a survey.

response bias The tendency of people to answer questions untruthfully or in ways that may be misleading.

structured interview An interaction where respondents are asked a standard set of questions in the same form and the same order.

unstructured interview An interaction where respondents are asked more flexible and open-ended questions.

---

42 Up

Dir. Michael Apted (1998). Beginning at the age of seven, English children were interviewed every seven years to find any changes that occurred throughout their lives. Now, at forty-two years old, the participants review their careers, marriages, and divorces with researchers. The film is a great illustration of the power of longitudinal interviews—repetitive interviews over a long period of time.

is structured, unstructured, or semi-structured, the interviewer often follows up on answers to gain more insight into the interviewee's thoughts and feelings.

Secondary Data Collection

Sometimes there is no time, money, or need to conduct brand new research to answer a research question. Sociologists often use secondary data analysis, which examines and interprets data gathered by another researcher or by the government. For example, for a small cost, researchers can buy computer-readable sets of data from the Census, the monthly Labour Force Survey, or the National Longitudinal Survey of Children and Youth. Statistics Canada currently makes available hundreds of high-quality data sets for both academic research and market research.

6. Data Analysis

Regardless of what type of method is used to carry out a research project, researchers are required to ensure that research results are both valid and reliable. Validity refers to accurately measuring a concept. For example, if we wanted to study the relationship between education levels and income earned, a valid measure of income would accurately represent how much money (in Canadian dollars) a person earned in a given year. Reliability refers to the extent to which a measure produces consistent results. In our example, people would report the same amount no matter if someone else asked the question, or if someone else were giving the

answer, or if the questions were asked a year later (assuming their income did not actually change). So, for example, asking a person to specify in dollars how much they earned last year would produce more *valid* and *reliable* data then asking them to answer on a three-point scale: "Not much money," "Some money," and "A lot of money."

7. Dissemination of Results

Once research has been collected and the data has been analyzed, social scientists are required to disseminate the knowledge to the public. Some write books and academic journal articles that are published in discipline-specific journals. Others hold public forums or attend conferences where they publicly share the outcomes of their research. In addition, research that is based on community needs is often shared directly to the community studied through pamphlets or by other easily accessible means.

Research Ethics

In Canada no sociologist is permitted to carry out public research without satisfying academic authorities and funding sources that their research is governed by ethical principles. The Canadian Sociology and Anthropology Association (CSAA) first published its code of research ethics in 1994. The ethical principles (statements of what is considered right and wrong in social research) and policies guide researchers during all phases of research. In colleges and universities, researchers are required to go through a research ethics board (REB) that assesses all potential research before it can begin.

Among other things, the guidelines require researchers to openly share their research truthfully. Thus, research ethics forbids falsifying research results, as well as stealing someone else's work and presenting it as one's own. Another basic principle is that research participants should not be harmed by the research (psychologically, emotionally, or physically). Protecting the participants of a study includes protecting their identity and allowing them to discontinue their participation in the research at any time.

secondary data analysis Examines and interprets data gathered by another researcher or by the government.

validity Refers to accurately measuring a concept.

reliability Refers to the extent to which a measure produces consistent results.

research ethics Governing principles that dictate standards of behaviour for the collection, analysis, and interpretation of data in order to ensure that undertaking these tasks does not do harm.

Practising Sociology

Conducting Research

This exercise requires you to do some small-scale original research. You will pick a topic that you want to research through unobtrusive observation. You must identify a hypothesis (such as "Females and non-binary people are more likely than males to hold the door for someone behind them") and the independent (females and non-binary people) and dependent variable (holding the door open). Once you have done so, you must pick two settings where you can go to do observations (such as the school library, a coffee shop, a cafeteria, hallways, the classroom). Remember that you must stay covert during the observation so as not to alter how people behave. Fill in Figure 2.4 with your findings.

Hypothesis		
Independent Variable		
Dependent Variable		
Location	Setting One:	Setting Two:
Describe location		
Observations: Record what you see		
Accept or Reject Hypothesis? Why?		
Ethical Issues:		

Figure 2.4 **Conducting Research Activity**

In the News

Unethical Research Carried Out on Indigenous Populations

Glen Aikenhead and Lillian Dyke published an article in the *Vancouver Sun* in August 2013 highlighting the unethical research that has

F. Royal/National Film Board of Canada/Library and Archives Canada

historically been conducted on marginalized communities without informed consent. Scholar Ian Mosby uncovered details of unethical testing performed by the Department of Indian Affairs on Indigenous children at six of Canada's residential schools (Mosby, 2013). The children were, without their knowledge, subjected to myriad medical and social testing throughout their time in the schools, resulting in the death of

some. The Truth and Reconciliation Commission has condemned these practices and contends that unethical research practices are but one of the many forms of abuse Indigenous populations have had to endure in Canada. Aikenhead and Dyke argue that Indigenous representation in science through Indigenous scientists is the best way to prevent something like this from happening again in the future.

A nurse takes blood from an Indigenous student at Port Alberni Residential School in 1948, during the nutrition experiments conducted there and at five other residential schools

---

These ethical principles are intended to ensure that researchers will balance the risks to participants with the benefits of the study to the wider community. Following are three examples of (non-Canadian) research that have been widely criticized in discussions of research practices.

Zimbardo's Prison Experiment

Social psychologist Philip Zimbardo was interested in the degree to which an environment, such as a prison, could affect or alter a person's sense of self. In short, Zimbardo asked, "What happens when you put good people in an evil place?" (Zimbardo, 2008). Since Zimbardo was unable to secure a real prison in which to conduct his study, in 1971 he constructed a mock prison in the basement of a building located on the Stanford University campus. Over summer break, he recruited and paid male students to participate in a two-week study, randomly assigning them to the role of either prisoner or guard.

The male students then role-played. "Guards" ordered the prisons to engage in a number of activities—told them when to eat and when to use the washroom, enforced strip searches, and at times sent "prisoners" to solitary confinement)—and the "prisoners" followed theses orders. After only six days, the study was terminated because of the deteriorating conditions of the participants. Many showed signs of psychological harm. Those playing "guards" had begun to act in brutal and aggressive ways, and those playing "prisoners" were experiencing severe mental distress. Such a study would not be permitted today.

The Experiment

Dir. Oliver Hirschbiegel (2001). Based upon the 1971 "Stanford Prison Experiment." Twenty males are hired to play the roles of prisoners and prison guards. The results of this seemingly harmless role-playing are shocking. The film highlights why ethical principles of research are so important to guide the behaviour of researchers.

Milgram's Obedience Study

In 1961, social psychologist Stanley Milgram wanted to study the effects of authority on obedience. Specifically, he was intrigued by the brutal treatment of minorities in Nazi Germany and wondered what could possibly cause seemingly good people to commit such atrocities. He then wondered whether he could induce participants in a study to administer increasingly painful electric shocks to an experimental subject, simply by exercising authority.

To find out, college men were recruited to participate in what they believed to be a laboratory study of the link between punishment and learning. They were instructed to administer an electric shock to a "student" whenever that student gave the wrong answer to a memory question. Subjects did not know that the student in the other room was actually a paid actor who was not in fact receiving any electric shocks at all.

As they made more "mistakes" in their learning task, the actors screamed for help and begged the subject to stop administering shocks. However, two-thirds of the subjects continued to administer shocks despite these pleas for help. They kept doing so because the experimenter in charge directed them to do so. This showed that even ordinary college students could behave in a cruel manner if someone in authority had justified and encouraged them to do so. An important ethical issue, raised after the research results were disseminated, was whether subjects were harmed by their participation in this research. Some might feel distressed when they realized the extent of their own cruelty and willingness to inflict pain on others.

The Experimenter

Dir. Michael Almereyda (2015). Based on the 1961 "Stanley Milgram Experiment." This dramatic film takes viewers through the entire research process, from start to finish, calling attention to the ethical concerns of this study.

Humphrey's Tearoom Trade

In 1970 sociologist Laud Humphreys (1970), doing his PhD research, set out to study secret sexual encounters between men in public restrooms (tearooms). This was at a time when homosexual behaviour was still against the law and largely hidden.

The first step of his research included participant observation, which allowed him to observe from a distance what was occurring near the washrooms. As the research went on, Humphreys became intrigued by the men's personal lives outside the tearooms. So, after a washroom encounter ended, he would often follow the men to their cars and record their licence plate numbers. Through the help of a friend who worked in the police department, Humphreys was able to locate each of the men's home addresses. Disguising himself, Humphries then went to each of these men's houses, pretending to conduct a survey. By this means, Humphries found out that most of the men he had followed were married and that a high proportion turned out to be Roman Catholic. This study brought to the forefront issues of privacy, confidentiality, and informed consent. Did the information gained by this study justify the intrusion by Humphreys into people's lives? Most would probably answer "No."

Critical Thinking

In addition to using empirical research methods and sociological theories, the process of critical thinking is key in helping develop the sociological imagination. Thinking "critically" does not mean improving your ability to criticize something. Rather, critical thinking describes several processes. It is first about the active, objective, and skilful gathering of information from, or generated by, observation, experience, reflection, reasoning, or communication. It is also about the process of then actively, objectively, and skilfully conceptualizing, applying, analyzing, synthesizing, and/or evaluating this information. Finally, it is about then using this information and analysis as a guide to belief and action. Critical thinking requires practice and takes time to build. The sociology classroom environment helps to facilitate this practice.

#Sociology

#AlternativeFacts

On 20 January 2017, Donald Trump was sworn in as the forty-fifth president of the United States of America. The inaugural ceremony took place at the US Capitol building. On 21 January, White House press secretary Sean Spicer held a press briefing and accused the media of underestimating the number of people in attendance at the inauguration. Spicer argued that it was "the largest audience to ever witness an inauguration—period—both in person and around the globe" (Cillizza, 2017). He stated that almost a half million people had taken the DC metro on that day compared to just over 300,000 in 2013—although he did not offer a source for his claim (Kesslar, 2017). However, the photographic evidence and the data available regarding public transportation to the event confirmed that attendance at Trump's inauguration was much lower than for Obama's inaugurations in 2009 and in 2013. Indeed, ridership data showed that only 139,000 people took the DC metro on the morning of Trump's inauguration while 319,000 people had taken it on the morning of the 2013 inauguration (Fandos, 2017).

To make matters worse, Kellyanne Conway, Trump's campaign strategist, defended Spicer's statement, stating that Sean Spicer had given "alternative facts." Many have since stated that there are no such things as alternative facts; rather, Spicer had simply lied. Since that time, the "alternativefacts" hashtag has exploded and has been used in reference to many claims that the Trump administration has made since coming into power. Without research methods and statistics, these "alternative facts" may have never been invalidated.

AP Photo, File

View of the crowd on the National Mall at the inaugurations of President Barack Obama, top, on 20 January 2009, and President Donald Trump, bottom, on 20 January 2017. Both photos were taken just before noon on their respective dates from the top of the Washington Monument.

Top 10 Takeaways

1 Common sense is the knowledge we gather from life experiences, which may or may not be reliable, while a theory is a set of propositions intended to explain a fact or phenomenon and is based on social research. — p. 20

2 Functionalist theory views society as a set of interconnected parts that work together to preserve the stability and efficiency of social life. — pp. 21–23

3 Conflict theorists propose that society is organized around inequalities that produce conflict between social groups. — pp. 23–24

4 Symbolic interactionists highlight the important ways in which meanings are created, constructed, mediated, and changed by individual members of a group interacting with one another. — pp. 25–26

5 Feminists share an understanding that women's experiences are different from men's experiences, a concern for eradicating women's oppression, and a desire to dismantle patriarchy. — pp. 27–30

6 There are seven steps to most research projects; idea formation, literature review, hypothesis formation, research design, data collection, data analysis, and dissemination of findings. — pp. 31–36

7 There are two main approaches to social research: quantitative and qualitative. Quantitative research refers to numerical data while qualitative research refers to non-numerical data. Some researchers may use a combination of these two methods simultaneously—referred to as mixed methods. — p. 32

8 There are several ways that data can be collected in sociology: through experiments, unobtrusive measures, secondary analysis, participant observation, content analysis, surveys, and interviews. — pp. 33–36

9 When we analyze data, we must ensure that our findings are valid and reliable. — p. 36

10 Every researcher must go through research ethics approval prior to starting a project in order to ensure the protection of their participants. — pp. 36, 38–39

Questions for Critical Thinking

1. What are the manifest and latent functions of elementary and secondary schools? What are some dysfunctions that arise in these institutions?

2. Use conflict theory to discuss one current local event and one current global event.

3. How might the symbolic interactionist approach be applied to your high school experience?

4. How would the different waves of feminism explain women's lower rate of pay across most job sectors?

5. If there are so many different sociological views about any social issue—so many approaches, so many theories—and some people may not even view an issue as a "problem," why do we spend so much time and money studying the problem and trying (often unsuccessfully) to fix it?

6. Formulate a hypothetical research project. List each step of the research in relation to your proposed project.

7. Researchers want to study crime in low-income neighbourhoods. Contrast how a quantitative and qualitative researcher would approach this question.

8. Imagine that you are interested in the effects that media may have on fashion. How would you approach this topic from each of the different methodologies?

9. How might you ensure that your research is both valid and reliable?

10. Jasmine's mother was an exotic dancer when Jasmine was a child. Because of this, Jasmine is very interested in studying dancers' experiences within strip clubs. What kind of ethical issues might Jasmine face in a study of this nature?

Recommended Readings

- **Ritzer, G., & Stepnisky, J. (2017).** *Classical sociological theory* **(7th ed.). Thousand Oaks, CA: SAGE Publications.** After providing a historical sketch of sociological theory, the authors review the ideas of major sociological theorists, such as Marx, Durkheim, and Du Bois.

- **Ritzer, G., & Stepnisky, J. (2017).** *Modern sociological theory* **(8th ed.). Thousand Oaks, CA: SAGE Publications.** This book examines some of the sociological theories we have discussed in this chapter, including functionalism and symbolic interactionism, in more detail.

- **Swedberg, R. (2017). Theorizing in sociological research: A new perspective, a new departure?** *Annual Review of Sociology, 43*(1), 189–206. Recent academic work highlights the emergence of a new role of theory in sociology.

- **Harris, D. (2014).** *The complete guide to writing questionnaires: How to get better information for better decisions.* **I&M Press.** This easy to read guide presents a comprehensive system for creating questionnaire items that will yield accurate data.

- **Huff, D. (1954).** *How to lie with statistics.* **New York: W.W. Norton & Company.** This classic book presents the issues associated with data analysis and how errors in interpreting statistics can result in errors in conclusions of studies.

- **Stephens, W.R., Jr. (1998).** *Careers in sociology.* **New York: Allyn & Bacon.** This book presents the diverse range of careers of over a dozen sociology graduates.

Recommended Websites

Dead Sociologists Index
http://media.pfeiffer.edu/lridener/DSS/
- The Dead Sociologists Index provides detailed information on 16 classical theorists, including biographical information, commentary on the theorists' ideas, and links to original works.

Marxists Internet Archive
http://www.marxists.org/
- The Marxists Internet Archive is a comprehensive site offering sources and links for Marxism as a worldwide movement. It offers the full text of various writings, as well as information about many theorists within the Marxist perspective and about many other thinkers.

Sociology Online
http://www.sociologyonline.co.uk/
- This site, produced in Britain, provides resources for students of sociology. There is a "Classics" link to the "selective tradition" that comprises classical theory. The "Sociology News" link has many items of interest.

Social Sciences and Humanities Research Council (SSHRC)
http://www.sshrc-crsh.gc.ca/home-accueil-eng.aspx
- The SSHRC is a Canadian federal research funding organization that encourages post-secondary research and studies in the social sciences and humanities.

Statistics Canada
http://www.statcan.gc.ca/start-debut-eng.html
- Statistics Canada is a Canadian federal government agency that produces up-to-date statistics and data trends concerning a multitude of characteristics about the Canadian population, including resources, economy, culture, and the like.

The Conference Board of Canada (CBOC)
http://www.conferenceboard.ca/hcp/aboutus.aspx
- The CBOC is a non-profit research institute that is dedicated to researching and analyzing organizational, economic, and public policy trends and issues within Canadian society.

Chapter 3

Culture

If you live in a large city, all you have to do is look around your classroom, or around the street, to see that Canada is undergoing rapid cultural diversification. Despite our official legislation on multiculturalism, we often hear people say things like "Immigrants to Canada need to accept 'Canadian' culture if they want to live in this country." This statement is an example of **xenophobia**—the fear and/or distrust of people and traits that are perceived to be foreign or strange. The targets of xenophobia change based on the social conditions of the time and place. Sometimes these fears are expressed as concerns about the threat of change, such as the fear that "sharia law" will be implemented in Canada. Other times, they are expressed as changes to law or society meant to prevent people from retaining their differences, such as attempts to create laws to ban head coverings. And sometimes these fears manifest as a hate crime: in Canada, hate crimes against Muslims increased 253 per cent from 2012 to 2016 (Statistics Canada, 2017).

> *xenophobia* The fear and/or distrust of people and traits that are perceived to be foreign or strange.

Understanding what culture is and how it is created is more than a theoretical exercise—it is essential in combating xenophobia.

Key Terms

counterculture
cultural relativism
cultural universals
culture
culture shock
diffusion
ethnocentrism
globalization
innovation
language
material culture
multiculturalism
nonmaterial culture/symbolic culture
norms
sanctions
Sapir-Whorf hypothesis
subculture
symbol
values
xenocentrism
xenophobia

Introduction

What exactly do we mean by *culture*? You may hear people refer to an individual as "cultured," or to a particular place as having "lots of culture." The non-sociological use of *culture,* then, often refers to specific kinds of art highly valued by social elites, such as classical music or impressionist paintings. That use of the term *culture* is different from how we are using it here, however. In sociology, we use *culture* to refer to all objects and ideas within a society, including classical music and impressionist paintings but also including slang words or phrases, such as a *dab* (either a popular dance move or a concentrated marijuana extract, depending on context) and *kills* (the number of individuals a person has had sex with). Sociologists consider both the music of Mozart and of Drake and the paintings of Picasso and an anonymous graffiti artist to be equally indicative of culture.

Perhaps in your college classroom you have met some students who come from different parts of the world or who grew up in families with a different cultural heritage than yours. Think about the differences between you and those other students. Do you dress and accessorize differently? Are there differences in the way you speak, not only in accent but also in the way you use slang or speak formally? Did you grow up watching the same television shows? Do you follow different religions and/or have different values? Perhaps your value system includes abstaining from alcohol, while your classmates discuss their weekend plans that include "getting wasted." All these differences are indicative of your diverse cultural backgrounds.

What Is Culture?

Culture is the shared set of influences (including beliefs, **values**, rules, behaviours, objects, media, and language) that we use to make sense of the world around us—they are passed on from one generation to the next, shaping us, and in turn we shape them as we pass them on to the future. Culture, then, includes the characteristics people acquire not through biological inheritance but, rather, through growing up in a particular place, with particular people, at a particular moment in time.

Culture also includes **norms**, which are both written rules (such as laws) and unwritten rules (that are taught and understood but are not legally binding). It also includes the ways in which people sanction or punish/reward one another for violating a norm. For example, holding open a door for the person behind you is a common social norm in Canada, and if you were to let a door swing back in someone's face, that person might glare at you or even exclaim in surprise or quietly judge you as being selfish. This is a relatively mild sanction, but you can see how you might be motivated to hold the door, even if you don't really want to, just to avoid the

culture A collection of beliefs, values, norms, behaviours, language, and material objects that are passed on from one generation to the next.

values Beliefs about ideal goals and behaviour that serve as standards for social life.

norms The rules and expectations by which a society guides the behaviour of its members.

fear of being yelled at or glared at in public or to avoid poor public opinion. On the other hand, if you did hold the door, the person might smile at you in thanks, which is an example of a positive **sanction**.

In other words, culture is learned and is socially transmitted and enforced. It is what we in sociology call "fluid"; that is, it changes over time and is influenced by people and events. Moreover, while some traditions may seem to stand the test of time, even they are likely to eventually change in some ways.

Individuals moving to Canada from Somalia are surrounded by a culture that is very different from their own. Evidence of these differences would be everywhere—the way that people dress and wear their hair, the types of institutions found in a city, and the city's infrastructure would provide a contrast to what they are accustomed to. In addition, the religious beliefs, values, languages spoken, slang used, gestures, and other assumptions

---

Wild Country

Dir. Maclain Way and Chapman Way (2018). A Netflix documentary series about a controversial Indian guru named Bhagwan Shree Rajneesh, who built a large community of followers called Rajneeshpuram in small-town Oregon. The series follows the cultural clashes that originally occur as a result of xenophobia and then turn into something much more ominous.

> **sanctions** Rewards for adhering to a norm and punishments for violating a norm.
>
> **material culture** The physical artifacts and objects found in a culture.

about the world would differ. These are all part of what sociologists refer to as material and nonmaterial culture.

Features of Culture

Material culture includes all the physical objects that members of a culture create and use. In its broadest sense, material culture

monkeybusinessimages/iStock.com

Canada has a reputation as a "land of opportunity" for immigrants, but reality often falls short. University of Toronto economist Philip Oreopoulos found that replacing an anglophone name with an Indian or Chinese name on a resumé reduced by 50 per cent the chance that an employer would offer that person a job interview (Oreopoulos, 2011). This manifestation of xenophobia is at least part of the reason why many highly educated immigrants are left out of the Canadian job force. We will say more about this study in Chapter 9.

includes all the physical and technological aspects of people's lives. For example, it includes all the material objects that fill up our home, our locker, the stores at the mall, the cars that we drive, the restaurants that we visit, and so on. Material culture is what we consume in a consumerist, materialistic society like our own. In a culture as committed to a high standard of living and consumer goods as ours is, we often derive a lot of information about one another from the material objects that surround us. These objects are as much our cultural masters as they are our servants.

Nonmaterial culture is the part of the culture that goes on in people's minds. It includes values, beliefs, philosophies, conventions, and ideologies—all of which are aspects of culture that lack a physical existence. Nonmaterial culture also includes tweets, song lyrics, ways of talking, and a variety of other "styles" of behaviour.

> ***nonmaterial culture/ symbolic culture*** The intangible and abstract components of a society, including a society's values and norms and religious beliefs.
>
> ***symbol*** An object, image, or event used to represent a particular concept.
>
> ***language*** A shared system of communication that includes both verbal and nonverbal gestures to convey meaning.

Sociologists sometimes refer to nonmaterial culture as **symbolic culture** because one of its principal components is the set of **symbols** people use to interact and communicate with one another. Our symbol systems include language, values, norms, and sanctions—even, as mentioned earlier, graffiti tags.

Analyzing aspects of material culture can give you a sense of a culture's nonmaterial traits. For example, material goods shape our social interactions, as dictated by our (nonmaterial) values and norms. Smart phones, haircuts, cars, purses, and shoes can all have a major impact on how we communicate with each other—but only because nonmaterial culture imbues these items with particular traits (desirable or not desirable). People in our society depend on information and information transfer for their education, recreation, social life, and livelihood. That's why the average household contains so many information-related devices: books, magazines, televisions, telephones, and computers, among others. People are also preoccupied with time, and that explains why we possess so many time-keeping devices: clocks, wristwatches, Fitbits, alarms, calendars, schedules, and datebooks, etcetera. Finally, most of us are obsessed with looking good: with being stylish and attractive. That's why, if we can afford it, we possess so many material objects of adornment: clothing for different occasions, accessories, cosmetics, and even fake body parts (braces, false eyelashes and nails, contact lenses). Indeed, people will manipulate their appearance to gain friendship, love, and success. In short, cultural objects tell us a lot about what people in a society value.

Language

Language is a system of symbols strung together for the purpose of communicating abstract thoughts. Language is universal in the sense that all human groups possess it, but there is nothing universal about the meanings given to certain sounds. Think for a moment about the letters *s-t-o-p*. There is no obvious relationship between these letters and the cessation of movement. The letters are symbols that English-speaking people have collectively agreed mean that something should end.

Although language is a cultural universal, differences are evident around the world even in places that primarily speak the same language. Think of the use of the English language in London, Ontario, Canada, and in London, England. In Canada we refer to the clothing we wear on our legs as "pants"; in the UK, however,

Some types of art are more valued in society than others. While graffiti art is part of culture, it is often not as appreciated or valued as other artistic expressions.

Zach Gray

these are "trousers," and "pants" mean underwear! In Canada we might tell a friend that we will "hit them up later," while in the UK they might say "I'll ring you up." In both instances, individuals are trying to convey that they will call the other person on the telephone. For a discussion of the importance of language to culture and identity, see the From My Perspective box on page 54.

There are also interesting differences in language between provinces within Canada. In British Columbia, if you were curious as to the location of a person whom you were speaking to on the telephone you would ask, "Where are you?" In Newfoundland, on the other hand, you would say, "Where you at?" Likewise, in Newfoundland if you wanted to know where someone was going, rather than asking "Where are you going?" many people say "Where you to?" As you can see, language is also shaped by location and culture.

There are also cultural differences in the meaning of certain words. For example, in most provinces across Canada the word *fish* refers to any cold-blooded vertebrate animal with gills and fins that lives in water. In Newfoundland, however, *fish* is used to mean *cod* because of the importance of the cod industry on the Newfoundland economy. Similarly, in Canada and most of the northern United States, *toboggan* refers to a type of sled. However, in the southern United States it means "hat"—the type Canadians refer affectionately to as a "toque." The word *toboggan* comes from a Mi'kmaq word that made its way into Canadian French and then into English. In the southern United States, it is believed that the term "toboggan hat" was shortened to "toboggan" because tobogganing was so foreign to the southern US, where it rarely snows. In these cases, the history of intermingling cultures, as well as the variety of pastimes (affected by weather), affected the cultural and therefore linguistic differences by region.

Sapir-Whorf Hypothesis

In the 1930s, two ethnolinguists named Edward Sapir and Benjamin Whorf were studying a group—the Hopi people—in the Southwestern United States. They came to realize that in contrast to many other languages (for example, English, German, French, and Spanish), the Hopi language did not provide words that differentiated between the past, present, and future.

This discovery led Sapir and Whorf to develop the Sapir-Whorf hypothesis: that language reflects cultural values and so it affects the way we look at and interpret the world. When we learn a language, we are

Sapir-Whorf hypothesis
The theory that language shapes reality.

Crash

Dir. Paul Haggis (2004). This movie tracks the tense interactions between 12 African-American, white, Iranian, and Hispanic Americans. All 12 people cause suffering to one another, and suffer themselves, as a result of racial and cultural prejudices.

also learning a way of thinking about the world, which in turn shapes the ways we behave. It also filters the way people see reality. When children learn to speak a language, they learn the cultural values and norms of that language as well. As a result, differences in the ways different languages discuss things can make communication across cultures difficult.

For example, there are many words that are deemed "untranslatable" between languages because while they may capture an experience that is universal (sociologists theorize), the experience is more prevalent or more important to the culture that has a word for it. For example, the Inuktitut word *iktsuarpok* describes the feeling of excited, anxious anticipation that drives people to check multiple times if someone is coming when they are waiting for someone to arrive (Smith, 2015). Because of this and other evidence, social scientists still take seriously Sapir and Whorf's belief that languages shape and reflect the reality of cultures.

Nonverbal Communication

Each culture uses gestures, or nonverbal communication, to convey meaning. Think of this scenario: you and your friends go out to a bar in a large Canadian city for some drinks on Saturday night. The three of you are standing at one of the tables, looking out at the dance floor, when your eye catches the gaze of a person standing a few feet away from you. When this person sees that you have noticed them looking at you, they lower their gaze to your feet and slowly raise their eyes until they meet your eyes again, smile, and wink. This person has in fact communicated a number of things to you without saying one word.

We were not born with an understanding of what any gestures mean; rather, we learn them over time from people who share our culture. Nonverbal communication does not have the same meaning in all cultures. And even when a gesture does have the same meaning, cultures may have different rules around where and when such a gesture is acceptable. Do you think there are distinctly Canadian forms of nonverbal communication?

In North America, sticking your thumb up while standing at the side of a road indicates that you want a ride somewhere; in other contexts, the gesture can mean "Good job" or "I agree." In other countries, however, the thumbs-up gesture is considered rude. In Greece, Italy, and parts of the Middle East, it is essentially the equivalent of sticking up your middle finger in North America.

In the News

What Makes Canada Canadian?

A nationwide Canada Day poll asked more than 1000 Canadians to identify what they thought was the best symbol "of what Canada really is" (The Dominion Institute, 2015). The frontrunner was the great Canadian wilderness. Of those surveyed, 83 per cent said the wilderness was a "good" or "great" reflection of Canada (The Dominion Institute, 2015). Most respondents also selected Canada's majestic landscapes as the thing they would offer as an example of Canada's finest attributes to someone from another country. The remaining top 10 symbols of Canada were the flag (81 per cent), the national anthem (74 per cent), hockey (73 per cent), the Mounties (66 per cent), medicare (65 per cent), the Arctic (60 per cent), the beaver (59 per cent), multiculturalism (52 per cent), and the military (46 per cent), all of which were acknowledged as "good" or "great" symbols of Canada (The Dominion Institute, 2015).

On 31 January 2018, the Canadian national anthem made headlines across the nation as the Senate passed legislation that the song should contain gender-neutral language (Tasker, 2018). The change from "in all thy sons command" to "in all of us command" sparked outrage in some people across the country, while many others were happy to see that Canadian women are now included in their country's national anthem (Tasker, 2018).

Do you think that changing the words to the national anthem affects its "Canadian-ness"? Does the song have to remain as you have always known it to remain a symbol of Canada? (In fact, the original version of the song is in French, and the original English translation of the line was "thou dost in us command" and was changed in 1914 to "in all thy sons command.") Is there anything else about the anthem that you would change if you had the chance?

World Events

Kneeling

Although culture is influenced by food and clothing, it is even more strongly shaped by the social world and, especially, by politics. Between 1999 and 2013, black people in the United States accounted for 27.6 per cent of deaths at the hands of police yet made up only 13.2 per cent of the population, a phenomenon in sociology called overrepresentation (Newton, 2018). This, along with general frustration with the legal system and harassment by officers (an issue in Canada as well; see the discussion of "carding" in Chapter 10) led to the emergence of the Black Lives Matter movement in 2013, represented by protests and political demonstrations (Clare, 2016). Furthermore, the movement's message, imagery, terms, hashtags, mantras, aesthetic, and practices (i.e., their culture) have spread to chapters across the US and in Canada as well (Clare, 2016).

Three years later, in 2016, US football player Colin Kaepernick chose to kneel as a sign of protest during the American national anthem—a powerful national cultural symbol in a fiercely nationalist country (Pogue, 2017). Not only did this form of protest spread to other teams and players within the league, but it also influenced protests in schools, political demonstrations, and social media. Furthermore, Kaepernick's protest immediately drew backlash from nationalist and conservative news sources, who accused him of disgracing one of the country's core national symbols and of bringing politics into sports, which they argued goes against the rules of sports culture.

This incident (and its resulting fallout) brings up a number of important questions that sociologists must consider: How are movements formed by culture, and in what ways do they produce their own movements? How do symbols become so imbued with meaning that they act as focal points for political action? Who has the power to shape, promote, influence, and change culture?

How Do Cultures Develop?

Most of your experiences of the world at large are very different from those of your parents when they were your age. Thirty years ago, many of us only learned about other cultures through school textbooks or through the National Geographic monthly publication. Today, however, we can get a peripheral experience of any culture simply by clicking our mouse. Thus, we continue to experience changes across cultures. Social scientists are interested in the practices that are found throughout cultures, as well as the ways in which cultures modify over time.

The Existence of a Universal Culture

In light of the visible differences between people in different societies, can we find anything that all cultures and societies require—something that unifies all human communities? Many generations of sociologists and anthropologists have thought about this question and searched for cultural universals to find an answer. They have concluded that there are indeed cultural universals—practices that are found in every known human culture (Murdock, 1949, p. 124).

Examples of cultural universals include language, sports, religious ceremonies, and ritual gift-giving. Perhaps these activities satisfy the human need for social interaction and group membership. Other universals identified by Murdock include laws, music, numbers and counting, personal names, sexual restrictions, and tool-making. Note, however, that sports, religious ceremonies, gift-giving practices, and other cultural universals are all different from one culture to the next. People in different cultures play different sports, celebrate different religions, give gifts in different ways, and so on. This shows that, for example, while the desire to play in an organized fashion may be innate to humanity, the specific desire to get a ball through a hoop is not necessarily innate.

These universals are also always changing over time. One such example is the use of names. Historically in Canada, names were given to either a boy or girl based upon their gender exclusively—for example, Christopher for a boy and Mary for a girl. Over time, however, a trend has emerged in Canada of giving girls names that historically were only given to boys. For example, in my own household all four daughters—and even our

> **cultural universals**
> Common cultural features found in all societies.

Practising Sociology

Describe Your Own Culture

Can you describe your own culture? As you have learned in this chapter, describing your culture means much more than stating where you are from and what your religious beliefs are. Using the chart below, discuss your own culture. State whether each component is part of your material or nonmaterial culture.

Attribute	Describe	Material or Nonmaterial
Languages spoken		
Nonverbal communication used		
Religion		
Norms/values/folkways		
Taboos/mores		
Holidays/festivities		
Music		
Foods		
Modes of dress (daily and at special occasions)		
Practices around marriage, birth, death		
Technology		
Symbols		

Reflection: Looking at all the different components of your culture, would you say that you practice culture the same way as your parents and/or your grandparents? In what ways does your practice differ?

Get into groups of six and share the different components of your culture with one another. Are there more differences or similarities than you may have expected? Explain. Discuss something new that you learned about another culture during the discussion.

Current Research

Pierre Bourdieu and Cultural Capital

French sociologist Pierre Bourdieu developed the concept of cultural capital in the late 1950s while performing his national service in Algeria. For him, cultural capital described the means by which certain groups in Algeria traded on the fact that some types of cultural "taste" enjoy more status than others (Bourdieu, 1986; Field, 2008). Bourdieu theorized that the ability to decode art, enjoy classical music, name-drop the people you know or the places you've been, or eat foods not common in your culture is not in itself a sign of superiority but, rather, "coinage in the cultural currency used by a particular social group in order to maintain superiority over other groups" (Field, 2008, p. 16). Bourdieu argued that while cultural capital was shaped by family circumstances and school tuition, it could to some extent operate independently of monetary possessions and could in some cases compensate for lack of money (Field, 2008). More recent research has since shown that cultural capital does result in real-world financial gains. For example, a study by Wolfgang Lehmann and Holly Trower showed that cultural capital (such as a student's being exposed to travel in his or her family) had a greater influence than financial resources on Canadian students' decision to study abroad, although studying abroad provides demonstrable employment benefits, particularly for underprivileged students (Lehmann and Trower, 2018). Can you think of examples of situations where you or your friends may have cultural capital that might compensate for or be more important than your financial resources?

filipefrazao/iStock.com

You may be surprised to learn that kissing is not a cultural universal phenomenon! Researchers have found that less than half the world's cultures kiss in a romantic way. The study looked at 168 distinct cultures and found evidence of romantic kissing in only 77 of them: "It's a reminder that behaviours that seem so normative often do not occur in the rest of the world . . . No ethnographer working with sub-Saharan Africa, New Guinea, or Amazonian foragers or horticulturalists reported having witnessed any occasion in which their study populations engaged in a romantic-sexual kiss" (Jankowiak, Volsche, & Garcia, 2015, pp. 535–39).

female dog—are named after boys: Talor (my brother's name is also Taylor), Madison (originally an English boys name), Ryleigh (also originally an English boys name), Kennedy (named after John F. Kennedy, Jr, whom I may have had a slight crush on in the late 1990s), and Bentley (the fur baby). However, we have not seen the reverse of this trend with boys receiving names that were traditionally meant for girls. (Consider this when we discuss gender in Chapter 7.)

innovation Occurs when existing cultural items are manipulated or modified to produce something new and socially valuable.

Innovation

Arguably, one of the greatest things about being human is our creative capacity. A beaver's dam in 2017 looks very similar to a beaver's dam in 1817 because beavers, like most animals, build on instinct.

Humans, in contrast, build homes out of all kinds of different products, in all different shapes and designs. Humans create new designs, materials, and features in order to improve the home or to make it better suited to the culture and environment in which it is built.

Materials, designs, and security systems continue to evolve as new **innovations** are discovered. Now, for example, we can monitor our houses from our cellphones at any moment of any day. We can also turn on and off lights arbitrarily throughout the day from our phone to give the appearance that we are home. If our homes are broken into, our systems can instantly dial emergency services and call us wherever we are to inform us that there is an intruder.

As technological and scientific advancements continue, we will see new innovations that will impact our culture. Think for a moment about your cellphone. Many of you own an iPhone or Samsung cellular phone and use it for most of your communication needs. However, rather than telephone your friend, or flirt with the person you are attracted to in person—as the author of this text had to do at your age—you can simply send a string of emojis that express your mood or feelings, or a Snapchat of an inanimate object with two words written across the screen; or you can simply swipe right. This is a significant cultural shift and one that most people over the age of 30 didn't

A great example of cultural diffusion is the Pokémon series of shows and games, all cultural artifacts from Japan that were exported to North America in 1996 and remain popular today (Assunção, Brown, & Workman, 2017). In this photo, people gather in Assiniboine Park in Winnipeg, Alberta, to play an augmented reality game for mobile devices called Pokémon GO. In addition to media and institutions, the market can be a powerful force of cultural diffusion.

experience in the same way. While many teens from my generation waited excitedly for a phone call, teens today sometimes experience anxiety when their phone rings, believing that something may be wrong. In addition, when I was a teenager if my home phone rang and someone left the table to answer it my parents would get angry as they perceived this to be very rude. Now that most people have a cellphone at their fingertips, it is considered much ruder if they do not respond to messages quickly.

Diffusion

Culture shifts do not occur solely based upon new discoveries and/or inventions. Cultures are also impacted through the process of **diffusion**—when cultural items or practices are transmitted from one group to another. For example, many of us frequently enjoy meals that originated in cultures other than our own (e.g., curry, sushi, jerk, Kung Pao, tacos, shawarma, pasta with meatballs), wear clothing that originated in other parts of the world (e.g., yoga pants and denim come instantly to mind), listen to music that was born out of another culture's struggles (e.g., reggae), and take part in holistic practices that are still considered "alternative" in North America (e.g., acupuncture, reiki).

Diffusion can occur through a number of avenues, such as exploration, trade, conquest, mass media, tourism, and the Internet. **Globalization**—the worldwide integration of government policies, cultures, social movements, and financial markets—has accelerated cultural diffusion.

Cultural Diversity

Even within a given society, many subcultures develop because of generational, class, occupational, or lifestyle differences. A **subculture** is a cultural group within society that shares elements of the dominant culture but also has its own distinctive values, beliefs, norms, style of dress, and behaviour patterns; it may even have its own language. Determining the number of subcultures in any given society may be impossible. Different regions of the country may have different subcultures, as is evident if we compare beliefs and lifestyles in Nova Scotia, Quebec, and Saskatchewan.

In fact, we could argue that teenagers have their own subculture as many engage in shared activities and values that are at least somewhat similar to one another but dissimilar to those of their parents. Imagine

---

diffusion The spread of invention or discovery from one area to another.

globalization The worldwide integration of government policies, cultures, social movements, and financial markets.

subculture A segment of a culture that has characteristics that distinguish it from the broader culture.

counterculture A subculture with values and norms that oppose the dominant culture.

---

for a moment your parent or guardian dressing in the same clothes to go to work that you do to go to school, or wearing the same outfit you wear to the club when they meet their friends for dinner. Now imagine that you apologize to your parent for coming in late and they respond with "It's all Gucci" or that they ask you if the party you attended was "lit." Imagine your parent referring to their partner as their "Bae" and letting you know that their plans for the night include "Netflix and chill."

In addition to language choices, many teenagers eat similar foods—fast, cheap, and deep fried—and take part in similar activities—sleeping, playing video games, texting, Snapchatting, partying, and, hopefully, going to classes. While teenagers may share a language, values, and norms that are slightly different than those of their parents, they still very much exist within and, for the most part, accept the larger dominant culture.

Within this framework, a **counterculture** is a subculture that rejects conventional norms and values and adopts alternative ones. This kind of culture is fundamentally at odds with the culture of the larger society. It is often found among younger and less advantaged members of a society. A counterculture develops among people with little reason to conform to the main culture. Such people are unlikely to get rewarded with praise, good jobs, or high incomes, even if they value what other people value and conform to other people's rules.

Like a subculture, a counterculture has its own beliefs, material culture, and problems of cultural integration. Even members of the Hell's Angels have their loyalties; even anarchists follow their own rules. Delinquents, punk rockers, and skinheads have their ideals, too. Like any culture, a counterculture contains contradictions between what its members say and what they do.

Culture Shock

Have you ever sat down to eat a meal in a different country or at a restaurant you've never been to and found that the featured dish is something that you would never imagine (or desire) eating? For example, if you travel to rural France from Canada, you might at first be afraid to consume dairy products as most never go inside the refrigerator and are not pasteurized. If you came to Canada from the United States, you might be shocked to see Canadians at the grocery store purchasing milk in plastic bags! If you travelled to Switzerland, you might be surprised to find out that

From My Perspective

Jessica Riel-Johns

As an adult educator and as an Indigenous woman, my own journey of discovery into my Indigenous culture led me to believe that the role to maintaining your cultural identity is by teaching and allowing your experiences to be guided with the guidance from elders, community, parents, and the individual to help self-identify all elements of culture.

Understanding Indigenous spirituality is the way of working, thinking, and communicating and how you perceive that world view. Indigenous spirituality is passed-down knowledge from generation to generation to allow Indigenous people to appreciate what they have in this world and to give thanks to the creator for what surrounds us. As an Indigenous person, you may feel like you have a deep spiritual connection with the land and land-based education. Indigenous spirituality encompasses many things—from a blade of grass to the sky—and this is just as important as being human, but this paradigm is opposite to Western society's spirituality.

Historically, in Indigenous culture, the language is an important identifier to your location and nation, and is seen as spiritual to many Aboriginal people, and many are trying to reclaim and restore the language for generations to come because this too was lost during the colonization era of Indigenous people. When the culture is lost so is the spirit within that component of the cultural context. There are tangible threats to Indigenous spirituality, much like the colonization era, but now it is done differently. The threats can be environmental loss, loss of sacred land and animals; environment factors like floods, ozone, and pollution can all contribute to the removal of culture and spirituality in the Indigenous world.

Indigenous spirituality is complex to those who do not understand or have the willingness to understand the culture. It is like learning a new language and having many misconceptions of the meaning. You need to have an open mind to have the window of opportunity to understand the culture and all complexities of the spiritual components. Others perceive Indigenous spirituality as an experience because it is something they do not practise on a daily basis and are foreign to the ceremonies, traditions, and practices but observe with respect. When I teach I try to introduce my students to learn in a more holistic way rather than the current classroom setting. I believe that incorporating my culture into my classroom not only reaches different types of learning styles but that it allows all students to feel inclusive to my classroom; thus in my perspective Indigenous spirituality is not only important to my culture but also to who I am as an Indigenous woman.

Jessica Riel-Johns

Jessica Riel-Johns, Three Fires Community Justice Program Coordinator; Anishinabe from Batchewana First Nation.

Source: Provided by Jessica Riel-Johns, used by permission.

Rather than valuing military might, financial success, and social conformity, the "hippie" counterculture of the 1960s valued peace, love, few possessions, and coexistence with the environment, and actively pushed to make its ideals more mainstream. In 2018, a movement is building that has some similarities, known as "minimalism." In direct contrast to mainstream Canadian culture, the main value of minimalism is to own *less*. However, unlike hippies, minimalists tend to function within mainstream culture rather than trying to actively change it, making theirs a subculture and not a counterculture.

one of their most beloved meals (and quite expensive at restaurants) is called *rosti* and is really just shredded potatoes cooked into a round shape. And, if you came to Canada from Uganda, you might be shocked to see the long lines of people waiting at Tim Hortons every morning for coffee (something easily and cheaply made at home!), on almost every street corner.

This feeling of feeling disoriented, out of place, and uncertain is known as **culture shock**. Culture shock can also happen within your own culture. A white Catholic student living in Vancouver, British Columbia, might experience culture shock if she were to visit a rural town in New Brunswick. To some extent all of us take our cultural practices for granted and may find it surprising to realize that other cultures have completely different customs that appear strange to us.

> **culture shock** The feelings of disorientation and uncertainty that people experience when they encounter unfamiliar cultural practices.
>
> **ethnocentrism** The tendency to assume that one's own culture and way of life represents the norm or is superior to all others.

Ethnocentrism, Cultural Relativism, and Xenocentrism

People are so emotionally involved with their own culture that they may not see that their personal values are just one approach to human life. They think that their point of view is the only natural or sensible view. Often, they fail to consider other ways of thinking or even to realize that these other ways *exist*. **Ethnocentrism** is a tendency to evaluate other cultures through the lens of one's own culture. People take their own culture to be the norm and consider it superior to all other cultures. For example, an ethnocentric Canadian tourist might look down

Zach Gray

This cartoon depicts just one of many ways in which culture—in this case, different norms around hair styles—affects our understanding and judgment of others.

on a country for not having a Tim Hortons or for only having espresso (and no brewed coffee) regularly available. Ethnocentrism can pose serious problems in a world filled with different values, languages, and perceptions.

For example, ethnocentrism played a significant role in several cases in Canada where black women have been discriminated against because of their hair. A female television reporter on a Canadian channel was told by her white male boss to straighten her hair if she wanted to keep her job on television (Cox, 2014). Similarly, in 2015 a female student was told to "do something" about her hair and that "no one would hire her with hair like that" (Da Silva, 2015). While these may seem like isolated cases, an American study by the Perception Institute (2016) found that there is explicit bias toward black women's hair: respondents stated that black women's hair is less attractive and less professional. Davis (2003) asserts that as a society we assign value to certain hair, viewing some types as good and others as bad, and that these values are so ingrained that they exist even within the black community itself. In 2016, the United States Court of Appeals ruled that an employer could discriminate against an employee based on dreadlocks (Kiwanuka, 2017). This sort of ethnocentrism may seem trivial to some but has disastrous consequences for black communities. Black women report having lower self-esteem, and research continues to find that they are less remunerated in the labour market (Kiwanuka, 2017).

The consequences of ethnocentrism can also be more explicit. For example,

during the initial phase of the war on terror, the images of oppressed, veiled Muslim women were widely and continuously circulated in Canadian media to justify the bombing of Afghanistan by the United States military. However, what was not circulated was the fact that women's groups in Afghanistan, prior to 9/11, were on the front lines of resistance against the Taliban and other extremist Islamic groups (Tickner, 2002). By judging Afghan culture to be "backwards" based on ethnocentric assumptions, Canada, the United States, Britain, and others effectively justified the war as being about the liberation of oppressed women and conveniently ignored the high number of civilian casualties (including women) that would occur over the course of the war.

In an attempt to counter our tendency to judge other cultures based on our own standards, we try to understand a culture on its own terms. This is called **cultural relativism**. Practising cultural relativism places a priority on understanding other cultures rather than merely dismissing them as strange or "exotic." Different social contexts give rise to different norms, values, and sanctions, and we must examine certain practices within the contexts of the cultures in which they are found. This sounds like a simple idea: obviously we cannot claim to understand other cultures by using our own ideas; we *must* take the time to understand all aspects of the other culture. But is that as easy as it sounds?

We can probably all agree that it is rude to tell someone who is sitting next to you

> **cultural relativism** An appreciation that all cultures have their own norms and values and thus should be understood on their terms rather than according to one's own cultural standards.

that the cultural food he or she is eating is disgusting, smells bad, or looks weird. We can also agree that wearing a hijab or niqab is not an oppressive religious requirement but, rather, something that is deeply embedded in culture and historical context. However, not all cross-cultural differences are that easy to understand on their own terms. What do you think of the practice of raising bulls for the sole purpose of stabbing them to death in front of shouting crowds? What about dogfighting? Or female circumcision?

Female circumcision is the ritual removal of some or all of the external female genitalia, and the procedure is typically carried out by a traditional circumciser with a blade or razor, with or without anesthesia. The practice is carried out in 28 countries in sub-Saharan and Northeast Africa, South America, Yemen, and to a lesser extent in other areas of Asia (Abolfotouh, Ebrahim, & Abolfotouh, 2015). More than 125 million girls and women alive today have undergone circumcisions (Abolfotouh, Ebrahim, & Abolfotouh, 2015). The age at which female circumcision is conducted varies from days after birth to puberty; however, approximately 50 per cent of women go through the procedure before they are five years old. North American feminists see the practice as an overt attempt to control women's sexuality that is rooted in gender inequality.

Practising cultural relativism is attempting to understand why this may happen rather than judging it. It certainly doesn't mean that we support or agree with all of the practices that occur across cultures. Instead, cultural relativism is an attempt to refocus our cultural lens and thereby appreciate and understand the complexities behind other ways of life rather than simply asserting that our way is the right way and insisting that others change.

Practising Sociology

Practising Cultural Relativism

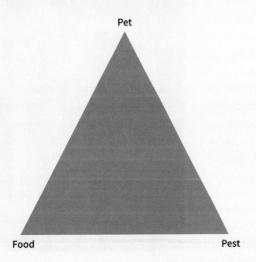

Consider how we think about animals in our everyday life. Try placing the following animals around the triangle above, and see if the person beside you agrees with where you put them:

- Cat
- Dog
- Rat
- Fish
- Cow
- Pig
- Insect
- Shrimp
- Horse
- Snake

Based on your own culture, where did you put each animal? How might this change from person to person? By culture? By religion? What situations might change their placement? What would change if you had not eaten in two days? Or if you were alone with lots of food but nothing else for company? Or if there were 5000 of each animal instead of one? Our perception is often tied to our cultural understanding and upbringing and can vary drastically from place to place as well as over time and context.

While people raised in Canada may find it difficult to understand why female circumcision is allowed to continue, many girls and women allegedly choose to have the procedure, and women have resisted and even opposed changing these practices in some countries (Althaus, 1997). Research reveals that, often, in the cultures in which female circumcision occurs, if a woman has not been circumcised she will not be viewed as marriageable and thus will live a life of poverty (Althaus, 1997). Additionally, attempts by England, the United States, Canada, or the United Nations to impose change are often seen by citizens of these countries where it is practised as patronizing and just another attempt at colonialism—the practice of acquiring control over another country and then exploiting it economically (Althaus, 1997).

> **xenocentrism** The preference for a culture other than one's own.

Another explosive topic is the treatment of animals. Bullfighting is a traditional spectacle in Spain, parts of southern France, and some Latin American countries in which humans (called matadors) fight one or more bulls in a bullring. Although in North America this practice is seen as cruel and unnecessary, within the areas where it is practised, bullfighting is considered a highly ritualized cultural event and art form, which some see as deeply tied to Spanish culture and identity. Dogfighting is also commonly practised for revenue in many places. Traditionally, the dogs fight until one dies and the owner of the winning dog earns all of the money. While this is illegal in many countries, it is common practice in some cultures.

An extension of cultural relativism is xenocentrism, whereby rather than merely attempting to assess another culture based on its own merit, people assume that everything about another culture is superior to their own. For example, even though the Niagara Region in Ontario and the Okanagan Valley in British Columbia are known for their wine, many Canadians assume French or Italian wines are superior (whether they drink wine themselves or not). Japanese electronics, German cars, and Swiss chocolate are also perceived to be superior to domestic-made products.

Canadian Culture

Is there a Canadian culture that distinguishes us from, for example, Americans—our nearest neighbours? Where researchers do find cultural differences between Canadians and Americans, they find Canadians to be less traditional and elitist. Both in our social policies, such as medicare, and in our attitudes toward the disadvantaged, Canadians are much more egalitarian than Americans. Other likely differences in preferences are between liberty (Americans prefer more) and order (Canadians prefer more).

The Tragically Hip are Canadian icons although they reached only minimal fame globally. Arguably, this is because their lyrics often focus on Canadian history and events, and challenge elements of Canadian identity. After frontman Gord Downie was diagnosed with terminal brain cancer, the band went on tour, ending in the band's hometown of Kingston, Ontario, in 2016. CBC televised the sold-out venue across Canada, and almost 12 million viewers tuned in. During the show, Downie begged Prime Minister Justin Trudeau to address the deplorable conditions under which Indigenous people are forced to live in Canada. Downie passed away in October 2017.

© Paul Mckinnon | Dreamstime.com

Secret Path

Gord Downie (October 2016). A 10-song record by Tragically Hip frontman Gord Downie that explores the story of Chanie Wenjack, a 12-year-old boy who died attempting to walk more than 600 kilometres home from the residential school he was placed in.

Still, some observers propose that Canadian culture may not exist at all. If it does, it is only as a collection of regional cultures, such as a Prince Edward Island culture, a Métis culture, or a Yukon culture. On various social and political topics, Quebeckers (as an example) consistently have shown the most progressive or liberal attitudes. They are as distinct a group as people in the American south, although far less conservative. Other North Americans are far less distinctive, whether they live in Toronto or Toledo, Winnipeg or Minneapolis, Vancouver or Seattle.

Nationalists propose that if we don't have a unified Canadian culture, the United States will take over our

> **multiculturalism** The freedom of individuals of all origins to preserve, enhance, and share their cultural heritage and to participate in society fully and equally.

economy, culture, and political world. Others say that Canadian culture is already strong enough to resist that possibility. Regionalists, such as Quebec nationalists, propose that cultural unification would negatively affect regional cultures that people care about. So, over 150 years of nationhood has failed to provide Canada with an unambiguously distinct national culture. What's more, given the forces of globalization, it seems unlikely that the future will lead to a distinct Canadian culture.

One of the things that Canada is most known for, however, is its multiculturalism. But despite being an integral part of Canadian identity, multiculturalism is a relatively recent political policy for the country. In the 1960s, Canada eliminated overt racism in its immigration policies, allowing the country to begin to diversify. The federal government, under Prime Minister Pierre Elliott Trudeau, declared in 1971 that Canada would adopt a multicultural policy. In 1982, multiculturalism was recognized by section 27 of the Canadian Charter of Rights and Freedoms. Prime Minister Brian Mulroney then enacted the Canadian Multiculturalism Act in 1985.

#Sociology

Hockey as Part of Canadian Culture?

When I ask my classes to tell me what they perceive to be the elements of Canadian culture, students inevitably yell out words such as *apologetic, nice, maple leaf, maple syrup, Tim Hortons, poutine, bilingual, Canada geese, beavers, moose, snow, lacrosse,* and *hockey.* The love of the game of hockey has long been associated with being Canadian and has at times been said to be closer to a religion than a sport (Keating, 2010). Indeed, social research into hockey has shown that in Canada the sport plays a vital role in how we understand gender, class, and community identity, and is significant

at both the local and national level (Lorenz, 2015).

Hockey continues to unite the country despite its immense diversity. As an extreme example, we can examine the tragic event of 6 April 2018 when a tractor-trailer collided with a bus carrying the Humboldt Broncos, a junior A hockey team, in rural Saskatchewan. The collision killed 16 people, including the bus driver, coach, assistant coach, a radio announcer, an 18-year-old stats-keeper, an athletic therapist, and 10 of the young players. Another 13 players were taken to the hospital with serious injuries.

The country mourned together, with many people showing their support through social media posts, including multiple number 1–trending hashtags, such as #JerseysforHumboldt, #HumboldtStrong, and #PutYourSticksOut. *Hockey Night in Canada* as well as rinks across the country offered tributes to the team. Perhaps most remarkably, within two days a GoFundMe page had garnered $5,401,296 to support the families affected by this tragedy. Would you argue that hockey is a part of Canadian culture? What other things would you say are deeply ingrained in us as Canadians?

The act affirms that every Canadian shall receive equal treatment by the government regardless of race or religion. While English and French remain the only official federal languages, the Multiculturalism Act recognizes the right to speak other languages, and official languages vary by province and territory.

The act also allows citizens to practise any religion and maintain their ethnic and social identities without the fear of persecution or discrimination. The policy, therefore, encourages mutual respect between ethnicities and acceptance of one another's personal beliefs. This policy mandates equality before the law, as well as protection from discrimination in all contexts, whether personal or professional. The Canadian Multiculturalism Act has two fundamental principles: (1) all citizens are equal and have the freedom to preserve, enhance, and share their cultural heritage; and (2) multiculturalism promotes the full and equitable participation of individuals and communities of all origins in all aspects of Canadian society.

In practice, however, racism, xenophobia, and inequality persist in Canada. Some scholars argue that this policy of multiculturalism is partly to blame for these ongoing inequalities. For example, Kubota (2015) claims that the assumption that Canada's multiculturalism policy has solved social inequality has ended up actually solidifying inequalities as they are harder to address when people don't know, or won't admit, that there is a problem. Kubota argues that we need to engage critically with social systems rather than assume that a perfect multiculturalism already exists.

Theoretical Perspectives on Culture

Functionalism

From a functionalist perspective, a cultural practice will continue if it performs functions that society needs to contribute to overall social stability. Talcott Parsons (1951) argued that human societies cannot exist without cul-ture as it is culture that allows people to communicate, understand each other, and work toward common goals. Thus, ethnocentrism helps to reinforce a group's solidarity.

Conflict Theory

Conflict theorists agree that a common culture exists among groups; however, they suggest that it serves to maintain the privileges of some groups. Culture, they argue, is merely a reflection of a society's dominant ideology. Conflict theorists suggest that ethnocentrism devalues groups in society and that countercultures develop in an effort to question the dominant social order. According to Karl Marx, the dominant ideology eventually becomes part of the values of the oppressed groups in society. These groups may begin to view their own culture as inferior and attempt to adopt the ways of the dominant culture.

Symbolic Interactionism

Symbolic interactionists are interested in the ways that culture is maintained through face-to-face interactions. For them, culture is perpetuated through daily interactions that define, and redefine, the norms and values for any given group. The values and norms surrounding motherhood, for example, are the result of mutual interaction and social definition. Motherhood is a social category created by interacting individuals and manifests itself in society through social interaction. There are many notions of what it means to be a mother—a woman, kind, nurturing, caretaker, selfless. Thus, people interact with women based on these notions.

Feminism

Feminists think that many aspects of culture have the potential to perpetuate social inequality as norms of behaviour may reinforce gender roles for men and women. They suggest that cultures often reflect society's view of men and women. Using cultural relativism allows an understanding of the myriad ways that men and women are viewed in different societies. For example, fathers staying at home to raise children is gaining prominence in Canada (albeit, slowly); however, this is rare in East Asia. These differences are largely due to East Asia's strict gender codes.

Top 10 Takeaways

1 Culture refers to all objects and ideas within a society. pp. 44–45

2 Each culture follows norms that are passed down generationally. These are instilled and reinforced through both positive and negative sanctions. pp. 44–45

3 Material culture includes all physical objects that a society creates and uses. Nonmaterial culture includes the values, beliefs, ideologies, and philosophies of any given group. pp. 45–46

4 The Sapir-Whorf hypothesis contends that language reflects and shapes a culture's understanding of reality. p. 47

5 Cultural universals are the practices that are known in every human culture and include language, sports, ceremonies, sexual restrictions, and personal names. pp. 49, 52

6 Cultures continue to expand through innovations and diffusion. pp. 52–53

7 Both subcultures and countercultures exist within every society. p. 53

8 Ethnocentrism—the tendency to evaluate other cultures through the lens of one's own culture—can be dangerous for society. Instead, we should attempt to practise cultural relativism. pp. 55–57

9 It is often debated whether Canada has a unique Canadian culture; however, some of our distinctness is that we are not American (Canadians are less traditional, less patriotic, less elitist) and that we have free health care and have two official languages, and are multicultural. pp. 58–60

10 Functionalists argue that human societies must have an understanding of culture to allow for communication and to work toward common goals. Conflict theorists argue that while culture exists among groups, culture is really a reflection of the dominant ideology of any given time. Symbolic interactionists are interested in the way that culture is maintained through daily interactions. And feminists are concerned with the ways in which the passing down of culture has the propensity to perpetuate inequality. p. 60

Questions for Critical Thinking

1. Discuss how the sociological definition of *culture* differs from our typical understanding of culture.

2. Outline some material and nonmaterial aspects of your own culture.

3. Discuss the importance of language—both verbal and nonverbal—to the preservation of culture.

4. Examining the ways in which girls and boys are expected to behave in society, can you think of some gender norms that you have been raised with as part of your culture? What were the positive and negative sanctions provided that ensured adherences to these gendered ideas?

5. Find someone in your class who has a different cultural background from you. Compare and contrast the way that the cultural universals have taken shape in each culture.

6. Give three examples each of things that you own or ways in which you play and/or act that are representative of cultural innovations and cultural diffusion.

7. During a 24-hour period, pay attention to the different crowds of people you encounter. Record the different subcultures you observe. Are there any readily visible countercultures in your community? Does your perception of your community as a cohesive group alter at all, or is it reinforced?

8. Can you think of a time you've viewed a situation from an ethnocentric perspective? Did you change your mind after thinking more openly about the topic?

9. What are the main distinguishing features of Canadian culture, if any? How are they changing as a result of immigration? How are they changing as a result of global communication?

10. Compare and contrast the theoretical approaches to the study of culture. Which one do you find the most compelling, and why?

Recommended Readings

- **Bourdieu, P. (1979).** *Distinctions: A social critique of the judgment of taste.* **Cambridge: Harvard University Press.** In this classic work on culture (which introduces the concept of "cultural capital"), eminent French sociologist Pierre Bourdieu examines the refined taste of the French bourgeoisie. In 1998, the International Sociological Association voted *Distinctions* as one of the 10 most important books of sociology of the twentieth century.

- **Chomsky, N., and Herman, E.S. (2002). Manufacturing consent: The political economy of the mass media. New York: Pantheon.** In this ground-breaking work, Chomsky and Herman argue that information obtained through the media is neither objective nor transparent. Rather, the media are always biased toward the opinions and agenda of the powerful upper class.

- **Lamont, M. (1984).** *Money, morals, manners.* **Chicago: University of Chicago Press.** In this in-depth look into the high culture of the upper-class elite, Harvard sociology professor Michèle Lamont looks closely at upper-middle-class white men in two different countries: France and the United States. Her point is that different parts of the population perform different versions of national culture.

- **Milner, M. (2004).** *Freaks, geeks, and cool kids: American teenagers, schools, and the culture of consumption.* **New York: Routledge.** This book chronicles the two years of fieldwork that sociologist Murray Milner conducted in one American high school. Milner finds that high school is the time where we begin to use material objects to define our immaterial identities.

Recommended Websites

Statistics Canada: Culture and Leisure
https://www150.statcan.gc.ca/n1/pub/11-402-x/2012000/chap/culture/culture-eng.htm
- The culture and leisure section of the Statistics Canada website contains studies about the personal cultural (and consumer) activities of Canadians, as well as the many creative industries that create and promote Canadian culture.

Office of Consumer Affairs
http://www.ic.gc.ca/eic/site/oca-bc.nsf/eng/home
- The Office of Consumer Affairs is affiliated with the Innovation, Science and Economic Development branch of the Government of Canada. The Consumer Affairs website contains helpful information for Canadian consumers, researchers, and businesses. Browse steps to get out of debt, research about the consumer practices of Canadians, or find ways to prevent identity theft.

World Values Survey Database
http://www.worldvaluessurvey.org/wvs.jsp
- The World Values Survey Database is a global research project that studies cultural and political change around the world through measures of the ways in which people's values and belief systems change over time. The first study was conducted by social scientists in 1981, and the most recent study was released in 2014. (Information about wvs obtained from:

http://www.eui.eu/Research/Library/ResearchGuides/Economics/Statistics/DataPortal/WVS.aspx)

The Broadbent Institute
http://www.broadbentinstitute.ca
- The Broadbent Institute is an independent, non-partisan organization based in Ottawa. It publishes research pertaining to environmental issues, income inequality, youth unemployment, electoral reform, and more.

Canada.ca
https://www.canada.ca/en/services/culture.html
- Canada.ca is a comprehensive website about all things pertaining to Canadian culture and heritage. Learn about Canada's history, find out about distinctively Canadian celebrations, apply to funding programs for the arts, sign up for cultural youth programs, and much more.

Global Affairs Canada
https://www.international.gc.ca/cil-cai/country_insights-apercus_pays/ci-ic_ca.aspx?lang=eng
- Curious about Canadian culture? This website provides answers about all aspects of Canadian customs—from how to hold conversation, how to build relationships with others, appropriate ways to dress, how to display emotion, and more.

Chapter 4

Socialization

Do you love or hate to read? Do you think your feelings about reading are purely related to your personal interests or to your intellectual abilities? If you love reading, can you trace where and when this love began? Researchers have found that reading to children every day improves their understanding of words and concepts at young ages and also improves their memories throughout their lives (Hutton, Horowitz-Kraus, Mendelsohn, DeWitt, & Holland, 2015). In addition to these positive developmental effects, spending this one-on-one time with a child helps to foster the parental bond, transmitting different types of knowledge such as how to parent and how to develop a routine. In this chapter you will learn how your interactions with different social agents, such as your parents, friends, school, and the media, have helped shape who you are today. You will begin to see how your relationships with people and your interests (such as reading) have been socialized into you from a young age.

▲ Michael Berman/Getty Images

Introduction

Socialization is one of the most important forces acting on us throughout our lives. Like culture, socialization is also essential for the survival and stability of a society. And as members of society, we must learn how to be active members of our communities to maintain the social structure. We need to learn how to follow rules and to develop a work ethic, and we also learn to purchase products to maintain capitalism. We also need to learn how to reproduce—not simply the act of having children, but the process of passing down our cultures from one generation to the next.

The Role of Socialization

Socialization is often defined as the social learning a person goes through to become a capable member of society. The learning is "social" because we learn through interactions with other people. These interactions teach us a society's language, skills, likes and dislikes, norms, values, and beliefs.

> **socialization** The learning process through which an individual becomes a capable member of society.

Although the techniques used to teach beliefs, values, and norms are somewhat similar in many societies, the content of socialization differs greatly from society to society. Our body language, way of speaking (including language, accent, and slang), food preferences, music tastes, and expected lifestyle are all functions of the culture in which we are raised. We are also, at the same time, influenced by other social influences, such as the class in which we are raised, our ethnicity, whether or not we are racialized by those around us, the religion in which we are raised, our

When it comes to Halloween, many women are expected to wear revealing costumes that emphasize physical attractiveness: maid, "sexy nurse," etcetera. Men, on the other hand, are expected to choose costumes that emphasize strength and competitiveness: superhero, policeman, doctor, and so forth. What does this tell us about how men and women are socialized differently? What are the consequences?

Pussycat Dolls, an all-female pop band, hit international stardom in the mid-2000s with songs such as "Don't Cha" and "When I Grow Up." By 2009 the band has sold over 54 million records and had amassed a large following of mostly young female fans.

ascribed gender at birth and whether it aligns with our gender identity, and our sexuality (among others). In addition, each of us has unique experiences in our families, our schools, and our friendship groupings, as well as different exposure to various media, including radio, television, billboards, websites, and video games. A lot of who we are and how we see and interpret the world depends greatly on the particular society and social groups that are there to influence us throughout our childhood. The kind of people we become is largely a product of our interactions with others during our development.

During lectures, I like to begin with a music video somehow related to the day's topic. The week of the discussion of socialization, I use the music video "When I Grow Up" by the Pussycat Dolls. I chose this song because its title epitomizes what socialization really is—the process of growing up. The chorus of this song includes lyrics such as "When I grow up / I wanna be famous" and "I wanna have groupies." The lyrics also assert that when they grow up, they "wanna drive nice cars" and "be in movies."

In addition to specifically discussing what the Pussycat Dolls hope to have by the time they grow up, this song had an impact on my own life.

I was standing in the grocery store with my then four-year-old daughter when "When I Grow Up" began playing through the store's intercom system. When I looked down I found my daughter dancing in the store singing loudly, "When I grow up I wanna have boobies,  great big boobies." Everyone in the store laughed hysterically, but I was in a wee state of shock. How did my daughter know the words of this song? (The lyrics are actually "I wanna have groupies" but were widely misinterpreted at the time as being "boobies" rather than "groupies."? How did she know that "great big boobies" were somehow perceived as a desirable attribute in society?

This moment had really made me reflect on the ways that our external sources contribute to our own development. Despite the fact that I was hyper focused on researching and writing about eradicating gender inequality and on teaching my children to be strong, independent thinkers, my daughter, like all other children, was growing up with a number of outside influences: her extended family, her friends, her schools, and the media have all greatly influenced who she is now as a teenager and will continue to influence her all her life—as they continue to influence you and me. Consciously or not, we are always taking in messages about what it means to be a member of society and what our role in society should be. Although raised by a strong, activist, single mother—this young girl was learning lessons through background music about what it means to be a girl in North American society. Learning about these processes helps us to understand the agents that are influencing what we want and who we become when we grow up.

Nature versus Nurture

To be human includes being aware of ourselves as individuals with unique identities, personalities, and relationships with others. As humans, we have feelings, ideas, and a value system. We have the ability to think and to make rational decisions—but also the capacity to make irrational decisions at times. But where does this humanness come from? Are we born with all these abilities, or do we develop them over time and through our interactions with the world around us?

When we are born, we are totally dependent on others for our survival. We cannot turn ourselves over, speak, feed ourselves, go to the bathroom ourselves, or do many of the things that are associated with being human. Although we can receive food in the form of liquid, can cry, and can go to the washroom, most small mammals also can do these things. What differentiates us from our non-human animal counterparts is that we lack instincts and the ability to survive on our own at birth. Survival is taught to us throughout our lives. Thus, to become fully functioning members of society we must be exposed to people and institutions invested in teaching us the necessary skills.

Nature Argument: Biology Is Destiny

The nature argument is that behaviour is determined by our genetic makeup. That is, we are born being who we are. Sociobiology is a scientific approach to human behaviour that incorporates evolutionary theory and

> **biological determinism**
> The idea that our behaviour is determined solely by our genetic makeup or other biological attributes.

genetic inheritance to examine the biological roots of social behaviour. This approach, known as **biological determinism**, looks for evidence of behaviour through biology. While it does recognize that behaviours change over time, rather than thinking that this is a result of the influences of society, it argues that behaviour evolves over time to secure the survival of the species. Social scientists argue that applying the "nature" argument to human behaviour disregards the ability of humans to think before they act.

Nurture Argument: We Are Products of Our Environment

So how important is social influence or nurture in human development? There is hardly a behaviour that is not influenced socially. Except for simple reflexes, such as when your doctor hits your knee with that little mallet and you immediately have a knee-jerk response, or the continuous blinking of your eyes, most human actions are, in fact, social. Let us consider the act of crying for a moment. When you were first born, you cried to alert your caregiver that you were hungry. When you were learning to walk, you most likely experienced many falls and would cry to tell your caregivers you were hurt. Somewhere around the age of five or six, however, the act of crying begins to change. Imagine there are two of you playing at a park as your fathers watch from the bench. One of you is female and the other is male. While chasing each other you both fall on the rocks and rip your knees open. You both begin to cry. Are you both comforted the same way? Generally, girls are comforted and their "boo-boos" are kissed better while boys are told to toughen up.

Over the course of childhood and the teenage years, these messages become more pronounced. Now imagine that you have just experienced a breakup with your significant other at your current age. Do you grab a box of Kleenex, play some Adele, and head over to your best friend's house to weep as your friend holds you and reassures you that your recent ex doesn't deserve you? Your answer will depend on how you were socialized—how the people around you responded to you when you cried throughout your life thus far. Crying, which at first appears to be biologically driven, in fact becomes sociologically driven. You are taught through everyday experience (as opposed to a formal classroom) when and where crying is acceptable, and by whom.

Sociologists argue, then, that our social environment probably has a greater effect than heredity on the way we develop and the way we act. However, heredity does provide the basic material from which other people help to mould an individual's human characteristics. Our biological and emotional needs are related in a complex equation. We know that children who receive care in affectionate homes tend to perceive the world in more positive ways than do children who receive less than adequate care or who are abused.

Social environment, then, is a crucial part of an individual's socialization. Even non-human primates such as monkeys and chimpanzees need social contact with others of their species in order to develop properly.

Isolation and Non-Human Primates

Researchers have attempted to demonstrate the effects of social isolation on non-human primates raised without contact with others of their own species. In the 1960s an American psychologist named Harry Harlow extensively researched the effects of maternal separation, dependency, and social isolation among infant rhesus monkeys who were separated from their mothers and isolated in individual cages. In this series of studies, Harlow created surrogate mothers for the monkeys made from different products. Each monkey became attached to its surrogate, whether made of wire or wood. In the next stage of the research Harlow and his colleague built surrogate mothers out of barbed wire and out of

One of the rhesus monkeys used in Harlow's experiment, shown here clinging to its stand-in mother.

cloth (Harlow, Dodsworth, & Harlow, 1965). The wire "mothers" were given bottles with food. The infant monkeys instinctively clung to the cloth "mother" and would not abandon it.

The monkeys were eventually reintegrated with other monkeys. Those that had been given access to these substitute mothers interacted better with other monkeys. They exhibited less violence and attempted to coexist, whereas the monkeys who had not had access to the substitute mothers attacked others (Harlow et al., 1965). This experiment shows the detrimental effects of isolation on non-human primates. Having been deprived of social contact with other monkeys during their first six months of life, they never learned how to relate or to become well-adjusted adults—they were fearful of, or hostile toward, other monkeys (Harlow et al., 1965). Obviously, interacting with others at a young age or even the perception of having another to interact with, in the case of the rhesus monkeys, is important for socialization.

Feral and Neglected Children

Because humans rely more heavily on social learning than monkeys or our pets do, the process of socialization is even more important for us. For obvious reasons—both moral and ethical—we cannot take human beings from their mothers and put them in isolation to measure the effect on their behaviour. (Some would argue we should also not do this to animals.) Thus, we need to rely on information that we have about children who have grown up in circumstances that have been seriously isolating. There are several examples of feral children and severely abused children that illuminate the importance of socialization from a young age.

People have always been intrigued by accounts of **feral children**: those who are assumed to have been raised by animals in the wilderness, isolated from human society. The Romans, for example, believed that the alleged founders of Rome (Romulus and Remus) had been raised by a wolf.

> **feral children** Human children who have lived in isolation from human contact from a very young age, some of whom are believed to have been raised by animals.

In the late eighteenth century, hunters in Aveyron, a rural area of France, reported that a boy was running naked through a forest on all fours (Itard, 1962). The "wild boy of Aveyron" was believed to be about 11 years old and to have lived alone in the forest for five or six years. Jean-Marc Itard, a young doctor, took the boy into his home, named him Victor, and attempted to socialize him. Itard studied the boy closely and recorded what he found.

The day Victor was found he had been caught digging for vegetables in a garden. Victor, who was almost naked, showed no modesty and was not housebroken. He would relieve himself wherever he wanted, squatting to defecate and standing to urinate. He could not speak and made strange, meaningless cries (Itard, 1962).

After spending five years with Itard, Victor lived another 22 years with a devoted woman named Madame Guerin in a little house near an institute for those who were deaf and could not speak. In this period, no one—not even Itard—tried to educate Victor further, and no one followed his progress closely. By 1816, the socialization process he had undergone while living with Itard had largely disappeared. Victor was once again fearful and half-wild, and still could not speak. He had few links to the rest of the community. A state pension kept Victor alive until he died at the age of 40.

In the late nineteenth and early twentieth centuries, other cases of feral children were reported in India, France, and elsewhere. These children were unable to talk, were afraid of other human beings, walked on all fours or slouched over, tore ravenously at their food, and drank by lapping water.

Social scientists generally agree that it is highly unlikely that feral children were raised by wild animals (Newton, 2004). They suggest that the children likely were abandoned in the woods shortly before they were found by others and that the children already may have been abused or isolated from most human contact before being abandoned (Newton, 2004). Indeed, several documented cases of child abuse and neglect indicate that human infants without adequate social interaction with other human beings are unable to develop fully human characteristics.

Two young girls were found severely neglected almost 40 years apart. Anna was found at the age of 6 in 1932, and Genie was found at the age of 13 in 1970. Both girls were unwanted children who were locked away from society and received minimal care. Anna was her mother's second unwanted, illegitimate child. Anna's grandfather was furious that her mother was expecting again, so her mother tried multiple times to give her away when she was born. However, Anna was born during the Great Depression, so no one was able to take her in. As a result, Anna spent the first six years of her life tied to either a chair or a cot in a storage room out of sight of her grandfather. She was never bathed, never taught to care for herself, and never touched in a loving way. When Anna was found, she could not speak, walk, or feed herself, nor did she have any comprehension of cleanliness. She was placed in a foster home, where she slowly started showing signs of improvement. At the age of 9 she was able to feed herself with a spoon and had started to develop speech. Unfortunately, Anna passed away at the age of 10 due to illness.

Similarly, Genie had been locked in a bedroom alone, alternately strapped down to a child's potty chair or straitjacketed into a sleeping bag, since she was 20 months old. She had been fed baby food and beaten when she made a sound. She had not heard the sounds of human speech because no one talked to her and there was no television or radio in her home. She had bone deficiencies because of a lack of sunlight and was malnourished. Genie was placed in a pediatric hospital, where reports indicate that she could not stand fully erect, salivated continuously, had no control over her urinary or bowel functions, could not chew solid food, and had the weight and appearance of a six-year-old. Extensive therapy was used to try to socialize Genie and develop her language abilities. These efforts met with limited success, however, and in the early 1990s (the last time her whereabouts were documented), Genie was living in a board and care home for mentally challenged adults. For researchers, Genie was considered a rare and interesting case that could assist them in understanding

The Wild Child

Dir. Francois Truffaut (1970). A movie that details Dr Itard's experiences with Victor—the "wild boy of Aveyron."

Wild Child: The Story of Feral Children

TLC (2002). A documentary that explores the story of Genie. Contrary to the title, Genie was not raised in the wild but was a victim of child abuse.

David and Louise Turpin made international news in January 2018 when one of their daughters escaped their home unbeknownst to them and called 911. On social media, the family of 13 children, ranging in age from 2 to 29, appeared to be living the high life, residing in an expensive home in California and taking multiple trips to Disney World—that is, until the police arrived at their home and found three of the children shackled to their beds and the rest of them sitting in the dark surrounding areas. All 13 children were very dirty and severely malnourished. Police reported that the children appeared 10 years younger than their actual ages because of the malnourishment and contended that they had a hard time believing that many were adults. Unfortunately, these cases are not isolated. Thirty-two per cent of Canadians are estimated to be victims of child abuse (Government of Canada, 2011). Furthermore, Canadian research suggests that even if children are socialized to an extent, child abuse can result in myriad mental health conditions, such as depression, substance abuse, and post-traumatic stress disorder and can even change brain structure, demonstrating how people's experiences in childhood can shape their entire life (Hopton & Huta, 2013).

These children clearly received contradictory messages about love and caretaking as they were treated to family vacations and yet simultaneously lived at least portions of their lives lacking care. Do you think these children and adults will be able to fully develop all human characteristics despite their inappropriate child socialization? What might explain why the older children, some well into adulthood, remained in the house despite their situation?

language, brain development, and human social psychology. However, some researchers posit that all the research and experiments performed on Genie were unethical since Genie could not speak, nor did she have the mental capacity to consent to such experiments (Dombrowski, 2011). See Chapter 2 for a more in-depth discussion of research ethics.

Cases of feral children and isolated and abused children highlight the importance of appropriate child-rearing processes when children are young. Clearly, what we are taught before the age of 10 lays the most important building blocks for our future. These cases underscore the sociological emphasis that we are more than just our DNA; we are, in fact, products of our socialization. Our socialization processes—how we grow up—shape who we are today and who we will become in the future.

Primary and Secondary Socialization

The stories of Victor, Anna, and Genie in the previous section illustrate that we also learn some of our most basic skills through the process of socialization. These children could not stand erect, stop salivating, chew solid food, or control their

primary socialization
The early socialization of children, much of which takes place in a family setting.

secondary socialization
The ongoing and lifelong process of socialization, including accumulated learning in adolescence and adulthood.

bowels, and they lapped water from their hands to drink. Clearly our interactions with others are extraordinarily important for our development. Primary socialization is learning that takes place in the earliest years of a person's life that helps form an individual's personality. This socialization also sets the tone for all future development. Often, primary socialization takes place within a family setting. Here, a young child learns many of the social skills needed to take part in a wide variety of social institutions (see Figure 4.1).

While the process of socialization begins at birth and is most intense during infancy, it does not end in adulthood. In fact, we are socialized throughout our entire lives. For example, consider the socialization that takes place when you get to post-secondary school: you learn how to engage in class discussions, speak to professors, take notes, and complete assignments. And consider the socialization that happens in the workplace, where you have to figure out proper "work etiquette," such as how to write emails to your boss or how to behave at a company party. We are always undergoing new experiences and, as a result, always learning new behaviours.

The socialization that occurs after childhood is called secondary socialization (Figure 4.1). It is much more limited than

- <18 years old
- Most intense in early life; usually takes place in the family; person learns language, body regulation, social skills, and social norms

+

- >18 years old
- Has less effect on our self-image; person learns specific roles and norms for adult behaviour (such as work role, parent role)

=

Figure 4.1 **Socialization**

primary socialization. Indeed, it has less effect on our self-image or our sense of competence than primary socialization. Even so, we should not underestimate its importance. Secondary socialization involves learning specific roles, norms, attitudes, and beliefs for different adult situations.

Theoretical Perspectives on Socialization

We will begin this section of the chapter by briefly discussing the way that four of our main theoretical lenses in sociology view the topic of socialization. We will also include a section on psychological approaches to the development of our selves as these approaches have offered us much insight into childhood development.

Jesus Camp

Dir. Rachel Grady and Heidi Ewing (2006). A film about the influence of a Christian summer camp, whereby children are taught that they have God-given gifts and are capable of "[taking] back America for Christ." Perhaps most importantly, this film depicts the dramatic effects of secondary socialization on an individual's attitudes and beliefs.

Functionalist Approach

Functionalists see the role of socialization as essential in establishing and reinforcing the rules of any given society. As we discussed in Chapter 3, growing up in specific cultures is accompanied by an internalization of norms and values—the more we understand these, the more smoothly a group will function. Functionalists refer to this as social integration. Socialization teaches people how to integrate into society. In the eyes of functionalists, human babies are like "blank slates," and society is like the artist that "paints" this blank canvas. Or, to use another art metaphor, like a sculptor, society moulds people into whatever shape it needs people to take. For example, it moulds children by teaching them a language and teaching them how to behave. In this way, society preserves itself and keeps itself going.

social integration
The internalization of norms and values that allow us to function well as a group.

One key functionalist scholar was Karl Mannheim. His "theory of generations"—that the historical and social context in which people live influence an entire generation's relationship to society and that those within a generation will, as a result, share similarities—led to the study of birth cohorts (Mannheim, 1952). Birth cohorts refer to groupings of individuals born at the same period of time and have thus experienced the same events at around the same age. These have become a key way that sociologists research the development of self, and one that the public also love to discuss. (For example, how many times have you heard someone say something negative about "millennials"?)

A popular form of sociological research looks at birth cohorts to help explain issues associated with changes in the family structure that have occurred over time. For example, young adults aged 18 to 35 are currently the subject of a girth of research that attempts to explain why this cohort is choosing to marry later, start families later, and move out of the family household later compared to previous birth cohorts (Downey, 2015; Ng, Lyons, & Schweitzer, 2016). For older adults aged 35 to 60, much sociological research is dedicated to what is referred to as "empty nest syndrome," the depression associated with retirement and with children leaving the home, and the associated isolation and loneliness (Mitchell & Lovegreen, 2009; Wister & Mitchell, 2015). Lastly, for individuals aged 60 and over, some sociological research focuses on exploring issues related to Canada's rapidly aging population and on how this change will impact pensions and health care in Canada, transitions related to retirement, as well as our understanding of "old age" (Beach, 2008; Denton & Spencer, 2010; Marshall & Mueller, 2002; see also Chapter 11).

> **gender socialization**
> The process of learning "appropriate" sex specific behaviour.

@gender_umd
A Twitter handle that focuses solely on gender socialization and its many effects.

Conflict Approach

For conflict theorists, socialization is about power and control. Primary socialization is one way that a powerful group exercises control over a less powerful group. It teaches less advantaged people their "place" in society and also convinces them that they cannot escape this place. Through such socialization, poor people learn to blame themselves for their misfortunes and to praise the rich for their successes. They blame themselves without realizing the ways that their misfortunes are the fault of a rigged system. In this way and others, socialization helps the dominant group maintain its power over subordinate groups.

Feminist Approach

Feminists have long critiqued functionalist notions of fulfilling roles and argue that viewing men and women in relation to the roles that they fulfill negates the role that structural inequalities play in their lives. For feminist sociologists, socialization is all about the structures of patriarchy that they argue shape the values and norms of our culture at a fundamental level (hooks, 2004). Feminists focus on how people are socialized based on their gender and learn a gendered identity, which is called **gender socialization**. Men are taught to act in certain "masculine" ways while women are taught to act in certain "feminine" ways, and those who do not fall neatly into these categories are typically treated as though they do by their agents of primary socialization (e.g., an intersex person being raised as a girl). Recall the earlier example of how we are socialized to cry (or not cry) and how this is often based primarily on our gender. Girls, often viewed as the "weaker sex," are taught that crying is acceptable whereas boys are taught that it is not a masculine attribute, and, as a result are, as bell hooks says, "denied . . . access to full emotional well-being" (2004, p. 20). Despite the work of feminists to dismantle gender norms, we are all still socialized into a patriarchal system (hooks, 2004). Many examples of the ways in which our genders are socialized and influence our socialization will be discussed in much more detail in Chapter 7.

Symbolic Interactionist Approach

Symbolic interactionists have one of the most interesting approaches to understanding the importance of socialization in our lives. Recall that the focus of this micro approach is on understanding everyday forms of social interaction. Interactionists are interested in the ways in which we act toward things based on the meaning we have for things and understand that these meanings have been taught through social interaction. For example, the word *mother* is a universal symbol that allows us to understand how we should behave in the presence of a mother, especially our own mother. We understand that "mothers" have been defined as nurturers, caregivers, and as loving, warm, and providing unconditional love. Even if our own mothers do not embody these preconceived notions, we still have come to understand or believe that they should. Thus, we judge our own mothers based on this understanding of what a mother "ought" to be.

We are taught through social interaction—our socialization process—what it means to be a parent and how to fulfill those roles in the same way that we are taught what it means to be a brother or sister, a student or an employee, or a son or daughter. Symbolic interactionists have spent considerable time investigating how we as individuals develop and modify our sense of self as a result of our social interactions.

George Herbert Mead

In Chapter 2, we discussed George Herbert Mead's conception of the self. Recall that he argues that the self is composed of two parts, the "I" and the "Me." He also proposed that the self emerges throughout three distinct stages in our lives: the preparatory stage, the play stage, and the game stage (see Table 4.1). Our sense of self continues to shift throughout these three stages of our development, as well as beyond.

Charles Horton Cooley

In the early 1900s, Cooley (who you may remember is our symbolic interactionist avatar, above) began arguing that it is through interactions with others that we learn who we are. He argued that a major part of this understanding is derived from our observation of how others perceive us. Cooley used the term the looking-glass self to encompass his belief that our self is the result of our social interaction with others. The looking-glass self contains three elements (see Figure 4.2). First, we imagine how we appear to those around us. Second, we interpret others' reactions and come to a conclusion about how others evaluate us. Lastly, we develop a self-concept based on our interpretation of how others view us.

looking-glass self A sense of oneself formed through interaction with others by assessing how they view us.

Imagine, for example, that you are a college professor. You try very hard to be humorous and engaging in your lectures, but every time you look out at the students some are falling asleep, surfing the Internet, or Snapchatting their friends. What might you think about your skills as a professor? Would you feel confident in your ability, or would you second-guess yourself?

The looking-glass self is particularly helpful in explaining adolescents' and teenagers' feelings about themselves. If, when you walk down the hall in high school, everyone fist-bumps you and hands out "bro' hugs" and smiles, you might easily develop high self-esteem, believing that you are perceived well by others. At the same time, however, imagine the opposite situation. If you walk down the hall in high school and very few people meet your eyes or even acknowledge that you are there, you might perceive that people don't like you. Unfortunately, many young people then deduce that they are "losers" or "uncool" and that there is something fundamentally wrong with them as a result. How we imagine others to perceive us undeniably has some impact on how we view ourselves.

Table 4.1 Mead's Stages of Development

Stage	Description	Example
Preparatory stage	Children imitate the behaviour of others.	Small children may grab their nose and wave their hand in front of their face every time they see a baby being changed. They are most likely unaware why they are doing this; they are imitating a behaviour they have seen an adult do at some point.
Play stage	Children begin to take on the roles of others.	Children begin to pretend that they are other people: nurses, doctors, mechanics, mommies and daddies, hockey players, superheroes, etc.
Game stage	Children have a more sophisticated understanding of the social world.	Children begin to understand their position within a social group. If they play a sport, such as soccer, they begin to understand that everyone on the field has a role to play in the game. At the same time, children learn that one person can have multiple roles. For example, mom is their caregiver but also their soccer coach and has a job as an engineer.

Figure 4.2 **The Looking-Glass Self**

According to Charles H. Cooley, we develop our sense of self by evaluating how we believe others perceive us. However, we often occupy many roles throughout our lives, and we are perceived differently depending on the individual doing the judging. How do we decide which "looking-glass self" to pursue?

Psychological Theories

Many of the psychological theories on the development of our personalities are in fact quite similar to those of the symbolic interactionists. The notoriety of these theorists and their ideas, however, warrants a discussion of them in this sociology textbook.

Sigmund Freud's Structural Model

Sigmund Freud (1856–1939) was a physician who founded a treatment protocol called psychoanalysis. This treatment was used for individuals who had serious emotional problems through long-term exploration of their subconscious mind. Freud proposed that the personality consisted of three elements; an id, an ego, and a superego (see Figure 4.3).

According to Freud, the ego is our neutral, balancing force that tries to prevent either the superego or the id from dominating. When our id gets out of hand, we are willing to break our society's norms in order to follow our desires for pleasure. When the superego gets out of control, on the other hand, we become overly rigid in following our society's norms, inhibiting our own lives for the sake of conformity. In an emotionally healthy individual, the ego succeeds in balancing these conflicting demands. Proper socialization that includes clear understandings of societal expectations of norms and values is taught through social interactions with our families, peers, schools, and the media (as discussed below), as ingrained in our superego.

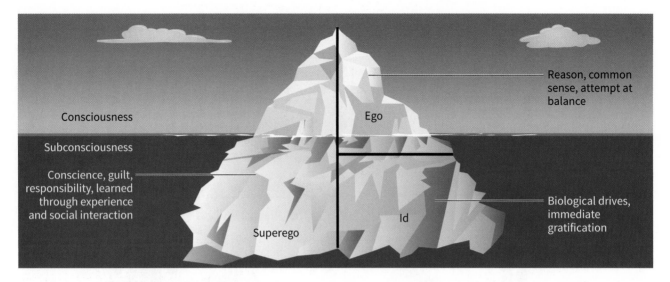

Figure 4.3 Freud's Structural Model

Labels in figure:
- Reason, common sense, attempt at balance
- Consciousness
- Ego
- Subconsciousness
- Conscience, guilt, responsibility, learned through experience and social interaction
- Biological drives, immediate gratification
- Superego
- Id

Jean Piaget's Cognitive Theory

After years of studying newborn babies, psychologist Jean Piaget (1896–1980) proposed his **cognitive theory of development**. He argued that there are four distinct stages of development of children's thought processes (see Table 4.2).

According to Piaget, social interaction is key to a child's successful development through these stages. To fully develop a personality, each person must be given the opportunity to interact with others. As we saw earlier in this chapter, Victor, Anna, and Genie were not given these opportunities for normal interactions and thus the consequences were severe.

> **cognitive theory of development** A theory by psychologist Jean Piaget that describes the development of abilities to think, believe, remember, perceive, and reason.

Agents of Socialization

Up until this point in the chapter we have discussed the importance of "growing up" with the proper social interaction and influences around us for optimal

Table 4.2 Piaget's Stages of Cognitive Development

Stage	Age Range	Description
Sensorimotor stage	0–2 years	Uses senses to make discoveries about the world Recognizes that objects still exist when out of sight Uses language for demands
Preoperational stage	2–7 years	Uses language Rather egocentric, only seeing things from own viewpoint Has the ability to pretend
Concrete operational stage	7–11 years	Begins to develop logical thinking Understands time, space, and quantity Has strong imagination
Formal operational stage	11 +	Capable of sophisticated abstract thought Strategizing and planning becomes possible Can create hypothesis and test it

Source: Adapted from Piaget (1952).

development. But how exactly does this process of growing up happen? Where and how do we learn to become functioning members of society? Sociologists believe that this process occurs through **agents of socialization**: the individuals, groups, and social institutions that influence our daily lives. While there are many agents of socialization, we focus on four principal ones here: families, peers, education, and mass media.

Families

Across societies, families are the most important agents of socialization in our lives. As we have seen through our examples in this text, the initial love and care we receive from our families are paramount to our cognitive, emotional, and physical development. Our caregivers are responsible for transmitting cultural and social values to us. Through them, we are also socialized into our specific social position within a society. We are taught our particular religious beliefs, gender roles, and are assigned to a particular socio-economic position. We are also born into a particular position within our own families. Are you a first child? A middle child? The last child? Are you one of many? Has the position in which you were born in the family affected your relationship with others and/or your personality in any way? An abundance of research suggests that it does (see, for example, Davis, 1997; Delroy, Paulhaus, & Trapnell, 1999; Salmon & Daly, 1998). Research by Wallace (1999), for example, shows that eldest children are often very ambitious and driven. They also often have the highest IQ's in a family as their parents were able to spend more one-on-one time with them than other children. Youngest children are the most likely to become entrepreneurs because they must find ways to blaze their own trail. They are also known to be much more relaxed as a result of parents being much less uptight with their youngest than they were with their firstborn (Wallace, 1999). Middle children often feel left out in their family and as a result develop much more active imaginations. They tend to become excellent negotiators and also have a tendency to be the most creative members of their family (Wallace, 1999).

While the family is the most important agent of socialization, it's not always the most effective or efficient one. Parents sometimes have little understanding of parenting; they may be unprepared emotionally, and their dedication and commitment to the task may be offset by competing considerations. Contrary to the idealized notion of family that is continually put forth in society,

agents of socialization
Institutions and other structured relationships within which socialization takes place.

The World's Strictest Parents

Multiple directors (2009–). A reality TV show in which uncontrollable teenagers are sent off to live with a strict family for a week in order to change their attitude and behaviour. The show encourages viewers to make a connection between socialization and families.

families or caregiver groups can be unsafe places for members. Almost daily, we hear horrific news reports of parents being charged with extreme abuse, attempted murder, and murder of their children. As well, much evidence indicates that parents may reproduce in their children the negative modelling those children experienced in their own upbringing.

Think for a moment about sexism, racism, classism, or homophobia. Where do the ideas that women are less valuable than men, that white people are more deserving than others, that poor people are immoral or unintelligent, or that homosexuality is a moral failing actually come from? Where do children learn these thoughts? Most often it is first learned in the home, passed down to children from their parents and extended family.

The ways in which we interact with each other are often direct consequences of the ways we have witnessed our parents interacting with others. Do you have road rage? If so, where does this behaviour stem from? Most likely, it is a result of witnessing your primary caregiver react in similar ways to stressful driving situations. So, while we learn many wonderful and important things from our families, we also learn some of our worst behaviours.

Schools

Schools play an enormous role in the socialization of young people. For many people in Canada, the formal education process is an undertaking that can last as long as 20 years. For some of us, it feels like it never ends! If your professor has a PhD, he or she went to school for a minimum of 24 years. If we don't count sleeping hours, on an average day those of us in school spend more time in a classroom than we do with our families.

What did you learn in elementary school? Of course, you learned to spell, do basic subtraction and addition and multiplication and division, and you learned to read and write. However, you also learned many concepts that were not listed in the curriculum.

These concepts are referred to as the *hidden curriculum*: the informal and unwritten rules that dictate social interactions, which are beyond the formal content consciously decided by the school. Recall in Chapter 2 that we discussed Robert Merton's explanations of the functions of social institutions. Education has both a manifest and a latent function. The manifest function of education is the teaching of spelling, math, and so on.

The latent functions of schools include how schools act as agents of socialization. Schools teach us that genders are different and not equal by constantly separating and sorting students by gender, for example. Did you use a different washroom than your sisters and brothers in your own homes prior to going to school? Did you play with friends of just one gender? When you enter into the school system, you learn that girls and boys not only use different washrooms but also require different equipment in those washrooms. Ideas of gendered modesty are also wrapped up in these separate washrooms. Urinals are placed in the open, side-by-side, for boys' use while females always have individual stalls. Sports teams at school are always divided along gender lines and there is often greater emphasis on boys' teams (hockey and football, especially) than on girls' teams.

Schools also have a profound effect on a child's self-image. Think of all the artwork you made prior to entering school. No doubt your family members praised you for your work and often displayed it on the fridge. You probably felt like Picasso even though you didn't yet know who he was, and your drawing probably resembled something like stick figures and a sun. As children enter school, they are for the first time evaluated and compared with peers by their teacher. They are graded on that artwork and sometimes discover that they are in fact not that talented in comparison to other children's abilities. Moreover, a permanent, official record is kept of each child's personal behaviour and academic activities.

While your parents pass down their socio-economic status to you upon your birth, it is at school that you learn what that means and where you sit in the hierarchy. Remember when your mom or dad went to Walmart and bought you those super cool blue Velcro shoes that lit up on the sides when they touched? Remember how much you loved those shoes? Then, you went to school and you learned very quickly that those Walmart shoes illustrated that you belonged to a particular social class. Alternatively, perhaps when you were young you spent the majority of your day with a nanny and you spent weekends and summers at the family cottage. It was most likely not until you went to school that you learned that your lifestyle was considered privileged compared to most others.

© Photogolfer | Dreamstime.com

School is the first place where we learn that while our parents' accolades of everything we've done—such as our many artistic endeavours—have given us the impression that we are amazingly smart and talented, we are not *as* talented as others in some respects (nor are we as talented as our parents led us to believe, in many cases). We begin to compare our abilities and ourselves to others once we begin school, which has tremendous impact on our self-esteem.

Peer Groups

Earlier we pointed out that our family is our most important socialization agent and has the most influence over us as young children. While the family does remain the most important agent, for a period of time in our lives our peers have an immense influence on us. A peer group is a group of people who are linked by factors such as age and social position, as well as by common interests such as similar hobbies. As soon as we are old enough to know and spend time with people outside our homes, most of us begin to rely heavily on peer groups as a source of information about the world and about expectations, as well as a source of approval about our social behaviour.

Peer groups include classmates in daycare, preschool, and elementary school. As we become teenagers, however, these groups typically are people with similar interests and social activities. For young people, establishing a peer group is necessary for creating a sense of belonging and identity, and for cultivating self-esteem (Matthews, 2005). But the successful establishment of a peer group does not always lead to positive outcomes. Research suggests that young people who belong to a peer group that is disruptive in school are more likely to become disruptive themselves (Berndt & Keefe, 1995). These findings support other research that suggests that peer involvement is fundamental in determining an adolescent's likelihood of participating in drug use and other delinquent behaviour (Donnelly, 2013). Later, as adults, we continue to participate in peer groups of people with whom we share common interests and comparable occupations, income, or social position.

Peer groups are an important agent of socialization because they contribute to our sense of belonging and to how we feel about ourselves. They also have great influence on our appearance. Consider the efforts young children make to dress like their peers, their older siblings, and parents, and even like the people they see on television. Their sense of who or what is stylish or beautiful comes from these sources. Again, their gender is also reinforced through these peer groups. The way in which girls and boys highlight their masculinity and femininity will depend on the group of peers they associate with. For example, in a study of "skater girls," researchers discovered that certain young women were actively constructing their identities in ways that challenged normative ideas of femininity. In doing so, these skater girls were able to distance themselves from misogynistic assumptions about women's ability in sport while creating a new identity for themselves. (Kelly, Pomerantz, & Currie, 2005)

peer group A group of companions with whom one interacts, particularly from late childhood through adolescence and into early adulthood, and who relate to one another as equals.

Like the family, peer groups also teach people about acceptable behaviour—however, this behaviour may differ from what children's caregivers have taught them is appropriate. As a result, conforming to peer demands frequently results in disagreements between children and parents. Children experience strong peer pressure during their school years. They may be under pressure to obtain certain material possessions (toys, games, technology), and they pass on this pressure to their parents through emotional pleas to purchase desired items. Caregivers may contribute to this peer pressure by purchasing items that their children desire even though less expensive similar products may be available. As an example, how old were you when you got your first phone? Did you receive either an iPhone or a Samsung despite the fact that much cheaper models and plans were available? Do your parents agree with your clothing choices, body art, piercings, choices of music, or what you do in your spare time? During adolescence, peers often influence all of these choices to a higher degree than parents.

Mass Media

Mass media have a profound impact on every one of us because we encounter media daily. Composed of large-scale organizations that use print or electronic means (such as radio, television, film, or social media) to communicate with large numbers of people, media function as socializing agents in many ways. Television and, increasingly, the Internet have become important agents of socialization for children, especially adolescents. The socialization function of media is even more subtle than the latent function of schools.

In 2013, 98 per cent of Canadian households had at least one television in their homes, and 94 per cent of those homes had cable, satellite, or some other television service (Television Bureau of Canada, 2014). The television has long been an important source of information

Frontline: The Merchants of Cool

Dir. Barak Goodman (2001). A documentary that explores the media influence and culture of modern-day teenagers and how corporations can exploit teens' attitudes via carefully constructed marketing strategies. The methodology used by corporations to determine exactly what teenagers want is further analyzed.

Current Research

The Face of Youth Gangs in Canada

Public Safety Canada put out a report in 2017 on the status of youth gangs in Canada (Dunbar, 2017). Wortley (2010) defines a youth gang as "the engagement by group members in delinquent or criminal behaviour, some of which may involve violence (as well as fear and intimidation) on a regular basis" (p. 3). Youth may join a gang for a number of reasons; the most common are to feel protected against any threats or potential threats, and for the sense of belonging, self-esteem, and identity that membership can provide (Dunbar, 2017). Additionally, gang membership offers constant companionship and support, acting at times as a substitute family (Dunbar, 2017).

While exact numbers are hard to ascertain on a national level because of the requirement of self-reporting, research suggests that while youth gang members cut across many ethnic, geographic, demographic, and socio-economic contexts, there tends to be a relationship between gender, race, ethnicity, and class structure that factors into the formation of particular gangs. The three most prominent gang populations are Indigenous youth, immigrant youth, and young women (Dunbar, 2017).

Use your sociological imagination to think about how peer group socialization and gang membership are related. Why do you think we may be seeing an increase in the formation of gangs among these populations? Do these three groups share any similarities, sociologically, that may make them more prone to gang membership?

---

as it provides us with information about events, an array of viewpoints on current issues, and introductions to a variety of people. Television shows model what a "typical" family, person, experience, and behaviour is like, which influences our expectations about our own lives. Television also makes us constantly aware, through advertising, of products and services that will apparently make us fashionable and accepted by others. However, the importance of television is quickly being replaced by the dominance of the Internet. Canadians between the ages of 18 and 34 spend over 30 hours a week online, compared to 16.6 hours watching television (Television Bureau of Canada, 2014). Estimates suggest that over 34 million Canadian use the Internet at home (Internet World Stats, 2019. Email, cellphones, and texts allow us to maintain close and almost constant connections with family and friends around the world.

In particular, social media, such as Twitter, Snapchat, and Facebook, are rapidly changing how we interact with one another and, thus, changing how we are socialized. Some of these changes have been negative while some have been overwhelmingly positive. For example, sociological research on social media websites such as Twitter and Facebook confirms that these networks assist high school and university students with social anxiety around connecting to their peers (Indian & Grieve, 2014). Other sociological research has explored the revolutionary aspects of social media, such as the ability to reveal abuse at the hands of police and government officials (Bentley, 2008). Furthermore, sociological research has assisted in understanding the impact social media memorial pages have on friends and family members of the deceased, who are now able to stay in "contact" with their loved ones by posting on their social media pages (Irwin, 2015). Other research, however, has exposed the dark side of social media. For example, research has revealed the negative effect social media use has on self-esteem, the positive association between social media use and narcissism, as well as how social media can be used to bully others and how it has no physical boundaries (Andreassen, Pallesen, & Griffiths, 2017; Vogel, Roberts, Rose, & Eckles, 2014; Boyd, 2015).

Furthermore, according to Nielson Music—the U.S. and Canadian music industry's leading consumption measurement service—in 2015 90 per cent of Canadians listened to music for 24 hours a week, while 95 per cent of teens listened to at least 31 hours a week (Nielsen Music Canada, 2015).

Taken together, all of these statistics indicate that whether we are consciously aware of it or not, we consume a heck of a lot of media per week! The messages that we receive, then, must have some effect on our socialization. And, indeed, media reinforce standards of behaviour and communicate expectations about social life.

While media can provide us with countless hours of entertainment and allow us distractions from our

How conscious are we of our own socialization? How conscious are we of our influence over those around us?

everyday lives, they also can be dangerous as socialization agents. Media generally provide one-sided information from the position of whomever owns the conglomerate.

The exacerbation of Islamophobia—the irrational fear of and/or hatred toward Muslims—is but one example of the dangers of media. Many people in the West get the bulk of their information about the rest of the world through media. Since the attacks on the World Trade Center in September 2001 (now referred to as 9/11), media outlets have reinforced prejudicial stereotypes of Muslim men as violent and of Muslim women as oppressed. While less than 2.5 per cent of all terrorist attacks in the United States since 1970 have been carried out by Islamic extremists (Center for Research on Globalization, 2013), Muslims continue to face severe scrutiny worldwide (Wilkins-Laflamme, 2018). In fact, if a non-white person commits a crime against others, the media quickly call the act terrorism without a clear indication of the motivation behind the crime. But when a white person commits a crime of the same or bigger magnitude, the media call this a mass shooting or the act of a mentally unstable person, even when there is evidence that it was intended to incite terror in a particular population. And word choice matters in shaping public opinion (see the "In the News" box).

Resocialization

Recall that socialization is a lifelong process and that all the agents described in this chapter will continue to influence you throughout your entire life. As we assume new positions, whether they be social, geographical, or occupational, we must at times unlearn previous socialization. For example, going from being single to living as part of a couple often requires us to discard former behaviours (unless you have an open relationship, hitting on others is just one example of what will need to change) and accept new ones (watching reality television when we would prefer a suspenseful drama, or vice versa). Sociologists refer to this process as **resocialization**.

Resocialization causes adults to adopt a new outlook on the world and to develop a new sense of self. Such major changes come about through learning new values, norms, and role expectations that are radically different from those learned earlier. For example, various studies have focused on the "adjustment period" when first starting

> **resocialization** A learning process that reshapes the individual's personality by teaching radically different values, norms, and role expectations, often within a total institution.

Media as Agents of Socialization

There is a debate about whether media reflects reality or whether reality reflects the ideas presented in media. Fill in the following chart using your three favourite current songs. Include the title of the song, and then write out a verse. When you have finished writing the verse, see if you can identify the theme of the lyrics (i.e., Is it about love? Hate? Relationships? Sex? Violence? Partying?).

Song	Lyrics	Themes
"Bad Guy"—Billie Eilish	"So you're a tough guy / Like it really rough guy / Just can't get enough guy / Chest always so puffed guy / I'm that bad type / Make your mama sad type / Make your girlfriend mad tight / Might seduce your dad type / I'm the bad guy, duh"	Gender roles Family Relationship norms Deviance Labelling

Reflection: What themes are present in the kind of music you listen to? Were you explicitly aware of all of the lyrics? What does this song tell you about the world around you? Do you think that music has the potential to influence young people? Why do you think that you are attracted to songs that have these particular themes in them? How do they relate to your life?

Figure 4.4 **Song Lyric Themes**

In the News

Media Representations of White versus Muslim Terrorists

On 1 October 2017, Stephen Paddock carried out the worst mass shooting in US history. He opened fire on 22,000 people who had gathered for a concert in Las Vegas, Nevada. Paddock killed 58 people and injured hundreds of others (Hernandez, McCarthy, & McGown, 2017).

News reports quickly stated that Paddock was a country music fan who liked to gamble and was enjoying his retired life. Reports separated his actions from broader society by emphasizing that he was a "lone wolf" who had mental health issues (Ruiz-Grossman, 2017). Within hours, President Donald Trump stated that the shooting was an "act of pure evil," and he sent "warmest condolences" to all those affected (Ruiz-Grossman, 2017). Politicians and the media tend to show violent white males as "unstable, angry, isolated people driven to mass murder" (Metzl, 2017).

In contrast, when the accused is a person of colour or a Muslim, his violence is treated as natural and expected because of his race and/or religion. For an example, let's examine the Pulse nightclub shooting in Orlando, Florida, on 12 June 2016, where Omar Mateen killed 49 and wounded up to 60. Within minutes of hearing of the tragedy, President Trump responded to this shooting by calling it "radical Islamic terrorism" (Wyrich, 2017). The media focused on Mateen's religion and avoided any discussion of the kind of music he liked, what his hobbies were, or where he worked. Because of his Muslim identity and Afghan roots, Mateen was automatically considered a terrorist.

Do you think that the choice of terms we use to describe people matters? Does calling white mass shooters "lone wolves" and brown mass shooters "terrorists" influence the way society views all Muslims, or all men and women perceived to be Muslim?

Fresh Off the Boat

Dir. Lynn Shelton (2015–). A sitcom about a Taiwanese family who move from Chinatown in Washington, D.C., to Orlando, Florida, to open a cowboy-themed restaurant. The father wholeheartedly adopts the American Dream, while the mother finds it difficult to make friends with other women in the community. The son, Eddie, has problems fitting into school. Watch how the whole family has to socialize into a vastly different culture.

university that can cause young adults to undergo a series of transformational changes as they adjust to campus life and negotiate a new set of expectations (Harris, 2016; Thuo & Madhanit, 2017). These studies found that high school students transitioning into university, especially females, were very concerned about how this resocialization would affect their social life. They mentioned worrying about maintaining social connections, navigating sexual harassment, and forming relationships with staff and faculty (Thuo & Madhanit, 2017). For international students, these anxieties

> **total institutions**
> Institutions in which people are monitored 24 hours a day, seven days a week, as they are in prisons, mental hospitals, and military barracks.

increase tenfold as they struggle to resocialize themselves not only into university, but also into Canadian culture (Wu, Guzman, & Garza, 2015). These studies prove that resocialization is a serious issue among recent high school graduates, and should be met with the necessary supports.

Resocialization can be voluntary. For example, resocialization is becoming more necessary for people who have trouble finding a job in their current industry. Other people, who seek psychological counselling or treatment of addiction, may intentionally try to be resocialized—to have their personalities "remade" into someone new. In both of these cases, resocialization is voluntary. In other cases, resocialization is involuntary, as it can be for people who are placed into total institutions—institutions in which people are monitored 24 hours a day, seven days a week, such as in prisons, hospitals, and military barracks. Sometimes entry into total institutions can be voluntary, such as nuns entering a convent or someone self-checking in to a psychiatric institution. In either case, these institutions cause major fundamental changes to the people who enter them. In these settings, people are totally stripped of their former selves—or depersonalized—through a degradation ceremony. In most of these circumstances, individuals are required to undress, wear assigned institutional clothing, and are assigned a number rather than a name. After stripping people of their

former identities, the institution attempts to build a more compliant person.

Does this mean our capacity for change is unlimited—that we can become any kind of person at all? For example,

#Sociology

Indigenous Resocialization: The Case of Residential Schools

Library and Archives Canada/PA-185530

Mi'kmaq girls in sewing class at the Roman Catholic–run Shubenacadie Indian Residential School in Shubenacadie, 1929. This photograph was part of the Department of Indian Affairs and Northern Development collection showing "success" stories of the integration of Indigenous people into the dominant society.

Canada has a long history of attempting to resocialize Indigenous children. Government-sponsored residential schools were run by Christian churches with the purpose of educating and converting Indigenous children into the ways of white settlers. The schools were first established in 1880, and the last one closed in 1996. An estimated 150,000 Inuit, Métis, and First Nations children attended these schools (see http://www.cbc.ca/news/canada/a-history-of-residential-schools-in-canada-1.702280). These children were stripped of their cultures, languages, customs, and values and were taken from their families and land. If this were not terrible enough, many became victims of horrific physical and sexual violence. After finishing at the schools, the young adults had a hard time returning to their Indigenous families and simultaneously did not fit in well in an urban setting because of receiving a substandard education.

These total institutions wreaked havoc on the lives of Indigenous people throughout Canada—the effects of which many are still dealing with today. In 2007 the federal government agreed upon a $1.9-billion compensation package for those who were forced to attend residential schools, and in 2008 the Truth and Reconciliation Commission was put in place to help bring together Indigenous peoples and Canadians in a process of reconciliation and renewed relationships based on mutual understanding and respect (Truth and Reconciliation Commission of Canada, 2008). The Commission was charged with documenting the truth of survivors, families, communities, and anyone else personally affected by the residential schooling system; it released its report in 2015. Days before the release, the hashtag #MyReconciliationIncludes was trending in Canada. People used this hashtag to share their vision of what reconciliation would look like. The hashtag #reconciliation is still used today to discuss the successes, failings, and ongoing work being done around the process of reconciliation.

In the case of residential schools, there is recognition that resocialization can and did have disastrous consequences. Can you think of negative consequences that other total institutions may face as a result of resocialization?

does it mean there are conditions under which a gentle person may willingly become a killer? The answer to this question is often yes. Military training (for example) does indeed teach gentle people to kill other people. As a total institution, the military trains recruits to kill enthusiastically and efficiently. In such circumstances, most recruits find ways to justify this new attitude and behaviour. While some individuals become effectively resocialized, others become angry and hostile.

The stated purpose of involuntary resocialization is to reform people identified as needing correction, with the goal of teaching these people to conform to accepted social standards of conduct after their release. However, the ability of total institutions to effectively modify anyone's behaviour in a meaningful or reliable way has been widely questioned. In many prisons, as one example, inmates are socialized to conform to the norms within the prison, but prison norms are very different from the laws of society outside of prison. Some argue that prisons are more likely to teach inmates new tricks of their illegal trades rather than give inmates the skills to be successful in society—in other words, prison teaches inmates to become better criminals rather than teaching them to be good citizens (see, for example, Schrag, 1954).

Top 10 Takeaways

1 Socialization is accomplished through social interaction with others. p. 64

2 While the most important socialization happens during infancy, socialization is a lifelong process. pp. 69–70

3 Our biological makeup (nature) determines some aspects of who we are; however, it is through the socialization process (nurture) that our key human qualities are developed. pp. 66–67

4 The rhesus monkey experiment and the findings presented from studying feral children (Victor) and severely isolated children (Anna and Genie) provide evidence in support of the importance of nurture in the nature vs. nurture debate. pp. 67–69

5 Functionalists focus on social integration as the purpose of socialization. Conflict theorists highlight the way that power is exerted in primary socialization as children are socialized into their positions in a hierarchy. Feminists see the patriarchy as a fundamental influence that underlies all the ways in which we are socialized. pp. 70–71

6 George Herbert Mead and Charles Horton Cooley are both symbolic interactionists who focus on the way our sense of self is developed. Mead argues that it is developed through three stages: the preparatory stage, the play stage, and the game stage. Cooley believes that our selves are developed through how we believe others view us—the looking-glass self. p. 71

7 Freud and Piaget are both psychologists who present influential theories that are closely linked to the sociological theories of the development of the self. Freud contends the self was made of three components: the id, the ego, and the superego. Piaget believes our sense of self develops through four stages: sensorimotor, preoperational, concrete operational, and formal operational. pp. 73–74

8 Families are the most important agent of socialization and socialize us into our social positions (religion, norms, values, social class). p. 75

9 Our schools, our peers, and the media have great influence as children age. Schools have a profound effect on our self-image (self-esteem, socio-economic status, gender). Peers and media influence our norms of behaviour and our understandings of gender and sexuality. Media are perhaps the most subtle socialization agents.

pp. 75–79

10 Resocialization is possible by learning new behaviours and norms. It can be either voluntary (changing jobs or going to therapy, for example) or involuntary (through total institutions and degradation ceremonies).

pp. 79, 81–83

Questions for Critical Thinking

1. Discuss the ways in which your identity has been socialized through social interactions.

2. Discuss ways that you are still being socialized into roles as a young adult and an adult.

3. Explain why sociologists believe that nurture has a stronger influence than nature on our behaviours and personalities.

4. How do the rhesus monkey experiments and the cases of isolated and feral children support the argument that nurture is more influential than nature in the development of functioning members of society?

5. How do the macrosociological approaches (conflict and functionalism) view socialization?

6. Relate Charles Horton Cooley's looking-glass self to your own experiences at home and in school. Who has been influential in shaping your understanding of yourself?

7. How do the psychological approaches of the development of the self differ from the sociological approaches?

8. Classify each of the following as an agent of primary socialization, an agent of secondary socialization, or a total institution, and explain your choice:
   a. Family
   b. College professors
   c. Employees
   d. The military
   e. Religion
   f. Boarding school

9. In what ways is prison a total institution? How does prison as a total institution impede the successful resocialization of prisoners as functioning members of society, upon their release? Could post-secondary schools be considered total institutions? Why or why not?

Recommended Readings

- **Crewe, B. (2012). *The prisoner society: Power, adaptation and social life in an English prison.* Oxford: Oxford University Press.** This engaging novel provides an in-depth analysis of the prison as a social institution. Crewe explores the lives of prisoners and shows how a prisoner is socialized into the prison culture. He then shows how different prisoners react and adapt to prison culture.

- **Erikson, E. (1950). *Childhood and society.* New York: W.W. Norton & Co.** This classic book explores the importance of socialization during childhood on an individual's life. The concepts of identity and culture are further explored in Erikson's engaging book.

- **Newton, M. (2004). *Savage girls and wild boys: A history of feral children.* New York: Picador.** If you are interested in learning more about feral children,

then this is the book for you. Newton explores multiple cases of wild and feral children in this study.

- **Scott, S. (2011). *Total institutions and reinvented identities.* Basingstoke, UK: Palgrave Macmillan.** Why might an individual willingly commit him- or herself to a total institution? Scott attempts to answer this question by introducing the concept of "reinventive institution" to Goffman's classic model.

- **Taylor, P.J. (2014). *Nature-nurture? No: Moving the sciences of variation and heredity beyond the gaps.* Arlington, MA: The Pumping Station.** The nature versus nurture debate is key to understanding the development of a human individual. In this book, Taylor presents both sides of the debate and tries to close the gap between people on each side of the debate.

Recommended Websites

Blackwell Encyclopedia of Sociology Online
http://www.sociologyencyclopedia.com/public/
- This website contains a large repository of information that enables you to search the most complex sociology theories. Upon searching, you will be presented with a clear, succinct and thorough summary of any theory that confuses you.

The Vanier Institute of the Family
http://vanierinstitute.ca
- The Vanier Institute of the Family is a charitable Canadian organization that is dedicated to understanding the importance and various roles of the family. This website presents a host of publications and studies that contribute to a thorough understanding of the social, economic, environmental, and cultural effects of the family.

Crown–Indigenous Relations and Northern Affairs Canada
https://www.canada.ca/en/crown-indigenous-relations-northern-affairs.html
- This Government of Canada website provides many articles and publications pertaining to Indigenous peoples. The effects of various agreements between the Canadian government and Indigenous nations is discussed and reported in detail. These agreements can be seen as agents of socialization in and of themselves.

Canadian Center for Policy Alternatives (CCPA)
https://www.policyalternatives.ca
- The CCPA is a Canadian non-partisan research organization that focuses on social, economic, and environmental justice. It provides hard-hitting news and busts open the myths about justice in our society. In addition, the CCPA presents a balanced debate between all viewpoints and provides alternative policy solutions aimed at benefiting Canadians.

The Truth and Reconciliation Commission Reports
http://nctr.ca/reports.php
- Hosted by the University of Manitoba, the Truth and Reconciliation Commission Reports are available for public reading. They can be difficult reading as they include testimony from thousands of Indigenous people and often contain upsetting truths. Most important of all to read are the "Calls to Action," which list the recommended steps for everyone in Canada to take (at varying levels) in order to move the country toward reconciliation with Indigenous peoples.

Chapter 5

Social Interaction, Groups, and Social Structure

The wildly popular American series *The Office* (2005–2013) is a "mockumentary" (mock documentary) about the lives of office workers. The show largely relies upon the social structure of the workplace, which is presented as an institution that is structured based on position. We see warehouse workers, office employees, managers, and bosses interact with each other and see how the power each one has affects these interactions. For example, who gets to sit where, what kind of privacy each person has, how people are treated based on where they sit, what some can get away with that others can't (such as Michael's extensive office desk toys), and how status both grants and is granted by where a person sits are all illustrations of social structure in action.

This structure is not only present in the workplace but also in other aspects of our lives: education, health care, religion, friendships, and family. Such social structures can be formal, such as a class schedule, or more informal, such as cliques in a classroom. In what ways are your own lives structured? Is structure a problem, or is order always desirable?

Learning Outcomes

1. Outline the elements of social structure

2. Compare and contrast the theoretical perspectives on social structure

3. Discuss the role of formal organizations in society

4. Identify the components of an ideal bureaucracy

5. Recognize the principles of McDonaldization in our current organizations

Key Terms

achieved status

ascribed status

bureaucracy

coalition

conformity

formal organizations

Gemeinschaft

Gesellschaft

in-group

master status

McDonaldization

mechanical solidarity

obedience

organic solidarity

organizations

out-group

primary group

reference group

role conflict

role exit

role strain

secondary group

social network

social scripts

status

Introduction

When you think of your future self—your 40-year-old self—what do you see? Do you hope to be married? To have children? To own a home and a vehicle? Has it occurred to you that you might be just as happy, or maybe even happier, to be on your own without a spouse? Have you ever thought that you would like to have children but that you do not want to co-parent with another person? Have you perhaps imagined, instead, a life of endless backpacking and camping?

Where do these ideas come from? Are we born with an inherited desire to marry, have children, and own property? Or are these ideas part of a social script that we learn from a number of influences, including popular culture, the media, school, friends, and family, all pushing us to find an acceptable place within the organization of society?

This chapter is about how society is organized in ways that bring order to our human relationships. Social structure is perhaps the key concept in our discipline, yet it is widely agreed to be the most elusive of sociological concepts. According to John Scott and Gordon Marshall in the *Oxford Dictionary of Sociology*, *social structure* refers to "any recurring pattern of social behaviour; or, more specifically, to the ordered interrelationships between the different elements of a social system" (Scott & Marshall, 2015). The authors go on to explain that the norms and values that we discussed in earlier chapters are what, as a whole, make up our social institutions. These expectations we place on one another hold us all to certain standards that then define roles and their relationship to one another. In other words, social institutions are invisible on their own, but we can see their outlines by observing the interactions between individuals within the structures: "It [social structure] is evidenced in the observable movements and actions of individuals, but it cannot be reduced to these" (Scott & Marshall, 2015). So, when looking at "social structure," we are looking for patterns that people express in their behaviour—patterns that reveal expectations they hold, which are based on social norms (or rules), which in turn are based on social values. As an example, finding and maintaining a monogamous, committed relationship (in Canada, often but not always formalized in marriage) is a cherished value in Canadian society. It represents order in a way that being single does not—hence, the pressure we may feel from a number of sources to meet social expectations by becoming part of a couple. Direct pressure from parents asking when you'll "settle down," to the more indirect way seating often appears in pairs, to governments offering tax breaks for couples all work to encourage the maintenance of this social structure.

Elements of Social Structure

All of our social interactions take place within a social structure. In this chapter, we break down social structure into five elements: statuses, social roles, groups, social networks, and social institutions. Think about construction on a new house: the builders need to complete the structure of the home before they can do anything else. First, they pour the foundation, then construct the walls and then the ceilings, before filling in doors and windows and doing the wiring and plumbing. Statuses, social roles, groups, social networks, and social institutions can be thought of in the same way—these are the elements that make up our social structure and are developed throughout the lifelong process of socialization, as described in Chapter 4.

Statuses

Sociologists use the term **status** to refer to socially defined positions within society. Within our society, a person can occupy the status of executive director, cashier, parent, pianist, student, friend, neighbour, and so on. In addition, a person can maintain a number of statuses at the same

> **status** A socially defined position within society.

time. For example, I am simultaneously a professor, writer, researcher, board member, mother, wife, friend, volunteer, and neighbour. Statuses are characterized by certain duties and privileges, and each status stands in a hierarchical relationship with other statuses. This hierarchy itself is, in turn, determined by the structure of society.

It is easiest to understand a status system in the context of a formal organization (which will be discussed below), such as the police. In the Royal Canadian Mounted Police, for example, the bottom status, or rank, is the special constable. Above special constable, the ranks, in ascending order, are constable, corporal, sergeant, staff sergeant, sergeant major, inspector, superintendent, all the

#*Sociology*

Stars on the Rise

© Touchstone Television / Courtesy: Everett Collection

Oprah Winfrey and Ellen DeGeneres have much in common in that they both came from poor and troubled upbringings, worked a variety of jobs throughout their lives, and later rose to stardom.

Oprah dealt with significant abuse as a child, had to switch schools multiple times, and was sent to live away from her mother (OWN, 2010). She worked at a local grocery store and eventually got a position as a news anchor at a radio station. She later won a full scholarship to Tennessee State University to study communication, eventually building her media empire into the internationally recognizable brand that it is today. She uses her platform to raise money and awareness for multiple causes, in particular providing education and opportunities for black women.

Ellen DeGeneres similarly came from a humble upbringing in Louisiana, working a variety of jobs growing up, such as retail, waitressing, house painting, hostessing, and bartending (Montag, 2018). As a woman interested in acting and stage work, she started in stand-up comedy and worked a variety of film jobs before eventually creating *The Ellen DeGeneres Show* in 2003, which is still wildly popular. Aside from her show, however, she is a prominent LGBTQ activist, animal rights advocate, and humanitarian, getting involved in activism and politics and using her show as a platform for her multiple causes.

Looking at these two women's lives, we can see examples of shifts in roles and status. They both worked a variety of jobs, changed their wealth status, and tailored their image over time. Both have had multiple relationships, some long and committed and some short. On the other hand, some of their statuses have not changed: Ellen's statuses as a white lesbian woman and Oprah's statuses as a black straight woman. Which of these positions would you say is their *master status*—that is, what dominates all other statuses in their own eyes or in the eyes of society in general? Do you think the master status for either of them has changed over time?

way up to the commissioner. Each of these ranks dominates all of the ranks below it; each has a set of duties and obligations, as well as a corresponding set of rights. These ranks also have particular role expectations. For example, someone occupying the status of staff inspector may play the roles of mentor to the officers in her charge, disciple to the superintendent she reports to, and colleague to fellow staff inspectors.

While we hold a number of different statuses within our lives, we generally also occupy a **master status**. According to sociologist Everett Hughes (1945), master statuses are society's way of dealing with the fact that we simultaneously hold multiple, and sometimes conflicting, statuses. Our master status is the status that dominates others and thereby determines a person's general position in society. Think of Barack Obama, for example.

Obama was a civil rights attorney, a lawyer, the forty-fourth president of the United States, a Nobel Peace Prize laureate, a son, a husband, a father, and also a black man.

> **master status** A status that dominates all others.

Despite all of Obama's astounding accomplishments in his life, his status as a black man remains his master status. In fact, studies have shown that while Obama was running for president against John McCain in 2009 his "blackness" was mentioned in 100 per cent of the articles that researchers reviewed surrounding the upcoming election, while McCain's "whiteness" was not once addressed (Seidman, 2008).

Our master status can also shift depending on our location at any given moment. When I am on campus, my master status is professor; however, when I am working in the community, my master status is researcher. When I enter my home, I can assure you that my children could care less about either of those two statuses. At home my master status is "mom" or "annoying mom" or "bank machine" depending on the circumstances.

Our society gives much importance to attributes such as gender, race, and ability; thus, these labels often dominate our lives. For example, when I walk down the street,

From My Perspective

Sabreena: PhD Student, Mother, Community Advocate

The popular narrative will have you believe that all Muslim women are oppressed. However, whilst many women are oppressed in this world, patriarchy and misogyny are not born of or isolated to Muslim communities. Whether it is about gender pay inequity or gender-based violence, unfortunately, women's oppression

Sabreena Siddiqui

occurs in all societies, even in Canada. But sadly, women's oppression too has been labelled a "Muslim problem" as of late. The global negative spotlight placed on Muslims has made it even more vital for those of us in leadership positions to highlight our Muslim identity in order to counter spurious and troubling stereotypes. As such, I have allowed my being Muslim to take centre stage and become my master status, but at times it has felt like a very heavy burden thrust upon me.

I am proud that as a complex, highly driven, multilingual, confident, and well-spoken British/American/Canadian/Afghani/Pakistani Muslim woman, I continuously shatter the conventional myths of representation and disrupt the status quo, but I hope for a future where my daughter does not carry the burden of resilience and representation that I have had to.

Source: Provided by Sabreena Siddiqui, used by permission.

strangers primarily see me as a white woman. These attributes are known as our **ascribed statuses**, which, generally, we attain at birth. How we are racialized, what gender we are assigned, and our age are examples of ascribed status. We are all also born into a particular social class. All of these characteristics are important mainly because of the social meanings they have within a given culture.

Contrary to our ascribed statuses, our **achieved statuses** come to us largely through our own efforts. Professor, lawyer, janitor, college student, guitarist, animator, and convicted offender are all achieved statuses. We must do something in order to acquire these statuses, whether that's by going to school, applying for a job, acquiring a licence, learning a skill, or committing a crime. However, our ascribed statuses often constrain our achieved statuses. As will be discussed in Chapter 7, being born female, for example, decreases the likelihood that a person will become the CEO of a Fortune 500 company.

Social Scripts and Social Roles

Social scripts are the culturally constructed, socially enforced practices that we are all expected to follow when we interact in social situations. Each situation or group has its own script in a given community or society. Most adult members of society are aware of these scripts because they have learned them through many years of observation and practice.

As we will see, social scripts constrain the ways that people relate to one another. They are the human, social factors that influence how social life proceeds—for example, how conflicts arise and how co-operation is negotiated.

Social scripts are built on a skeleton of social *norms* (see Chapter 3): rules about how people are to behave in particular situations. They may be formal and explicit, but more often they are informal and unwritten, and they vary over time and across cultures. Rules of etiquette are one such set of norms or scripts: use this fork, not that one; send a thank-you note after receiving a gift; wait your turn in line; and so on. Even behaviours we sometimes think of as natural or automatic are actually learned norms—or social scripts—that some people may take time to catch on to. Failure to observe a norm may result in a *sanction*—a glare, a verbal rebuke, an anonymous

ascribed status Advantages and disadvantages assigned at birth.

achieved status Attributes that individuals gain throughout their life based on effort.

social scripts The culturally constructed, socially enforced practices that we are all expected to follow when we interact in social situations.

role conflict A situation that occurs when incompatible expectations arise when one individual holds two or more social positions.

role strain The difficulty that arises when the same social position imposes conflicting demands and expectations.

note slipped under your door, or worse: a slap in the face, being barred from entering a building, or social rejection (see Chapter 10 for a discussion of sanctions).

On any given day, you will follow a number of different social scripts, mostly unconsciously, because you play a variety of roles. As you read this, you are likely meeting the expectations associated with the role of student, but you may also be a sibling, a son or a daughter, a best friend, a teammate, an employee, and so on. These roles may come into conflict: for instance, imagine having suddenly been given a promotion at work. At work we may build friendships with our co-workers where we cover for each other and "talk smack" about our bosses. Being shifted to a supervisory role may fundamentally alter that relationship and result in **role conflict**—are you your subordinate's friend, or are you his or her boss? Can you be both?

Social scripts often guide our decision-making, telling us, for example, that letting it slide that your friend has missed a shift is norm-violating behaviour. But what if the friend just received particularly upsetting news? It can be difficult to negotiate a pathway between these conflicting social scripts. As another example, think about the role conflict that you may feel as a student: Is it difficult to be a good student, an available friend, a dedicated athlete, a family member, and an employee all at the same time? Research shows that while many post-secondary students struggle to balance both school and work, there are factors that can lessen this conflict, such as having more control over the workplace, and how well work and school fit together (Creed, French, & Hood, 2015). How do you balance work and school? What makes it worse? What makes it easier for you?

Sometimes in life we also come across situations where we deal with **role strain**, which occurs when one of our social positions has conflicting demands and expectations placed upon it. Think, for example, of the role of being a mother—in society mothers are expected to be caretakers of their young children, to be nurturing and attentive, and to put their children's needs first. At the same time, raising children requires access to an income. A working mother may feel the strain of being considered both a "good" mother because she is providing for her child and a "bad" mother because she is not giving her child all of her attention. As another example, as a student you may experience the role strain of wanting to seem smart and engaged to your instructor, while not wanting

Thodoris Tibilis/Shutterstock

Many of us must balance the expectations of numerous people at the same time. Mothers, for example, are often expected to be nurturing and to be the disciplinarian for their children, work outside the home, clean the house, feed the family, manage the household budget, etc. These competing and demanding expectations often cause role strain for the working mother.

to seem like a know-it-all or a "suck-up" to your classmates. The dual expectations of how you, as a student, should behave can be stressful and can get in the way of meaningful classroom discussion.

We also enter and leave roles throughout life, which means that we take on new identities and shed old ones over time. Changing or leaving a role sometimes means leaving a community, which can have a profound effect on a person's identity. In her book *Becoming an Ex: The Process of Role Exit*, sociologist Helen Ebaugh (1988) reminds us that the shift to important new roles can be difficult and stressful, especially when that shift occurs suddenly as the result of unwanted changes. This kind of sudden move, known as **role exit**, may result in social dislocation and a sudden need to learn and practise new social roles.

For example, when you graduate from your program you will exit your role as student. Ebaugh (1988) argues that there are four stages of role exit. First, you will experience *doubt*—often when people exit school they experience something known as "imposter syndrome." This is when they doubt their own accomplishments and believe that others will find out that they aren't as prepared or as knowledgeable as they seem. Even your professors experienced this when they first exited their role as students. The second stage is the *search for alternatives*—most likely by attempting to find employment. The third stage is the *action stage or departure*—the turning point at which people realize they must take the next step forward. For you, it may be accepting a

permanent job. The last stage of role exit involves the creation of a *new identity*—for most of you, this coveted step will involve things like buying work-appropriate clothing, setting and maintaining a new sleep schedule, changing the frequency or manner in which you party with your friends, and learning how you fit in socially to your new work environment. While most of you can't wait to be finished school, most of you will in fact miss it and mourn at least some parts of the loss of your student identity.

Groups

We rarely live our lives in isolation even if at times we feel rather alone. We in fact belong to many different *groups*—people with similar norms, values, and expectations who interact with one another—some that are primary groups and some that are secondary. Coined by Charles Horton Cooley (1909), the term **primary group** refers to a small, intimate group characterized by face-to-face interactions and co-operation. A family living in the same dwelling is an excellent example of a primary group. Primary groups are largely responsible for our socialization process and how we develop roles and statuses. With the exception of our teen years, when we tend to be the most rebellious, we most closely identify with those in our primary group. We are also all part of multiple **secondary groups**, which tend to be formal and impersonal with little social intimacy, common in workplaces and schools. Look around your college classroom; by this point in the semester you most likely have become friendly with many people in this particular class, as well as in other classes throughout the school. While these relationships are undoubtedly important to your overall experience as a post-secondary student, they are rarely characterized by close bonds.

Groups are also often relational. We often feel as

> **role exit** The process of disengaging from a role that is central to one's self-identity in order to establish a new role.
>
> **primary group** A small group characterized by intimate face-to-face interactions.
>
> **secondary group** A formal impersonal group with little social intimacy.

though we belong in some groups while we feel alien in or outcast from others. Think of the many different groups that made up your high school experience. A typical high school will be made up of students who feel most comfortable with the "jocks," "geeks," "art kids," "stoners," or "outsiders," or those who identify as "floaters." An **in-group** is any group or category to which people feel that they belong. If you identified as a jock in high school, this was most likely your in-group. Belonging to a particular in-group implies that there is also an **out-group**, which is a group to which you feel you do not belong. In-group members typically feel distinct from and in some way superior to out-group members. "Stoners," for example, may view the "geeks" as "goody two-shoes," "narcs," and "keeners." The fact that the geeks are perceived as caring more about their grades and following school rules and less (or perhaps not at all) about smoking weed or doing poppers results in the stoners looking down on geeks for not being as cool or fun. In return, the geeks may view

> **in-group** A group or category to which people feel they belong.
>
> **out-group** A group to which people do not feel they belong.

the stoners as lazy, unmotivated, or even criminal, and thus feel a sense of superiority for having their priorities "straight." Significantly, these statuses also constrain behaviour. For example, a stoner who is excited about a particular assignment may hide from his friends that he is working hard on a school assignment. Similarly, a geek who is interested in smoking weed may hide this from her friends in order to maintain her in-group status.

While in- and out-groups during high school can be difficult for teenagers to negotiate, they are rarely as dangerous or have as many consequences as broader groups within society can become. Think of the war on terrorism that has led to a clear distinction between who belongs to the "in" group and who belongs to the "out" group in North America and Europe. The discussions surrounding terrorism around the world have often taken the form of a push for aggressive action. Aggressive actions are more readily justified when aimed at an out-group (see, for example, McDonald, Navarrete, & Van Vugt, 2012).

Kayden Chan

In elementary school, children in the same class tend to interact with one another during and after school. Once high school begins, however, specific groups tend to form and students sort themselves based on similar interests. The group that you identify with is referred to as your in-group while the other groups are your out-groups.

As we learned in Chapter 4, our family, friends, schools, and media impact our socialization process. Indeed, these socialization agents can drastically influence the way we think and behave. Sociologists refer to any group that individuals use as a standard for behaviour as their **reference group**. Often two or more reference

> **reference group** Any group that individuals use as a standard for evaluating themselves.

groups will be influencing an individual at the same time. Our families, for example, may be acting as a reference group for our morals and values and our desire to pursue education and a career, while our peers may be modelling behaviour and modes of dress required to fit into a particular group. Our reference groups continue to

World Events

Initiations Gone Too Far

Monkey Business Images/Shutterstock

Male sports teams around the world have a long history of initiation rituals. Historically, these practices have included some humiliation and physical abuse (Nuwer, 2000). These initiation practices—known as hazing—are almost exclusively related to adolescent-aged males. Although hazing practices have long occurred as a rite of passage, evidence suggests that these practices have become more dangerous, with recruits being coerced into degrading, abusive, deviant, and high-risk behaviours (Johnson & Holman, 2004).

In one extreme example that recently made headlines, the Baylor University football team made the news for a string of sexual assaults against female students at the school between 2012 and 2016. Linebacker Tevin Elliot was sentenced to 20 years in prison in 2014 and defensive end Sam Ukwuachu was sentenced to 180 days in jail and 10 years felony probation for two counts of sexual assault. These cases prompted an investigation into the Baylor football program, which found that there were accusations that players had committed 52 rapes, including five gang rapes

> **obedience** The notion that an individual will adhere to a set of rules or social codes.
>
> **conformity** When individuals or members of a group seek to be similar in terms of dress and behaviour.

between 2011 and 2014, and that the coaching staff had often intervened to quiet the accusations (Bonesteel, 2017). As a result, the head football coach was fired, the athletic director resigned, two additional members of the football staff were fired, and the president of the university was demoted and then resigned.

A lawsuit against Baylor claimed that new recruits were hazed by having them bring freshmen women to parties so that they could be drugged and raped as a player "bonding" experience. A woman identified as Jane Doe alleged that football players photographed and videotaped two female students being assaulted by many members of the team. The videos were then circulated among the players. Many argue that assaults such as these are an ingrained part of the football team's culture (Bonesteel, 2017).

And this is not just an American phenomenon. One study of athletes at seven Canadian universities showed that 92 per cent of participants experienced hazing, with 72 per cent involving alcohol. Those involved in collision sports, such as football, were far more likely to experience hazing (Hamilton, Scott, & O'Sullivan, 2013).

Sociologists argue that incidents like these show the dangers associated with complete **obedience** to some in-group and reference groups. Acceptance to a varsity team is a coveted position for many; as a result, a desire to **conform** to expectations may overtake common sense. While not all hazing rituals are this extreme, many have called for a stop to the practice altogether. What do you think causes this type of behaviour? Have you participated in a hazing ritual? Should hazing be made illegal? Are there other ways that broader groups, such as university campuses or cities, control whether hazing is a desirable or acceptable activity?

change as we take on different roles and statuses during our lifetime.

Sometimes groups in society find common ground, and **coalitions** begin to develop. Coalitions happen when groups align toward a common goal. For example, not-for-profit organizations fighting food insecurity through their own separate groups might join together to develop a national alliance to reach long-term goals. In times of a federal or provincial or territorial election, if the "right" (Progressive Conservative Party) party is winning in the polls, there is often talk of the "left" (New Democratic Party) party joining together with the "middle-to-left" (Liberal Party) party to form a "coalition government." People also join forces once in a while to meet short-term goals. For example, think of any "reality" game show you have seen. The most successful contestants on shows like *Survivor*, *Big Brother*, or *The Amazing Race* are those who make temporary coalitions to go further in the game.

Social Networks

As we go through life, we belong to several different groups and through our

coalition The aligning of groups toward a common goal.

social network A network of individuals (such as friends, acquaintances, and co-workers) connected by interpersonal relationships.

The Social Network

Dir. David Fincher (2010). A movie about the beginnings of Facebook, a social media site that changed the way individuals around the world form and maintain their social networks.

acquaintances make connections with people in all types of social circles. These connections are known as our **social network**. Networks can be real, in the sense that they are made up of people who interact in face-to-face relationships, or they can be virtual, meaning that face-to-face interaction is unnecessary. Our networks are important both socially and economically—such networks can help people living in rural areas survive harsh conditions and share risk, and can be a way to help people in urban areas find jobs with a sustainable income (Bloch, 2011).

With the spread of the Internet and social media, we have seen the proliferation of virtual as well as real social networks. Among younger generations in North America, about 71 to 81 per cent say they have a profile on at least one social networking site (Pew

Current Research

Sociological Research on the Importance of Social Networks

The adage "It's not what you know, it's who you know" is often used in reference to people who are able to climb the career ladder quickly. Social networks do much more than simply give us a sense of belonging; they also bring opportunities that can mean the difference between barely scraping by and living comfortably.

From 2005 to 2011, I conducted a longitudinal study of 42 lone mothers living in Toronto, Ontario (Cumming, 2014). All the women who participated in my study were receiving social assistance (welfare) and had at least one child under the age of 18 living with them. At this time, Ontario Works—the Ontario social assistance program—required that all people receiving social assistance take part in a number of programs to facilitate entrance into the workforce and to build self-sufficiency. I began the project with the idea that I would interview the women once every year for five years to explore their experiences with the different programs. I had hoped to shed light on which programs were effective and which were a waste of time

and money to draw policy-maker and funder's attention to invest in the best programming possible.

After five years, few women had reached the stated goal of self-sufficiency through participation in the labour market. Regardless of which programs the lone mothers entered, which skills they updated, and how many resumés they were required to submit, they were not finding and maintaining employment that could help them exit from social assistance. After closer examination of those who had been able to leave social assistance through work (30 per cent), I discovered that these particular lone mothers had all found employment through their social networks rather than through the official programs and skills development offered through Ontario Works (Cumming, 2014).

Social networks are indeed important in many ways. How did you get your most recent job? How did you find out about your apartment? How did you meet your significant other? Where did you learn about the career you are working toward? It is very likely that social networks played a part in making these connections for you.

Table 5.1 Social Networking Sites

	Facebook (%)	Instagram (%)	Twitter (%)
Total (adults)	68	35	24
Ages 18–29	81	64	40
Ages 30–49	78	40	27
Ages 50–64	65	21	19
Ages 65+	41	10	9
Total (13-18)	71	52	41

Source: Adapted from Pew Research Centre Internet and Technology, 2018. https://www.pewinternet.org/2018/03/01/social-media-use-2018-appendix-a-detailed-table/

Institute, 2018; see Table 5.1), and an increasing number of adults are joining networking sites like LinkedIn and Facebook for both professional and purely social reasons. As of June 2018, Facebook continues to remain the most popular social network site with a total of 2 billion active users (Statista, 2018). Instagram has 700 million users, and Twitter has 328 million (Statista, 2018). The greatest proportion of users of these sites are under the age of 30; however, we continue to see a rise in adult and older adult use. Some researchers argue that these social worlds may have detrimental side effects as individuals disengage from the real world in favour of social networking sites. How many times today have you scrolled through Facebook, Twitter, or Instagram? How many people have you Snapchatted with or texted with on WhatsApp? How many of those same people have you seen or spoken to in person?

We cannot know the precise size and composition of any one person's network, whether real or virtual; likely, it comprises hundreds or even thousands of indirectly linked individuals. Probably, the virtual networks are larger than the real networks because there is little cost associated with joining and maintaining membership in a virtual network.

Social Institutions

Schools, the government, the economy, the family, mass media, and the health care system are all examples of social institutions found in Canadian society. Social institutions are behavioural and relationship patterns that are persistent, interlinked, and function across society. They also regulate the behaviour of individuals in important areas of society, including family, relationships, education, training, labour market, economy, law, governance, politics, culture, media, and religion. Much of the remaining chapters of this text will discuss social institutions in Canadian culture. But first we shall examine some of the sociological approaches to social structure.

Kayden Chan

Many young people have hundreds upon hundreds of "friends" on their social media sites and spend their days counting "likes." One study showed that over 90 per cent of its youth participants used social media, for example (Byrne, Vessey, & Pfeifer, 2018). Consider how social media allow us to form connections outside our traditional institutions, which can weaken the influence that our traditional institutions have over our lives. While for many these connections can be positive, social media can sometimes come with negative results (such as online bullying). How would your life be different without social media? Would it be better or worse?

In the News

Six Degrees of Separation

You have probably heard the phrase "six degrees of separation." This idea—that all people are six or fewer social connections away from each other—has been used in popular discourse in innumerable ways. One of the latest permutations of this phrase was the streaming service Netflix's claim that any two subscribers, anywhere in the world, will likely share six or more shows in common (Feldman, 2019). But did you know that this common phrase was popularized based on the results of a sociological study?

To examine the social networks that link large numbers of people, Milgram (1967) set up an ingenious experiment. He selected a target, or "end-point," person in Boston—let's call him John Doe—and then randomly selected starting points: people in Omaha, Nebraska, or in Wichita, Kansas, thousands of miles away from Boston. Milgram sent information packets containing postcards to these starting-point people and asked them to send the packet to John Doe in Boston, if they knew him personally. Otherwise, they were to send the packet to an acquaintance they thought would know John Doe or would know someone else who knew John. When they passed along the packet, they were also to sign a roster and send Milgram a postcard to let him know the material had been passed along.

As you might expect, many people declined to pass the packet forward, and in those cases, the chain never reached its target destination. However, many chains *did* eventually reach the target person in Boston. For completed chains, the average length (or number of connections between starting-point and target) was 5.5 links, yielding nearly six degrees of separation between randomly chosen North Americans.

What do we learn from this experiment? First, and most surprisingly, if this study is representative, nearly everyone in the United States—over 320 million people—is connected to nearly everyone else in the US at a relatively small number of removes. Second, this "six-degrees" phenomenon depends on a few extraordinary people—connectors—with a large network of contacts, friends, and acquaintances. These connectors link a vast number of otherwise unconnected individuals. As a result, the "big world" is really a set of connected "small worlds." Everyone is therefore connected by people whom sociologists call "stars" or "brokers."

Theoretical Perspectives on Social Structures

Functionalism

According to the functionalist viewpoint, all social systems—from groups and organizations up to communities, societies, and empires—have universal, self-maintaining features that enable them to survive, to move forward, and to achieve their goals. Systems are made up of regular people interacting with one another, but in order to keep the system functioning, some of these people need to take on special roles. People assume these roles unconsciously, often out of necessity, since allowing these roles to go unfilled would result in the breakdown of the system. In essence, according to the functionalist approach, social systems persist independently of the efforts and intentions of individuals; they force us to conform whether we are aware or unaware, willing or not.

In his book *Division of Labor* (1933), Émile Durkheim argues that social structure is very much dependent upon the division of labour in a society. He contends that the way that tasks are distributed in any society will affect all social structures. For example, in agricultural societies there was a minimal division of labour—the family farm produced the meat, eggs, dairy, vegetables, and fruit, and family members made clothing and other necessities. According to Durkheim, this kind of society has a sense of group solidarity, which he terms **mechanical solidarity**. He argues that since all are engaged in similar work and have few options for what to

> **mechanical solidarity**
> Characteristic of societies with a minimal division of labour and group solidarity.

do with their lives, they stay focused on group rather than individual needs.

Over time societies became less agricultural and more technological, resulting in a greater division of labour. Suddenly people were less able to rely on their own farms and families and had to start to depend on others. For example, how many of you grow your own food? Sew your own clothing? Fix your own cars? According to Durkheim this resulted in a shift from mechanical to organic solidarity. This shift also resulted in much more specialization—farmers grow only certain types of crops or raise specific livestock, doctors specialize in specific ailments or types of bodies, teachers specialize in one or two subject areas. This reliance on one another shifts social structures in a way that interdependence is necessary for group survival.

Similarly, Tonnies, a German sociologist, had conceptualized the notions of *Gemeinschaft* and *Gesellschaft*, describing how society is organized in the past and present (Bond, 2011). **Gemeinschaft** refers to the past, when society was more communal and small-scale, but also refers to the rule of the monarchy used to establish order (Bond, 2011). **Gesellschaft** refers to society as a collection of free citizens who are no longer restrained to one village their whole lives and are governed by constitutional governments rather than monarchies (Bond, 2011).

For sociologists, these terms are similar but relate more to the ties that hold social groups together. *Gemeinschaft* for Weber refers to solidarity related to kinship, neighbourhoods, religious orders, and other small-scale, communal forms of organization based on a shared past (Waters & Waters, 2010). In contrast, *Gesellschaft* relationships are formed through contract and market exchange, competition and economic law, and are more modern and not based in emotions or a shared past (Waters & Waters, 2010). While Weber acknowledges that *Gesellschaft* is the dominant form of relation in our present society, the two still co-exist to some extent, often in conflict with each other (Waters & Waters, 2010).

More recent is the work of functionalist Talcott Parsons, who is concerned largely with how order is kept in society and how systems influence people's actions and behaviours. Rather than focus on how society changes over time, like Weber and Durkheim, Parsons wanted to understand how social systems could be maintained and understood when so many of us have competing interests in society. He sought to take into consideration social, cultural, and individual aspects of people's lives and the systems in which they live and how these societies function effectively.

> **organic solidarity**
> Characteristic of societies with a large division of labour and group interdependence.
>
> **Gemeinschaft** Past society as defined by a shared past and communal networks, such as family and religious institutions.
>
> **Gesellschaft** Present society as defined by market relations, business contracts, individuality, and competition.

Conflict Theory

While conflict theorists generally agree with functionalists that social institutions meet basic social needs, they critique the notion that they are efficient or even desirable. Conflict theorists argue that our major institutions serve to maintain the privileges of the most powerful in society.

Using the family as an example, conflict theorists argue that the "traditional" patriarchal family in North American culture serves to perpetuate inequality. Throughout history and in most cultures, husbands have exercised overwhelming power and decision-making. Men continue to maintain advantage as long as we privilege the nuclear, "breadwinner" family ideology.

Using education as a second example, we know that property tax dollars fund our public education system. This, then, means that more affluent areas have better funded schools than low-income areas. As a result, low-income children are rarely given the same opportunities as children from high-income areas. Exposure to culture, art, and even a variety of sports is limited by funding. For example, did your high school have a rowing club? Thus, from a conflict perspective, our current structures are unfair, discriminatory, and self-perpetuating.

More recently, critical disability studies have developed as a means of analyzing how social institutions perpetuate the exclusion of disabled people from full and meaningful participation in society (Devlin & Pothier, 2006). Building on critical theory, critical disability studies question the assumption that our physical infrastructure should inevitably be built for able-bodied individuals exclusively or that students with exceptionalities should be segregated from their peers. The goal of this approach is to make clear the ways in which *disability* is a social construct meant to intentionally exclude those who are different rather than an inherent inability in disabled people to fully participate in society (Devlin & Pothier, 2006).

Symbolic Interactionism

In contrast with functionalism's orderly maintenance of clearly defined roles, symbolic interactionism argues that, every day, people are creating and revitalizing "the social structure," which would not exist without their intentional, co-operative efforts. Indeed, people actively take part in social institutions all the time; they take on roles with accompanying statuses wherever they go. Think of your school, for example: the social role of being a professor occurs within the larger context of the education system. The "status" of a professor stands in relation to the status of a student, janitor, lab assistant, and dean. What prevents you from, for example, sitting in class with a colouring book and colouring during lecture rather than taking notes? You all entered college out of an elementary and a secondary school where you first learned all of these roles as well as the information required to enter into post-secondary education. All of these schools work in relation to one another. Most "correct" student behaviour is so encoded in people, after so many years of experience with it, that to break this social contract does not even occur to anyone! Thus, the education system derives its significance from the roles people carry out in social interactions.

Symbolic interactionist researcher Goffman (1959) suggests that we all take part in social performance, where we present an ideal version of ourselves rather than the real version (Kerrigan & Hart, 2016). Furthermore, we have multiple front-facing selves as well, depending on the social constraints present in whatever situation we are performing (Kerrigan & Hart, 2016). For example, you may have a different front-facing self for your friends, your boss, your teachers, and your parents, and all of these will likely vary from how you are on your own. This performance is called *impression management*, and it is not so much that people change their identity but that all these identities come together to form the people that we are, with some of them holding *master status* as described earlier, and others being secondary or abandoned entirely over time (Kerrigan & Hart, 2016).

> **organizations** Large groups that have a collective goal or purpose.
>
> **formal organizations** Deliberately planned groups that coordinate people, capital, and tools through formalized roles, statuses, and relationships to efficiently achieve a specific set of goals.
>
> **bureaucracy** Formal organizations that thrive in both the public and private sector.

Feminism

While feminists align closely with the conflict theorists' analysis that social structures work to maintain and enforce the power and privilege of some, they highlight the ways that many social structures remain gendered and disadvantage girls and women. To use education again as our example, girls and boys are often given different messages at school. Girls have traditionally been encouraged into the social sciences (nurturing and caretaking professions) while boys have been pushed into the STEM (science, technology, engineering, and math) subjects (discussed further in Chapter 7). These professions are not only segregated by gender but also by income, with STEM jobs paying substantially higher wages than social science jobs. Anti-racist feminists, such as Patricia Hill Collins, pay particular attention to the ways that social institutions (and not just individuals) operate to maintain gendered and racist divisions through socialization (Collins, 1990).

Organizations and Bureaucracy

As technology advances and social structures become more complex, we have seen a rise in secondary groups referred to as formal organizations. **Organizations** are large groups that have a collective goal or purpose. An organization can be a giant multinational corporation, a small corner variety store, a political party, a government, a church, a school, a sports club, or even a search party. **Formal organizations** are deliberately planned groups that coordinate people, capital, and tools through formalized roles, statuses, and relationships to efficiently achieve a specific set of goals. Within formal organizations, formal roles and statuses provide the skeleton for all communication and leadership. Often, formal organizations have multiple goals, and they usually have a long lifespan.

The most successful form of organization in the past century or so has been the **bureaucracy**. Although the term has negative connotations for most people, bureaucracies are merely formal organizations that thrive in both the public and the private sector and in both capitalist and socialist societies. Whatever their setting, bureaucracies are the main organizational form because they are comparatively efficient and effective. Max Weber (1978 [1908])—the first sociologist to study bureaucracies—developed the earliest, indeed classic, description of bureaucracy as an "ideal type."

According to Weber (1946), the ideal bureaucracy has six defining characteristics:

1. *Division of labour*. Everyone in the organization performs a specific task. In a restaurant, for example, the greeter seats you, the server takes your order, the cook

prepares your food, and the bartender makes your drinks. By performing these individual tasks, each becomes (or hopes to become) skilled at a particular task and thus carries out the job with maximum efficiency.

2. *Hierarchy of authority.* In an ideal bureaucracy, positions are ranked so that everyone knows who reports to whom. In the same restaurant, there may be an assistant manager, a manager, a front staff supervisor, a sous-chef and chef, and an owner. Everyone in the organization knows who to report to.

3. *Written rules and regulations.* In an ideal world making rules clear and concise would offer employees clear standards for expected performance.

4. *Written documents.* Having extensive documentation and policy in writing makes it possible to enforce rules.

5. *Impersonality.* In an ideal bureaucracy, everyone carries out each of their roles without giving personal consideration to people as individuals. This is intended to support equal treatment.

6. *Hiring and promotion based on technical merit.* Hiring for all organizations should be based on technical and/or educational qualifications rather than on favouritism or bias. Written documents should outline what individuals must do to get promoted.

So far, we have been looking at the features of bureaucracy as an "ideal type." Yet, often, bureaucracies do not behave rationally in terms of their long-term interests and survival. As sociologist Robert Merton (1957) points out, bureaucrats are under pressure to act in ways that, in the long run, weaken the organization as a whole. In particular, bureaucracies force their members to conform to rigid bureaucratic rules that may no longer make sense. Bureaucrats may also fail to see their clients as people with unique wants and needs, framing them instead in impersonal terms or as mere categories. This viewpoint is harmful to the organization because it often results in the bureaucrat's failure to meet the unique needs of individual clients. In the end, this creates hostility in the public and weakens the organization's authority and legitimacy.

"Do What You Love (The Bureaucrat Song)"

By Matt Groening. From the popular cartoon *Futurama* that involves the character Hermes singing about his love of bureaucracy. https://www.youtube.com/watch?v=rcnV1Eimet0

Overall, then, the problem with bureaucracy—even in its "ideal typical" form—is that it tends to be rigid, unresponsive, and slow-changing when it operates as intended. To remedy this in practice, workers on the front lines often break the rules to overcome these shortcomings.

McDonaldization of Organizations

In his book *The McDonaldization of Society*, American sociologist George Ritzer (2015) described the way that the principles that underscored the success of the McDonald's hamburger chain have come to dominate more and more sectors in societies throughout the world. There are four principles of **McDonaldization**:

1. *Efficiency.* Find the best route to the goal you have in mind.
2. *Predictability.* Your experience is the same from one time to another or from one place to another.
3. *Calculability.* The emphasis is on quantity over quality.
4. *Control.* Any time that automation (non-human technology) can do the job, it should.

This model appears to make sense in the fast-food industry where getting orders out through automated processes helps the restaurant to be efficient and predictable, and to put out large volumes.

You may have noticed that Max Weber's defining characteristics of a bureaucracy are also apparent in fast-food chains. Taking orders, preparing food, cleaning the store, doing bank deposits all reflect a *division of labour*. This division of labour is kept in check by a *hierarchy of authority* that goes beyond the shift supervisors, managers, and owners to the corporate board. At McDonald's, there are *written rules and regulations* that govern everything from policies around food waste and employee consumption, to how much ketchup and how many pickles go on every burger. The atmosphere of a fast-food restaurant allows for little interaction between the server and the customer, thereby creating a high level of *impersonality*. Employees go through days of training so that they can be *qualified* to carry out the tasks to which they are assigned.

Ritzer (1993) contends, however, that the real significance in this model is that it has seeped into all types of bureaucracies, changing the way business is done, how organizations are run, and the way that people live their lives. For example, think of the way that our busy lives often result in us swinging by a fast-food drive-through on our way home rather than cooking our own meals.

Practising Sociology

Bureaucracy Assessment

Does your college live up to Max Weber's characteristics of an ideal bureaucracy? Are there elements of your education that have become "McDonaldized"? Fill in the chart with any examples you can think of, and answer the critical reflection questions.

Characteristic/Principle	Examples	Yes/No (Is the characteristic/ principle present?)
Division of labour		
Hierarchy of authority		
Written rules and regulations		
Written documents		
Impersonality		
Hiring/promotion based on merit		
Efficiency		
Predictability		
Calculability		
Control		
Reflection: After filling out the chart, reflect on the positives and negatives of following the model of an ideal bureaucracy. Discuss the advantages and disadvantages of McDonaldization, especially in reference to the education sector.		

Figure 5.1 **Practising Sociology Bureaucracy Assessment**

Top 10 Takeaways

1 All of our interactions take place within a social structure. *Social structure* refers to recurring patterns of social behaviour and the interrelationship between the different elements in the social system. — pp. 88–89

2 Social structure can be broken down into five elements: status, social roles, groups, social networks, and social institutions. — pp. 88–96

3 *Status* refers to our socially defined positions within society, for example, son, daughter, student, employee. *Master status* is the position that dominates all others. For example, Barak Obama's master status is being black, despite his also being a former president of the United States. — pp. 89–91

4 We follow a number of social scripts in the variety of roles we play. At times we experience role conflict (e.g., when we are friends with but also the supervisor of employees in our workplace), role strain (e.g., mothers), and role exit (e.g., leaving school and becoming a full-time employee). — pp. 91–92

5 We belong to primary groups (small intimate groups, such as our family) and secondary groups (formal and impersonal groups like those in one of your classes). We also have an in-group (the group to which we belong), an out-group (to which we do not belong), and a reference group (the group we look to for our standards of behaviour). — pp. 92–95

6 Social institutions are behavioural and relationship patterns that are persistent, interlinked, and function across society. They also regulate the behaviour of individuals in important areas of society: family, relationships, education, training, labour market, economy, law, governance, politics, culture, media, and religion. — p. 96

7 Functionalist Durkheim argues that social structures are dependent on divisions of labour in society. He refers to societies where people rely on the land and themselves for survival as experiencing mechanical solidarity. Highly industrialized societies have what Durkheim refers to as organic solidarity as individuals must rely on each other to meet the needs of survival. Symbolic interactionists are more interested in the ways that social structures are maintained and reproduced through social interactions. We all take on roles and statuses within institutions. — pp. 97–98

8 Conflict and feminist theorists both contend that social structures serve to maintain the privilege and power of some while disadvantaging others. — pp. 98–99

9 Organizations are large groups that have a collective goal or purpose. An organization can be a giant multinational corporation or a small corner store. Formal organizations are deliberately planned groups that coordinate people, capital, and tools through formalized roles, statuses, and relationships to efficiently achieve a specific set of goals. — pp. 99–100

10 Max Weber argues that the ideal bureaucracy is the most successful kind of organization. Ideal bureaucracies have six defining characteristics: division of labour, hierarchy of authority, written rules and regulation, written documentation, impersonality, and hiring and promotion based on technical merit. George Ritzer added to Weber's account, arguing that many of today's bureaucracies are experiencing McDonaldization. — pp. 99–100

Questions for Critical Thinking

1. How does the structure of our society exacerbate the problem of role strain? For example, are socially disadvantaged people more likely than others to experience role strain? If so, why?

2. Explain the five elements that make up a social structure, and provide one example.

3. Reflect on the statuses that you hold. What is your master status? Does it differ depending on where you are?

4. Recall one of your own experiences with someone violating a socially scripted rule. Describe the situation and the reactions of the people involved. What can you conclude about the ability of social scripts to shape or control human interaction?

5. Are primary groups, secondary groups, in-groups, and out-groups found in all formal organizations? What functions might these groups serve for a formal organization?

6. Discuss the ways in which the government as a social institution regulates members of society.

7. Durkheim argues that social structures are characterized by the division of labour in society. Using this idea, how and why has the division of labour in institutions (for example, the family and school) changed?

8. Pick any three social structures (for example, marriage, education, media) in society and critique their structure using a feminist and/or conflict perspective.

9. Do you consider organizations such as Rogers, Amazon, Google, or Facebook to be bureaucracies? Why, or why not? Choose one and list the main characteristics of a bureaucracy that you see, and identify the characteristics that you think are absent.

10. Can you think of other types of organizations that are experiencing McDonaldization? What are the advantages and disadvantages of this to both the business owner and the customer or employee?

Recommended Readings

- Angouri, J., and Marra, M. (2011). *Constructing identities at work*. Houndmills, Basingstoke, Hampshire: Palgrave Macmillan. This edited collection presents new research on the process of identity construction in different realms. The chapters explore the construction of identity in professional and institutional contexts, from corporate workplaces to courtrooms, classrooms, and academia.

- Bouchard, M. (2015). *Social networks, terrorism and counter-terrorism: Radical and connected.* New York: Routledge. This book argues that networks should be at the forefront in analyzing terrorists and when assessing the responses to their actions. This unique volume looks at the role of the Internet in the process of radicalization and in recruitment more generally.

- Brake, M. (2013). *Comparative youth culture: The sociology of youth cultures and youth subcultures in America, Britain and Canada.* London: Taylor and Francis. Drawing on symbolic interactionism, the author argues that subcultures develop in response to social problems that a group experiences collectively. Brake also shows how individuals draw on collective identities to define themselves.

- Graeber, D. (2015). *The utopia of rules: On technology, stupidity and the secret joys of bureaucracy.* Brooklyn: First Melville House. Graeber traces the unexpected ways we relate to bureaucracy today and reveals how it shapes our lives. The book provides insight into the ways that institutions rule over us.

- Papacharissi, Z. (2011). *A networked self: Identity, community and culture on social network sites.* New York: Routledge. This book brings together new work on online social networks by leading scholars from a variety of disciplines. The focus is on the construction of the self and what happens to self-identity when it is presented through networks of social connections in new media. The core themes of the book are on identity, community, and culture, including a central theme of social network sites.

- Quan-Haase, A. (2013). *Technology and society: Social networks, power, and inequality.* Toronto: Oxford University Press. This book examines self-presentation and social connection in the digital age. Quan-Haase brings together work on online social networks by leading scholars from a variety of disciplines. The book looks at the construction of the self and what happens to self-identity when it is presented through networks of social connections in new media. Theory, research, and practical implications of online social networks are explored.

- Zenko, M. *Red team: How to succeed by thinking like the enemy.* **New York: Basic.** This book explores "red teaming"—the practice of rigorously challenging plans, policies, systems, and assumptions by adopting an adversarial approach. In *Red Team*, national security expert Micah Zenko provides an in-depth investigation into the work of red teams, revealing the best practices, most common pitfalls, and most effective applications of these modern-day devil's advocates.

Recommended Websites

Global Dialogue: **Magazine of the International Sociological Association**
http://globaldialogue.isa-sociology.org/the-representation-of-african-american-women-an-interview-with-patricia-hill-collins/
- *Global Dialogue* covers all kinds of interesting topics. This specific article is an interview with Patricia Hill Collins on the representation of African-American women.

Purdue University's Online Writing Lab: Critical Disability Studies
https://owl.purdue.edu/owl/subject_specific_writing/writing_in_literature/literary_theory_and_schools_of_criticism/critical_disability_studies.html

- Purdue's Online Writing Lab (OWL) contains a multitude of resources, including citation style, research suggestions, and backgrounders on key topics. This specific article goes into the history of critical disability studies from the 1990s to present day.

Veritasium: The Science of Six Degrees of Separation
https://www.youtube.com/watch?v=TcxZSmzPw8k&feature=youtu.be
- *Veritsaium* is a YouTube channel run by Australian-educated Canadian Derek Muller. In this episode, he goes into the criticisms of Milgram's "six degrees of separation" experiment, discusses how social media is shrinking this distance between us all, and suggests a six degrees of separation experiment you can try for yourself.

Chapter 6

Class Inequality

It is estimated that roughly 35,000 Canadians experience homelessness on any given night (Gaetz, Gulliver, & Richter, 2014). Importantly, these same researchers suggest that 80 per cent of Canada's homeless population may be "hidden" (i.e., couch surfing, seeking refuge in abandoned buildings and temporary accommodations). While these numbers provide some general context, the academic community and those who provide services for people experiencing homelessness agree that there is a lack of quality data. This, coupled with the challenges of comparing data between regions within a province or territory, makes any attempt to quantify homelessness in any province problematic. With this in mind, a one-night count in Toronto in 2013 counted over 5000 people living on the streets.

While the causes of homelessness are multiple, precarious employment, economic hardship, unequal access to opportunities (employment/education), and a general lack of affordability within the housing market are major contributing factors that push people in Canada onto the streets. Because these issues affect so many, Canada's homeless population is diverse. In a country with such wealth, the homeless population is a constant reminder of how class inequality shapes one's life circumstances and chances.

Learning Outcomes

1. Define social stratification
2. Understand the different systems of stratification
3. Discuss the different theoretical approaches to social class
4. Explain the different ways that social class is measured
5. Clarify the difference between blaming the system and blaming the victim

Key Terms

absolute poverty

blaming the system

blaming the victim

caste system

clan system

class

class system

classism

conspicuous consumption

Davis-Moore hypothesis

elite

false consciousness

low income cut-off (LICO)

low income measure (LIM)

market basket measure (MBM)

meritocracy

poverty

prestige

relative poverty

social mobility

social stratification

socio-economic status (SES)

Introduction

One of the key insights of this course thus far, and of sociology in general, is that our realities are socially constructed through varying agents of socialization. Our understanding of the world and of ourselves is framed through our interactions with others. Consider this scenario: you have been assigned a group project at school, and you have a group of new friends you have made in the class to work with. One of the friends suggests having the group over to her house on a Tuesday to organize the project, and another offers his house up on Thursday. When you approach each classmate's house, you are not simply registering the fact that there is a building with doors, windows, and a roof. Rather, you are unconsciously running through socially constructed meanings—meanings that are embedded in patterns of social inequality. The location, age, size, and upkeep of the home are all instantly noted. The fact that your female classmate lives downtown in a two-bedroom high-rise apartment with her parents and three siblings evokes a range of social reactions that are very different from those you experience upon seeing your male classmate's home, which is a 10,000-square-foot lakefront estate.

> **class** A social hierarchy based on the unequal distribution of material resources.

This example highlights the centrality of class and status inequalities in our daily experiences. When we see a home, we generally make assumptions about the social class of the people who live in it. The lakefront home gives us the impression of wealth and economic well-being while the apartment, whether rightly or wrongly, conjures up images of poverty.

Let's think of other examples where we unconsciously make these assumptions based on material objects. When you get into someone's car for the first time, do you notice the make, model, and upkeep? What about when you notice people's shoes? Or purses? Or their technology, or lack thereof? Clearly, one of the most important sorting devices that have been socially constructed in our daily reality is the division between those who have and those who have not.

Of course, our responses to each of our friends' homes may vary depending on our own social class. While some of us may feel more comfortable in our classmate's apartment than in the lakefront estate, we are still likely aware of the relationship between having a lot of money and holding power in society. You have probably noticed in your own life the relationship between holding assets, such as land and property, and having power. Just think of the election of Donald Trump as president of the United States. President Trump had no political training, had never held any position in government, and did not have the normal level of education of a president—however, he did have many assets. The idea that he was successful in business trumped (pardon the pun) his lack of experience. Thus, Trump had a high level of power prior to the election (and has even more now). Understood in terms that are relevant to all of you: generally, those at the top of the economic hierarchy are in excellent positions to dictate what others do and, as a result, have a lot of control over the lives of those who are less well off.

In the News

The Super-Rich and the Rest of Us

Oxfam Canada, a part of the Oxfam Confederation, consists of 20 organizations networked in over 90 countries that aim to improve the lives of those living in poverty. In January 2017, findings on income inequality in Canada made national news headlines as it was reported that the two richest businessmen in Canada, Galen Weston Sr. and David Thomson, hold the same wealth as 11 million Canadians (Noakes, 2017). As of 2017, Galen Weston Sr. had a net worth of US$13.55 billion, and David Thomson was cited as the wealthiest Canadian in the Forbes 2018 list, with a net worth of US$28 billion. Meanwhile, the median Canadian net worth was

Romolo Tavani/Shutterstock

just under $300,000 when taking all assets into consideration (Evans, 2017). At the same time, over 15.5 million Canadians earn less than $40,000 per year (Statistics Canada, 2016a). Why might this type of rising income inequality be an issue for Canadians?

@inequality.org & @inequalitymedia

Two Twitter handles that engage the public in discussions about the realities of inequality in the world. Also check out the hashtags #inequality and #incomeinequality, which are continually trending on Twitter.

Social Stratification

This hierarchical arrangement of individuals based on wealth, power, and **prestige** is known as **social stratification**. Social stratification affects almost every aspect of our lives—from the clothes we wear, to the location of our homes, to the level of education we obtain, to the method we use to commute to work or school every day. Even our health and well-being are influenced by our location in the social hierarchy (see Chapter 12). Thus, when we are considering social stratification, we are focusing on the ways that groups are layered in society into social classes rather than on individual

> **prestige** Honour and respect; a type of stratification that is separate from income, authority, or class position.
>
> **social stratification** A system of inequality that integrates class, status, and domination with other forms of differentiation, such as gender, race, ethnicity, ability, religion, and sexual orientation.
>
> **meritocracy** A system of rewards based purely on demonstrated ability.

circumstances. Your individual position within a social class is referred to as your status. Your status may be achieved or ascribed (as discussed in Chapter 5).

When you hear someone listing the virtues of living in Canada, the idea that we live in a **meritocracy** often comes up. A meritocracy is a system based on achievements rather than on ascribed status. The idea that the American (or in this case Canadian) Dream is attainable by all who work hard and put in the effort required to change their life circumstances is in fact a bit problematic. A complex relationship exists between our ascribed and achieved statuses that is extremely difficult to escape. For example, arguably the chance to improve your life circumstances through attending school, getting the appropriate credentials, and obtaining a good job are equally available to everyone living in Canada. Yet, research shows us that the best indicator of university entrance is family income (Mueller, 2008; Frenette, 2017) and that those most likely to attend university are those whose parents also attended (Finnie & Mueller, 2008;

The University of Toronto ranks as the top post-secondary institution in Canada and the thirty-first in the world (QS Top Universities, 2018). In theory, schools such as the University of Toronto accept the "best of the best" in terms of academics; however, the yearly tuition, residence, and books and other supplies are expected to cost $19,775 annually for most programs, while for international students that cost jumps to $62,795 per year (University of Toronto, 2018). And that does not take into account living in Toronto itself. With few exceptions, only the very wealthy can access this type of education.

Statistics Canada, 2016b). Furthermore, if Canada were truly a meritocracy, we would expect to see a high degree of social mobility—the ability to move between social classes—yet research shows that most people stay within the social class they were born into (Greenstone, Looney, Patashnik, & Yu, 2013).

Even when we can change our socio-economic status, we are often still constrained by other measures related to wealth—such as school loans, credit card debt, car payments, etc. For example, as you know from earlier chapters I was raised for most of my childhood by a single mother in poverty. We received social assistance (welfare) from the government, had no car, and lived in a rural area with no public

social mobility The movement of individuals among different levels of the occupational hierarchy. Movement may be vertical or horizontal, across generations or within a generation.

socio-economic status (SES) A method of ranking people that combines measures of wealth, authority (or power), and prestige.

transportation. I finished secondary school and went straight into the workforce until the time my first daughter was 18 months old, at which point I went to university. I completed three degrees and all of the other requirements to obtain my PhD and get my "doctor" status. Up until this point my journey does indeed describe a meritocracy, where, through my own effort and hard work, I was able to achieve a social status different than the one I had been born into. However, as discussed in Chapter 1, I graduated with a very large student loan. In fact, my student loan payment per month was more expensive than many people's housing costs. While my colleagues who were born into higher socio-economic statuses were building equity, buying homes, saving for their children's education and their own retirement, I was still paying for my education. My ascribed status will continue to affect my economic well-being for the rest of my life. By the time my student loan was fully paid off, I was behind my colleagues in investments by 12 years. Thus, there is a strong relationship between our two statuses despite effort and achievement.

That being said, compared to other countries around the world, Canada has a relatively open stratification system. Although difficult, it is in fact possible for a young person who has grown up in poverty, such as I did, to access student loans and scholarships to attend post-secondary school. Through hard work, people of all backgrounds can earn credentials and obtain a high-paying job. From a global perspective, Canada does offer more opportunity for upward mobility; however, ascribed status limits these opportunities for many groups in Canada.

Global inequality is a popular research topic spanning entire decades of academic work in order to find out the extent of the issue, its causes, and what can be done about it. Early work on this topic focused mostly on the inequality within a country, or between countries, often using a measurement tool called the Gini coefficient (Niño, Roope, & Tarp, 2017). This coefficient is a score that each country has, ranging from 0 to 1, where 0 means the country has no inequality whatsoever and 1 is absolute inequality, where one person made money and everyone else made nothing (Niño, Roope, & Tarp, 2017).

More recently, these concepts have been applied to the world as a whole, rather than just using countries as the unit of measurement for inequality. Research finds that from

World Events

Global Inequality

According to the 2018 "World Inequality Report," wealth inequality continues to grow. The largest amount of growth in wealth has occurred in North America and Western Europe in the top 1 per cent of earners (Biswas, 2018). In other words, the rich continue to get richer (see Figure 6.1).

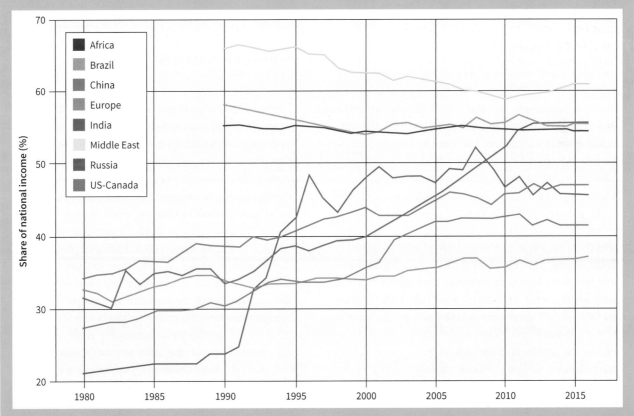

Figure 6.1 **Share of National Income Held by Top 10 Per Cent of Earners, by Country, 1980–2016**
Source: https://inequality.org/facts/global-inequality/

1975 to 2010 inequality increased substantially in North America, Africa, and South Asia, while in Europe and Central Asia it has been on the decline since 1995 (Niño, Roope, & Tarp, 2017). Evidence demonstrates that while global inequality measures are still quite high, some improvement has occurred over the past decades largely due to economic growth in India and China (Niño, Roope, & Tarp, 2017). However, calculating and accounting for global inequality is complex, and evidence can change based on which standards of measurement are used, which countries are taken into account, and the general availability of data.

Systems of Stratification

In Chapter 3, we learned that there are a few cultural universals—practices found in all human cultures—such as language, sport, ceremonies around birth and death, and sexual restrictions. Another cultural universal is social stratification. All human groups have a system by which they rank members of their group, and these systems have different levels of social mobility. Some are open systems—those that allow for a degree of social mobility; others are closed systems—those that allow for limited or no possibility of individual social mobility. There are four different types of stratification that occur worldwide: the class system, slavery, the caste system, and the clan system.

The Class System

The **class system** has been discussed up to this point in the chapter. The class system is a social ranking based primarily on economic position within society that often begins at birth when an individual is ascribed a status. The class system is considered an open system as there is room for an achieved status. Other systems of stratification tend to result in prolonged inequality.

Slavery

One of the most extreme forms of social stratification for individuals and groups is slavery. The ownership of some people by others has been common throughout history. During colonization of what is now called the United States (1628–1759), there were not enough workers to meet the growing need for labour. Colonizers turned to the Dutch, English, and Spanish slave trades for workers. While initially slavery was based on religious and political grounds (Catholic governments enslaved those who were captured by war and/or would not convert), this practice was not found to be sustainable, particularly in

America, where religious freedom was the reason many of the colonizers were there in the first place (Wood, 2003). During this period, an ideology was formed that Africans were somehow inherently inferior to the rest of the population and at times were not even viewed as human (Berlin, 2003). With this philosophy, white slave owners were able to justify hereditary slavery (where a child born from a mother who was a slave became a slave as well), which led to all black people in America, regardless of status, being treated as slaves. Often, freed black people would find themselves captured and enslaved again (Wood, 2003). Thus, with this ideology in place, a cheap and renewable labour source was gained, on the basis of extreme inequality rooted entirely in ascribed statuses (Berlin, 2003).

This type of slavery never developed in Canada to the same extent it did elsewhere, mostly because of the short growing season and the cost to house and feed someone over winter. However, slavery still existed. While the slave trade ships never came to Canada to sell the people they had kidnapped, colonizers who came to Canada brought their slaves with them, and so there were African people living as slaves in Canada from the early 1600s until the abolition of slavery on the first of August 1834 (Henry, 2019). During the same time, many attempts were made to enslave Indigenous people. In fact, between one-half to two-thirds of slaves in New France are estimated to have been Indigenous (Lawrence, 2016). Although slavery was eventually abolished in Canada and in the United States, various methods of legal discrimination remained for years to come. In Canada, for example, Indigenous people were not fully able to vote until 1960 (Moss & Gardner-O'Toole, 1991).

While slavery has been abolished in most places around the world, it continues to exist in some countries as well as in our own backyards. Today's slavery is most often known as human trafficking—the practice of illegally transporting people from one country or area to another for the purposes of forced labour or commercial sexual exploitation. I live in the Niagara Region in Ontario, Canada, very close to the famous Niagara Falls. In 2018, 75 per cent of all human trafficking victims were reported to have passed through Niagara Falls at some point in their journey when being trafficked within Canada (Knox, 2018). Most are young girls who are coerced into having sex with multiple men, usually through violence. Girls under the age of 16 are said to bring in the most money for those who enslave them, who often earn in the neighbourhood of $280,000 per year for every enslaved girl (Forsythe, 2018). While we like to think of slavery as something from the past and of Canada as a more equitable and responsible place, slavery continues here well into the twenty-first century.

> **class system** A hierarchy of groups with different market conditions, work situations, and life chances. In Marxist theory, classes stand in different relations to the means of production.

The Caste System

The third type of social stratification is the caste system, which is rooted in religion and is based on a division of labour. Broadly speaking, the caste system placed individuals in occupational groups. In this system a person's status is determined at birth and is lifelong. The practice was rooted in the Hindu religion. In Hinduism there are four major castes or varnas: priests, teachers, doctors, and other scholars (Brahman); warriors and politicians (Kshatriya); merchants and artists (Vaisya); and workers in the service industry (Sudra) (Howard, 2006). Members of a fifth caste are referred to as outcastes, Dalits, or the "untouchables" and are considered so unclean that they have no place in the caste system. Each caste is clearly defined, and endogamy—marriage within one's own group—is required. This

caste system A hierarchy of groups separated from each other by rules of ritual purity and prevented from intermarrying, changing status through social mobility, or carrying out particular jobs (as determined by one's status).

clan system Where every individual is connected to a large network of relatives.

type of hierarchical arrangement leaves no room for social mobility as it is a completely closed system. People's castes determines every element of their lives—whom they can marry, what job they can perform, what houses they are allowed to enter, even what clothes they are permitted to wear. While the caste system was legally abolished in 1949, it remains part of life in India. Centuries-old ideologies are difficult to eliminate in any society.

The Clan System

The final type of social stratification, the clan system, is most prevalent in agricultural societies, such as Scotland. In the clan system, every individual is connected to a large network of relatives. This extended family shares a common status among their society, and allegiance to the clan is a lifelong obligation. Interestingly, unlike in the caste system,

From My Perspective

Anjana: Wife, Mother, Full-Time Student

I was born into the caste system in Nepal. The majority of people in Nepal follow the Hindu religion, and it is this religion that distinguishes castes as superior or inferior.

Anjana Dhungana Dhakal

Growing up I remember feeling very lucky as I was born into the Brahmin caste—the caste that is held in the highest esteem in my country. In the majority of Brahmin families, children are taught that education matters most, and education is considered a tool to improve your societal status. The women from lower castes, in contrast, have to follow the tradition to which their caste is assigned. For instance, they are supposed to help Brahmin families by washing their dishes, looking after their cattle, ploughing their fields, sewing their clothes, etc. They have many restrictions upon them including when they may go to temple, what types of jobs they are permitted to do, whom they can associate with. In addition, lower castes are forbidden from entering a Brahmin house.

Now that I live in Canada and am attending post-secondary school, I no longer live under the caste system. However, while inequality may not be as predetermined as it is in the caste system I grew up in, I still experience it in my daily life in Canada. I have moved from the highest caste in Nepal to one of the lowest groups in Canadian society. I am hoping my quest for a Canadian education changes that.

Source: Anjana Dhungana Dhakal, used by permission.

marriages can cross clan lines, and in the past was at times encouraged to forge alliances between clans. While clans can still be found in Scotland, they generally provide a shared sense of identity—most clans have their own tartan patterns found on kilts, plaids, sashes, and ties—rather than a fixed position within society. In most circumstances, the clan system of stratification has been replaced by the class system.

You may have noticed a trend throughout this section. Slavery has been mostly abolished, although legal and illegal versions of it still exist today: in fact, an estimated 40.3 million people were enslaved around the world in 2016 (Global Slavery Index, 2018). The caste system, too, has already technically been abolished, although culturally it still functions to this day. The clan system, moreover, has mostly been replaced by the class system. And the class system, which we live under in Canada, continues to create and maintain social inequality. All four systems still exist within the culture, if not the law, of some groups around the world.

Theoretical Perspectives on Stratification

Functionalism

From a functionalist perspective, social stratification is found across societies, and so it must serve a social function. In discussing the universality of inequality, Kingsley Davis and Wilbert Moore (1945) developed what became known as the Davis-Moore hypothesis. Their argument is that every society requires people to fulfill all different kinds of roles. We need doctors and lawyers, accountants and financial advisors, professors and teachers, but we also need service industry workers, cleaners and janitors, tradespeople, and factory workers. People must be compelled to fill all of these jobs in order for society to continue to function properly. Also, all of these positions require different levels of commitment in education and training; therefore, those who require the most investment tend to be rewarded with higher levels of pay. Consider brain surgery. If you are going to have surgery on your brain, you want it done by someone who is skilful. You want to know that this person has a steady hand, a good knowledge of the human body, and an up-to-date familiarity with surgical techniques. This amount of education and training is a significant

> **Davis-Moore hypothesis**
> The belief that inequality is a functional and essential part of society.
>
> **false consciousness**
> Marx's term for when the working class mistakenly identifies with the capitalist class.

investment that the surgeon must make with the hope of being rewarded in the future. We may agree, then, that brain surgeons are important to society and thus should be better paid than, let's say, baristas.

However, we may have trouble applying the same logic to explaining the rewards gained by participating in organized crime, professional sports, and popular entertainment. Why is Kim Kardashian so rich, for example? Or, for that matter, LeBron James? Likewise, we would have a hard time explaining why teachers, nurses, librarians, and ambulance drivers gain so few monetary rewards compared to brain surgeons and Kardashians. And, even if we could get past *that* hurdle, we would have trouble using the functional theory to account for non-occupational inequalities. For example, why is only one CEO of the top 100 companies in Canada a woman (Erlichman, 2018); and only four CEOs of the companies in the Fortune 500 in the US black (White, 2017)? The Davis-Moore hypothesis does not fully explain these inequalities.

Conflict Theory

Recall from Chapter 2 that Karl Marx was the first to deeply explore the class system that emerged after the Industrial Revolution. Marx argues that the bourgeoisie provide capital—they own the companies, factories, land, and equipment (means of production) that the proletariat use to create products. The bourgeoisie control the labour of everyone else and can hire and fire people whenever they deem necessary. There are far more people who work for pay (proletariats) than those who own the means of production (bourgeoisie). The proletariat cannot survive without selling their labour to the bourgeoisie, so they often have to accept poor wages and conditions.

It's easy to understand why poor, powerless people worry about day-to-day survival. They spend less time thinking about the future than people with more wealth and power because they are focused on keeping a roof over their heads and food in their family's mouths. However, Marx argues that gradually people in the same class begin to share class consciousness with one another (see Chapter 2). Once they recognize their common fate, they begin to act to protect their interests. Workers form unions to protect their interests, and, as they do so, they gain even more awareness of their situation. Marx argues, however, that many proletariat fall victim to false consciousness—the belief that if they work hard enough they too can become a member of the bourgeoisie.

From a sociological standpoint, this theoretical perspective challenges us to question and interrogate the status quo. Who benefits from the wealth gap between rich and poor? What policies, behaviours, and beliefs maintain this gap? In what ways does the state protect private property, sometimes at the detriment of the people it governs? Conflict theory seeks to investigate these questions and analyze how inequality is socially produced rather than being a function of natural order or individual difference.

Max Weber, also mentioned in Chapter 2, is an early sociologist who theorized about class inequalities as well. For Weber, social position was not defined by one's relation to the means of production, as Marx thought, but rather through a combination of wealth and status. Therefore, to be of high standing one must have money or income, as well as an important title, position, or role that bestows status (and therefore power) upon a person. Here we can also see how a person could have one without another: a community religious leader may be poor but have status, or a factory worker may win the lottery and thus gain status without changing jobs. Wealth differs from income: someone could have little income but have inherited massive wealth. On the other hand, I earn what would be considered an upper-class income but have relatively little in terms of wealth and property ownership, and student debts prevent me and thousands of others from attaining wealth despite higher-than-average income. Weber's conception of class is the one that sociology and statistics generally follow, and it is where we get our conceptions of lower, middle, and upper classes.

Symbolic Interactionism

Rather than attempting to explain why stratification exists or how conflict is created because of class inequality, symbolic interactionists are interested in how people maintain class distinctions and inequalities through social interaction. They are especially interested in the use and meaning of "status symbols." In *Theory of the Leisure Class* (1899), Thorstein Veblen (1857–1929) suggests that there is a distinct difference between the productiveness of the manufacturing industry and the greed of business. Business, he argues, exists only to earn profits for a leisure class.

Veblen maintains that the main activity in which the leisure class engages is conspicuous consumption—the purchasing of expensive goods and services primarily for the purpose of putting wealth on display. Such purchases are status symbols—various signs that identify a particular

> **conspicuous consumption** The purchasing of expensive goods and services primarily for the purpose of putting one's wealth on display.

social and economic status or position. Diamond tiaras, massive country estates, and large retinues of servants would all be status symbols in Veblen's era. Not surprisingly, he not only draws attention to this conspicuous consumption, but given the dire poverty that characterized that period of US history, he also harshly criticizes the waste and excess that accompany conspicuous consumption.

Today, status symbols remain apparent everywhere, although they may manifest themselves differently depending on culture and location. Expensive houses, luxury cars and clothing, along with exotic vacations and elite sports still communicate wealth and social position. Symbolic statements about wealth are apparent throughout universities, with brands such as Lululemon, Coach, Jordan, and Apple dotting the hallways even though similar, less expensive products are widely available. Today, conspicuous consumption, even at the risk of indebtedness, has become an epidemic, as suggested by the multi-billion-dollar industries dedicated to helping the millions of North Americans live beyond their means, industries ranging from payday loan companies to the credit card divisions of banks and credit unions.

Feminism

Feminists argue that to understand inequality it is necessary to consider gendered patterns of domination both at home and in the workplace. Feminist sociologists stress the interaction between inequalities, including those based on class, gender, race, ability, and sexual orientation, at home and in the workplace—an interaction called *intersectionality* (first discussed in Chapter 2).

One cannot usefully study class and status inequalities without recognizing the importance of gender differences. In part, that is because women tend to have very different experiences in the world, particularly in the workforce and at home compared to men (see Chapter 7).

> ### *Us and Them*
>
> Dir. Krista Loughton and Jennifer Abbott (2016). A documentary that follows the lives of four chronically homeless individuals in Victoria, British Columbia. The film problematizes misconceptions about why people live on the streets and highlights why the "Pull yourself up by your bootstraps" rhetoric is flawed.

The four theoretical approaches presented in this book look at poverty through different lenses. Functionalists see poverty as a necessary part of society in order to entice people to take on different roles. Conflict theorists see poverty as a result of exploitation of the poor by the rich. Feminists note the gendered nature of poverty and inequality. Symbolic interactionists are interested in the ways in which we display our wealth, or the imagery of wealth, through our consumption patterns.

Class in Canada
The Wealthy, Elite, and Super Rich

Looking at those who hold disproportionate financial and other assets is important for a full understanding of social inequality. The elite have long fascinated most of us; just think how popular television shows like *The Simple Life* with Paris Hilton and Nicole Richie were, or the current array of *Real Housewives* shows. We strive to understand their lives and often aspire to have as much as they do some day. Social theorists have also long been interested in studying the elite members of society to shed light on the maintenance of power generationally.

> **elite** A small group that has power or influence over others and that is regarded as being superior in some way.

C. Wright Mills—who is, as you'll recall from Chapter 1, the author of *The Sociological Imagination*—played a prominent role in establishing the elite as a social research topic. His book *The Power Elite* (1956) challenges the idea that there are minimal class differences among Americans. Rather, Mills argues that the elites in the US are extremely powerful, bringing attention to the ways in which the leaders of the military, corporations, and political figures are interwoven. He argues that the elites control the democratic process, rendering the average citizen powerless and subject to manipulation (Mills, 1956).

John Porter is the most famous Canadian sociologist to study power among the elite. As mentioned in Chapter 1, he authored *The Vertical Mosaic* (1965), which provides a surprising analysis of the concentration of corporate power in the hands of a few people, whom he identified as mostly white, Anglo-Saxon, Protestant (or WASP) males. In 1975, Wallace Clement advanced Porter's work in his book *The Canadian Corporate Elite* (1975). Clement reveals that, in several respects, those holding economic power in Canada have become a more diverse group (e.g., more religiously diverse and more ethnically though not racially diverse), but that many of the traditional structures that bound the elite together, such as private schools and cultural and charitable organizations, persist.

More recently, Jamie Brownlee's *Ruling Canada: Corporate Cohesion and Democracy* (2005) pulls together much of the more recent information on the "ruling class." Brownlee argues that think tanks, such as the Fraser Institute, overlap with other boards, which results in drawing the Canadian corporate elite together. Also notable among contemporary researchers is sociologist William K. Carroll. His *Corporate Power in a Globalizing World* (2004, 2010) looks at how the social ties from shared membership in elite clubs interlocks with universities that integrate the elite into every facet of Canadian society. What does all of this mean in simple terms? Canada's elite are a very interconnected group with powerful positions in some of our most important institutions.

A small number of Canadians are extremely wealthy and powerful (see Table 6.1). In 2015, the wealthiest 1 per cent of Canadian tax filers held 11.2 per cent of the national total income—up considerably from the 7 per cent they had held in the early 1980s (Statistics Canada, 2017a). To have a better understanding of what this wealth means, consider Linda McQuaig and Neil Brook's illustration: if the Thomson

Television is overloaded with shows that display both real and fictional wealth. Reality shows such as *The Real Housewives* series (Beverly Hills [pictured above], Atlanta, New York, New Jersey, Orange County, Vancouver, Toronto), *WAGS*, *Rich Kids of Beverly Hills,* and *Keeping Up with the Kardashians* showcase wealth among famous people (or those married to or born to famous people). Fictional shows such as *Billions, Gossip Girls,* and *Empire* also have millions of viewers who tune in to watch the lives of the wealthy. Why do you think that we as a society are so enthralled by these types of shows?

Table 6.1 Canada's Top Income Earners, 2018

Ranking	Name	Worth	Company
1	Thomson Family	$41.4 billion	Thomson Reuters
2	Joseph Tsai	14.36 billion	Alibaba
3	Galen Weston	13.55 billion	Weston, Loblaws, Holt Renfrew
4	Rogers Family	11.57 billion	Rogers Communication
5	Saputo Family	10.41 billion	Saputo
6	Garrett Camp	8.58 billion	Uber, StumbleUpon
7	Desmarais Family	8.38 billion	Power Corp of Canada
8	Irving Family	7.38 billion	Irving Oil
9	Richardson Family	6.55 billion	James Richardson & Sons
10	Jimmy Pattison	6.41 billion	The Jim Pattison Group

Source: Adapted from Canadian Business's *Canada's Richest People 2018*. http://www.canadianbusiness.com/lists-and-rankings/richest-people/top-25-richest-canadians-2018/

family, one of Canada's wealthiest families, started to count their wealth at $1.00 per second and counted non-stop day and night, they would have it all counted up in approximately 700 years (2010). This is wealth beyond most of our wildest imaginations.

Further, the very wealthy, as Mills, Porter, Clement, Brownlee, Carroll, and others have pointed out, do not simply function as isolated individuals; they tend to be bonded together by important shared experiences. Many were themselves born into wealthy families. These families tend to live in exclusive neighbourhoods, vacation at elite resorts, belong to the "best" clubs, send their children to exclusive private schools, and join other wealthy families in participating in specific philanthropic and cultural events. In addition, out in the more public domain, they sit with one another on corporate boards, university governing councils, and political organizations. These shared experiences inevitably lend themselves to friendships, family intermarriage, and a common perspective on social issues. The research on elites shows us that rather than Canada being a true meritocracy, the rich tend to stay rich and money passes down generationally.

The Middle Class

Most people believe themselves to be middle class. The median family income in Canada in 2015 was $70,363 (Ontario Ministry of Finance, 2017). Only 20 per cent of the population can be considered "true" middle class with an income that ranges between $63,000 and $77,000 (Statistics Canada, 2017b). The middle class generally includes semi-professionals and managers who have post-secondary educations (for example, teachers, police officers, human resource managers, social workers) as well as those in non-retail sales, such as insurance and financial services. Also included in this category are those with semi-skilled positions in areas such as manufacturing or clerical. There is evidence that the middle class is shrinking as the number of low-income earners increases. University of Toronto professor David Hulchanski studied income in Toronto, Ontario, and found that there was a drastic increase in very-low-income neighbourhoods, from five in 1980 to 88 in 2015. Hulchanski attributes this in part to the disappearing middle class (Smith, 2018). Looking at the income divide in Toronto, he found that while low-income earners and high-income earners are increasing, middle-class earners are rapidly disappearing (Smith, 2018).

He compared the average Toronto income earners in 1980 to 2015 and found that there was an almost doubling of both high-income (from 12 per cent to 21 per cent) and low-income (from 28 per cent to 51 per cent) individuals while middle-income earners decreased by more than 50 per cent (60 per cent to 28 per cent) (Smith, 2018).

Economist Lars Osberg also analyzed the Canadian middle class and found that economic growth experienced by this class has happened at a much slower rate than the growth experienced by the elites, meaning that inequality between the elites and the middle class has continued to get worse since 1980 rather than better (Osberg, 2018). Sociologists D.W. Livingstone and Brendan Watts analyzed the attitudes of the middle class and found that one result of this increasing inequality is the "proletarianization" of professional workers, who once had unique attitudes toward work but whose attitudes are now becoming closer to those of traditional working-class employees (Livingstone & Watts, 2018). All of this is to say that the "middle class" has been both financially and ideologically disappearing.

The Poor and Economically Marginalized

How do we define *poverty*? In order to qualify as poor, do people have to be homeless, jobless, and receiving social assistance? Can someone be poor and have a smartphone? What causes some people to be poor?

This next section will attempt to navigate through some of these much-reported myths about the poor and illuminate how poverty rates are determined in Canada.

Poverty Measures

The word poverty is often used as an all-encompassing term to describe situations in which people lack many of the opportunities available to the average citizen (Levitas, 1998). There is no shortage of ways to measure and define poverty. The Canadian federal government has developed five measures, while social planning councils, individual researchers, non-profit organizations, and others have developed their own measures (deGroot-Maggetti, 2002). The most common distinctions made between these definitions of poverty are the terms *absolute* and *relative*. Absolute poverty definitions refer to a lack of basic necessities, while relative poverty definitions emphasize inadequacy compared to average

poverty The state of lacking sufficient material resources to live a life that is considered normal or comfortable in a society. See also *absolute poverty* and *relative poverty*.

absolute poverty A way of defining poverty based on an individual's ability to afford the basic necessities (food, shelter, and medicine, for example) for physical survival. See also *relative poverty*.

relative poverty A way to define poverty that compares an individual's circumstances against the general living standards of the society or group in which they live; a low standard of living compared to most. See also *absolute poverty*.

living standards (Mitchell & Shillington, 2002; Sarlo, 1996). Teasing out the differences between absolute and relative definitions of poverty, Ross and Shillington (1994) suggest that the first approach assumes that we can ascertain an absolute measure of poverty by calculating the cost of goods and services essential for physical survival, and then using this number to assess whether someone is poor or not. The relative approach, in contrast, is grounded in the belief that any definition of poverty should take social, physical, and mental well-being into account. This approach argues that people who have noticeably less than their surrounding community will feel disadvantaged, even if they are able to afford everything they require in order to survive (Ross & Shillington, 1994, p. 4; Roberman, 2015).

The most common method of poverty measure is the **low income cut-off** (LICO). This method identifies income thresholds of families who are likely to spend a larger proportion of their income on necessities than an average family of similar size (Statistics Canada, 2013). For example, let's say a middle-income family of four might devote, say, one-fifth of its household income to housing expenses, such as rent or a mortgage. Meanwhile, a family living *below* the LICO might spend one-half or even three-quarters of its household income on housing expenses. Of course, one-half of a person's income is a dangerously high portion of income to spend on housing expenses because it leaves little for the other necessities, such as food, clothing, transportation, daycare, etc. The LICO thresholds are based originally on 1992 consumption patterns of Canadians. They are updated each year to ensure that their values are in line with the current cost of living (Murphy, Zhang, & Dionne, 2012).

A second measure of low income is the **market basket measure** (MBM). The MBM calculates how much income a household requires to meet its needs. This includes subsistence needs, such as basic food and shelter. It also includes what it needs to satisfy community norms. For example, this measure would take into account the kind and quality of clothing people typically wear in that community (Canadian Council on Social Development, 2001). People whose income falls below the MBM's calculated value are considered low income Canadians.

The third and final measure is the **low income measure** (LIM). This measure calculates the low-income threshold of a household as one-half of the median income of a household of the same size in a similar-sized community (Government of Nova Scotia,

2008). This measurement counts households according to their relative poverty. In other words, it doesn't measure households by what they can or can't afford to buy. Rather, this measure looks at how much less some households have than others. Of course, households with different numbers of members, in different-sized communities, will have different cut-off points (since they have different expenses).

Statistics Canada also completes income surveys that highlight the gap between the rich and the poor in Canada. The latest data indicated that in 2013 the average after-tax income of the wealthiest Canadians was $183,000, while the average after-tax income of the poorest Canadians was $9000 (Statistics Canada, 2015b). This distribution of wealth means that 4.6 million Canadians (13.5 per cent of Canadians) lived in households defined as "poor" according to the after-tax low income measure (Statistics Canada 2015b).

The Canadian government has recently begun looking to redefine how we understand poverty by implementing the market basket measure (MBM) as the official measurement of poverty in the nation (Statistics Canada, 2019). What measure do you think is the best way to define poverty?

Populations Facing Highest Income Inequality in Canada

Regardless of what measurement we use, research continues to point to five groups that face the highest level of income inequality in Canada: women, unattached singles, Indigenous people, immigrants and visible minorities, and disabled people.

Women are the poorest of the poor, especially those raising children as lone parents and those living as unattached seniors. According to the latest census, in 2016, there were 1,114,055 lone-parent families making up 19.2 per cent of all families (Statistics Canada, 2017c). And lone mother-led families account for 905,630 of all lone-parent families (Statistics Canada, 2017). The low-income rate is much higher for mother-led families (42 per cent) compared to father-led families (25.5 per cent) (Statistics Canada, 2017c).

As an example, a single mother living in Calgary, Alberta, will receive $18,416 in total income per year while receiving social assistance (see Table 6.2). A search of Rent Board Canada reveals that the average one-bedroom apartment in Calgary is $1119 per month and $1284 for a two-bedroom.

> *low income cut-off*
> **(LICO)** A method of defining poverty that identifies income thresholds of families who are likely to spend a larger proportion of their income on necessities than an average family of similar size.
>
> *market basket measure*
> **(MBM)** A method of defining poverty that calculates how much income a household requires to meet its needs. This includes subsistence needs, such as basic food and shelter. It also includes the needs to satisfy community norms.
>
> *low income measure*
> **(LIM)** A method of defining poverty that calculates the low-income threshold of a household as one-half of the median income of a household of the same size in a similar-sized community.

Table 6.2 Yearly Rate of Social Assistance for a Single Mother with One Child, 2016

Province	Total Welfare Income
Newfoundland and Labrador	$22,908
Prince Edward Island	$20,116
Nova Scotia	$17,727
New Brunswick	$19,245
Quebec	$21,057
Ontario	$20,530
Manitoba	$20,815
Saskatchewan	$20,681
Alberta	$18,416
British Columbia	$19,120

Source: Tweedle, A., Battle, K., & Torjman, S. (2017). *Canadian Social Report: Welfare in Canada 2016*, Caledon Institute, 50–53.

If this single mom shares her bedroom with her child, she will pay on average $13,428 per year just for rent. If her child is older and requires his or her own room, she will pay $15,408. This means that this family will far fall below the LICO as they will be required to pay 72 to 84 per cent of their income on shelter (see the Practising Sociology activity in this chapter).

Similarly, 28.2 per cent of elderly women (aged 65 and older) living alone lived in poverty (LIM-after tax) (Statistics Canada, 2015a). Women's low lifetime earnings in conjunction with the likelihood that women will live longer than men (83 years compared to 79, see Chapter 12) puts them at the greatest risk of poverty as seniors (HOOP, 2017).

Although the Pay Equity Act came into effect in 1987, making it illegal to pay a woman less than a man to do the same job, women continue to face barriers to employment and equal wages (McInturff & Lambert, 2016). For example, women continue to face inequities in their homes as they undertake the lion's share of household duties despite the number of hours they work. As well, their paid work remains undervalued and they are segregated into "female" jobs within the workforce (see Chapter 7). Even women working full time continue to earn 20 per cent less than men, an inequity that is even greater for Indigenous, racialized, and immigrant women (McInturff & Lambert, 2016).

Perhaps unsurprisingly to many of you, the second group facing the highest level of income inequality in Canada is unattached singles—28 per cent of whom live in poverty (Statistics Canada, 2015b). Attempting to find housing on one income is extraordinarily difficult across Canada. Many of you may have first attempted to live on your own after high school and quickly discovered that the only way that you could afford to live away from home was with roommates. This is perfectly acceptable in your late teens and early twenties but what happens when you are in your thirties and not coupled?

The third group that experiences poverty in Canada is Indigenous people (particularly Indigenous women); indeed, they experience the highest rates of poverty in Canada, which is exacerbated when living on reserves. The average income of all Indigenous people is 25 per cent less than that of non-Indigenous people (Statistics Canada, 2017c). For Indigenous women, the gap is even greater, with their incomes averaging 55 per cent of that of non-Indigenous men (Statistics Canada, 2017d). Looking closer at Indigenous groups, First Nations individuals fared worse, on average, with incomes 66 per cent of that of non-Indigenous men.

When looking at reserves, Statistics Canada (2017c) reports that of the 367 reserves for which data was collected, 297 communities fell far below the income measure. At the lowest end, 27 communities reported median incomes below $10,000 (Statistics Canada, 2017d). As well, a recent Canadian study found that one in four Indigenous people experiences food insecurity (Arriagada, 2017).

The fourth group of people who experience high rates of poverty are immigrants and visible minorities (Morisette & Galaraneau, 2016). They are at greater risk of low income, unemployment, and lower wages than comparable Canadians, despite having significantly higher education and more potential earners per household (Morisette & Galaraneau, 2016). In 2015, the poverty rate for new immigrants and refugees was 31.4 per cent (Citizens for Public Justice, 2017), and the average total income of recent immigrants was 63 per cent of that of non-immigrants (Block, 2017). Women who are recent immigrants had a total average income that was 41 per cent of that of non-immigrant men in 2015, meaning that there is a 59 per cent income gap between immigrant women and non-immigrant men in Canada (Block, 2017).

Intersecting with recent immigrant status is visible minority identity. Since in recent years the overwhelming majority of Canadian immigrants have been visible minorities, there is often an overlap between these two elements. Between 2006 and 2016, the racialized

Inequality Research

A study by Davies, Maldonado, and Zarifa (2014) suggests that, in the province of Ontario, having certain social characteristics—such as being female, being of Asian origin, and attending high school in wealthier neighbourhoods—results in easier access to prestigious and highly ranked universities. On the other hand, the studied implied that students who self-identify as black and male and who come from lower-class backgrounds often do not get the chance to enter such institutions (Davies, Maldonado, & Zarifa, 2014, p. 23). This inequality in access to education leads to future inequalities, where students who attended well-resourced and well-known universities get access to better paying, more stable jobs.

Canada's Indigenous population is particularly under-represented in institutions of higher learning. The Canadian post-secondary attainment level—the percentage of people between the ages of 25 and 64 who have graduated with some form of post-secondary education—is 54 per cent, whereas the Indigenous level is only 39 per cent. But why does this large gap exist? Indigenous students face a lot of difficulties in accessing higher education, including "inadequate financial resources, poor academic preparation, lack of self-confidence and motivation, absence of role models who have post-secondary education experience, lack of understanding of Aboriginal culture on campus, and racism on campus" (Restoule et al., 2013, p. 1). The long history of colonialism and residential schools has also led to Indigenous distrust of authority groups. Policy recommendations by researchers are that the government should focus on encouraging Indigenous students to enter post-secondary institutions because their doing so would increase their future economic prosperity (Wang, 2013, p. 60).

population in Canada increased from 5 million to 7.7 million (Block, 2017).

However, the income gap between racialized and non-racialized Canadians isn't budging; rather, it has slightly widened. Racialized Canadians earn 26 per cent less than non-racialized Canadians (Block, 2017). However, even greater differences emerge when we add an analysis of gender. Racialized women earn on average 47 per cent less than non-racialized men (Block, 2017). You can see this increase in inequality in Figure 6.2: note that the average income for white women and men increased between 2011 and 2014 while the average for racialized women and men decreased, resulting in increasing inequality.

The fifth and final group of people facing high levels of poverty are those who are disabled. In 2012, 3.8 million Canadians (almost 14 per cent of the population) relied on disability supports in order to live independently in their communities (Torjman, & Makhoul, 2016, p,. 1). Despite these supports, almost one in five Canadians living with a disability earn a low income (Crawford, 2013, pp. 10, 11). Breaking this down, 17 per cent of those with a physical disability, 27 per cent of those with a mental or cognitive disability,

> **classism** Prejudice against people of a certain standing in the social hierarchy based on their material wealth and power.
>
> **blaming the victim** A perspective that holds individuals accountable for their circumstances.

and 35 per cent of those with a combination of both physical and mental disability live in low income (Wall, 2017). Moreover, the low-income rate is over 50 per cent for lone parents who are disabled and persons living alone who are disabled compared to 8 per cent for those living with a partner or spouse (Wall, 2017). In fact, lone parents and unattached people between the ages of 45 and 64 who are disabled account for one-quarter of the total low-income population in Canada (Wall, 2017).

Understanding Poverty

Many people believe that we all start out with the same chances of obtaining the "American Dream"—a good job, marriage, family, home ownership, nice car, and yearly vacations. This belief system is grounded in classism—bias, prejudice, and discrimination on the basis of social class—and often results in blaming the victim rather than the system. Coined by William Ryan (1971), "blaming the victim" is a view that holds individuals entirely responsible for any negative situations that may arise in their lives. Because there is an implicit understanding in

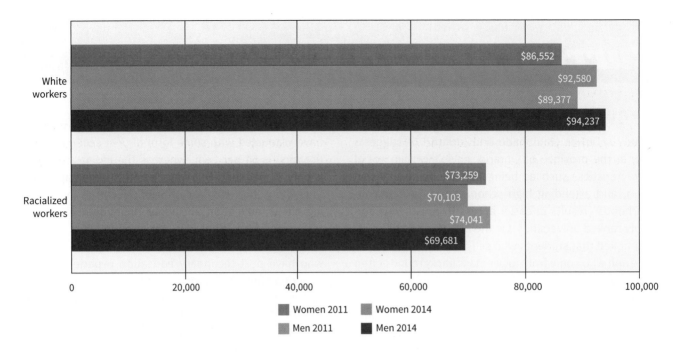

Figure 6.2 Average Household Income by Sex and Race, 2011–2014

In the Poverty and Employment Precarity in Southern Ontario (PEPSO) study, researchers investigated employment and income, finding disparities based on gender and race. (Note that Indigenous populations in this study are covered under "racialized" as well.)

Source: https://pepso.ca/documents/precarity-penalty.pdf, p. 40. With permission of PEPSO.

Canada that individuals who work hard should be able to prosper, those who do not succeed are seen as at fault and are criticized as lacking the motivation or the skills to help themselves.

In a classical, now heavily criticized, study on poverty, Oscar Lewis (1966) examined the lives of the poor and argued that those who live in poverty make up a subculture with different value systems than the rest of society. He argues that they are often incapable of improving their situation due to living in a "culture of poverty," which results in their feeling inferior and helpless. In this approach, the responsibility for changing the circumstances of impoverished people lies directly with the individual. Contemporary analysts argue that

Shameless

Prod. John Wells (2011–*present*). An American drama-comedy series that focuses on the Gallaghers—a large dysfunctional family led by an alcoholic father but raised mostly by the eldest child. While the show is fictional, it is unique in that it focuses on the lives of deeply impoverished people and the choices they are presented with in life to get by.

the classism and blaming-the-victim stance embedded in Lewis's analysis have contributed to policies that exacerbate rather than improve economic inequalities (Seabrook, 2014). This approach to poverty overlooks the facts, which show that poverty is strongly influenced by structural issues. For example, better legislation on welfare rates and increased minimum wages would eradicate a great deal of poverty. This is supported by research that indicates that despite fears about employment loss, ensuring a living wage—one that takes into account the cost of living in certain areas rather than just a set minimum wage—would have positive effects in terms of alleviating poverty (Harris, Janmaat, Evans, & Carlaw, 2018). Moreover, the individual-focused thinking that "poor people should be able to surpass their social environment demands a higher standard of behaviour and sacrifice from people who are poor than from people who are not" (Swanson, 2001, 3). Jean Swanson argues that much of poverty has to do with wealth distribution and furthers this argument by urging society to stop blaming individuals for their impoverished circumstances so that "we can expose the policies, laws, and economic system that force millions of people in Canada and around the world to compete against each other, driving down wages and creating more poverty" (2001, 8).

Practising Sociology

Monthly Budget of a Single Mom

Pretend that you are a single parent living in your current hometown. When your child was born, the other parent chose not to participate, thus leaving all financial responsibilities to you. You have no family supports who are able to help financially or with providing free child care. Fill out the corresponding chart based on the income information provided in Table 6.2 along with your own research on approximate monthly costs for a single mother and one child to survive in your city.

Family Type: Single mom, one child	City and Province:	Monthly Social Assistance:

Bill	Monthly Cost	Total Income Remaining (subtract as you go)
Rent		
Utilities (hydro, gas)		
Phone		
Groceries		
Cable/Internet		
Vehicle/transportation		
Insurance		
Life insurance		
Recreation (sports/gym memberships, etc.)		
Clothing		
Birthday presents or other holiday costs		
School supplies		

Reflection: Were you able to purchase all of the necessities that your family required? Which things did you choose to cut from your monthly budget and why? What are the repercussions for you and for your child from cutting those particular items? What could you do to "pull yourself up by your bootstraps"? Is it possible for people in this situation to make their lives better? Why or why not? Are there other costs missing from this list?

Swanson employs a perspective often referred to as **blaming the system**. This approach is much more consistent with a sociological view, as it takes environmental factors into consideration and recognizes the systemic discrimination that exists within society when considering an individual's circumstances.

> **blaming the system**
> A perspective that views environmental factors and systemic discrimination as responsible for an individual's circumstances.

The Florida Project

Dir. Sean Baker (2017). A documentary that centres on a run-down motel that houses poor families in Florida. The motel is located close to Walt Disney World and provides the characters with constant reminders of their economic position. The film examines the cycle of poverty that is created and the coping skills that children develop to deal with their social position.

Top 10 Takeaways

1 Social stratification is the hierarchical arrangement of individuals based on wealth, power, and prestige. — pp. 107–112

2 Most assume Canada to be a meritocracy—a system whereby if you work hard you have equal chances for success. — pp. 107–108

3 There are four systems of stratification: slavery, caste, clan, and class. — pp. 110–112

4 The four theoretical approaches look at different elements of inequality. Functionalists use the Davis-Moore hypothesis to argue that inequality is functional and necessary for the well-being of society. Conflict theorists argue that inequality is a result of the bourgeoisie exerting their power over the proletariat. Feminist theorists are concerned with the gendered patterns of inequality apparent both in the home and in the workplace. Symbolic interactionists highlight the ways in which people display their wealth through conspicuous consumption. — pp. 112–113

5 Most of the elites in Canada were born into their wealth and continue to pass it down generationally. — pp. 114–116

6 The middle class is slowly disappearing in Canada. — p. 116

7 Poverty is a term used to describe situations in which people lack opportunities available to the average citizen. Absolute poverty refers to the inability to afford particular goods, while relative poverty refers to the perceived difference between your own circumstances and those around you. — pp. 116–117

8 The most common measures of poverty are the LICO (an absolute measure based on the percentage of income spent on necessities), LIM (a relative measure that is calculated based on 50 per cent of the median income, adjusted for household sizes), and MBM (an absolute measure based on the cost of a set of goods representing a modest standard of living). — p. 117

9 The five most disadvantaged groups in Canada are women, single adults, Indigenous people, visible minority and recent immigrants, and disabled people. — pp. 117–119

10 There are two prominent explanations for poverty. One blames the victim, stating that individuals are responsible for their life situations. The second blames the system, which takes environmental factors into consideration. — pp. 119–120, 122

Questions for Critical Thinking

1. Think about your own social class and discuss the different areas of your life that social stratification impacts.

2. In what ways are we encouraged to believe that Canada is a meritocracy? Think about various agents of socialization (your family, school, the media) when answering.

3. Compare the four systems of stratification. Explain which are open and which are closed systems of stratification. Which has the potential to produce less inequality and why?

4. Which theoretical paradigm best describes social inequality? Explain why.

5. Research the top five wealthiest Canadians. How did they obtain most of their wealth? Reflect on whether you have the same chances of reaching these high levels of success.

6. What has been happening to the middle class in Canada?

7. Discuss the pros and cons of each measure of poverty. Explain which you feel is the most effective and why.

8. What kinds of policies could be put in place to help the most disadvantaged groups in Canada ameliorate some of the hardships they face as a result of their disadvantage?

9. Go online and read through newspaper headlines during any election period in any country. Discuss the ways that different political parties explicitly either blame the victim or the system as part of their campaign strategies. Reflect on why this might be.

10. What kinds of social class messages are embedded in your day-to-day experiences at college?

Recommended Readings

- **Crompton, R. (1993).** *Class and stratification.* **Cambridge: Polity.** Crompton argues that class processes are not the only factors contributing to the maintenance and reproduction of inequality; rather, cultural practices are deeply involved in both its reproduction and its maintenance.

- **Dahrendorf, R. (1959).** *Class and class conflict in industrial society.* **Stanford, CA: Stanford University Press.** Dahrendorf believes that in an age in which property and control have become separated in the industrial world, it is not property but the exercise of or exclusion from authoritative control that establishes class position.

- **Grabb, E.G. (2007).** *Theories of social inequality: Classical and contemporary perspectives* **(5th ed.). Toronto: Harcourt.** Grabb provides an overview and analysis of theories of social inequality, including theorists such as Marx, Weber, Durkheim, Lenski, Poulantzas, Wright, Parking, and Giddens.

- **Lenski, G. (1966).** *Power and privilege: A theory of stratification.* **New York: McGraw-Hill.** Lenski contends that classes are aggregations of persons in society who stand in similar positions with respect to some form of power, privilege, or prestige. He shifts from a focus on class structure to processes that generate structure.

- **Li, P.S. (1992). Race and gender as bases of class fractions and their effects on earnings.** *Canadian Review of Sociology and Anthropology, 29*(4), 488–510. Li examines the joint effect of race and gender on income and argues that gender fractionalizes class in two important senses: as the occupational structure changes, gender provides the ground for segregating occupations into men's and women's jobs, and women have become more proletarianized than men in the labour force.

- **McMullin, J.A. (2010).** *Understanding inequality: Intersections of class, age, gender, ethnicity, and race in Canada* **(2nd ed.). Toronto: Oxford University Press.** McMullin outlines the ways in which opportunities are distributed differentially in society on the basis of class, age, gender, ethnicity, and race and argues for an intersectional understanding of inequality.

- **Porter, J. (1965).** *The vertical mosaic: An analysis of social class and power in Canada.* **Toronto: University of Toronto Press.** Porter argues that there is a hierarchical structure of material rewards that acts as a barrier to equal opportunity. He argues that in Canada there is an establishment of a vertical mosaic of class and power, with the Anglo-Saxon charter group at the top of the class and power structures, recruiting their offspring and social equals as future elites.

- **Wright, E.O. (1997).** *Class counts: Comparative studies in class analysis.* **Cambridge: Cambridge University Press.** Wright outlines his conception of social class and argues that class analysis is based on the notion of exploitation conceived as an antagonistic interdependence of material interests. He contends that there are three basic classes: capitalists (exploiters), workers (exploited), and petty bourgeoisie (neither exploited nor exploiter).

Recommended Websites

Canada Without Poverty
www.cwp-csp.ca
- This organization is a not-for-profit charitable organization dedicated to the elimination of poverty in Canada.

Who Rules America
http://www2.ucsc.edu/whorulesamerica/
- This site highlights the work of G. William Domhoff, a research professor at the University of California, and presents an abundance of information on wealth and income distribution in the US.

Make Poverty History Canada
http://www.makepovertyhistory.ca
- This site provides information about poverty across the world and includes information and resources for anti-poverty activism.

Oxfam International
http://www.oxfam.org
- Oxfam is an international confederation of 17 organizations working together in more than 90 countries to ensure that poor people can improve their lives and livelihoods and have a say in decisions that affect them.

Ontario Coalition Against Poverty (OCAP)
http://www.ocap.ca
- OCAP is an anti-poverty organization located in Toronto. It provides advocacy for individuals combating organizations (such as the Ontario Disability Support Program and social assistance and public housing authorities) that make it difficult for poor people to receive what they are entitled to.

Organisation for Economic Co-operation and Development (OECD)
http://www.oecd.org
- The OECD brings together governments from around the world to support sustainable economic growth, boost employment, raise living standards, maintain financial stability, assist other countries' economic development, and contribute to growth in world trade.

Report Cards on Child and Family Poverty
https://campaign2000.ca/1106-2/
- This site offers useful data on child and family poverty in Canada.

SocioSite
www.sociosite.net/topics/inequality.php
- The section "Social Inequality and Classes" offers a comprehensive list of sociological resources on social inequality, class, stratification, and poverty.

Chapter 7

Gender

Fraternal twins born into a family should for all intents and purposes have the same life chances and similar socialization processes. The same parents, with the same socio-economic status and parenting style, should theoretically raise the twins in the same manner. Research shows us, however, that fraternal twins will in most cases be raised very differently based solely on the sex assigned to them at birth. Being born with visible female or male sex organs drastically changes one's life circumstances (Wallis & Kwok, 2008). This chapter explores the ways in which one's biological sex influences socialization processes. In addition, we problematize the binary categorization of males and females by Canadian society.

Introduction

Each of you at some point in your life has been asked to fill out a survey—it could have been a survey to gather feedback about a particular sport or program you participated in, to determine customer satisfaction, to evaluate your courses, or to fulfill the Government of Canada's census. One of the very first questions that most surveys ask is that you identify either your sex or your gender by ticking one of two boxes: Male or Female. A more recently developed survey may offer a third option: Other. The wording of these questions is problematic for a number of reasons that will be discussed in this section.

Defining Sex and Gender

Sex is a biological concept. The biological differences between humans are anatomic, genetic, and hormonal. Perceived physical differences between humans have resulted in the arbitrary division of the human population into two categories: male and female. Categorizing people into two groups suggests that these groups are diametrical opposites—thus, the terminology "opposite sex." This division is known as a binary construction, meaning that people can only fit into one of two mutually exclusive, and opposite, groups. However, in reality the human body is complex and rarely falls into the perfect definition of female or male sex. There is no set hormone threshold at which someone becomes "female" rather than "male." Chromosome configuration can be complicated (e.g., XX, XY, XYY, XXY), and most hospitals do not test a baby's DNA for chromosomes before assigning a sex. Further, there is no scientific proof of biologically based psychological differences (such as a "maternal instinct") based on sex. Generally, these biological differences have few (if any) inevitable effects on modern-day social life. For example, having a working womb does not mean that a person necessarily has the desire to become pregnant and give birth to a child; it also does not mean that the person would be a particularly nurturing parent.

In contrast to biological sex, gender refers to the cultural beliefs, assumptions, and structures around biological sex. Gender roles are learned patterns of behaviour that a society expects of men and women: in other words, masculinity and femininity. These roles are a widespread fact of social life although, like all sociological constructs, they differ over place and time. Wherever you go, people are likely to expect different behaviours based on the categories that society uses to construct gender. We will use the gender binary here, as this is what Canadians are most familiar with. From men, people will expect behaviour that is "masculine," and from women, they will expect behaviour that is "feminine."

sex The social construction of categories based on physical and biological characteristics; in the hegemonic Canadian society, these categories are male and female.

binary construction The classification of a concept (in this case, gender or sex) into one of two mutually exclusive groups.

gender Human traits (including behaviours, roles, attributes, personality, physical appearance, and values) that a culture associates with a particular sex.

gender roles The attitudes and activities that members of a culture typically expect, or desire, of other members of that culture based on their perceived sex.

By masculinity, then, we mean qualities that people associate with men. By femininity, we mean qualities that we associate with women. Individuals are expected to behave in accordance with their assigned gender role in every aspect of their lives, including in their relationships, educational pursuits, and work lives.

Interestingly, there is no single form of masculinity and femininity in North American society; however, there are dominant forms. According to Connell (1987) these forms are known as hegemonic masculinity and emphasized femininity. Hegemonic masculinity is the "ideal" form of masculinity that boys are supposed to strive to achieve by adulthood. In North America, masculinity includes strength, athleticism, assertiveness, and aggression. Moreover, masculinity has been tied to heterosexuality. Likewise, emphasized femininity is the most culturally valued form of femininity. Thus, emphasized femininity includes attractiveness: feminine women are expected to look their best at all times, to accentuate their femaleness with dresses, skirts, and high heels—and also supportiveness, enthusiasm, and the ability to accommodate men's desires.

An important part of gender is that we *learn* our gender, but we don't have to learn our sex. That is, we learn *how* to be masculine or feminine and also learn that we should be one or the other. We are not born with the idea that girls should play with dolls and that boys should play with cars and trucks. Instead, we learn these expectations. We learn which toys to play with at preschool by watching children's televisions shows and from what our parents (and other relatives) tell us.

As a social construction, the performance gender varies across societies. And, like all social constructs, gender is largely a social construction that is forced upon us. We violate the rules at our own risk.

Problematizing the Binary Construction of Sex and Gender

Current theorizing on the historical binary construction of sex and gender problematizes the male/female and masculine/feminine opposition as false. There are many examples of individuals whose biology and/or gender display question our understanding of these categories as diametrical opposites.

Intersex individuals, for example, are people who are born with indistinct genitalia and/or a combination of chromosomes that do not allow for an easy categorization of male or female at birth (Newbould, 2016; Joanna et al., 2018). Prior to the availability of advanced medical testing, the decision about whether to surgically intervene to ensure that a baby fit into the male or female category was often done based upon the presence of testes and the length of the penis (Newbould, 2016). If they were deemed to be of "suitable" length and functionality, surgery would be performed, taking away any evidence of female genitalia and organs, and the child would be raised as a male (Newbould, 2016). Most current medical experts encourage parents to raise intersex children with the genitalia and chromosomes that they are born with and allow them to make their own decision about what gender (if any) they most closely align with when they age (Roen, 2018).

Current research suggests that between 1 in 1500 and 1 in 2000 births are of intersex children (Blackless et al., 2000). Furthermore, 1 in every 100 births deviates from "standard male and female" (Blackless et al., 2000). Considering the relative frequency of this phenomenon, wouldn't this imply that the categorization of two sexes is incorrect? If we had three sexes—male, female, and intersex—would individuals feel the need to surgically alter themselves to fit into either the male or female category?

Transgender is a term that has been used in mainstream media with much more frequency in the past five years than ever before. Caitlyn Jenner (retired Olympian), Laverne Cox (who played Sophia on the popular Netflix series *Orange Is the New Black*), and Jazz Jennings (reality star of *I Am Jazz*) were propelled to celebrity status because of their transition from their biological sex to a different (or, in the binary construction of popular culture, "opposite") gender. *Transgender* is an umbrella term for a range of individuals who do not easily fit, or categorize themselves, into the normative categories of male and female. The term *trans* implies that one is in transition;

masculinity The sets of traits (including behaviours, roles, attributes, personality, physical appearance, and values) that are associated with being a man in any given culture; these change over time and place.

femininity The sets of traits (including behaviours, roles, attributes, personality, physical appearance, and values) that are associated with being a woman in any given culture; these change over time and place.

hegemonic masculinity The idealized or most highly regarded traits associated with being a man; in our current Canadian culture, this includes being strong, capable, financially successful, and heterosexual.

emphasized femininity The idealized or most highly regarded traits associated with being a woman; in our current Canadian culture, this includes being attractive, compliant, caring, and available to men.

intersex An umbrella term that applies to someone who is born with one of several possible variations in sex characteristics from the discrete gender binary categories; these differences can be chromosomal, gonadal, hormonal, or related to visible genitalia.

transgender An umbrella term for people whose gender identity does not align with the sex that they were assigned at birth.

Well-known Belgian model Hanne Gaby Odiele recently opened up about being intersex. Odiele was born with testicles; her parents decided to have them surgically removed when she was 10 (McNamara, 2017). She also reported that she had to undergo vaginal reconstruction surgery, which was extremely traumatic (McNamara, 2017). Odiele has become a spokesperson for avoiding unnecessary surgeries, arguing that sex and gender exist on a spectrum rather than according to strict imposed categories and that intersex people should not be seen as abnormal (McNamara, 2017). How would society change if we didn't have such strict constructions of biological sex?

however, this transition does not always include the physical body. Some trans individuals have no desire to alter their bodies, and others do, while some prefer to present themselves in a more ambiguous or non-gender-specific manner.

In circumstances where trans individuals feel the need to align their physical body with their understanding of self, they may decide to undergo sex affirmation surgery. This means that individuals take hormone replacement protocol and have surgery (usually multiple surgeries) to transition from the sex they were born with to the sex

doing drag Performing (in public or on a stage) while embodying a gender identity that does not align with the sex that the performer was assigned at birth.

two-spirit A modern umbrella term used by some Indigenous peoples within North America to describe people within their communities who fulfill one of many traditional non-conforming roles that transgress the hegemonic gender binary (including a third gender, multiple genders, and transgender identities); as with all identities related to gender, the identity of two-spirit is distinct from sexual orientation.

Southern Comfort

Dir. Kate Davis (2001). An award-winning documentary that follows Robert Eads, a trans man dying of ovarian cancer who is refused medical treatment.

that they identify with. These surgeries may include facial reconstruction, genital realignment surgery, and/or chest reconstruction or augmentation surgery. Some individuals reject the label "trans" because it is tied to a medical discourse as something in need of treatment—implying that there is something wrong with individuals who require this surgery.

Sexual orientation refers to people's identity as it relates to the gender(s) they are attracted to. People's sexual orientation (who they are sexually attracted to) is distinct from their gender identity (what gender they identify as). In addition to sexual attraction (or in the absence of it, as in the case of asexual individuals), some individuals vary in terms of whom they are romantically attracted to. For example, a person may enjoy having sex with people of a particular gender identity but prefer to commit to long-term relationships with people of a different gender identity.

"Doing drag" refers to stylistic performances where individuals dress up as a different gender than the one they were assigned at birth. These individuals, however, do not necessarily identify with or want to be another sex. Drag is a performance rather than a change in identity. For many drag performers, gender identity is fluid depending on their gender presentation although others may identify as a single gender, or as no gender, no matter how they are dressed. For example, RuPaul, host of *RuPaul's Drag Race,* has shown an indifference toward gender-specific pronouns throughout his career: "You can call me he. You can call me she. You can call me Regis and Kathie Lee; I don't care! Just as long as you call me" (RuPaul, 1995). When uncertain, it is always best to ask individuals which pronouns they prefer.

In white settler colonies, transgender individuals have historically been viewed as somehow deviant or abnormal; however, in other cultures being born with both masculine and feminine traits is seen as a gift. Indigenous peoples of North America, for example, have many different terms for members of their communities whose gender identity is unique; the modern umbrella term used for these varying identities is two-spirit, which

From My Perspective

Justice, 30-Year-Old Man, Full-Time Employee in the Service Industry

Much to everyone's excitement, I was the first biological female-born grandchild to both my mother and father's side of the family. As a result, I was spoiled rotten. I was always dressed up in dresses and had long, curly hair. When I was old enough to start dressing myself, I started dressing less feminine and was quickly labelled a tomboy. I knew even from a young age that dresses, pink stuff, and frilly things just didn't feel right to me. Those years were extraordinarily difficult for me as I always felt something was off, and while I didn't have the words to properly articulate it, I just never felt comfortable with myself.

In my early twenties I became friends with a person who identified as transgender. I had never even heard of this before and couldn't recall ever being exposed to the concept. I was not consciously aware of ever even having heard of this in school or in the media. When I learned that this friend was in fact a trans man, it felt like a whole new world opened up to me. I started questioning myself and thinking through my continual inner confusion throughout my life to date. It was like everything I had felt suddenly made complete sense to me. I struggled for a long time before coming to terms with and accepting myself as a trans man. It took me 10 years to finally come out to my family.

When I did come out, I felt so many emotions simultaneously. First, I felt a sense of relief at finally being my true self. Second, I felt immense fear of rejection. In fact, it took my family almost a year to finally even talk to me at all. This was a very tumultuous time in my life as I struggled to go through the process of transitioning without any family by my side. I had grown up my entire life surrounded by family and the Catholic Church and suddenly felt very isolated. It was very tough on my mental health and well-being.

I didn't think my family would ever understand—and quite truthfully, I still don't fully understand the how's and why's of it all. However, it has now been two years and I am in a committed, healthy relationship, and we spend holidays with my family. This past Christmas was like nothing had ever happened and we were all back to being the loving family we were pre-transition. I am very grateful to have their love and support.

Every culture has preconceived notions of how its members should act and look, whom they should love and how that love should be enacted. These constructions make it very difficult for people like me to feel okay with ourselves and to be the contributing members of society we want to be.

Source: Provided by Justice Dion, used by permission.

---

describes how a person's sexual, gender, and/or spiritual identity includes both a masculine and feminine spirit (Laframboise & Anhorn, 2008). This term is exclusive to specific Indigenous communities and should not be used by non-Indigenous people. The existence of two-spirit individuals shows us that viewing transgender identity as abnormal is a social construction. Moreover, this term encompasses some traditional third gender roles within some Indigenous communities, illustrating nicely that the gender binary, too, is a social construction.

Lady Valor: The Kristin Beck Story

Dir. Sandrine Orabona and Mark Herzog (2014). A documentary that follows the life of Navy SEAL elite special force member Christopher Beck as she begins a new mission in her personal life. Beck's transition to Kristin is followed as she begins to live her true identity despite an abundance of fear and discrimination.

YouTube: PrincessJoules

Julie Vu, a transgender beauty vlogger from BC. She records makeup tutorials as well as information about her own transition.

Podcast: Transmission

An interview podcast in which YouTuber and trans man Jackson Bird makes space for trans people to tell their own stories on their own terms.

Laverne Cox (left) is the first openly transgender person to ever be nominated for an Emmy (twice!) in the acting category for her role on *Orange Is the New Black* and the first to appear on the cover of *Time* magazine. Jazz Jennings (right) is a YouTube star, reality TV star, model, and one of the youngest publicly documented people to identify as transgender. In 2007, at the age of six, she appeared on ABC's *20/20*, explaining her trans identity. Can celebrities make a difference in the lives of non-celebrity transgender people?

In the News

Can We Live in a Genderless World?

In 2011, a news story first hit local news stations and then quickly claimed international air time. A couple living in the Greater Toronto Area gave birth to a healthy, beautiful baby, whom they named Storm. The happy parents already had two sons and had witnessed that their sons' decisions not to conform to normative standards of masculinity (they wore their hair long, liked to wear pink, and at times wore clothes and played with toys that are traditionally viewed as feminine) resulted in their often being ridiculed and treated poorly. As a result of these experiences, the parents sent a message to their friends and family announcing Storm's arrival. In the message they stated that they had decided not to share Storm's sex as "a tribute to freedom and choice in place of limitations" (Poisson, 2011). One of the people who received the message was outraged and shared it with the media.

The media in Canada and the United States quickly began debating the couple's motives in choosing to raise their child without conventional social norms regarding gender. Many news outlets reprimanded the couple for conducting an unfair social experiment at the cost of their child's well-being. Others applauded the parents for attempting to break social norms. Is it possible to raise a child in North America without a public gender? Consider some of the difficulties and consequences of this choice.

Reproducing Gender: Gender and Agents of Socialization

In Chapter 4, we discussed our socialization agents. Here we discuss how three of these agents—families, education, and the media—perpetuate our understandings of what it means to be a girl or boy.

Families

In today's era of gender-reveal parties, gender socialization begins even prior to birth. The moment an obstetrician reveals the perceived sex of a fetus, parents begin the process of indoctrinating their yet-to-be-born child into their assumed gender. Walls are painted in soft shades of either pinks or purples for girls or blues, greens, and greys for boys, and the purchasing of gender-specific accessories begins. The moment the baby is brought into the world, the doctor congratulates the new parent/s on the arrival of their new baby boy or girl. The first job of the parents is then to give the child a gender-specific name. Friends and families come to the hospital or home to visit the new arrival with their arms full of gifts. Despite the gifts generally being the same for boys and girls (flowers, balloons, blankets, sleepers, teddy bears, soothers, etc.), the colours and decorations of these gifts tend to be gender-coded—even though babies don't even develop colour vision, and can't see details, for several weeks!

These gendered interactions continue and become more pronounced throughout a child's life. Research shows that parents interact with their children differently based upon their sex: boys are left to cry longer than girls (Kimmel, 2004) and are punished more often (Armstrong, 2004). Girls are more likely to be given toys that reinforce nurturing (dolls and kitchen sets, for example) while boys are more likely to receive toys that strengthen problem solving and activity (building blocks, video games, and sports equipment, for example) (Francis, 2010). Often, household tasks that are assigned to children are gendered activities: children identified as male are instructed to take out the garbage, shovel the driveway, and cut the grass, while children identified as female are expected to do the dishes, dust, vacuum, and do the laundry. What tasks were you first assigned in your home? How does your current home break up household activities?

Education

Some of you may have had incredibly progressive parents who raised you as gender-neutral, exposing you to

© Alexmak72427 | Dreamstime.com

Have you ever been to a large children's toy store? In the "boys" section, you will find action, adventure, construction, automotive, and sport-themed toys. You will also find weapons in this section (fake guns and swords). In the "girls" section, you will find nurturing- and caretaking-themed toys. You will also find beauty-related products (jewellery, makeup, and gowns). Were you able to tell, even without being able to see the details in this photo, whether this is a girls or boys section? How does this social construction of gender reinforce inequality?

toys that were designed for any gender, dressing you in gender-neutral clothing, and enforcing your equal participation in all household labour. However, even if you were raised this way, the moment you entered the educational system you would have been exposed to gendered expectations. Think through some of the basic design elements of a school. Girls and boys are taught to use gender-specific washrooms, with the implicit message that boys need specialized equipment that girls do not. There are also gender-specific change rooms, sports teams, and recreational activities. Gym is often separated by gender. As well, when directing students to line up to go somewhere, often teachers ask them to line up according to their gender. Some private schools are exclusive to one gender. Immediately, then, school teaches us that only two genders exist, that these two genders are different, and that these differences matter.

Research continues to show that boys and girls are treated differently in the classroom. There is an expectation that girls will complete their work and will be respectful while doing so, and, as a result, more attention is aimed at encouraging boys to focus on their schooling (Renzetti & Curran, 1999). Girls are praised for being neat, quiet, and polite, while boys are praised for completing work and for their intellectual prowess (Nelson, 2009). As discussed in Chapter 4, these unconscious and informal differences in the ways that genders are treated in school are collectively known as the *hidden curriculum*.

While I have been either learn-ing *or* teaching about these very real gendered practices for two decades now, coming up with tangible examples of how teachers treated the girls and boys differently when I went to school was difficult for me. This, of course, is in part because it has been a very long time since I was in elementary and secondary school but also because these gendered practices often happen so covertly that we don't even notice them. A few years ago, my family had a holiday get-together. My mother was in the process of moving into a smaller home and, as a result, was purging many of the items she had been collecting over the years. She came to the get-together with a bag for each of her four children that contained all of our artwork, medals, awards, and report cards from when we went to school. My brother and I are 18 months apart in age and would often have the same teacher for specific grades. We both had the same grade 3 teacher, so for fun we pulled out our report cards from the year and compared them. I started with my grades; A, A+, A, A-, C (music), B- (physical education), C (art), A, A+. My brother then read his out loud; C, C-, D+, C+, A (physical education), B+ (art), C, C, D. I then did what most older sisters would do (when they are 12, not 40) and started laughing at my brother and bragging about how smart I was. (This is an ongoing joke between my brother and me as I went to university for 15 years and he went to college for two, and yet makes much more money than I do!) We then decided to read the teacher's feedback, written to help us work on our shortcomings. My brother read his first: "*We are so delighted with the improvement in Taylor's work this year. He is working hard and is staying focused. Great job, Taylor.*" Then, I read mine: "*Sara is by far the messiest child I have ever taught. Her desk is a disgrace and her penmanship is very sloppy.*

I suggest Sara work on her cursive at home after school" (cursive turned out to be a really useful skill, didn't it?). I was not praised at all for my academic achievements; instead, my shortcomings in being neat and tidy (i.e., feminine) were highlighted. These gendered messages were permeating our lives as children without any of us really understanding *or even noticing* them.

By the time we hit post-secondary school, then, our gender socialization is well underway. Interestingly, female participation rates in post-secondary education have continued to rise, with women constituting almost 60 per cent of all undergraduate students (Statistics Canada, 2015). However, the types of programs that females and males enroll in clearly illustrates the impact of gendered socialization. When looking at undergraduate degrees, females dominate in the health and social sciences fields, while men dominate in the engineering and math fields. Overall, women hold approximately 27 per cent of all PhDs in Canada but are underrepresented in fields that are traditionally dominated by men, including science, engineering, computer science, and math (Statistics Canada, 2015). In recent years there has been a push to get women to enter the STEM (science, technology, engineering, and math) fields (see Figure 7.1), with more scholarship money available and programs at some schools designed specifically for women. However, research continues to show a low level of retainment of women in these studies (Catalyst, 2018). Women who have exited STEM programs cite discrimination, sexual harassment, and anxiety associated with being perceived as intellectually inferior in the field (De Welde & Laursen, 2011; Easterly & Ricard, 2011; Beasley & Fischer, 2012). These barriers, however, are not limited to women studying and working in STEM areas. Women in the wider labour market also face discrimination, sexual harassment, and perceived inferiority. We will get into this a bit later in the chapter.

Media

We interact with numerous forms of media from the time that we are very young. And media have rarely been neutral in their depiction of gender. The socialized differences between men and women are apparent in everything that we see and hear—from children's books that we read, programming that we watch, advertisements that we see, songs that we stream, etcetera, we are continually bombarded with masculine and feminine images.

A trend that appears universal among international and domestic students alike is exposure to Disney movies at a young age. The masculine and feminine roles that have been portrayed in the majority of movies produced

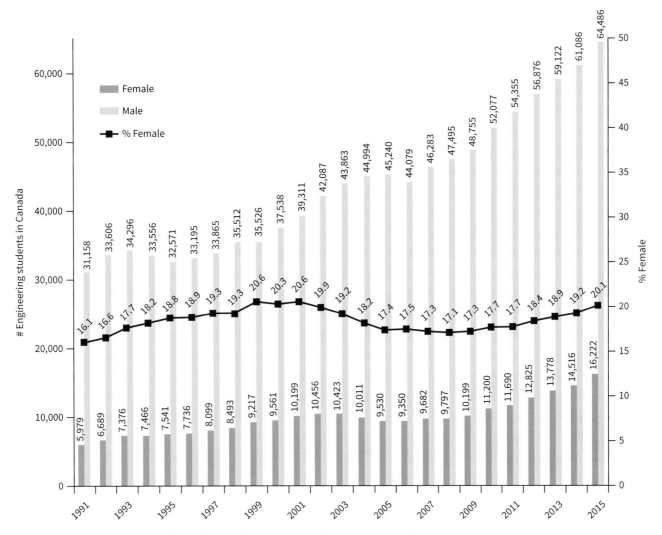

Figure 7.1 Number of Engineering Students in Canada, by Gender, 1991 to 2015

Source: Adapted from Canadian Engineers for Tomorrow: Trends in Engineering Enrolment and Degrees Awarded 2013-2017. Engineers Canada report by Vinicius Rossi, 2017: https://engineerscanada.ca/publications/canadian-engineers-for-tomorrow-2017

Instagram: @kimkardashian and @kyliejenner

The Instagram accounts of Kim Kardashian and Kylie Jenner. The Jenner/Kardashian family have become fashion and beauty icons for girls around the world, with millions of followers each in 2019. Kim Kardashian is the most famous—her Instagram has 141 million followers. Kylie Jenner has a makeup and skin care line—her IG has 137 million followers. What do these accounts tell us about what is beautiful/desirable femininity?

by Disney are clear examples of hegemonic masculinity and emphasized femininity and highlight how expectations in life are different for girls and boys. Think about the classic Disney princesses: Belle, Aurora, Cinderella,

Snow White, and let's add in Ariel as well. What do the stories have in common? In four of the stories, the princesses are motherless, and in three of those, they are raised by absentee fathers and "wicked" stepmothers. All of the princesses share the physical features of slim waists, an hourglass shape, mid-length to long hair, and whiteness, and all are identified as "beautiful" in their stories. In addition, they are so very in touch with nature that when they sing (beautifully, we might add) animals are drawn to them and share in their melodies. Perhaps the most problematic issue in Disney is the portrayal of the princesses as incapable of taking care of themselves and as destined to be victimized. In each case, a white, rich prince comes to the rescue (usually on a horse) to save the poor, weak, damsel in distress with true love's kiss. Let's really think about this scenario, particularly in *Snow White* and in *Sleeping Beauty*: a strange male comes along and starts kissing a beautiful, passed-out female.

Ariel gives up her voice to be with a man, and Belle falls in love with her captor. There are obvious messages to both boys and girls in these films—that women are incomplete and incapable without a man and that men must fulfil the task of taking financial and physical care of women. Examine how these learned gender roles might have played out in your own relationships, or those of other people in your social network.

Current research suggests, however, that Disney is now creating more dynamic female characters. Female

> **ideology of gender** A set of widespread social beliefs that gender is a binary and that there are "natural" differences between men and women (i.e., hegemonic masculinity and emphasized femininity). This ideology is entirely socially constructed and is harmful to everyone.

leads are at times shown to be independent and brave, such as the characters Merida (*Brave,* 2012), Elsa and Anna (*Frozen,* 2013), and Tiana (*The Princess and the Frog,* 2009; D'Ambrozia, 2017). In addition, for most of these female leads, finding love was either not a priority or never appeared in the film at all (Man-Hsin & Tso, 2014). Think about something (television or film) that you've seen recently. Do you think the shifts in gender portrayals in some Disney films are corresponding to shifts within the wider media landscape, and to shifts in society at large?

Advertising is another medium that is deeply gendered. Often, women are sexualized and treated as objects while men are masculinized, shown as strong and capable. Jean Kilbourne is an activist filmmaker who has produced films and spoken internationally about the need for media literacy. In her renowned documentary series *Killing Us Softly,* Kilbourne uses thousands of current media images to illustrate the ways in which women are often portrayed as objects and pieces of their bodies used to sell products. She notes that racialized women in particular are sexualized and dehumanized in advertisements, portrayed as both exotic and animal-like (Kilbourne, 2010). Kilbourne is just one of many activists and academics who argue that the treatment of women as sexualized objects is dangerous in a world where domestic violence remains deeply gendered (see below). Jackson Katz, PhD, is an educator, author, and filmmaker who problematizes the version of masculinity that is often portrayed in media in his documentary series *Tough Guise.* Katz argues that media play a major role in socializing men into believing that aggression and violence are part of being a man.

The Ideology of Gender

The **ideology of gender** is a set of widespread social beliefs that gender is a binary and that there are "natural" differences between men and women. For example, this ideology assumes that men are naturally more aggressive, competitive, and rational than women. As a result,

The popular erotic novel *Fifty Shades of Grey* topped the bestseller list and sold 125 million copies prior to becoming a film. If we remove the sexual activity from the storyline, is it that much different than the older Disney films discussed above? Anastasia Steele (played in the film by Dakota Johnson, right) is a white, thin, beautiful, kind, young female who is moving through her mundane life until the billionaire, handsome, white, Christian Grey (Jamie Dornan, left, in the film) comes along and sweeps her off her feet. Are these fantasies harmless?

> ### Queer Eye
>
> From Netflix (2018–). A makeover show where stylists not only encourage self-expression as beauty but also demonstrate the necessity of male connection, vulnerability, and empathy.

Practising Sociology

Analyzing Ads

Advertising is a multi-billion-dollar industry. And every single day in the Western world, each of us is inundated with messages about what it means to be male and female. Using the Internet, look up ads from Nike as well as nine other companies that you typically purchase, or aspire to purchase, your clothing from, and describe the advertisements for these companies. How are females and males portrayed by each company? Do any of the companies have non-binary ads?

Were people of each gender portrayed differently (various physical positions, activities, level of dress, etc.) by each company? What were those differences? Is there a difference between how people of various ethnicities are portrayed? Discuss any similarities or differences between the portrayals in advertisements and the lessons you have learned in your life about being a particular gender.

Company	Describe Advertisement	Gendered Messages
Nike		

men more naturally invent, explore, and explain reality, which is why (according to this ideology) men make better scientists. Conversely, women are more naturally passive, supportive, emotional, dependent, and sexually available than men. So, it is natural, according to this ideology, for women to nurture and to not be ambitious. Moreover, this ideology considers these feminine traits to be negative while these masculine traits are considered positive.

When men are taught this ideology of gender, they learn to justify their inherited privileged and authoritative role in society. At the same time, women learn to tolerate their subordinated role in society. For example, people learn to expect women to be submissive. If women do otherwise, they risk being labelled unfeminine or "bitchy." Conversely, people learn to expect men to be dominant. If men act submissively, they risk being called a "sissy" or a "wimp" or, even more likely, having their sexual orientation called into question. In this way, gender differences become part of the structure of society. Think about all of your professors, for example. Do you have different expectations of your male and female professors in terms of their attitudes and behaviours in class? Have you ever accused a female professor of being "bitchy" for being strict with deadlines or other classroom rules or not listening to your complaints? Have you ever accused a male professor of the same?

"Toxic masculinity" refers to the harmful attitudes and behaviour of men that occur as a result of hegemonic masculinity (Pascoe, 2007). Or, in other words, the term refers to the consequences of socializing men to be unemotional, violent, and sexually aggressive. Some of the more apparent outcomes of toxic masculinity are the impact it has on others. For example, socializing men to be sexually aggressive toward women leads to increased sexual harassment and assault (discussed below). However, much of the impact of toxic masculinity is felt by men. Toxic masculinity prevents men from openly expressing their emotions, from hugging or having any sort of physical contact with other male loved ones, from developing meaningful relationships with other men (or expressing appreciation to one another for the relationships they do have), and so forth. It also prevents men from developing certain skills, such as future planning and emotional support of a loved one, that are relegated to women. Thus, while much of the conversation surrounding toxic masculinity tends to focus on the negative consequences it has for women, men also experience negative consequences of these societal expectations, and these consequences are felt more acutely by men who deviate from hegemonic masculinity.

Patriarchy

The ideology of gender is related to *patriarchy,* a system of social organization in which men hold power and women are excluded from power. Indeed, it is the ideology of gender that justifies patriarchy. And since patriarchy is built on social constructs like gender and the ideology of gender, it varies in strength from one society to another. In patriarchal societies, men have more decision-making power than women and reap more rewards as a result— and the more "masculine" the man, the more rewards he reaps.

While most patriarchal laws have been struck down by the Supreme Court, Canada remains a patriarchal society. Chapter 2 discussed an example of the way that the ideology of patriarchy continues to play out despite legislation demanding equal rights for women: recall the example of the heterosexual union with the father walking the bride down the aisle and "giving her away" to the husband. In most provinces (excluding Quebec, where this is actually illegal), the wife will then commonly take on her new husband's last name. While these practices are not law, they continue because of patriarchal ideology. There are also examples of the law continuing to enforce patriarchal assumptions in Canada. Until very recently, "Indian status" was legally only passed down through male lineage. The original Indian Act defined First Nations as "a male Indian, the wife of a male Indian or the child of a male Indian" (Kassam, 2018). If a First Nations woman married a non-Indigenous man, she would lose her First Nations status as well as any benefits that came with the status. However, First Nations men who married non-Indigenous women were able to pass down their status to their children (Kassam, 2018). In 2017, Prime Minister Justin Trudeau's government passed legislation to amend this law, making it closer to being gender equitable—however, it did not undo all of the past biases of the Indian Act, and no timeline has been placed on the amendments, leaving First Nations women fearing that change will take years (Kassam, 2018).

In September 2017, Saudi Arabia made international news when King Salman issued an order to allow women to drive, with new guidelines to be created and implemented by June 2018. Up until that point, Saudi Arabia remained the only country where women were legally forbidden from driving. Salman has also relaxed some of the long-held traditions by allowing women into sports complexes for certain events. Despite these changes, Saudi Arabia remains a deeply patriarchal society where women need men's permission to do many things. In fact, there is a guardianship rule that stops women from making any decision without the assistance of a male relative, even if that relative is her young son.

Gender Inequality in Canada

You may be thinking that gender inequality is an issue of the past or of other places. It is true that the dramatic increase in women's labour force participation in the past 50+ years has signalled a major change in gender roles in hegemonic Canadian culture (more on this below). However, in their paid and unpaid labour, most women still do "women's work." This is part of what sociologists call a **gendered division of labour**, which refers to the fact that women are more likely to have jobs that pay less, have lower prestige, require longer hours of work, and are less likely to be full-time (i.e., to have benefits) than jobs in which most workers are men. The gendered division of labour is part of a system of **gender stratification** that still exists in Canada today. Whatever social situations we are in, we see gender differences and, often, we are made to feel obligated to maintain existing gender inequalities.

Gender Inequality in the Workplace

The past 40 years have seen women make important gains in the labour market, especially in labour force participation (Budig & Hodges, 2010; Youngjoo & Weeden, 2014). However, a **gendered wage gap** continues to persist. In the early 1960s, female labour force participation remained below 30 per cent (Fortin & Huberman, 2002); in 1967, women working full-time, full-year, earned on average 58.4 per cent of what men earned (Heisz, Jackson, & Picot, 2002). By 2015,

gendered division of labour The cultural categorization of work (whether inside the home or in public) by gender.

gender stratification A hierarchical system of categorization based on gender. Traits associated with masculinity are considered positive, while traits associated with femininity are considered negative. Any deviations from these categories are understood as not just negative but dangerous. These classifications and associated power imbalances apply to all different aspects of social life.

gendered wage gap The difference in the amount of money that is earned by different genders. See also *pink ghettos*.

female labour force participation had risen to 76 per cent (Drolet, Uppal, & LaRochelle-Cote, 2016). In April of 2018, Newfoundland held the lowest rate of women working, at 49.4 per cent, and Alberta had the highest rate, at 63 per cent (Statistics Canada, 2018). The gap between men's and women's wages narrowed in that time, but, despite pay equality and pay equity legislation in most Canadian jurisdictions, in 2017 the average earnings for women working full-time, full-year, were $52,500 compared to $70,700 for their male counterparts (Statistics Canada, 2017). In other words, a woman working full time in Canada in 2017 earned approximately 74 per cent of what a man earned in the same year. This gap is much worse for black women, Indigenous women, and disabled women (McInturff and Tulloch, 2014).

Consider the work relationship between nurses and doctors. Traditionally, the nurse has been the doctor's assistant. The doctor is viewed as having expert knowledge, authority, and prestige over nurses, and the nurse is expected to carry out the doctor's wishes. She must do so with an attitude of obedience, competence, selflessness, and loyalty, all while displaying total dedication to caring for patients. In short, the nurse serves as an "instrument" or "tool" of the doctor—not as the doctor's co-worker with her own experience and knowledge.

As we would expect, this occupational gendering and underlying ideology has economic consequences. For example, a registered nurse makes only about a fraction as much money (average pay ranges from $58,831 to $78,000 annually) as a doctor (average pay is $339,000 annually) (Canadian Institute for Health Information, 2017; Registered Nurses' Association of Ontario, 2019). Even within doctors, there

Colin Woods/Shutterstock

In this ceremony, graduating medical students receive their medical doctor certificates at the Canadian Family Medicine Forum in 2017. What are your aspirations for your future career? Can you pinpoint ways in which your gender has influenced (or been a barrier to) your aspiration?

are pay gaps within specialties, with higher paid specialties being dominated by men. For example, in 2016 there were 958 male and only 315 female ophthalmologists across Canada—the highest paid surgical specialty (Izenberg, Oriuwa, & Taylor, 2018).

Critics of the sociological explanation of the gendered wage gap, including University of Toronto professor Jordan Peterson, contend that the gendered wage gap exists as a result of personality differences in men and women: they contend that women self-select into nurturing roles and roles that provide them with the time to care for their families (i.e., part-time service work, which is typically the most underpaid form of labour), while men do not. Peterson qualifies this statement by stating that since the gendered wage gap still exists in contemporary, fully developed societies, it must be a natural fact that proves irreducible differences between men and women (Peterson, n.d.). Sociologists, however, do not accept that women simply "choose" to enter into low-paying, precarious work.

> **pink ghettos** Employment areas dominated by women, characterized by lower average wages, more precarious work (e.g., part-time, high turnover), and being undervalued in society.

Instead, sociologists seek to investigate the factors underlying women's decisions to engage in these forms of work. For example, does the woman in question have affordable access to child care that meets her hours of work? Are there other family members whom she is expected to take care of, such as elderly parents? Has she been socialized to believe that she is inferior at math and science, thus preventing her from accessing these high-paying fields? Do her employers pay her less than her male counterparts because they undervalue female labourers? Does her spouse provide adequate help with household tasks, or is she expected to complete those in addition to her work outside the home? These are all important questions to ponder when considering the role that gender socialization has on our future in the labour market.

Pink ghettos represent one facet of the gendered wage gap issue. While women are entering occupations previously closed to them, many jobs remain as segregated by gender as they were in the 1950s (Williams, Muller, & Kilanski,

2012). Women dominate the non-manual sector and, in particular, the less desirable occupations within the sector, such as sales, service, and clerical positions (Korkki, 2011). The fact that higher paying occupations continue to be male dominated accounts for some of the gender pay gap. But when women do enter into traditionally male-dominated positions, they encounter a glass ceiling—an invisible barrier that prevents them from receiving promotions. By contrast, the glass escalator is a semi-invisible *advantage* that men encounter.

Another issue impacting the gendered wage gap is gender stereotypes. For women, gender stereotypes often work against them (Cognard-Black, 2004; Budig, 2002). For men, on the other hand, gender stereotypes often work in their favour. For example, the few men who do go into female-dominated areas of work, such as care work, enjoy "hidden advantages" that help them gain higher paying, higher status, and more authoritative positions (Kullberg, 2013). In other words, many men enjoy an easy ride up the so-called "glass escalator" in female-dominated professions. This is not the case for women in male-dominated professions. Researchers have concluded that (white) men are granted higher wages and quicker promotions even in fields where they are "occupational minorities" (Galabuzi 2006).

Significantly, women are simply paid less than men for the same labour. Looking at earnings in the same industries, with comparable education, experience, and title, women in Canada are paid approximately 96 cents for every dollar earned by men (Chamberlain, Zhao, & Stansell, 2019).

In addition to inequality within and between particular fields, women are also expected to perform domestic duties at home, perform and/or pay for child care, care for elderly and/or disabled family members, and so forth (Bezanson & Luxton 2006). Indeed, the demands of paid work are often intertwined with family life in a way that they are not for men. A woman's family obligations may limit her ability to work for pay, while work obligations may intrude on her family relations. All of these factors combine to create and maintain the gendered wage gap.

The Family and Domestic Inequality

Whether or not they work for pay outside the home, most women also work hard (for no pay) within the home. We have experienced an increase in egalitarian attitudes in Canadian society, yet the distribution of household

> **glass ceiling** Invisible barriers to advancement that women face in the labour market. These can be related to unconscious bias as well as to reduced qualifications because of gendered expectations (such as which school program to complete or expectations of labour at home).
>
> **glass escalator** The invisible benefits granted to men in the labour market, especially white heterosexual men who embody hegemonic masculinity.
>
> **second shift** The double burden of work and housework experienced by women; coined by Arlie Hochschild.

responsibilities remains more unequal than anticipated (Lachance-Grzela & Bouchard, 2010). Even when studies find that couples believe themselves to be egalitarian, the actual effects on household labour are in fact quite small (Cohen, 2007). Regardless of how many hours a woman may work outside the home, research shows that, in heterosexual couples, men on average contribute less to the household labour (Bittman, England, Sayer, Folbre, & Matheson, 2003; Statistics Canada, 2017). Women employed outside the home continue to contribute on average 50 per cent more than their male partners (Statistics Canada, 2017). Even more interesting, while the gap is slowly narrowing, in households where women out-earn their male partners, they are responsible for even more household labour than in other types of economic situations (Bittman et al., 2003; Doucet, 2007; Nakhaie, 2002).

Household tasks are not inherently gendered, yet due to the gendered division of domestic labour, tasks are often labelled as "masculine" or "feminine." Stereotypical female tasks tend to be "routine tasks," those daily chores that are ongoing and time consuming, while stereotypical male tasks tend to be "intermittent tasks," which are done occasionally, are less time consuming, and are more flexible in nature (Lachance-Grzela & Bouchard, 2010). Indeed, women are responsible for about two-thirds of routine household tasks (Greenstein, 2009; Knudsen & Waerness, 2008) and are also responsible for managing, planning, and organizing all tasks (Mannino & Deutsch, 2007). As a result, wives in the paid labour force have often suffered from responsibility overload (Bianchi, Sayer, Milkie, & Robinson, 2012; Brines, 2006 Koivunen, Rothaupt, & Wolfgram, 2009). Terms like the "double day" or the second shift describe the double burden of work and housework that women in the labour force experience (Hochschild, 1989).

Interestingly, research on gay and lesbian households show a more equal division of household labour (Brewster, 2017; Goldberg, Smith, & Perry-Jenkins, 2012). Lesbian households tend to have the most equal distribution of tasks, while males in gay households are more equal than heterosexual couples but not as equal as lesbian couples (Kurdek, 2007).

Violence and Victimization

One of the most severe consequences of gender inequality in our society is violent victimization. Women are more likely than men to suffer violent victimization at the hand of their intimates: dates, boyfriends, lovers, husbands, and ex-husbands, for example. According to the 2014 General Social Survey (GSS), women are twice as likely as men to report having experienced severe forms of domestic violence (being sexually assaulted, beaten, choked, or threatened with a weapon). In particular, violence and victimization are experienced at a greater rate by Indigenous women and girls within Canada than by any other group. Indigenous women and girls are nearly *three times* as likely to self-report sexual assault and spousal violence and are more likely to fear for their lives in comparison to white women (Department of Justice, 2017). The Native Women's Association of Canada has estimated that over 4000 Indigenous women have been murdered or gone missing since 1980 (Native Women's Association of Canada, 2016). The National Inquiry into Missing and Murdered Indigenous Women and Girls concluded that this and other violence against

> **sexual harassment**
> Any behaviour that is of a sexual nature (this can be conduct, comment, gesture, or touching) and that is likely to cause offence or humiliation or that might be perceived as demanding something sexual of a person in order to receive an opportunity or advancement. Note that this definition relies on perceptions and expectations of the person being harassed, as well as on how the behaviour will be seen by the wider social audience (i.e., what might cause humiliation); therefore, which behaviours fall under this term have changed over time.

Indigenous peoples throughout Canada's history amounts to genocide (National Inquiry into Missing and Murdered Indigenous Women and Girls, 2019).

Sexual harassment, another form of gendered violence, is still prevalent in schools and workplaces. The Supreme Court of Canada defines workplace sexual harassment as "unwelcome conduct of a sexual nature that detrimentally affects the work environment or leads to adverse job-related consequences for the victims of the harassment" (Janzen v. Platy Enterprises Ltd., 1989). This is a deliberately broad definition to encompass any unwanted sexualized behaviour. Recently, there has been a dramatic shift in how the public views sexual harassment with the #MeToo campaign gaining prominence (see #Sociology box). The large number of celebrities who have been publicly shamed for sexually harassing or sexually assaulting female co-workers has brought sorely needed attention to a long-ignored issue.

In the News

Gendered Violence between Strangers

On 23 April 2018, a van driven by 25-year-old Alex Minassian sped through a busy street in Toronto, Ontario, deliberately attempting to hit pedestrians. He killed 10 people and injured another 14, some critically. Minassian was arrested a few minutes after the van stopped. While there appeared to be no immediately clear motivation for the attack, one day later a Facebook post was found, allegedly written by Minassian moments before the attack, which was linked to an online group of men who feel victimized because they are "involuntarily celibate." The post states, "The Incel Rebellion has already begun! We will overthrow all the Chads and Stacys! All hail the Supreme Gentleman Elliot Rodger!" (Casey, 2018). "Chads" is a term used to describe muscular, popular men, while "Stacys" describes feminine, attractive women who are only attainable by Chads.

An online community of men use the term "incel" to express their anger at women as a group for not being willing to have sex with them. These men use online communities to talk about overthrowing feminism and plotting violence against women, including advocating for state-sanctioned rape (Samotin & Dancygor, 2018). Elliot Rodger was 22 years old when he killed six people and then himself in 2014. Before his attack, Rodger wrote a manifesto, outlining his hatred of women and his anger that they refused to have sex with him.

While there have always been cases of men who blame women for their issues, prior to the Internet these men mostly acted alone (for example, in the Montreal Massacre in 1989, where Marc Lépine killed 14 women and then himself after he blamed the equal rights movements for his not being accepted into the program he wanted to attend). The Internet has allowed a space where these angry individuals can find each other and fan each other's hatred.

What aspects of the ideology of gender are reflected by the beliefs of "incels," as described above?

#MeToo

In October 2017, news broke that Harvey Weinstein, film producer and cofounder of Miramax, was accused of sexual abuse. Within a few weeks, over 80 women in the film industry had spoken out about Weinstein, with horrific tales of sexual misconduct. After many statements of denial, Weinstein officially stepped down from his own company and was expelled from the Academy of Motion Picture Arts and Sciences. This case prompted women (and some men) to come forward against other men in positions of power.

Shortly after the Weinstein accusations were revealed, actress Alyssa Milano used the hashtag #MeToo as a symbol of solidarity and a way to express just how widespread the sexual abuse of women is around the world. The phrase came from social activist Tarana Burke, who, in 2006, used the phrase to empower women of colour who had experienced sexual abuse. Burke says that she was inspired to use the phrase after a 13-year-old girl confided to her that she had been sexually assaulted. She contends that rather than not knowing what to say or do for the young girl, she wished that she simply would have said "Me too" (Ohlheiser, 2017). In the same spirit as Burke's original statement, Milano Tweeted, "If all the women who have been sexually harassed or assaulted wrote 'Me too' as a status, we might give people a sense of the magnitude of the problem." Within one week, #MeToo had been Tweeted 1.7 million times (Park, 2017).

Powerful men are not immune to sexual abuse in Hollywood. Actors Terry Crews, Michael Gaston, Alex Winter, and Brendan Fraser have all reported being victims of sexual abuse in the workplace. Many of these men said that they initially felt humiliated about the incident and felt that they wouldn't be believed since our gender socialization tells us that men are supposed to be the sexual aggressors or strong enough to fight off an aggressor. Terry Crews describes his experience coming forward as being behind "enemy lines": "You are a problem that needs to be eradicated . . . because there's a whole system in place, and you're about to upset the whole thing" (Bradley, 2018).

How does our gender socialization prevent us from seeing male sexual assault victims as true "victims"? How do we ensure that male victims of sexual assault are not left out of the #MeToo movement?

Theoretical Perspectives on Gender

Functionalism

Functionalists treat gender differences as though they are natural and assume that gender differences benefit society as a whole. In their opinion, gender roles support and contribute to the cohesiveness of society. Men are  expected to fulfill what functionalists call the *instrumental roles* in society—whereby they provide financially for their families and provide stability—whereas women are responsible for what they call the *expressive roles*—bearing and raising children, taking care of the household, and providing love and emotional support.

For that reason, functionalists think that a society with traditional gender roles will run more smoothly, so gender roles are worth maintaining. Functionalists see gender inequality from a positive perspective, to say the least. Because of this, they ignore some harsh realities— namely, that men's and women's roles are not only different, they are also *unequal*. Consider the women who work in the labour market and also do the majority of household work. Because functionalists have not considered housework to be "real" work, they have been unable to see women as being unfairly burdened by the domestic division of labour. Their approach also does not account for extremely unequal societies that experience social unrest.

Conflict Theory

Conflict theorists tend to see gender differences as largely a consequence of class and property relations. Friedrich Engels (1820–1895), for example, who often wrote with

Marx, linked gender inequality to the development of private property (Engels, 1962). According to his theory, it wasn't until we were worried about inheritance that male domination reached its peak. The Industrial Revolution forced  women into the role of working homemaker with no pay, while men went out to work in waged labour. In this view, traditional gender roles will change, and gender equality will develop, only with the elimination of capitalism.

Symbolic Interactionism

Symbolic interactionists are interested in the ways that people embody and perform gender. As discussed earlier, children learn gendered expectations of themselves through their socialization agents. Their families, their education systems, and the media  they consume all work to offer role models of how to behave as a particular gender. Interactionists argue that this occurs through **operant conditioning**, whereby gender-appropriate behaviours are rewarded and signs of gender deviance are punished. When people assigned a female gender at birth are dressed up in feminine attire, such as frilly dresses, and have their hair and nails done, they are repeatedly told how pretty they look. When people assigned a male gender at birth fall down and hurt themselves and cry, they are repeatedly told to "stop acting like a girl" or that "big boys don't cry."

Candace West and Don Zimmerman (1987) argue that gender is something that we "do" in our everyday lives. They argue that in "doing gender" we actively create differences between gender categories. Over time these differences have become so taken for granted that we see them as biological differences rather than as social constructions. Doing gender draws our attention to all the ways that these differences have been socially constructed and reinforced.

Feminism

Some early women sociologists, such as Harriet Martineau in the nineteenth century, stressed the significance of gender relations in society. But, until the late twentieth

operant conditioning
A method of training that rewards compliant behaviours and punishes deviant behaviours.

matrix of domination
The ways that race, sexuality, and class (among other inequalities) intersect with gender, making inequality not just more pronounced but unique for each individual based on their circumstances; coined by Patricia Hill Collins.

century, there were not many women sociologists. Because of this, gender analysis was not part of the mainstream of sociological work. A rapid increase in the number of female sociologists in the 1970s, however, led to a  widespread rejection of traditional, male-centred sociology. These women sociologists developed a new view of society—a feminist sociology that is grounded in women's experience of inequality in everyday life. This has led to a greater awareness of the role of gender in society among all sociologists, both male and female.

In only four decades, feminist sociologists have done a lot to promote equality in our society and in the discipline of sociology. A key contribution of the feminist approach has been to show that gender roles are social constructs and to explain how we maintain these social constructs over time. Judith Butler, a well-known gender theorist, wrote the book *Gender Trouble* (1990), where she questioned the idea that our genders are natural or that they are intrinsically linked to our sex. Furthermore, she asserted that our sexuality is not tied to either our gender or our sex. Rather, Butler argues that our sexuality and our gender are both a performance, and our ideas about the links between gender and sexuality have been culturally constructed through repetition. For example, when we are continually confronted with masculine men who desire women (both in our everyday lives and in media representations), we begin to see this as an essential or biologically natural way to act. Her ideas surrounding identities as flexible rather than rigid, and as a performance rather than essential, are the foundation of queer theory.

Additionally, feminists such as Patricia Hill Collins (2000) have drawn our attention to the ways that race, ethnicity, class, and disability intersect with gender, making inequality even more pronounced for those who experience these multiple sources of inequality. Collins refers to this as the **matrix of domination**.

"Shrinking Women"

Lily Myers (Author). A spoken word poem performed by Myers at a slam poetry competition at Barnard College in New York. The poem, easily accessed on YouTube, outlines the ways in which we reproduce gender inequality without necessarily ever realizing it.

Top 10 Takeaways

1 Sex and gender are social constructions; one is based on physical traits, while the other is based on self-expression. Both are arbitrarily binary constructions in Canadian society. pp. 126–130

2 Hegemonic masculinity and emphasized femininity are the idealized forms of the gender binary that we are all taught to try to achieve. p. 127

3 The existence of groups of people who do not fit within our predetermined categories of sex and gender problematize that there are only two ways to exist. These groups include intersex, transgender, and two-spirit people. pp. 127–130

4 *Transgender* refers to people who identify as a gender that does not correspond to their assigned sex at birth. Drag performers are individuals whose gender identity (usually) aligns with their sex assigned at birth, but they enjoy expressing themselves as other gender identities generally through dress and performance. pp. 127–128

5 We learn our specific gender roles through socialization agents, such as our parents, our schools, and various media. pp. 131–134

6 The ideology of gender is a set of widespread social beliefs that gender is a binary and that there are "natural" differences between men and women (i.e., hegemonic masculinity and emphasized femininity). This ideology is harmful to everyone. pp. 134–136

7 Patriarchy is a system of social organization in which men hold power and women are excluded from power. p. 136

8 Women are often responsible for working a double shift, where they work in the labour market (for less pay than men) and then carry the lion's share of the household labour at home. p. 139

9 Women, particularly Indigenous women, are the victims of disproportionate amounts of domestic violence and sexual harassment. pp. 139–140

10 Functionalists believe that men fulfill instrumental roles and women fulfill expressive roles in order for society to function harmoniously. Conflict theorists argue that the development of private property in society is what led to inequality among the sexes. Symbolic interactionists contend that we learn how to "do gender" through operant conditioning. Feminists assert that gender roles are social constructs that lead to unfair disadvantages for women and that these disadvantages are made worse for poor, black, Indigenous, and disabled women through the matrix of domination. pp. 141–142

Questions for Critical Thinking

1. Explain why both sex and gender are considered binary social constructions.

2. Can you think of examples in film or television of individuals who illustrate hegemonic masculinity or emphasized femininity? Discuss how these characters "do" their gender.

3. Discuss the variances that exist within sex and gender.

4. Explain how transgender individuals complicate traditional notions of sex and gender.

5. Describe the ways in which your own gender has been shaped by your interactions with your socialization agents throughout your life course. How do you "do" your gender?

6. Do you think that you live in a patriarchal society? Explain why or why not.

7. How might we reorganize so that women are not responsible for the majority of household tasks while simultaneously earning less in the labour market?

8. Using the American 2016 presidential election, discuss how the glass ceiling and glass escalator may have been at play.

9. Critically reflect on the #MeToo movement in relation to college campuses. What are some examples in the media of serious victimization of women across Canadian and American college and university campuses?

10. How would functionalists, conflict theorists, and feminists approach women's disadvantage within the labour market?

Recommended Readings

- **Bezanson, K., and Luxton, M. (2006). *Social reproduction: Feminist political economy challenges neo-liberalism*. Montreal: McGill-Queen's University Press.** *Social Reproduction* is a contributed volume that takes a political economic feminist approach—in other words, the essays analyze how patriarchy and the gender ideology function in Canadian society to limit the power and financial health of women.

- **Doucet, A. (2007). Stay-at-home fathering. *Community, Work and Family, 10*(4), 455–473.** Doucet did critical work on how gender roles alienate men from their own homes and their own children. Her research compares Canadian and Belgian households and shows how mandatory shared parental leave leads to more equitable household work sharing in heterosexual couples, and also leads to more satisfaction in men.

- **Hochschild, A. (1989). *The second shift*. New York: Viking Penguin.** Hochschild coined the term "the second shift" in this book; she outlines intensive qualitative research done over decades to explore the "leisure gap" between men and women at home. It is also worth noting that Hochschild is also the person who coined the term "emotional labour." Her work is still used today to help contextualize the more hidden inequalities that women continue to face in North America.

- **Butler, J. (1990). *Gender trouble*. New York: Routledge.** Butler's work is part of the core foundation of queer theory. She clearly outlines how gender is performative. She draws parallels between the universality of what "woman" meant to feminism at the time to what "masculine" meant to the patriarchy and makes clear that the concept of "woman" is complicated by class, ethnicity, and sexuality. She also talks about drag, and how drag does important work by making explicit the performative aspect of gender.

- **Collins, P.H. (1990). *Black feminist thought: Knowledge, consciousness, and the politics of empowerment*. Boston: Unwin Hyman.** Collins goes into the work of key black feminist thinkers, such as Angela Davis, bell hooks, Alice Walker, and Audre Lorde to produce a comprehensive overview of black feminist canon at the time. She discusses how black women, being excluded from the power structures of white women, can bring a more nuanced approach to feminism and social theory. As well, Collins describes how oppressions are structurally organized and intersectional to form a matrix of domination, so the experiences of black women differ based on age, sexuality, and socio-economic status.

- **Stolenberg, J. (1989). *Refusing to be a man: Essays on sex and justice*. Portland, Oregon: Breitenbush Books.** Stolenberg writes about masculinity as a political and ethical construction that earns advantages based on injustice. He writes in response to the reactionary "men's movements" that grew as a response to feminism. He argues that men need to refuse, deconstruct, and actively work against masculinity in order to free everyone—women and men—from its construction.

Recommended Websites

Status of Women Canada
http://www.swc-cfc.gc.ca/index-en.html

- Status of Women Canada is an organization run by the federal government that promotes equality of women through their full participation in economic, social, and civic life.

Gender Spectrum
https://www.genderspectrum.org/quick-links/understanding-gender/

- Gender Spectrum is an organization dedicated to helping families and institutions develop their understandings of gender to create a gender-inclusive world for all children.

InterAction
https://www.interaction.org/blog/celebrating-women-and-girls-around-the-world/

- InterAction is part of the Commission on the Advancement of Women and is focused on advancing female empowerment and gender equality in policy and practice.

Equality Now
https://www.equalitynow.org

- Equality Now is dedicated to four main principles: (1) gender equality—females are equal to males; (2) universality—everyone, everywhere in the world, has the right to live without violence; (3) partnership—strong relationships with organizations who collaborate to champion equality; and (4) speaking up and speaking out—activism and change.

Chapter 8

Families and Intimate Relations

Thomas Beatie made international headlines as the first (known) pregnant man. Thomas was misgendered as a woman at birth, but he has stated that he always wanted to be a man. In his twenties, he began the process of transitioning to a male body (Tremblay, 2008). While taking testosterone Thomas met and married his partner Nancy. As he was transitioning, the couple discussed their desire to have children. Nancy was unable to conceive, so Thomas decided to postpone his transition so that the couple could potentially conceive a child. He underwent artificial insemination, and in 2008 he gave birth to the couple's first child, quickly followed by their second and third (Beatie, 2008).

Thomas has since separated from Nancy. When petitioning an Arizona court for a divorce in 2012, the two were denied on the grounds that 'same-sex marriages" are not recognized in that state (Witheridge, 2016). Despite the fact that Thomas was legally a man married to a woman, the judge ruled that birthing children necessarily meant that he was in fact a woman (Witheridge, 2016). A higher court overturned the decision and awarded the divorce in 2015.

The Beatie family draws our attention to how we define a family, the ways in which our social structures and constructions (such as gender) play a role in these understandings, and how the two can clash.

▲ David McNew/Getty Images

Learning Outcomes

1. Define the family

2. Explain the structures and functions of family

3. Describe descent and authority patterns

4. Differentiate between the sociological approaches to understanding family

5. Describe the types of exchanges that occur within the family

6. Recognize the different aspects of mate selection and union formation

7. Discuss the ways that child bearing and rearing affect relationships

8. Understand the trends in family life

9. Highlight the changes in society that have resulted in the restructuring of the work–life balance for most families

10. Discuss family violence as a social issue

Key Terms

affinal
bilateral descent
cohabitation
divorce
egalitarian family
endogamy
exogamy
expressive exchanges
extended family
family

Introduction

In 1949, the anthropologist George Murdock defined family as "a social group characterized by common residence, economic cooperation, and reproduction. It includes adults of both sexes, at least two of whom maintain a socially approved sexual relationship, and one or more children, own or adopted, of the sexually cohabiting adults." At that time, the functions of a family were considered to focus on sexual relationships, reproduction, the socialization of children, and economic dependence. More recently, however, sociologist David Popenoe (1993) stated that changes in the structure of society—resulting in the increase of single parent, divorced, and gay and lesbian families—require a shift in definition of the family. Popenoe argued that to be considered a family, there must be at minimum one adult and one dependent child; the parents do not have to be married, nor does their sex matter. While recognizing that families could look different, he contended that the functions of the family were similar to Murdock's functions: procreation, socialization, sexual regulation, and economic co-operation. However, Popenoe added the provisions of care, affection, and companionship to the functions of a family.

Defining **family** in the legal and social realms is important for all of us as individuals but also for how we navigate our social institutions. For example, who is allowed to visit family members in an emergency situation, such as hospitalization? Or who is entitled to property should a relationship end in separation or death? Who is covered under workplace benefits, etc.? (See "Practising Sociology" box.) As sociologists, we strive to find appropriate definitions of family that encompass all of the variations. Must a household have children in order to be considered a family? Should the definition of family be extended to include those members of our networks who are "family by choice" rather than by blood?

> **family** A social group containing two or more people who function as a unit for the purposes of economic co-operation, socialization, procreation (in some cases), companionship, and emotional support; may refer to one household or to a wider group of people related by blood.

While the definition of family continues to evolve, the two concepts that sociologists continue to use in their discussions are "function" and "structure" (Georgas, 2003). The *functions* of a family are many and refer to how a family takes care of its physical and psychological needs to survive as a group (Georgas, 2003). For example, families provide and maintain shelter and provide economic sustenance, food for its members, clothing, and care. Raising children is also an important function of the family that includes socializing them into their culture and traditions and educating them. These are some of the major functions of the family, which are universal across all societies in the world (Georgas, 2003). However, there are variations in these functions in different cultures.

The *structure* of the family refers to the members and positions of those members (mother, father, daughter, son, grandmother, etc.). The people who are considered to make up a family differ across cultures, as do the roles that particular members are expected to take. For example, it is legal and even common practice for some men to marry more than one woman throughout West Africa and parts of Asia. It is legal to marry someone of the same sex in North America, most of South America, Australia, and parts of Europe and Africa. In Canada, it is illegal to be married to more than one person at a time—though the sex of the two does not matter—but some people still practise polygamy within Canada (see "In the News" box). Even between provinces and territories, family structure varies, with the majority of couples in Quebec choosing to form civil partnerships but forgoing marriage (Statistics Canada, 2017c). These examples illustrate that there are many variations on what it means to be a family, yet families—as an institution—are cultural universals.

homogamy
incest
instrumental exchanges
kin group
matriarchy
matrilineal descent
nuclear family
patrilineal descent
single-parent (or lone-parent) family

Family Composition

Kinship

Historically, the relationship between parent and child was a subset of a broader set of relationships called kinship relations. The total network of people related by common ancestry or adoption is called a **kin group**. This group would include (at the least) a person's parents, children, grandparents, uncles, aunts, cousins, nephews, and nieces.

> **kin group** A group of people related by blood or marriage.

In many societies, what we consider "the family" is embedded in this broad web of kinship relations, and a household is likely to include numerous kin. In other societies, such as our own, most households consist only of a set of parents and their unmarried children. These two main

Families can come in many shapes and sizes.

Kayden Chan

In the News

Bountiful, British Columbia

In July 2017, two former religious leaders were found guilty of polygamy after marrying more than two dozen women and fathering over 160 children (CBC News, 2017). Both men were part of a fundamentalist sect of Mormonism that practises plural marriages, despite the fact that the Mormon Church banned polygamy in 1890. Winston Blackmore, age 60, had 24 wives and more than 145 children while James Oler, age 53, had 5 wives and 15 children at the time of their convictions.

The two were members of a group known as Bountiful that reside in the Creston Valley of British Columbia. The group officially became known as Bountiful in the 1980s after Winston Blackmore became the bishop (Perrin & Palmer, 2004). In the late 1990s the population of Bountiful was estimated to be approximately 600 people; however, it has since grown to approximately 1000, with only approximately half a dozen men. This sect of the church first came under intense scrutiny when Warren Jeffs, the sect's leader, was charged with the rape of two girls, 12 and 15 years old, the latter of whom he fathered a child with (BBC, 2017). He was convicted and sentenced to life in prison in Texas in 2011.

Multiple marriages, and sex with minors, are both illegal in Canada. However, Jeffs, Blackmore, and Oler have consistently argued that this is against their constitutional right to practise their own religion. They also argue that the females in their sect willingly, and excitedly, take part in these marriages as they understand the benefits of this type of familial arrangement. The BC Supreme Court ruled that the Canadian law against polygamy does not infringe on religious freedoms. In June 2018, Blackmore was sentenced to six months of house arrest while Oler was given three months (Kane, 2018).

Should we be permitted to arrange our families in any way that we see fit? What are some of the issues with the arrangement of families that live in Bountiful (and others like them)?

Sister Wives

Prod. Deanie Wilcher (2010–). A TLC television series that follows the lives of Kody Brown, his four wives, and their combined 18 children to give us a glimpse inside a polygamist family. The family attempts to live as "normal" as possible in a society that stigmatizes their lifestyle.

---

nuclear family A kinship structure consisting solely of two parents and their children.

extended family A broad social group that includes everyone with whom one has kinship; this can include multiple generations (e.g., grandparents, great-grandparents) as well as more tenuous kinship links (e.g., cousins, second cousins).

bilateral descent A system of family lineage in which the relatives on the mother's side and on the father's side are equally important for emotional ties and for transfer of property or wealth.

patrilineal descent A system of passing down wealth and power that counts only kin relationships through male family members.

matrilineal descent A system of passing down wealth and power that counts only kin relationships through female family members.

---

forms of family household are referred to as the extended family and the nuclear family, respectively.

The **nuclear family** is the most common type of family household in our society. It includes one or at most two generations of family living together: typically, one or two parents and their children (se Figure 8.1). This nuclear family is also a *conjugal* family, meaning that it gives priority to marital ties over blood ties. An **extended family** household, on the other hand, is one in which two or more generations of relatives live together. It may include grandparents and/or grandchildren, uncles, aunts, and cousins.

There are three ways of determining kinship based upon descent. In Canada, people generally follow the system of **bilateral descent**, which means that both sides of your family are regarded as equally important. For example, your father's brother is equally as important as your mother's brother. Many societies, however, follow **patrilineal descent**, meaning that only members of the father's side of the family are important and pass down property and inheritance and are responsible for maintaining emotional ties. **Matrilineal descent**—whereby the mother's side of the family is dominant—is less common but still exists. The descent pattern that people follow is often related to the authority patterns within society but can sometimes be different. For example, while the Queen of England lives within a society that is

Practising Sociology

Who Benefits from Benefits?

You have been tasked with developing a new policy for health coverage for a Fortune 500 company. The company is rather generous with its package; however, the company requires you to define who constitutes "family" for the purpose of coverage. The company's employees have a wide range of households: some live in nuclear heterosexual families; some, in nuclear homosexual families; some, in extended family households with grandparents, aunts, and uncles; while others have taken on responsibility for children that are not biologically theirs and that they have not legally adopted. Some live with roommates who share household responsibilities and costs but are not in a sexual relationship. Most of the families also have household pets. Discuss below who should be covered under the definition of "family" for the purpose of work health benefits.

Beneficiaries for Health Benefits Hereby Include the Following:

Do our current understandings of what constitutes a family capture all of the realities of Canadian families? If a household depends on one or even two people's finances to survive, should the other members of that household be considered dependants regardless of their age and relationship?

primarily patriarchal in nature, the power within her family now flows through matrilineal descent.

Authority Patterns

Most of you are young adults and have started to think about your futures. Marriage and children may be a part of that plan. How will you make decisions about the following?

- Where will you live?
- What kind of home will you live in?
- What style will you decorate your house in?
- How will you split the household chores, such as cleaning and cooking?
- Where will you vacation?
- How much money will you keep in the bank at all times?

> **egalitarian family**
> A family where both partners are equal and, as a result, contribute equally to decision making.

- How much money will you spend on entertainment?
- Will you have, or adopt, children, and if so, how many?
- Will you have a pet?
- Who will have the power to make final decisions?

As you start to work through these questions in your relationships, you will also be working through issues of power. For example, if one member of your household really wants two big dogs, and one does not want any animals, who gets their way?

The egalitarian family is what most of us hope to have, where spouses are regarded as equals. In an egalitarian household, for example, family members split responsibilities (both financial and domestic) equally regardless of their gender. Benefits are also divided equally among egalitarian household members. This does not, however, mean that each decision is shared within the family.

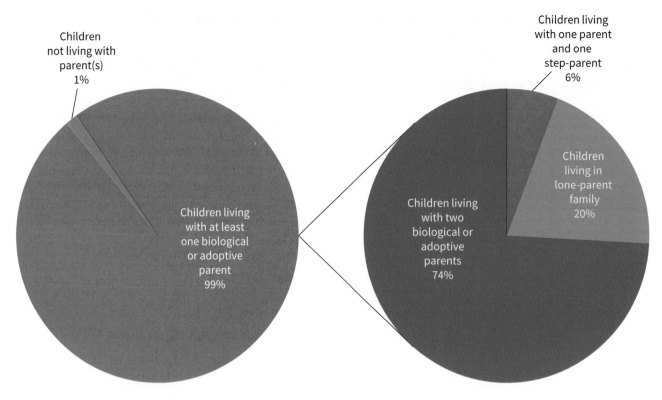

Figure 8.1 Children in Canada, 2016

The left pie chart illustrates that almost all children are in households with at least one parent. The right chart shows that, among those, the vast majority are in two-parent households, and in most of those both parents are biological or adoptive parents.

Source: Adapted from Statistics Canada, Census of Population, 2016.

Modern Family

Creators Christopher Lloyd and Steven Levitan (2009–2020). A show that highlights the complexities of family and showcases nuclear, step, multicultural, and gay families. The show offers an often hilarious perspective of family life in the 2000s.

Spouses may hold authority in different spheres. The egalitarian family is slowly replacing the patriarchal family. However, evidence suggests that this shift is occurring quite slowly as women continue to be responsible for the majority of household labour in addition to their waged labour (Bezanson & Luxton, 2002; see Chapter 7).

If family decisions are made primarily by the male, it is referred to as *patriarchy*. Individual family structures are influenced by the larger societal structures and

matriarchy Systematic gender inequality in favour of women. Women are favoured or exclusively granted power, such as political decision-making authority, control of resources, and ability to inherit wealth.

therefore may be limited by legal imbalances. For example, in some countries women cannot inherit or own property. As mentioned in Chapter 7, Canada is still a patriarchy, although efforts are being made to make the country more egalitarian.

In contrast, in a **matriarchy** women have greater authority than men. Although this type of family is relatively uncommon, there are six modern societies that are considered matriarchies: the Mosuo in China, living near the border of Tibet; the Minangkabau of West Sumatra, Indonesia (Sanday, 2002); the Akan people of Ghana; the Bribri, a small Indigenous group living on a reserve in the Limón province of Costa Rica; the Tibeto-Burman-speaking Garos tribe in India; and the Nagovisi in South Bougainville, an island west of New Guinea (http://mentalfloss.com/article/31274/6-modern-societies-where-women-literally-rule). Some Canadian Indigenous societies were matriarchal in nature prior to colonization (Abbott, 2003). As mentioned, a family power structure can be limited by, but also may be distinct from, the surrounding societal power structures.

Theoretical Approaches to Families

Functionalism

The functionalist perspective focuses on the family's various functions in society, that is, the roles that families play in helping society at large to survive. Functionalist William E. Ogburn (1933) argued that the family performs six functions in society: reproduc-  tion, protection, socialization, sexual regulation, affection and companionship, and social and economic status. Functionalists note that human infants depend on others—especially their parents—for several years before they can survive on their own. Indeed, human children rely on adults more than children of any other species! In addition, families, through socialization, promote people's integration into their surrounding culture and society. When families carry out these and the other listed functions above, they ensure the survival of both the individual and their society. This makes the family a uniquely important social institution.

Symbolic Interactionism

Interactionists focus on primary socialization, especially the inter-actions among family members that lead to the emergence of identity and the "self" (see Chapter 4). Equally important, interaction-  ists study the family as a specific social setting. Within the family setting, family members make important decisions about their lives. For example, interactionists study how parents decide—with one another and with their employers—who will stay home when their child gets sick. They are also interested in things such as the role of the step-parent and step-siblings in the family, and how a child may change his or her behaviour while at home and when with peers.

Conflict Theory

Conflict theorists argue that industrialization drastically changed the functions of families. Most families are no longer self-sustaining, nor do most live within agricultural societies where the entire family works as a unit of production. As family farms disappeared, children could no longer help their parents work. Instead, their parents went to work in factories and, eventually, office jobs while children went to school or stayed at  home. This shift changed the relationship between men and women as men were now the primary income earners, and women focused on the household. As a result, men gained power over women and children.

As times have changed and we have moved closer to the egalitarian family, we still see economic relations causing conflict in family relations. A prime example is the conflict that workers—especially women—experience meeting family and paid work demands simultaneously. More often than not, women miss work to care for sick children and reduce work hours to accommodate family needs (see Chapter 7).

Furthermore, conflict theorists argue that the family is an economic unit that contributes to social injustice. It is in the family that socio-economic status, power, property, and privilege are passed down generationally. All of these factors have substantial consequences for the lives of children and for their future life chances.

Feminism

Feminists argue that the family is not just a major social insti-tution: it is also an *unequal* and *gendered* social institution. That is why conflict within families is not just a product of capitalist class relations; it is also the product of  gender relations. What's more, conflict within families is not simply the result of what happens outside a household's gate. Rather, conflict can be built right into the structure of family relations. These are the reasons we need a feminist analysis to bring gendered inequality into our understanding of how family members divide up the work, share the responsibilities, and resolve the conflicts they face in making a family work successfully.

Canadian feminist Margrit Eichler has pointed out that the way in which the family has been studied throughout history has often contained biases. One is a *monolithic bias,* which assumes families are all the same rather than diverse. Another is a *conservative bias,* which presents the family as a haven and ignores the negative aspects of some families, such as physical and sexual abuse. Families have also been studied from an *ageist bias,* which assumes that both the young and the old are not fully contributing members. If we look at the expectations of mothers versus fathers, we can clearly see a double standard in the form of a *sexist bias.* In addition, most studies include a *heterosexist bias,* which either ignores same-sex families altogether or treats them as deviant. One of the most problematic biases is that of a *racist bias,* which assumes that the form of family found among the dominant culture is the "proper" structure of a family that others should aspire to.

Mating and Union Formation

Two social relationships are central to the family. The first is an **affinal** (or chosen) relationship between spouses. Spousal

affinal A family relationship by marriage.

relationships can be made up of any two non-related consenting adults who are not already married to anyone else in the North American context, though many states still specify the gender of both parties on marriage applications, potentially excluding non-binary people. (In Canada, marriage licences do not specify an applicant's gender.) What's more, these spouses may be legally married or merely cohabiting. In any case, these relationships result from what sociologists call "union formation." The second important family relationship is the relationship between a parent and child: the relationship that ties family members together over generations. In what follows, we will consider both relationships in turn.

A central feature of union formation in Canada is a commitment to the ideals of romantic love. Of course, practical concerns always play a part in intimate relationships—and more in some than in others. Nevertheless, most people who embark on a long-term relationship do so mainly because they feel love for their partner. Indeed, many people even believe in soulmates, thinking that we are destined to be with one special someone for the rest of our lives. Yet, for all this belief in fate, most of us also feel the need to assist the process. So, we spend an enormous amount of time and money on our personal appearance and on searching for our perfect other half—hence, the preponderance of dating (and hook-up) apps, such as Happn, Bumble, Coffee Meets Bagel, POF (formerly PlentyOfFish), Grindr, and Tinder (see Figure 8.2).

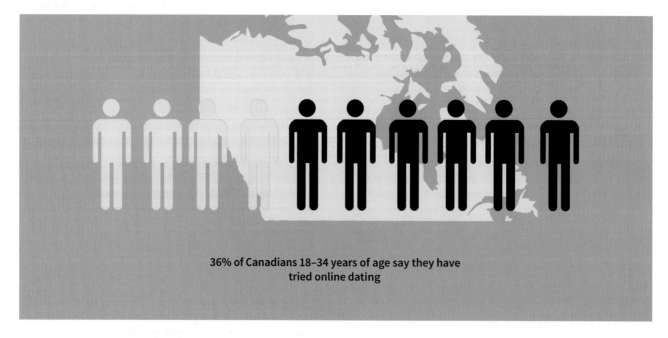

36% of Canadians 18–34 years of age say they have tried online dating

Figure 8.2 Online Dating

Source: Author-generated using Canva; using statistics cited in https://nationalpost.com/news/stop-wasting-time-with-undesirables-conservatives-only-dating-site-announces-move-into-canada

Romantic love does not play a big role in intimate relations everywhere, however. Indeed, in many parts of the world, romantic love plays a minor role in union formation, or is nonexistent. In some places, love is seen as irrelevant to marriage or just a matter of luck. These cultures view marriage as a mainly practical arrangement. What matters most is whether the union will supply the family and kin group with children (especially sons) and financial stability.

The exchange perspective sees marriage as a matter of give-and-take, in which each spouse both gives and gets. In this way of thinking, a relationship depends on how well spouses maintain a stable balance in this exchange. Expressive exchanges in marriage are exchanges of emotional services between spouses. They include hugs and kisses, sexual pleasure, friendship, a shoulder to lean on, empathy, and understanding. Such exchanges affirm the affection and love each spouse has for the other. By contrast, instrumental exchanges are non-emotional. They maintain a household in practical ways. For example, these exchanges include sharing the housework; paying the bills; and looking after children, elder adults, or other dependants.

As you would expect, every family relationship contains a mixture of expressive and instrumental exchanges. As well, every culture values both types of exchange. But cultures differ in that some value one type of exchange more than the other. Hegemonic culture in Canada considers expressive exchanges to be more important in marriage than instrumental ones for happiness and success in life. While recognizing the importance of material security, parents urge their children to marry someone they love. Think about the message in most romantic Hollywood movies. Even if the love interest is rich or powerful, the movie will make a point to show that the protagonist feels an emotional connection to the love interest, in order for that union to qualify as a happy ending.

So, in our society, people—especially young people—are urged to marry someone they love, not just someone who would help out in practical ways. Yet no matter how much two people may love each other, married life always involves practical matters and economic concerns. Instrumental exchanges may be more important than expressive exchanges during tough economic times. In the past four decades, most families have needed two incomes to support a middle-class lifestyle that one income would have supported in the past.

Economic concerns, then, are more important for marriages than ever before. Today, economic concerns lead many people to delay marriage, forgo intimacy, or cohabit instead of marrying.

Mate Selection

From a sociological perspective, how do people select their mates? The term "mate selection" may seem like an odd choice. Do we really "select" the person we will love or marry? The answer seems to be . . . yes. Every society, including ours, has laws about whom we can marry or with whom we can have legal sexual relations. We cannot legally decide to marry a close relative or have sex with a child, for example. Note, however, that these definitions vary somewhat from one society to another. (For example, as in *Game of Thrones,* in some societies in different historical periods incest was much more common.)

However, many societies have much more specific rules about who can marry whom. For example, some societies practise endogamy. This is the requirement or expectation that people will marry within their own social group, such as their own tribe, religion, or ethnic group. For example, Orthodox Judaism requires that both parties be Jewish in order to be married, with only some Jewish traditions allowing for conversion of the non-Jewish party.

On the other hand, other societies practise exogamy. This is the requirement or expectation that people will marry *outside* one's social group. For example, some villages in India require that their men marry women outside of their villages (Goode, 1970).

Canadian society has no rules of endogamy or exogamy. Nevertheless, the mating pattern sometime seems endogamous since most people fall in love with and marry people who are like themselves in important ways. People who marry or cohabit tend to be similar in age and education, physical attractiveness and appearance, class and social status, religion, and ethnicity. For example, in Canada, only 4.6 per cent of couples who responded to the General Social Survey of 2011 comprised people from two different racial groups (although that number seems to be increasing) (Statistics Canada, 2017b). Sociologists call this tendency for similar people to marry homogamy.

There are good reasons why most people are homogamous. First of all, people mostly interact with those within their own social

---

expressive exchanges
Exchanges of emotional services between spouses, including emotional support, love, affection, friendship, and companionship.

instrumental exchanges
Exchanges of practical or technical services between spouses that do not include emotions but do include money and labour.

incest Sexual activity between closely related members of the same kin group.

endogamy The practice of marrying *within* one's own group (class, caste, ethnic group, religion, etc.).

exogamy The practice of marrying *outside* one's own group (class, caste, ethnic group, religion, etc.).

homogamy The tendency of people with similar characteristics to marry each other.

network; and within their social network, they are likely to meet others who are (at least socially) like themselves. Second, we tend to like people who think the way we do and act the way we expect them to. This makes us feel comfortable having them around. Third, people who are similar find it easier to balance instrumental and expressive exchanges. That's because they bring similar, and thus more equal, qualities and resources to the marriage.

The importance of educational homogamy for mate selection has increased over the course of time. However, the importance of ascriptive (inborn) similarities, such as religion, ethnicity, and social class, has been decreasing over time. In short, we tend to mate with a person who is usually the same race, roughly the same age, with roughly the same education as we have.

Arranged Marriages versus Love Marriages

Arranged marriages take place in societies that take control of erotic property out of the hands of the prospective spouses and put them under kin group control. For most of history, in most societies, marriages have been based on the needs, beliefs, or desires of a couple's relatives, and *not* on love and sexual attraction. Arranged marriages are most common in societies where we find extended family homes and where ideas about the importance of family continue to prevail.

In these societies, rights to land and other possessions are passed from one generation to the next—typically, from father to son. Since marriage is an arrangement between families in these societies—and not just between individual mates—marriages are arranged in a way that protects family assets. Parents want to keep their property in family hands and also want to minimize conflict between the families that will be joined together by their children's marriage. For these reasons, the choice of marriage partners is far too important to be left to the whims of youth. Spouses are chosen because the union is economically advantageous or because of friendship or kinship obligations. Under this system, people occasionally even marry someone they have never met.

Proponents of arranged marriage state that it eliminates the stress from dating, helps to guarantee financial support throughout the marriage, and encourages harmony between in-laws (Bradby, 1999). Indeed, arranged marriages still persist: an estimated 60 per cent of all marriages worldwide are arranged, a figure that increases up to 90 per cent in places such as India (Toledo, 2009).

The modern North American hegemonic ideals about marriage and cohabitation—based on romance and free choice—have their own complexities and raise a host of new problems in the relations between spouses. Here, arranged marriages are viewed as inferior when compared to romantic marriages, a symptom of Eurocentrism. We will return to this issue after looking at another crucial family relationship: the one between parent and child.

Child Care and Child Rearing

Styles of child-bearing and child rearing (or parenting) vary from one group to another. Within Canada, different regional, ethnic, and religious groups raise children in somewhat different ways. Sociology is interested in how child rearing varies from culture to culture and in studying the outcomes of these different parenting styles to determine how they affect children. Sociological research shows us that certain ways of raising children will produce better outcomes for the child in adulthood, regardless of social background or type of family.

Research by Diana Baumrind (1991) and others has shown that children do best when they receive a lot of love and a lot of supervision; Baumrind calls this the "authoritative" parenting pattern. By "doing best,"

Do you think parenting style effectiveness depends on the wider social structure in which people are parenting, or are there "universal" parenting styles that are more effective?

we mean that children who receive this kind of parenting tend to remain mentally and physically healthy, do well in school, stay out of trouble with the law, and get along well with other children. Children whose parents are neglectful, unloving, harsh, or abusive are much less likely to "do well," at least according to North American research (Steinberg, 2001; Pinquart & Kauser, 2017). It is possible that other styles of parenting work well in other societies, but so far, there is insufficient research that proves this is so (Steinberg, 2001; Keshavarz & Baharudin, 2009).

Good parenting is possible in any family, whether same-sex, heterosexual, or non-binary, cohabiting or married, first marriage or remarriage, nuclear household or extended household, two-parent or single parent, and so on. A variety of family problems—poverty, conflict, violence, addiction, and the like—can make it hard for a family to parent well. However, there is little research support for the notion that family structure per se is the problem. But family structure and surrounding culture do affect parenting practices. In other words, some families find it easier or harder to parent effectively—to interact, communicate, negotiate, resolve conflicts, and so on.

The onset of parenthood is usually a trying time. Often, raising small children strains the marriage (Nomaguchi & Milkie, 2017). New parents have many additional chores and usually don't get enough sleep or relaxing time. Quarrels become more common, both partners feel they get less companionship from their mate than they once did, marital satisfaction declines, and the enjoyment of parenthood may be slight (Lawrence, Cobb, Rothman, Rothman, & Bradbury, 2008). No wonder we find that, at all ages and marital durations, women *without* children report being more satisfied with marriage than women *with* children (Twenge, Campbell, & Foster, 2003; Umberson, Pudrovksi, & Reczek, 2010).

A decline in parenthood has been going on for over a century. The potential strain on relationships, as mentioned, may help to explain why many couples choose to limit their child-bearing. Additionally, it has become gradually harder to live a comfortable, middle-class urban life with many children (Livingston & Cohn, 2010). The financial problems that affect parents and strain the spousal relationship can strain parent-child relations as well. Economic hardship can lead parents to provide inconsistent and harsh discipline (Nomaguchi & Milkie, 2017). The stress that arises between parent and child can, in turn, cause the child emotional distress and long-term social and emotional harm. Given the choice between having more children and having more disposable income, most Canadians over the past 100 years have chosen the second option. At the same

time, the development of new contraceptive technology has made the wish for a smaller family easier to fulfill. High quality contraception, such as is provided by "the pill," has made it easier for people to have only as many children as they want, when they want them (Reed, 2014).

That being said, there is still a demand across Canada for assisted reproductive technologies. This refers to treatments for infertility that involve eggs and/or sperm (for example, in vitro fertilization, or IVF) (American Society for Reproductive Medicine, 2019). Indeed, an estimated 15 per cent of the Canadian population will seek infertility treatment in their lifetime, with the most common group being women aged 35 to 44 (Bushnik, Cook, Hughes, & Tough, 2010).

Trends in Family Life

As we have seen, there have been many important changes in the Canadian family over the past 40 years (see Figure 8.3). These changes include an increase in the number of families with both parents working for pay, a decline in child-bearing and family size, and—another result of the decline in child-bearing—the aging of the Canadian population (see also Chapter 11). Divorce and remarriage rates are high in our society, as are rates of domestic violence. But the most striking feature of Canadian families today is their variety. Perhaps most surprising is the number of people living alone in Canada—28.2 per cent of all census households—and the 51.1 per cent of couples residing without children (Statistics Canada, 2017c).

Cohabitation

In the past 40 years, rates of first marriages have fallen to an all-time low in Canada (Statistics Canada, 2017a). The falling national rate has been led by large declines in Quebec, which has one of the lowest marriage rates in the world. On the other hand, there has been an increase in young people who choose common-law unions over marriage. Across Canada, 21.3 per cent of unmarried couples cohabitate (Statistics Canada, 2017b). This increase partly explains the decrease in legal marriages. However, most people are *delaying*, not *rejecting* marriage. So, another result of this change is that the average age at first marriage is increasing (Statistics Canada, 2017b).

Cohabitation is an arrangement in which an unmarried couple lives together to find out if they are suitable, to cut down on living expenses, or as an alternative to marriage. The major difference between marriage and cohabitation is that the former is an explicit legal commitment while the latter is not. Even so, Canadian law regards cohabitation that continues for more

cohabitation Two or more adults who live together, share expenses, and have a sexual and/or romantic relationship without being legally married.

From My Perspective

Katie and Jess

Unlike the majority of couples we know, we are high school sweethearts! We were both known as jocks in high school and quickly became inseparable friends at the age of 14. Feelings developed on both sides just as they would in any other typical young romance. For us it was quite simple—we met, we dated, we fell in love—just like we see all couples falling in love in the media. It was, however, not that simple for society.

Being a same-sex couple meant that we had to "come out of the closet." Such a ridiculous concept when you don't feel as though you were ever *in* a closet to begin with! Our "coming out" story is a lot less terrible and dramatic than many others we know of; however, it was still accompanied by the loss of some friendships and the loss of communication with some family members. There were feelings of exclusion and people stumbling over words because they seemed to no longer know how to speak to us, as if the fact that we were gay changed the people we had been our entire lives. Some people overcompensate while trying to be careful to not offend, and others just throw out offensive remarks freely.

Katie and Jess, a 33-year-old married couple currently living and working in Yellowknife, Canada.

As the stages of life progressed, we watched siblings and cousins enter heterosexual relationships and new partners were welcomed into the family fold with no questions asked. There was an almost immediate banter about marriage and babies with these couples, but nobody ever jokes or speaks about these things with us. Most people likely do not even realize they are doing this.

Society says that the next step in a relationship is marriage, so that is what we did. Please don't get us wrong—we loved each other and were very committed to one another, but the internal desire to follow the norm was an influencing factor in the decision to legally marry. Contrary to popular belief, lesbian relationships go through all the same kinds of difficulties as straight relationships. Life happens, people change, we forget to put each other first, we don't equally share the household responsibilities, partners are taken for granted, and marriages struggle. We ended up needing to go see a counsellor, which should have been a simple process of looking up local practitioners, phoning, and making an appointment. However, for gay couples, the process is a little more complex as we must first find out which counsellors are open to working with same-sex couples.

After a lot of work and self-reflection, reconnecting, and refocusing on what is truly important, we have decided to start a family! We are surrounded by nieces and nephews and have known for a long time that we wanted our own child. We want nothing more than to welcome a little bundle of joy into our lives that will eventually become a teenager and make us question every life decision we have ever made (we have watched our siblings struggle through their children's teen years with half their sanity intact). For most heterosexual couples starting a family, it is as simple as no longer using your method of birth control. As a same sex couple we had far more decision making ahead of us: Would we adopt or carry? Which one of us would carry? Would we both carry? Where and how would we get the semen? How do we choose the donor? How do we pay for the insemination? If we adopt, which agencies support gay adoptions? How long are the lists? How much money will it cost?

We are still on this journey and can tell you that it is very difficult to continuously be jumping over hurdle after hurdle in our quest to be a family.

Source: Provided by Jess Collins, used by permission.

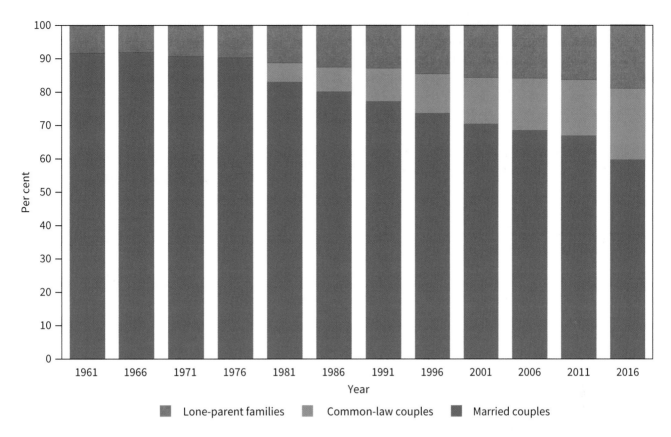

Figure 8.3 Family Composition 1961 to 2016

Source: Adapted from https://www12.statcan.gc.ca/census-recensement/2011/as-sa/98-312-x/2011003/fig/fig3_1-1-eng.cfm and https://www 150.statcan.gc.ca/n1/daily-quotidien/170802/dq170802a-eng.htm

than three years (or one year if there is a child) as a legally binding relationship in certain respects, and is considered a common-law partnership. Long-term cohabitants owe each other support obligations (though not the sharing of communal property) in the event of a breakup.

Divorce

Another significant change in North American family life is the increase in divorce (Statistics Canada, 2017b). Divorce is the legal, formal dissolution of a legal marriage. Among other things, it frees the spouses to remarry.

Divorce is widely accepted today as a valid and fitting way to end an unhappy marital situation. Current research shows that there are a few, but important, gendered differences in divorce outcomes, however (Amato, 2000; Wu & Schimmele, 2005; Thomas, 2018). Men tend to be more vulnerable to short-term consequences of divorce and generally experience a greater decline in well-being (Thomas, 2018). Women, however, are at greater long-term risk following a divorce (Amato, 2000; Wu & Schimmele, 2005; Thomas, 2018). They experience disproportionately

higher levels of poverty and single parenthood for many years following a divorce (Amato, 2000; Wu & Schimmele, 2005). Furthermore, studies suggest that women lose approximately 40 per cent of their pre-divorce income while men gain 5 per cent and that women face up to a 45 per cent risk of living below the poverty line several years after a divorce (Thomas, 2018). Interestingly, the same studies find that women experience greater satisfaction with household labour as the time spent on household chores decreases after a divorce, while men indicate an increase in overall time spent on household tasks (Thomas, 2018). Men are more likely to re-partner quickly while women are more likely not to re-partner at all (Wu & Schimmele, 2005).

Today, researchers project that newly married couples run a (roughly) 40 per cent risk of future divorce (Statistics Canada, 2017c). These projections assume that rates of divorce will continue to rise, or at least stay high, among young and middle-aged people. What causes marital breakdown, whether it ends in divorce or not? One problem may be too much pressure on the nuclear family. In the event of a crisis, people in nuclear families have few

> **divorce** The legal ending of a marriage by a court of law.

people to rely on for comfort and support. Another reason may be the over-romanticized expectations of love, as discussed earlier in this chapter (recall also the discussion of Disney in Chapter 7). Because of mythologized images of marriage, many people feel their marriage has failed when it loses its freshness and romantic passion. Finally, researchers note the growing economic independence of women, which means that more women can leave unhappy marriages today than in the past (Ruggles, 1997).

Single-Parent Families

As more marriages end in separation or divorce, single-parent families increase in numbers. A **single-parent (or lone-parent) family** is a family in which only one parent lives with dependent children.

> **single-parent (or lone-parent) family**
> A family in which only one parent lives with dependent children.

Both parents may provide child care and child support, but typically the custodial parent—most often the mother, when one is present—provides the majority of child care and support. The main problems facing such a family are economic, reminding us of what sociologists call the feminization of poverty. As we noted in Chapter 6 on class and status inequality, the "poor" in Canada are mainly women and children. These women include single mothers living on welfare, those living with a disability, or those who cannot work because they cannot afford daycare for their children. These women also include elderly women who spent their lives as homemakers and could not contribute to a pension plan that would support them in their old age. These problems are especially marked among racialized, Indigenous, transgender, and immigrant women.

Blended Families

My household, like many of yours, consists of a blended family. My husband and I each had two daughters prior to our starting our lives together. When the girls were younger, we all resided together under one roof with my children visiting their father, and my husband's daughters visiting their mother, on weekends. This family type is now relatively common, with 10 per cent of children living in this arrangement (Statistics Canada, 2017c). This type of family is particularly difficult to navigate as parents often have different types of parenting styles, and differential treatment of children is hard to avoid.

Same-Sex Families

Same-sex families are on the rise and yet continue to largely be ignored when teaching children about the

different types of families that exist. My sister is a lesbian and has been in a relationship with the same woman since she was in high school (see the "In My Perspective" box), so my children have always understood that you can fall in love with anyone, regardless of their sex. I moved with my two daughters to a town approximately 90 minutes from my hometown to complete my PhD. My oldest daughter was in grade 3 when I received a call from the principal of the school requesting a meeting as soon as possible. I was very anxious about what my precocious, loud, opinionated daughter may have done at school that day! When I got to the office, the principal proceeded to tell me that the teacher was doing a lesson about family that day. She had asked the class to describe the type of family you could live in. Students were answering things such as "I live with my parents and brother" or "I live with my parents and grandparents" or "I live just with my mom." The teacher proceeded to tell the class that these families were called "nuclear," "extended," and "single-parent" families. I was waiting to hear what my daughter had done (and quite honestly fearing that she had told the class in graphic detail how babies were made, or something to that effect) when the principal informed me that Madison had raised her hand and told the class that you could have two moms or two dads. The teacher quickly said that she was of course right; if parents got divorced you could have a mom and a stepmom. The principal then explained that Madison stated, "No, like two moms, no dad—you know lesbians." I laughed out loud in sheer disbelief that this was why I had been called into a principal's office! Despite the fact that many children are living in this structure of family, education systems often continue to ignore this type of family. According to the 2016 Census, there are 72,888 same-sex couples in Canada and over 12 per cent of them have children (Statistics Canada, 2017c).

Problems Related to the Family

Work–Family Balance

Two big shifts in society have affected how families negotiate the competing demands of earning an income and taking care of the family (see Figure 8.4). As has been discussed, historically this was easily negotiated for heterosexual two-parent families as men entered

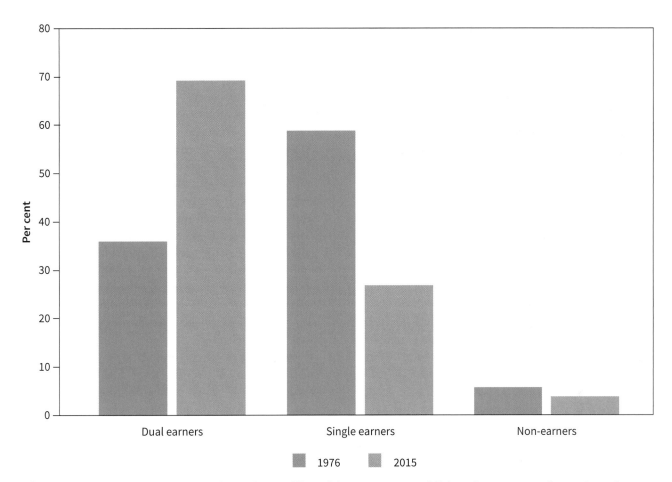

80

70

60

50

Per cent
40

30

20

10

0

Dual earners　　　　　　Single earners　　　　　　Non-earners

■ 1976　　　■ 2015

Figure 8.4 **Employment Status of Couple Families with at Least One Child Under 16 Years of Age, Canada, 1976 and 2015**

Source: https://www150.statcan.gc.ca/n1/pub/11-630-x/11-630-x2016005-eng.htm, Chart 1

into the labour market and women were relegated to the home. However, in recent decades, the number of hours of paid work required to run a household has continued to rise. The need for more income has translated into primary caregivers—primarily women—working more hours outside the home. According to Statistics Canada (2016), the percentage of families in Canada with two working parents has doubled in the past 40 years. During the same time period, the proportion of families where just one parent earned a paycheque dropped from 59 per cent to 27 per cent (Statistics Canada, 2016). The second major shift has been the major cutbacks in government support to schools, health care, and social service agencies, which have resulted in an increase in caregiving needs falling to the family (Luxton & Corman, 2001). For example, cuts to elder care and to health care have resulted in older adults relying on family members for care. As we have seen in Chapter 7, these shifts have not resulted in equality within the home. Although there have been some moves toward a more egalitarian approach to household activities, women continue to

shoulder the greatest percentage of the work (Yavorksy, Dush, & Schoppe-Sullivan, 2015).

Workload problems affect people differently depending on their cultural or social group. In Canada, mothers from higher socio-economic backgrounds are more likely to enter and stay in paid employment, even if they have children. Mostly due to their ability to pay someone else to do household and child-care labour, high-income women are better able than poorer women to deal with the dual burden of work and marriage. For example, many women of colour immigrate to North America to work in the households of white, upper-middle-class women, a phenomenon referred to as the "global care chain." This downloads the problem of work–family overload onto newly immigrated women of colour, who are some of the most socially vulnerable women. Many women who immigrate to Canada have never done paid work before because of household responsibilities and strict gender roles that have limited their opportunities. Yet, after moving to Canada, some have no choice but to pursue employment to support their family (Remennick,

2007). Given the opportunity, some women are even tempted to leave their husbands and seek economic independence, having only stayed with them because of cultural ties and economic dependency (Hyman, Guruge, & Mason, 2008). However, not all people who immigrate to Canada come from patriarchal societies who predominately subscribe to these traditional gender roles. In addition, many people who were born and raised in Canada also structure their family according to these rigid traditional values. Women from Canadian families that subscribe to traditional gender roles also have difficulty leaving spouses and/or entering into the labour market (Hyman, Guruge, & Mason, 2008).

On the one hand, a woman's transition from a traditional, patriarchal society to a more egalitarian society may be beneficial to her because she gains more autonomy (Hyman, Guruge, & Mason, 2008). On the other hand, this loss of patriarchal power may not be beneficial for her husband. Males who are used to being dominant may become insecure when they lose this role. In turn, this insecurity may lead to domestic conflict and even violence (Hyman, Guruge, & Mason, 2008).

However, if a husband encourages more egalitarian gender roles and task-sharing, the wife's marital satisfaction and well-being increase greatly (Arends-Tóth & Van de Vijver, 2007). Some men from patriarchal societies are willing to encourage their wives to find a fulfilling job or career. However, many are still reluctant to do so, in part because it might oblige them to take on roles traditionally associated with the female gender, such as child-care obligations and housework.

Family Violence

In Canadian society, the family is considered "private." Because of this, when violence occurs, often few outside the family know about it. Only recently have people begun to realize that violence is a pervasive part of family life and that it leads to negative social outcomes. In the past, it was taken for granted that parents had a right to use physical force to discipline their children. Violence between spouses was less acceptable, at least in public, but many men in particular thought that they had as much right to hit their spouses as to discipline their children.

The change in attitudes toward abuse within the family is illustrated by the Canadian law's failure to recognize marital rape as a crime until 1983. That marital rape was not considered sexual assault tells us that it was taken for granted that wives should be sexually available at their husband's will (as only heterosexual marriage was legal at the time). What's more, it shows us that violence

by men was considered acceptable when directed against their wives. Conversely, the change in law that eventually did make it a crime suggests declining support for the idea of the wife as "erotic property."

Feminists propose that spousal abuse and child abuse are two aspects of the same phenomenon: they both stem from patriarchy. What's more, reported incidents of physical abuse against children who receive hospital attention reveal that spousal abuse is also the most common context for child abuse (Stark & Filtcraft, 1988). As you can see in Figure 8.5, while both men and women experience family violence, women are far more likely to report being sexually assaulted, beaten, choked, pushed, grabbed, shoved, slapped, or threatened with a deadly weapon, while men were more likely to have been kicked, bitten, hit, had something thrown at them, or threatened to be hit. In other words, men are more likely to experience the less serious forms of violence; and women, the more serious forms of violence.

Verbal aggression is another type of family violence. It commonly results from a flaw in communication skills. That is, people are unable to express their grievances in helpful ways. The worst type of verbal abuse is attacks on the character of the other person (Infante, Sabourin, Rudd, & Shannon, 2009). Statistics link character attacks with physical violence more highly than any other verbal aggression (Infante et al., 2009).

Another form of family violence we are just beginning to learn about is elder abuse: mistreatment directed toward older adults by their children and grandchildren. In many cultures, family violence is not seen as acceptable. Such behaviour violates the expectation that family members will co-operate with and help one another. Cultural rejection of family violence is weaker in North America than elsewhere, however. Far from being a safe haven in a difficult world, the family has been, for many North Americans, a source of pain, shame, and anger. The psychological consequences of living with the terror of family violence are only beginning to be explored.

Despite changes in laws and people's attitudes, a lot of family violence still goes unreported. As a result, we do not have good statistics on the prevalence of such violence. However, homicide statistics, which are quite complete, confirm that people are at a greater risk of physical injury from a spouse or family member than from a stranger (Sinha, 2012; Miszkurka, Steensma, & Phillips, 2016).

Domestic violence is found in the richest homes as well as in the poorest ones. Some research suggests that while abuse happens as frequently in affluent communities as in

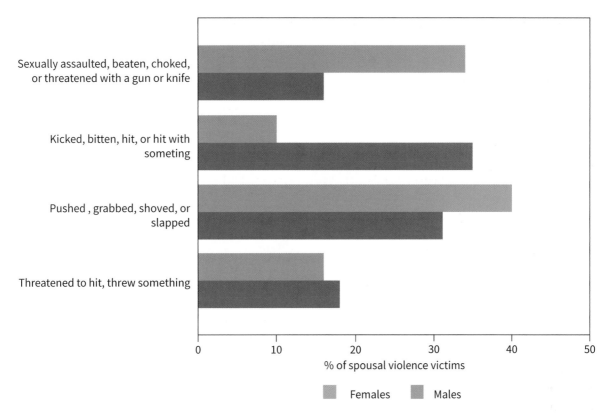

Figure 8.5 **Self-Reported Spousal Violence, 2014**

Source: https://www150.statcan.gc.ca/n1/daily-quotidien/160121/cg-b001-eng.htm

World Events

Domestic Violence vs. "Honour Killings"

Since the War on Terror began in 2001, people living in North America have been inundated with political rhetoric and media images denouncing Islam and those who practise it. While we touched briefly on cultural differences in previous chapters, it is worth looking at the more recent issue of "honour killing" that media and politicians have latched onto in order to push their respective agendas. However, there are approximately the same number of honour killings carried out in a single year in the Middle East and South Asia as there are intimate partner deaths in Canada (Abedi, 2018). The question is, why do we consider these North American acts of violence a problem of a few disturbed individuals, while we consider acts of family violence in the Middle East and South Asia a systemic cultural issue?

The commonalities between domestic violence and honour killings are disturbingly similar. For instance, in both cases perpetrators are overwhelmingly men, victims are overwhelmingly women, and the perceived transgression the family member commits to trigger the violence crosses some sort of boundary that the perpetrator objects to and therefore perceives that the partner or family member needs to be punished (Winegar, 2016). As well, both domestic violence and honour crimes include relatives and/or intimate partners, and sexual assault, psychological abuse, and murder are just some of the acts of violence carried out against the victim (Winegar, 2016).

It is true that there are stark differences between domestic violence and honour killings regarding the resources available to victims and the legal ramifications for perpetrators. However, this perceived difference between the two cultures gives the false impression that women are safer in North America than in other places. How might these different ways of characterizing similar crimes affect how perpetrators are treated in media coverage? How might it affect how victims are perceived? How might it affect how neighbours perceive a racialized, Islamic family vs. a white atheist household? What assumptions might neighbours make?

impoverished communities, the abuse is often more hidden and less disclosed (Haselschwerdt & Hardesty, 2016). It seems that people who have experienced many "stressful" life events are more likely to abuse their spouse or partner (Reese, Parker, & Peek-Asa, 2015). These stressful events include both personal and financial stress (Weatherburn, 2011; Reese, Parker, & Peek-Asa, 2015). But this does not mean that stress caused the violence. Committing violence in this way shows that the abusive partner was socialized to express his or her negative emotions through violence.

Top 10 Takeaways

1 Families have both structure and functions. pp. 148–149

2 The two main family households in Canada are nuclear and extended families. p. 150

3 Kinship is determined based upon three different types of descent: bilateral, patrilineal, and matrilineal. pp. 150–151

4 Authority patterns are related to descent practices. Families are either egalitarian, patriarchal, or matriarchal. pp. 151–153

5 Functionalists focus on the various functions the family fulfills in society. Interactionists are focused on the socialization processes that occur within the family as well as on group dynamics. Conflict and feminist approaches both contend that the family is a site of inequality. pp. 153–154

6 Union formations include both expressive and instrumental exchanges. pp. 154–155

7 There are rules about who can marry in each society. Mate selection may be based upon endogamy (within a closed group), exogamy (between groups), or homogamy (between people with similar traits). pp. 155–156

8 We are seeing many changing trends in family life in Canada, such as cohabitation, divorce, blended families, and same-sex families. pp. 157–160

9 Shifts in the labour market and in government spending have resulted in an increase in women working outside the home. This has resulted in work and home balance issues for most families. pp. 160–162

10 Contrary to popular media portrayal, families are sometimes sources of violence rather than sources of safety. p. 162

Questions for Critical Thinking

1. Why is developing a universal definition of family so difficult? Can you come up with a definition that encompasses all family forms and could be accepted by social policy?

2. Describe the structure of your family. What functions is your family fulfilling?

3. Explain the relationship between descent and authority patterns in families.

4. Examining your own family structure, what type of authority pattern exists? Explain examples that support your conclusion. Discuss whether the same authority pattern exists over generations of

your family (between your great-grandparents and grandparents, for example) and whether different sides of your family exhibit different patterns.

5. Discuss the relationship between gender socialization, the family, and gender inequality from a feminist perspective.

6. It has been suggested that adults who wish to have children should apply for a licence first, in order to reduce the number of dysfunctional homes. If we were to require a license to have children, what should the requirements be? Is there an age, sex, type of relationship, education, and/or income level that you think should be required? What are some of the pros and cons to this approach?

7. Explain why, despite living in "multicultural" Canada, we continue to find homogamy to be the norm in union formation.

8. How is domestic labour organized in your household now? Does it differ from how it was organized as you were growing up? Has studying gender socialization, inequality, and the family led you to think differently about domestic labour?

9. What structural inequalities make some women more able to balance work and family successfully while others cannot?

10. How is domestic violence within the family connected to age and gender inequalities in society?

Recommended Readings

- **Bezanson, K., and Luxton, M. (2006).** *Social reproduction: Feminist political economy challenges neo-liberalism*. **Montreal: McGill-Queen's University Press.** This edited collection explores the different ways that women bear the costs of and responsibility for caregiving. The book provides evidence that caregiving needs to be placed at the centre of analysis when looking at households, the state, markets, and communities.

- **Doucet, A. (2015). Parental responsibilities: Dilemmas of measurement and gender equality.** *Journal of Marriage and Family, 77*(1), 224–242. Doucet reveals persistent patterns of gender differences in parental responsibilities. She argues for a conceptualization of parental responsibilities that shifts away from a measurement of time and tasks and toward assessing a set of practices that unfold relationally across time and social spaces of parenting.

- **Fox, B. (2013).** *Family patterns: Gender relations* **(4th ed.). Don Mills, ON: Oxford University Press.**

In the fourth edition of *Family Patterns*, Fox and contributors explore the ways that gendered relationships continue to play a major role in the structure of today's families. The book provides a cross-country analysis as it presents contemporary readings from Canada, the US, and the UK.

- **Luxton, M. (2011).** *Changing families; new understandings*. **Ottawa: Vanier Institute of the family. https://vanierinstitute.ca/wp-content/uploads/2015/12/CFT_2011-06-00_EN.pdf** Meg Luxton, a pioneer in feminist studies of the family in Canada, explores differences in family forms. She argues that the way people understand families is central to how family practices are either normalized or rejected.

- **Ward, M., & Belanger, M. (2015).** *The family dynamic: A Canadian perspective* **(6th ed.). Vancouver: Langara College.** Ward and Belanger offer a broad introduction to the sociology of families.

Recommended Websites

Stop Family Violence
https://www.canada.ca/en/public-health/services/health-promotion/stop-family-violence.html
- Stop Family Violence is a Government of Canada website that provides a one-stop source of information on family violence.

The Childless by Choice Project
http://www.childlessbychoiceproject.com
- This advocacy site provides information that supports the decision to stay childless.

Family Service Ontario
http://www.familyserviceontario.org/
- This organization provides access to services and programs in a range of areas, such as relationship counselling, financial management, mental health and addictions, domestic violence, and support for LGBTQ families.

Vanier Institute of the Family
https://vanierinstitute.ca/
- The Vanier Institute is a national organization dedicated to promoting the well-being of Canada's families through research, education, and advocacy.

Chapter 9

"Race" and Racialization

From 1990 to 2019, the Canadian government was involved in over eight different international conflicts. Many of these conflicts grew out of ethnic, religious, and racial conflict among different groups. For example, Canada's role in the war in Afghanistan (2001–14) was largely justified by pointing to the role of Muslim religion and culture in the subordination of women. What is often not considered is the Canadian and US government's role in the establishment of patriarchal social relations via the political and economic destabilization of Afghanistan. This was neither Canada's first nor last involvement in racial and ethnic conflict. Indeed, the creation of the Canadian state began with the intentional, systematic genocide of Indigenous Peoples. Indigenous people are still disproportionately killed today, as demonstrated by the Idle No More movement, the Missing and Murdered Indigenous Women and Girls Inquiry, and other Indigenous-led activist movements. Other notable ethnic and racial conflicts in the past 30 years include the Rwandan genocide, the Bosnian genocide, the genocide of Yazidis (Iraq), and the Darfur genocide (Sudan). These remind us that racial and ethnic conflict continue to be important factors in contemporary life, even though we might think of racism as existing "in the past" or "not in Canada."

Key Terms

apartheid

assimilation

charter groups

contact hypothesis

discrimination

ethnicity

exception fallacy

exploitation theory

genocide

Islamophobia

othering

pluralism

minority groups

prejudice

race

racism

reserve

segregation

stereotype

systemic discrimination

visible minority

Introduction

Ethnic, religious, and racial problems are all around us. As discussed at the start of the chapter, intergroup conflicts around the world today hint at the global need to explore political arrangements that honour ethnic differences, rather than erase them.

Unfortunately, this is not just an "us" versus "them" problem. Canada's colonial past is still negatively affecting our present. Indigenous communities have long been the targets of violence, and other groups have become targets of conflict at different points of time throughout Canada's existence. Earlier in Canada's settlement, Chinese (and visibly "Asian" people) were so disliked that they were prevented from coming to Canada at all. More recently, post 2001, many Christian-based countries, including people within Canada, view Muslim populations around the world, regardless of their sect, as suspect—and view those racialized as "Arab" to be Muslim, regardless of their actual faith. Black individuals, especially young black men, continue to face many difficulties in Canada and the United States, particularly regarding being suspected of criminal behaviour. These examples will be discussed in more detail throughout the chapter, but are used here to highlight that intergroup conflict is not something that happens somewhere else. It's happening in all of our towns and cities across Canada and has very real consequences. Thus, understanding what these categories are and how they function in society is paramount to co-residing in peace.

In earlier chapters, we noted that societies and social institutions are social constructs. That is, people re-create social and institutional culture every day by imagining and then performing it. Ethnic and racial differences are also social constructs. Scientific studies have shown that there is little—if any—difference in the genetic makeup of different races or ethnic groups (Kolbert, 2018). Humans are all, essentially, the same, genetically, and ethnic and racial differences are imaginary, not real! Yet, the consequences of these socially constructed categories are very real.

The Concepts of "Ethnicity" and "Race"

As mentioned, from a sociological point of view, both ethnicity and race are social constructs. People have assumed that inherent traits, similarities, and differences can be determined through visible variations in the way that a stranger looks, and they have imbued these differences with authority that has no basis in fact. Yet these ideas affect how we interact with one another.

Ethnicity and race share some similarities. Both terms refer to social constructs, and both influence how a person is perceived by others; and, because the latter is so, both unite those in each category through the shared experience of being treated like someone in that category. For example, while being black means little in terms of whether two people are genetically similar, there is a distinct, shared experience of being black in a given location at a given time (though these experiences are also shaped by other factors, such as gender, gender orientation, sexuality, and ability).

World Events

Fraternal Twins

Lucy and Maria Aylmer are fraternal twins from Gloucester in the UK. Eighteen years ago, the girls were born to a Caucasian father and a half-Jamaican mother. Because their mother carried the genes for both black and white skin, Lucy was born with white skin and Maria with black. These girls have experienced first-hand the very real ways that the social construction of race impacts people's day-to-day lives.

Ken McKay/ITV/Shutterstock

Lucy (left) and Maria (right) Aylmer on *Good Morning Britain* in 2015.

However, the two terms mean different things. **Ethnicity** refers to people with a common culture, language, religion, and/or national origin, as well as to people who share memories of colonization and migration. Members of an ethnic group feel they are culturally and socially united. Often, people outside that ethnic group also perceive those members as a coherent group. For example, I live in a small city that comprises a large Italian population. Most speak Italian as their first language, are Roman Catholics, cook plentiful meals of pastas and meats, and cheer on the Italian team during the Fédération Internationale de Football Association (FIFA) World Cup. My neighbours refer to me as a "mangia-cake"—a term that means "cake-eater," used to highlight the apparent differences in white people's food choices versus Italian food. (By the way, I don't eat cake ever, but I do love pasta!) Being Italian is very much my neighbours' ethnic identity, and it comes with a sense of pride.

> **ethnicity** A shared set of cultural traits—such as language, religion, national origin, traditions, and historical heritage—leading to a sense of collective existence or belonging.
>
> **race** A group whose members are defined as sharing the same physical characteristics, especially skin tone. Personality and cultural attributes have been assigned to these different racial categories in ways that justify and perpetuate white supremacy.

In contrast to ethnicity, **race** is defined in terms of shared (or similar) physical characteristics and appearance, not a shared history, culture, or genetics. Indeed, scientists have confirmed that there are more genetic differences between two individuals of the same race than there are between individuals of different races (McGettigan & Smith, 2015). Members of a race are categorized through their visible physical attributes. Different cultures, predominantly white, have then assigned personality and cultural attributes to these different racial categories in ways that justify and perpetuate white supremacy.

Since these concepts are different, they may or may not overlap. The "Caucasian," or white, race, for example, can include members from many ethnic and social backgrounds. It can also include white people from countries where Caucasians represent a racial minority. And who counts as "white" has changed over time—for example, for many years, in North America, Irish people were not considered white.

People who consider themselves (for example) ethnically French or German can be of any race so long as they have immersed themselves in the ethnic culture—although someone who is racially coded as not white may have a difficult time being accepted as a member of this ethnic group. There are, in other words, no clear definitions of each race or ethnicity; rather, they reflect people's assumptions, biases, and stereotypes, and they change over time. For example, consider a child with one white and one black parent. Is this child black or white? Historically, in the Southern United States, this was determined by law in the "one-drop rule" (Sweet, 2013). If a child had even a single drop of "black blood" that child would be considered black. Depending on what he or she looked like, the child may have been considered white before the

One of the first things you will notice in this photo is that the women in it are from different racial groups. You will have instantly, and most likely subconsciously, categorized these women based upon the tone of their skin. While the categories themselves are constructions, the effects of them are very real. In Canada, the white woman is more likely to be hired, to be considered pretty, and to be trusted. The other three women are likely to experience the world differently, by being more likely distrusted, underappreciated, and otherwise disadvantaged.

law went into effect. In other words, the same person may have been white one day and black the next.

If people see themselves, and others see them, as members of a unique category, then in practice they form a race. Race is real only in the sense that people treat it as real, and so its effects are real. As we will see, people often make many important decisions based on race. They might choose their friends, potential partners, places of work, places to live, people to hire, and whom to vote for on the basis of the "race" they perceive themselves and others to be.

The same is true of ethnicity. Ethnic origins—whether Ecuadorian, Welsh, West African, Ukrainian, Vietnamese, or otherwise—are not biologically meaningful. However, they *are* socially meaningful. As discussed in Chapter 3, culture can have significant influence on us as individuals. Shared cultural traits, such as language, learned history, and traditions, are important for social bond formation.

> *minority groups* Those groups that have less power and control over their own lives than the dominant group in a society.

Minority Groups

Rather than being a particular race or ethnicity, sometimes you'll hear someone referred to as a "minority." You may at first think that this is referring to numerical minority, but that is not quite right. A numerical minority is any group of people that makes up less than half of some population. If you think of the population of the city you are from, for example, there will be many numerical minorities, including those with green eyes, those who are left-handed, those who are librarians, those who have pink hair, or those who play basketball on a school team. However, we do not use this definition in sociology—this is because being a numerical minority in and of itself is relatively meaningless when it comes to the sociological reality of a society's connections, biases, and power structures. For sociologists, minority groups are those groups who have limited economic and

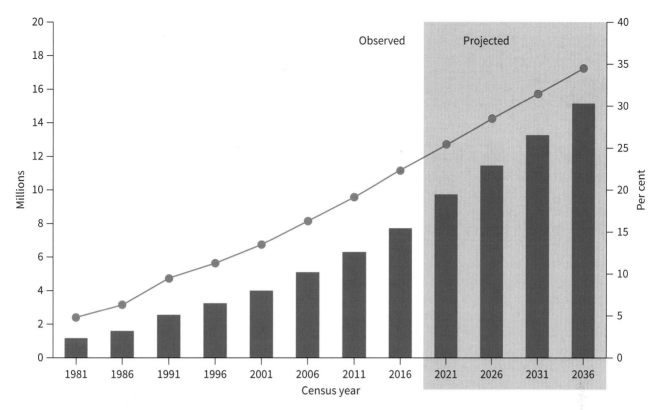

Figure 9.1 Number and Proportion of Visible Minority Population in Canada, 1981 to 2036

Source: https://www.statcan.gc.ca/eng/dai/btd/othervisuals/other010

social power and, therefore, limited control over their own lives. A minority group is subordinate to the dominant (or majority) group. In Canada, we use the term **visible minority** to refer to those Canadians who are neither Indigenous nor white (see Figure 9.1). Again, it is worth noting that while we categorize people based on other visible traits (such as perceived gender and perceived ability), the term "visible minority" has a specific sociological definition that is used to analyze Canadian society. Because the term has been criticized for using whiteness as a reference and default, insinuating that white is "normal," the term is falling out of favour and BIPOC (Black, Indigenous, and people of colour) is sometimes used.

Prejudice and Discrimination

Many people confuse the two terms, but social scientists treat prejudice and discrimination as different things.

> **visible minority** Racial groups that have less power and control over their own lives than the dominant group in a society. In Canada, this refers to anyone who is not white and who is non-Indigenous (not because Indigenous Peoples are a dominant group but because Indigenous Peoples have enough unique traits to be considered separately within the sociological study of Canada).
>
> **prejudice** A negative or hostile attitude toward members of a particular group simply because they belong to that group, based on assumptions and stereotypes about their characteristics.
>
> **stereotype** A broadly believed idea or trait about a particular group, in which the trait is assumed to apply to all members of that group.

Prejudice

Prejudice is a negative, hostile social attitude toward members of another group. Under prejudice, all members of the other group—because of their group membership—are assumed to have unsuitable qualities.

An important element in prejudice is the use of **stereotypes**—fixed mental images that prejudiced people think encompass all members of a given group. When we make use of stereotypes, we categorize people on the basis of only some characteristics, which we exaggerate in importance (see "Practising Sociology" activity later in this chapter). At some point you may have heard someone in your life say "Stereotypes are stereotypes for a reason." The underlying rationale is that people have been stereotyped because of behaviours or actions that they have been observed displaying over time. While these stereotypes may in fact be accurate for some members of a group, assuming that all members of a group fall under this same generalization is, by definition, prejudiced.

Once we are made aware of a stereotype, we are more likely to notice when we see examples that corroborate that stereotype. This is known as the **exception fallacy**. For ex-ample, for many years I commuted to work with a person I would label as extraordinarily prejudiced. Being a commuter, it is common to see accidents on the highway. In a one-week period there were four accidents within the same stretch of highway. At the first accident, we saw a middle-aged white woman holding a child and crying at the side of the road. My colleague stated that he hoped the child was not hurt. At the site of the second accident we saw, a senior white man was standing beside his damaged vehicle. Once again my colleague expressed his concern for the elderly gentleman. The third accident involved a group of mixed-race youth. My colleague exclaimed that they were most likely driving recklessly. In the final accident that we witnessed that week, there was a woman, whom my colleague racialized as Asian, standing at the side of the road. My colleague threw his arms in the air and exclaimed, "Urgghh, Asian women are the worst drivers." There was no evidence in our daily commute that Asian women were particularly bad drivers (or that the youth were driving any more recklessly than the rest of the drivers). In fact, based on this poor study sample, Asian women had the same probability as white women, senior men, and youth of varying races of being in an accident; however, my colleague was quick to interpret what he saw as evidence of that particular stereotype.

This is no less dangerous when people use positive stereotypes, such as "Asians are good at math." While a comment like this one may initially seem like a compliment, it actually serves to reinforce prejudice through the assumption that these traits are connected to race and are biologically inherited. Moreover, such a statement diminishes the accomplishments of individuals racialized as Asian who are good at math and shames those who are not. Stereotypes distort our perception of those around us as well as our perceptions of ourselves. In doing so, they justify prejudice.

Discrimination

In contrast to prejudice, **discrimination** refers to actions carried out against another person or group because of his or her group

membership. In particular, discrimination means denying opportunities that people would grant to equally qualified members of their own group. Prejudice is an opinion or belief, and it may be inevitable. People categorize things all the time and make snap judgments based on limited evidence and past experience. It is when our prejudiced views and feelings are acted upon that they turn into discrimination: for example, job segregation, unequal pay for equal work, denial of promotion, among others. It is hard to measure the effects of discrimination as they are often subtle. When people with the same ability receive different rewards for doing the same work, we can claim that, logically, discrimination exists.

Racism

A common form of discrimination, and the most relevant to this chapter, displays itself as **racism**. People are often treated differently based upon the prejudice that there is some type of biological difference related to ability and/or character that is visible in a person's skin tone and phenotype. However, the term *racism* does not simply refer to all discrimination based on perceived race. Rather, it refers to circumstances where prejudice, or holding opinions based on stereotypes about a particular racial group, is infused with *power* (Smith, 2000). In other words, racism refers to circumstances where prejudice and discrimination are supported and encouraged by social structures and is, therefore, systemic. For example, a white individual may experience prejudice when overhearing a group of people discussing their personal distaste for white people based on some stereotype; or that white individual may experience discrimination when told they are not welcome in a particular store because they are white. However, that same white individual cannot experience **systemic discrimination** based on his or her race. Racism refers to when a stereotype reinforces, and is reinforced by, an entire social structure that, in turn, (for example) justifies segregating people of colour into low-income areas with poor schooling through the selective lending practices of banking and insurance industries; denies people of colour access to decent work and equitable health care through blatant discrimination; rationalizes the disproportionate amount of unarmed people of colour murdered by police officers, and so forth (Zenou & Boccard,

exception fallacy A flawed principle of logic in which an observer makes conclusions about an entire group based on observed behaviour of a non-representative sample of individuals (e.g., one or two people's actions being used to form stereotypes about an entire group).

discrimination Unjust actions taken as a result of prejudice that favour one group over another group.

racism Systemic prejudice and discrimination by the dominant racial group against subordinate racial groups in a society.

systemic discrimination Biases against subordinate groups that are so deeply embedded in a society's institutions and customs that they are hard to see but are enforced across the society and create perpetual disadvantages for the subordinate group.

Trinity, 18-Year-Old Ivy League Student, World Record Holder

As a young girl in school, I was spit on, had books thrown at me from teachers in grades 2 and 3, told I wasn't smart, and pushed off the playground more times than I can count. I remember my mom having to tell the principal at my school that these incidents were wrong and violent. She was seen as causing a problem, and asking for any kind of apology was viewed as aggressive and time-consuming.

When I was 15 years old, my English teacher decided to lead a class discussion on race. She was inspired by the story *To Kill a Mockingbird* that we were reading as part of the curriculum. She handed out a news article that highlighted black-on-black crime statistics. She stood at the front of the class, pointed to a very light-skinned mixed-race girl and said, "You see, we have white mixed people and we have black mixed people like Trinity." She then pointed to me and said, "Trinity, you probably know more about this stuff, why don't you

Trinity Arsenault

read the first paragraph." I was embarrassed, confused, and didn't understand why I was so close to crying.

I responded to these moments in my life by getting involved. In 2014 and 2016 I set open water swimming records on Lake Ontario and the English Channel. These swims raised money for kids in single-parent families who need help covering the costs of organized sports. The majority of kids who access this fund identify as racial minorities. I have finished up high school and I am attending an Ivy League school in the United States for pre-medical sciences and biology—of course, with a minor in medical sociology. My brown skin provided me with many opportunities to not listen to teachers or guidance counsellors at school. When I was told I wasn't smart I just studied harder and I finished high school with a 93 per cent average.

I've grown up in a primarily white, conservative city in Ontario, Canada, that is very segregated. I'm biracial and have been raised solely by my white mother. This left me extremely removed from any understanding of my own identity as a black woman. My mom is comfortable with me identifying as a "person of colour" or a "visible minority." She becomes very uncomfortable when I tell her I am a black, light-skinned woman. I love that she is open to understanding this moment and we have many conversations about why she feels this way. Watching her identify white privilege and her inability to make sure I have that privilege is interesting. I am continuously letting her know that I don't want "this" privilege. It's embedded in power relations from colonization and slavery. You can unlearn and be an ally but that doesn't mean you don't benefit from it.

Never let anyone else's misconceptions of you become your perception of yourself. Do what you came here to do.

Source: Provided by Trinity Arsenault, used by permission.

1999; Galabuzi, 2011; Johnson, Bottorff, Browne, Hilton, & Clarke, 2009).

Often, the very existence of racism is denied through the benefit of white privilege. White privilege refers to inherent benefits and advantages that are possessed in a racially unequal society by virtue of being white. These benefits are countless and often difficult to measure. They range from benefits gained in simple, day-to-day interactions to more complex benefits that relate to overarching social structures, such as the economic system, employment, and so forth. For example, white individuals benefit from white privilege by virtue of knowing that their neighbours won't complain or worry about their presence based solely on their race, that security guards will not look at them and assume they are "up to something," that they will be able to see people of the same race on television in positive roles, and so forth (McIntosh, 1989). As we can see, these processes are easy to miss if you are not targeted by them personally—white privilege often functions in the absence of the detriments of racism and through historical benefits that have carried through to today (such as a parent or grandparent not being negatively impacted by racist laws that barred others from holding property, allowing them the ability to accrue wealth through home ownership). For that reason, a person who experiences white privilege may never realize, and would

> **othering** The classification of a group of people as "not one of us," i.e., different and therefore lesser; intentionally used on a political level to dehumanize a group of people in order to make it morally acceptable to discriminate against them.

also then not know about, the experience of those who are targets of racism.

Moreover, when one group of people defines another as inferior, they are able to reinforce their own sense of superiority. This process often includes othering—when we classify someone as "not one of us"—and results in people outside our social group being seen through the prism of stereotypes associated with their group. When someone is classified as "other," they lose their individuality and humanity in another person's eyes, making it easier to attribute negative and broad-sweeping assumptions about them. For example, "others" are often seen as "lazy," "violent," "dirty," "cheap," and a whole host of descriptions with negative connotations. This can make those who benefit from privilege assume that they deserve it and that those who experience racism deserve poor treatment.

The Story of Bob and Race, by Barry Deutsch. The benefits of racism to white people are often invisible, if you're white. What are some of the ways that racism has impacted you?

In the News

Racial Profiling in the Service Industry

In April 2018, two black men were arrested for sitting in a Starbucks in Philadelphia. The story made international news as the men were arrested for trespassing. Protestors gathered the following day to prevent the Starbucks location from making any money (Gayle, 2018). People expressed their outrage across Canada and were quick to point their finger at the US for the continued reports of racial profiling that happen in that country. Ironically, however, Canada has its own laundry list of blatant acts of racial profiling in the service industry. In March 2018, a Toronto restaurant was ordered to pay $10,000 after asking black customers to prepay for their meals (Bundale, 2018). Shoppers Drug Mart was ordered to pay $8000 after a worker targeted a black woman and accused her of stealing. In Saskatchewan, Giant Tiger and Canadian Tire employees were suspended after allegations that the employees were following Indigenous men around their stores and accusing them of shoplifting (Bundale, 2018). In Halifax, the provincial human rights commission found that a Sobeys store blatantly discriminated against a black woman when the store falsely accused her of stealing (Bundale, 2018).

Sojourner-Campbell, a consumer racial profiling expert, argues that for black, Indigenous, and other people of colour, this is a daily experience across Canada. Sometimes the profiling is discreet and other times it's blatant, but the "crime" is always the same—"shopping while black" (or not-white).

Seven Seconds

Prod. Veena Sud (2018). A Netflix crime drama that centres on a hit-and-run accident that kills a 15-year-old black boy. The aftermath includes a police cover-up and a lawyer who prosecutes the case as a hate crime.

Racism and othering are often perpetuated by media. This is especially true of news media. For example, hurricanes and other natural disasters often lead news media to report on survival methods in a racially divisive manner (The Sentencing Project, 2014). White individuals who are seen taking supplies from stores are described as "finding" the supplies while black individuals who are doing the same thing are accused of "looting" (Kahle, Yu, & Whiteside, 2007). For a more in-depth discussion of racism in the news media, refer to Chapter 10.

The region that I live in has been referred to as "Vanilla Land" for as long as I can remember due to its lack of diversity. Approximately 18 per cent of the region's total population comprises recent immigrants and approximately 10 per cent identify as members of a visible minority. Discrimination is often discussed in this area. (The young woman  showcased in the "From My Perspective" box lives in the same region.) My best friend of 33 years is married to a black Canadian-born man. They have been together for almost two decades and have two teenage daughters. He has a very good job earning much more than the average Canadian income. She was a stay-at-home mom for most of the children's childhood, although she is now back in the labour market full-time. In 2014, they were looking for a home to rent while they waited for the home they had purchased to be ready to move into. My friend went with her children and looked at several houses and put in applications for a few. When she was phoned back to say that her application had been accepted she informed the landlord that she wanted to bring her husband by to see the house first. Their children are very light skinned and thus pass for white; her husband, however, is easily identified as black. After he visited the house, they received a phone call telling them that someone else had rented it. This happened a couple of times before she came to me in frustration and asked me what she should do. I told her that I suspected that they were being discriminated against due to the colour of her husband's skin. She did not want to believe me but agreed not to take him to the house viewings for the remainder of the week. Their family was offered every house they looked at.

Discrimination at times is hard to pinpoint or understand. It is sometimes subtle in its expression. However, by using the sociological imagination, and our specialized

#*Sociology*

#racisminCanada

One of the myths that Canadians like to tell themselves and the world is that racism does not exist—or at least, is getting better—in Canada. However, a recent poll showed that nearly 50 per cent of Canadians admit to racist thoughts, and 32 per cent said they feel more comfortable expressing those racist thoughts than in the past. At the same time, 47 per cent said that racism is a serious problem, which is down from 69 per cent in 1992 (Elliott, 2019).

The hashtag #racisminCanada is just one of the ways that people use social media to try to make racism, which is so often invisible to those not experiencing it, visible. However, those who post about racism often become targets of racial slurs and attacks. In order to help with this, the hashtag #trollcollector was started by allies (e.g., non-black, non-Indigenous, non-trans people) in order to move the vitriol that can take place online away from those who are most vulnerable (i.e., black and Indigenous

women) and onto the pages of allies so that the person who is posting the vitriol can still be interacted with and reported if necessary. If you see someone posting racist comments on the feed of a black person, an Indigenous person, or a person of colour, particularly a woman or a trans person, untag the person being targeted/harassed and take on those battles to help stem the tide. If you are being attacked by racist trolls online, use the hashtag #trollcollector to signal to allies that they should come and help!

---

toolkit of methodologies, we study groups at the macro level, as well as the micro level, and are able to highlight the patterns and systemic forms of discrimination that pervade.

For example, while we know that discrimination has existed in the labour market for a long time, it took field experiments by Henry and Ginzberg (1985) to show the *true* extent of race-based job discrimination. When all else was equal, the researchers found that white applicants were three times more likely than black applicants to be offered a job.

More recently, Decheif and Oreopoulos (2012) conducted a follow-up study to earlier work (Oreopoulos, 2011) that found that significant discrimination existed within the Toronto labour market based on ethnic names. They examined callback rates from resumés sent to online job postings across multiple occupations in Toronto, Montreal, and Vancouver, and interviewed recruiters to ask why they believe name discrimination occurs. Oreopoulous and Decheif (2013) found that people with Indian and Chinese names experience significant discrimination. Furthermore, they discovered that recruiters believed that an "ethnic" name was a signal that an applicant might lack language or social skills.

These studies (and others like them) illustrate that racial discrimination is not the result of a few bigoted employers. There is instead a widespread racist bias in the labour force against hiring anyone assumed to be non-white. Employers believed that they were functioning on

DavidShankbone/Creative Commons license (CC BY-SA 3.0)

Derrick Albert Bell Jr. (1930–2011) was an American lawyer and civil rights activist. He is considered one of the founders of critical race theory, which explores how the status quo (including social institutions, such as the law) operates as an instrument of racial oppression. Critical race theorists are committed to ending racism. Bell Jr. insisted on recognizing the experiential knowledge of people of colour when analyzing social structures (Lawrence, Matsuda, Delgado, & Crenshaw, 1993). In other words, Bell Jr. argued that we must listen to and believe the people who experience racism to understand how it functions.

"logic" rather than on racist assumptions. Often unintended, systemic discrimination is so deeply embedded in a society's institutions and customs that it is hard to see or prove on a one-on-one basis. (For example, any one person with an "ethnic" name would be hard-pressed to prove that he or she had been discriminated against during a hiring decision.) Systemic discrimination is often perpetrated by people who are implementing longstanding practices whose fairness and necessity are taken for granted by the cultural majority, and whose hidden assumptions are not questioned until (and if) they experience the discrimination first-hand. In this hiring example, assuming that someone's language skills are poor based solely on the way their name is spelled is an unconscious bias that becomes a widespread, racist hiring practice.

Theoretical Perspectives on Race and Ethnicity

Functionalism

Functionalists stress that all people share common desires for work, family life, health, safety, and so on. For this reason, functionalists expect that most ethnic differences will eventually disappear from society. Those that remain, they assert, are largely "symbolic" (Parsons, 1975). That is, they are a part of a person's identity but have few practical consequences for everyday life. A second generation Italian Canadian may feel pride when an Italian athlete wins an Olympic event, but most of the time, an Italian Canadian would be sociologically indistinguishable from any other Canadian.

Functionalists have also pointed out four dysfunctions that are associated with racism: (1) discrimination results in a society's not maximizing its resources; (2) social problems, such as poverty, delinquency, and crime, are aggravated; (3) society spends too much time and money putting barriers to full inclusion in place; and (4) prejudice and discrimination have the tendency to impact relationships between nations. Functionalists also therefore tend to think that racism will resolve itself.

contact hypothesis
A symbolic interactionist theory that contends that contact between people who are from different racial or ethnic groups but who are otherwise of equal status will result in a reduction in prejudice.

exploitation theory
A conflict theory that contends that racism keeps minority group members in low-paying jobs, supplying the capitalists with a cheap reserve of labour.

Symbolic Interactionism

Symbolic interactionists focus on the personal experience of minority status. Interactionist researchers ask questions like these: What impact does a negative ethnic stereotype have on a person's sense of self? How, for example, does a young Sikh boy feel (and respond) when classmates mock his ceremonial turban and kirpan? How does a black (or Chinese or Indigenous) person feel about the lack of role models on television or in politics?

In other words, symbolic interactionists stress the links between race, ethnicity, and identity. They are especially interested in how we create and maintain these race and ethnic-based identities. Interactionists also believe that the more time that people spend with others from different backgrounds, the less prejudiced they will become. The contact hypothesis contends that interracial and inter-ethnic contact between people of equal class status will result in their abandoning previous stereotypes and becoming less prejudiced and less racist. People will begin to see one another as individuals rather than defaulting to learned stereotypes.

Conflict Theory

Conflict theorists can see the many harmful consequences that race- and ethnicity-based prejudice and discrimination have on society. These theorists use a Marxist approach to explain the basis of racial subordination. The exploitation theory contends that racism keeps minority group members in low-paying jobs, supplying capitalists with a cheap reserve army of labour. This view on race relations has remained persuasive, as we continue to see racialized minorities in low-paid, dangerous work since what is now Canada was colonized. However, Marxists have been criticized for reducing racism to a class dynamic even though, as we have seen and will continue to see in this chapter, it is more complex than simply a tool for financial gain (Leonardo, 2004).

Practising Sociology

Examining Invisible Privilege

Often, racism is portrayed as an individual act, not as an "invisible system" that confers dominance over others (McIntosh, 1989). White privilege is an important part of this invisible system. The term refers to inherent benefits that are conferred to white people in a racially unequal society, which in turn perpetuates white supremacy. Examine the list of instances of white privilege below identified by Peggy McIntosh (1989). Consider how this puts white people at an advantage and racialized people at a disadvantage.

Reflect on these instances of white privilege. Consider how they translate into advantages for white individuals and disadvantages for racialized individuals. How do these instances perpetuate white supremacy? Why is it important to be accountable to privilege?

Instance of White Privilege	How Does This Put White People at an Advantage?	How Does This Put Racialized People at a Disadvantage?
I can turn on the television or open to the front page of the paper and see people of my race widely represented (McIntosh, 1988, p. 2).		
I can avoid spending time with people whom I was trained to mistrust and who have learned to mistrust my kind or me (McIntosh, 1988, p. 2).		
I can take a job with an affirmative action employer without having co-workers on the job suspect that I got it because of race (McIntosh, 1988, p. 3).		
I can choose blemish cover or bandages in "flesh" color and have them more or less match my skin (McIntosh, 1988, p. 3).		
I am never asked to speak for all the people of my racial group (McIntosh, 1988, p. 3).		
I can easily buy posters, postcards, picture books, greeting cards, dolls, toys and children's magazines featuring people of my race (McIntosh, 1988:, p. 3).		
I can go shopping alone most of the time, pretty well assured that I will not be followed or harassed (McIntosh, 1988, p. 2).		
I can swear, or dress in second-hand clothes, or not answer emails, without having people attribute these choices to the bad morals, the poverty, or illiteracy of my race (McIntosh, 1988, p. 2).		
I can criticize our government and talk about how much I fear its policies and behaviour without being seen as a cultural outsider (McIntosh, 1988, p. 2).		
If a traffic cop pulls me over or if the government audits my tax return, I can be sure I haven't been singled out because of my race (McIntosh, 1988, p. 2).		

Feminism

As we have seen throughout the previous chapters in this textbook, feminists have diverse perspectives. Some feminists have been critiqued for performing analyses that apply only to white, cisgender, middle-class, heterosexual, and able-bodied women. One early example is in regard to the fight for the right for women in Canada to vote. Women's suffrage is often celebrated as having been won in 1918, although Asian women did not gain the right to vote until after World War II, and Indigenous women living on reserves did not gain the right to vote until 1960 (Strong-Boag, 2016). Further, Emily Murphy, Nellie McClung, and Louise McKinney (three of the Famous Five women who took the "Persons Case" to the Supreme Court of Canada, winning some women the right to vote) were also largely responsible for the Sexual Sterilization Act in Alberta, a provincial eugenics program in which over 4000 Albertan women who were deemed of a "lower" genetic makeup (based on race, ethnicity, indigeneity, class, religion, and perceived ability) were sterilized without their consent and sometimes without their knowledge (Yedlin, 2018).

> **reserve** A section of land set aside for a particular Indigenous band or nation by the Canadian government. Rules about reserves are set by the Canadian government, despite Indigenous Peoples' demands for sovereignty.

However, anti-racist and critical race feminism, thanks to the contributions of black, Indigenous, and other racialized women, continues to illustrate that gender is not the sole source of oppression; rather, gender identity and expression, race, age, ability, and sexuality all intersect to produce many different experiences of inequality.

Ethnic Groups within Canada

There were over 250 ethnic origins and ancestries reported to the 2016 census, and even these are larger categories that include subgroups (Statistics Canada, 2017b). Though they all can't be covered here, there are a few important categories worth highlighting to provide some context for the racialized differences we see in sociological data from Canada.

Indigenous Peoples

So far, this book has discussed Indigenous Peoples as a single group; however, Indigenous Peoples within what is now Canada come from various geographic locales, nations, cultural backgrounds, and ethnicities. Historically, the Canadian government has tended to treat these nations as a collective, and, as a result, there is a shared Indigenous identity within Canada that comes from experiencing the systemic barriers, discrimination, and attempted genocide by the Canadian state.

The umbrella term *Indigenous* comprises three different subpopulations: First Nations, Métis, and Inuit. First Nations applies to a large and diverse group of over 618 First Nations. Within these communities, there are over 50 cultural groups and 50 different languages (Government of Canada, 2017).

The second subpopulation of Indigenous people is the Métis. In the early years of colonization, the word *Métis* was used to describe people who were the offspring of varied combinations of settlers and First Nations. Different combinations included a mix of English or French, as well as Ojibwa, Cree, Algonquin, Mi'kmaq, and Wuastukwiuk ancestry. These children of mixed parents formed their own communities and languages in the 1600s to 1800s. Today, the word *Métis* encapsulates a set of cultural groups with histories, languages, and cultural practices that are distinct from First Nations and from one another.

Inuit, the third subgroup of Indigenous Peoples, mainly live in what is referred to as "Inuit Nunangat"—which translates to "the place where Inuit live." This vast region—a full third of Canada's total land mass—is home to 53 recognized Inuit communities (Government of Canada, 2017). Though small in terms of population, these distinct Inuit communities speak different languages, practise different cultural traditions, and have different historical and present-day experiences.

To complicate things even further, some Indigenous people in Canada are "Registered Indians" while others are not. Indigenous people who are Registered Indians (also called Status Indians) are registered with the Government of Canada. People on this registry are entitled to rights and benefits as outlined in the Indian Act, first created in 1876. Representatives of the Government of Canada are, in their own words, "the sole authority for determining which names will be added, deleted or omitted from the Register" (Government of Canada, 2011). This means that many

The Inconvenient Indian

Author Thomas King (2012). This text reflects on what it means to be an "Indian" in North America.

people who consider themselves to be Indigenous may not be included on the registry. Some have been excluded through the requirements laid out by the Government of Canada. Other Indigenous people chose not to register with the government even though they "qualified" for status. According to *The Inconvenient Indian* by Canadian author Thomas King (2012), "the [Indian Act] itself . . . has been the main mechanism for controlling the lives and destinies of Legal Indians in Canada, and throughout the life of the act, amendments have been made to the original document to fine-tune this control" (p. 71).

Just under five per cent of the population of the country is Indigenous (Statistics Canada, 2017a). Geographically speaking, Indigenous people are not evenly distributed in Canada. Most live in Ontario, Manitoba, Saskatchewan, Alberta, and British Columbia, and the majority of the populations of Nunavut and the Northwest Territories are made up of Indigenous people (Statistics Canada, 2017a).

The Indigenous population in Canada is, on average, young and growing. Children aged 14 and under make up one-third of the Indigenous population (Statistics Canada, 2017a), and the Indigenous population is growing four times more quickly than that of the non-Indigenous population, growing 42.5 per cent from 2006 to 2016 (Statistics Canada, 2017a).

As seen in Chapter 6, Indigenous people are much more likely than white, non-Indigenous Canadians to live in poverty and less likely to obtain post-secondary education (although their rate of educational attainment is growing faster than in the non-Indigenous population). Indigenous people are also more likely than other Canadians to die of heart disease, stroke, and diabetes (Heart Research Institute, 2016). And as we will see in Chapters 10 and 12, Indigenous people also have disproportionate suicide rates and interactions with the criminal justice system compared with other Canadians (Statistics Canada, 2016b). Because of these and other factors, Indigenous mortality rates are much higher than the national average, and life expectancy at birth is much lower for Indigenous people than for non-Indigenous people in Canada (HRI, 2006; see also Chapter 12). These are just a few of the statistics that help sociologists to expose the ongoing racism of the Canadian state against Indigenous Peoples. When large, significant differences in outcomes exist for whole populations, it is clear that systemic rather than individual factors are at work.

Throughout Canada's history, Indigenous people living within its borders have made concerted efforts to fight against the injustices that they have experienced. Following Canadian Federation in 1867, the Canadian government attempted to parcel out Rupert's Land, which had been purchased from the Hudson's Bay Company in 1868. The Métis inhabitants opposed the surveyors' system of parcelling out land that the Métis lived on. Led by Louis Riel, Métis took control of the territory and created a provisional government. In 1870, under Riel's leadership, the Red River Colony entered into Confederation as the province of Manitoba. In response, Canada sent a military expedition to Manitoba to re-enforce federal authority through violence and then through treaty. When the Métis began starving in the 1880s because of the decimation of bison herds, Riel tried to re-establish a provisional Métis government but was eventually forced to surrender. He was hanged for high treason on 16 November 1885 (Dickason & Newbigging, 2019).

The Oka Crisis was also a land dispute—this time between the town of Oka, Quebec, and Kanienkehaka (Mohawk) from Kanesatake, Kahnawake, and Akwesasne reserves—that lasted 78 days in total. In 1959, a private nine-hole golf course had been built on a portion of land that the Kanienkehaka had claimed as an important meeting place and burial ground, but the claim had been rejected by the courts. In 1989, the golf course decided to expand with the addition of nine more holes and condominiums. The Kanienkehaka people went to court again to lay claim to the land and prevent development; however, the court again ruled in favour of the developer. As a result of the ruling, the Kanienkehaka communities constructed barriers blocking access to the area. The protest quickly turned violent between the police and the Kanienkehaka protestors, resulting in the military and the Canadian Royal Mounted Police being called in by the Canadian government to "diffuse" the situation. The Oka Crisis resulted in the development of a national First Nations Policing Policy in an attempt to prevent future incidents from escalating, and brought Indigenous issues to the forefront in Canadian politics (Marshall, 2013).

Beginning in 2012 and currently ongoing, Idle No More has been the largest Indigenous mass movement in Canadian history to date. It calls on all people to join together to honour Indigenous sovereignty and to protect their land and water. This grassroots movement originally began as a protest to what was perceived as the abuse of Indigenous treaty rights by the Stephen Harper government. Beginning as a National Day of Action on 10 December 2012, the movement has since sparked hundreds of rallies, teach-ins, and protests across Canada. The movement continues to draw millions of people to social media accounts in an effort to reaffirm Indigenous inheritance rights to sovereignty and to protect land and waters from ongoing corporate dissemination. By 2013, the Assembly of First Nations and other chiefs began using the Idle No More movement to press Ottawa on treaty rights and improved living standards (Bradshaw & McCarthy, 2012).

Johl Whiteduck Ringuette is chef and owner of Anishinabe restaurant NishDish in Toronto, Ontario. NishDish offers traditional Indigenous foods as part of a larger goal to bring traditions back and keep them alive while also encouraging knowledge sharing between Indigenous and non-Indigenous communities. Riguette says of his restaurant, "It's really a reclamation of our food sovereignty, bringing back our food, what's best for our community." Individual projects like this one work alongside larger projects to retain and reclaim Indigenous knowledge and culture.

Important Indigenous organizations, such as the Assembly of First Nations (AFN) and the Inuit Tapiriit Kanatami (ITK) act on behalf of their member nations. Nations also work individually to gain sovereignty and uphold their treaty rights. There are also countless individual activists, artists, lawyers, and more, who work to improve the conditions and attitudes their communities face.

On 11 June 2008, Prime Minister Stephen Harper, accompanied by 11 Indigenous leaders, addressed a filled House of Commons to present a formal apology to First Nations, Métis, and Inuit peoples for the trauma caused by the residential school system and for the effects that persist to this day. In conjunction with some survivors of these schools, the Assembly of First Nations and several other Indigenous organizations, a settlement agreement was reached. It granted survivors "common experience payments," education credits, social support programs to aid in the healing process, and commemorative activities allowing for "the opportunity to pay tribute to, honour,

educate, remember, and memorialize their experiences by acknowledging the systematic impacts of the residential school system" (Indigenous and Northern Affairs Canada, 2014). This was a small first step. Nonetheless, it was an achievement worth noting for those who have worked hard to address the dark legacy of the residential school system. Prime Minister Justin Trudeau has extended that apology to those in Newfoundland and Labrador (Bartlett, 2017).

Because of the efforts of the Idle No More movement, the Truth and Reconciliation Commission, the

"Stories from the Rivers Edge"

Host Gillian Findlay, *The Fifth Estate* (2011). A documentary by the CBC that presents a stark look at the Indigenous high school system in Thunder Bay, Ontario.

Final Report of the National Inquiry into Missing and Murdered Indigenous Women and Girls, and countless others, there has been movement toward seeing Indigenous Peoples as partners and allies, separate but equal, in the spirit of the original treaties.

> **charter groups** Canadians of British and French ancestry; so named because settlers from England and France first came to what is now Canada with royal permission to trade and settle (i.e., royal charters).

The Charter Groups

The **charter groups** are made up of ethnically British and French people. Charter status makes these groups politically, economically, and socially dominant over everyone else within what is now Canada. The source of this status is historical: *charter groups* are the groups that set up the institutions and rules for the new society. Often, they ignored or intentionally suppressed the claims of those who were conquered, colonized, or subsumed into the new government. While Indigenous Peoples were pivotal to the foundation and success of Canada as a country, the agreements made with them in the form of treaties were regularly disrespected or unfairly interpreted, and because of the actions and inactions of the Canadian state, many Indigenous people died. Both the French and British charter groups shaped Canada's institutions during the country's first century of nationhood.

Despite being a smaller fraction of the population today, charter group members still exercise a dominant influence on Canadian society for several reasons. For one thing, they remain the largest of Canada's ethnic groups: indeed, 32.5 per cent of the Canadian population report as ethnically originating from the British Isles, and 13.6 per cent report French origin; also, 32.3 per cent of the country report their ethnic origin as "Canadian" (Statistics Canada, 2017b). As well, some of Canada's other ethnic groups have spread themselves unevenly (and sometimes thinly) around the nation. By contrast, most French Canadians are in Quebec, where they make up over 80 per cent of the population (Statistics Canada, 2012). In Quebec, this numerical majority has helped maintain French Canadian control over the provincial government, allowing them to take steps to clinch their political, economic, and cultural control.

It is primarily the maintained control over systems of power that have helped to maintain English and French dominance within Canada. Immigrants from other ethnicities, primarily European, have also benefited from this dominance by being seen as "white," or closer to white, and therefore more desirable to the dominant group than visible minority immigrants. While some of these groups also experienced discrimination (such as Ukrainians in World War I, who at the time were not seen as truly white [Luciuk, 2018]), they still benefited from their whiteness in being accepted as immigrants to Canada at all and have since been more accepted in the dominant group. A few of the many ways in which the Canadian state has explicitly and implicitly ensured that structures and systems benefit white Canadians has already been discussed, and will be discussed further below.

Visible/Racialized Minorities

Some of the first non-Indigenous people to come to what would become Canada were racialized, although the history of Canada often excludes these people from the story. Black slaves were brought by slave owners settling in Canada as early as 1629, and many black people came to Canada to flee slavery in the US between 1834 (when slavery was abolished in British colonies) and 1865. Chinese people were also major settlers in the 1800s (along with Ukrainian, German, and other European settlers) and were instrumental in creating the railroad that spanned both coasts.

Anxiety about culturally and racially different immigrants has been a feature of Canadian life for as long as settlement has occurred here. One sign of this anxiety was the head tax imposed on Chinese immigrants, which came into effect in 1885. This tax, a prohibitive fee on anyone from China entering Canada, was implemented once the railway was complete as an attempt to keep out Chinese immigrants (McRae, 2017). When this was deemed not effective enough, the Chinese Immigration Act was passed in 1923. Until 1947, this act continued to bar all but a few new Chinese immigrants from settling in Canada. After the Second World War, this repressive immigration act was finally abolished and Chinese immigrants were accepted in large numbers (McRae, 2017). Similarly, black immigration was seen as unwanted, and a proposal to ban black immigration to Canada was written and signed by Sir Wilfrid Laurier in 1911, although it was not enacted as it was an election year (Skelton, 1965). Still, border agents at the US–Canada border did everything they could to discourage black immigrants to Canada (Skelton, 1965).

These are just two examples of a more widespread general dislike or distrust of racialized minorities throughout Canada's history. After the changes to immigration laws and reduced restrictions that came in the 1960s, racialized immigrants began to come to Canada in much higher numbers. And as we have seen in Chapter 6, despite having high credentials at the time of immigration, immigrants, especially visible minority and racialized immigrants, remain highly disadvantaged in Canada.

Current Research

Experiences of Senior Immigrants to Canada

Mandell, Lam, Borres, and Phonepraseuth (2018) examined the experiences of senior immigrants in Canada. Their research first relied on census data to map economic security among seniors in different regions and ethnicities in Canada. Secondly, they held 13 focus groups with 110 participants from different ethnicities: Asian, South Asian, West Asian, Caribbean, South American, and European. Lastly, they held interviews with 31 individuals spanning the 13 focus groups.

Their research revealed that senior immigrants experience aging differently from the rest of the population because of the intersection of gender, race, and migration. Mandell et al. (2018) argue that racialization has a profoundly negative impact on the life courses of senior immigrants. Their participants communicated numerous examples of racialization in schooling, employment, and everyday encounters in their lives. Racialization took different forms, from overt discrimination in workplaces to covert discrimination on the basis of language and communication (Mandell et al., 2018). Perhaps most troubling were the incidents reported of difficulties in conversing with persons in authority, which led to ongoing negative encounters throughout their lives. These included interactions with school officials, teachers, doctors, police, and lawyers.

Furthermore, racial profiling and discrimination were described as commonplace throughout the racialized immigrants' lives in Canada. Black participants told stories of being called "chocolate" and being told that they "come from the same place as Ganja." Participants also told stories describing blatant racism directed toward Asians and blacks in the workplace.

All of these experiences contributed to the economic insecurity that immigrants, but especially racialized immigrants, experience as they become seniors in Canada.

All Saints

Dir. Steve Gomer (2017). An American film that tackles the story of Burmese immigrants who settle in a small Tennessee town and help revive a Christian church.

Indeed, research has shown that employers prefer to substitute recent immigrant employees with native-born minorities (Waters & Eschbach, 1995). Moreover, immigrants to Canada are often racially profiled and are, thus, disproportionately targeted by police compared to the rest of the population (Hanniman, 2008). This is just to name a few additional barriers and forms of discrimination that racialized immigrants face in Canada today.

These difficulties are not only experienced by new immigrants to Canada. Canadian-born visible minorities also continue to face disadvantage in the workforce. According to the Conference Board of Canada (2017), university-educated, Canadian-born members of a visible minority earn on average 87.4 cents for every dollar earned by their Caucasian peers. This gap changes depending on ethnic ancestry—for example, individuals of Japanese ancestry earned 3.7 per cent more, while individuals of Latin American ancestry earned on average 31.7 per cent less than their white peers (Conference Board of Canada, 2017). On average, black Canadian-born men earn 80.4 cents for every dollar of a white Canadian-born man (see Figure 9.2). And despite being just as likely to attend university, racialized individuals continue to earn less and be unemployed more than white Canadians (Conference Board of Canada, 2017). Again, these are just a few of the systemic inequalities that sociologists look to in order to find where and how racism works within Canada.

As with Indigenous groups, visible minority Canadians have fought for equal rights, political representation, and justice throughout their history within Canada. To provide just a few examples, during the 1783 American Revolution, as many as 10,000 escaped slaves fought alongside the British in exchange for their freedom. Once the war ended, the majority were relocated to Nova Scotia with almost 1500 moving to Shelburne County—most of whom ended up in Birchtown. Birchtown had the largest free population of black people in North America. In 1784, however, a group of settlers attacked Shelburne County, targeting the black population in what became known as the first race riot in North America. The black population soon came to the realization that their "freedom" did not mean that they would receive equal treatment. Not only were they unprotected from attack, the land they had

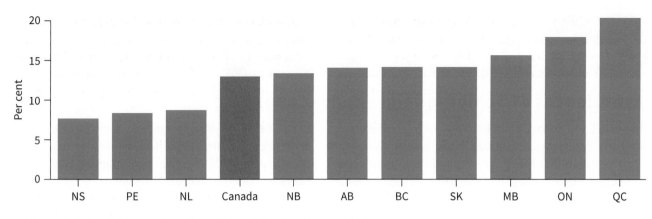

Figure 9.2 **Racial Wage Gap, Canada and the Provinces, 2010**

Source: http://www.conferenceboard.ca/hcp/provincial/society/racial-gap.aspx

been promised was slow to be allocated and was always in worse locations than that of the white population. More than half of the free black people of Birchtown left for Sierra Leone in 1792 and helped to found Freetown, the nation's capital city.

Chinese Canadians also worked hard to end the Chinese Immigration Act. After volunteering for service in the Second World War, and raising $10 million for victory bonds between 1939 and 1943, Chinese Canadians demanded an end to the Chinese Immigration Act. In 1947 they demanded enfranchisement (the right to vote) (Roy, 2008).

Racialized communities were also instrumental in rallying for the removal of racist barriers to immigration in the 1960s.

In 2013, social media lit up with the use of #BlackLivesMatter after George Zimmerman was acquitted in the shooting death of unarmed teen Trayvon Martin in Florida, leading to the formation of the Black Lives Matter movement in the United States. In 2014, 33-year-old Jermaine Corby was shot to death in a routine traffic stop in Brampton, Ontario, and in 2015 Toronto police killed Andrew Loku, a 45-year-old Sudanese father of five who was suffering from mental illness. These two

World Events

Islamophobia

Countries from around the Western World are all suffering to some extent from persistent Islamophobia—open hostility toward all Muslims based on fear. In September 2001, the actions of a small number of extremists captured the attention of media outlets worldwide and reinforced the stereotypes of Muslim men as violent and evil. Just as there are many denominations in Christianity or any other religion, there are various branches of Islam. There are secular and progressive Muslims who generally do not make headlines, and at the extreme end of the spectrum one finds a minority of radical and extremist Muslims—those whose actions the media generally fixates upon (Marcote, 2010). As a result, Muslims—or anyone perceived to be Muslim

based on racist stereotypes—are "othered," which has reinforced the status of Arabs living in non-Arab countries as the "enemy within" (Fleras, 2010).

In fact, less than 2.5 per cent of all terrorist attacks in the United States from 1970 to 2012 were carried out by Islamic extremists (Centre for Research on Globalization, 2013); similarly, a little under 8 per cent of all terrorist attacks across Europe were linked to Islamic extremists (Europol, 2015). In spite of these official statistics, Muslim men and women continue to face severe scrutiny worldwide because of Islamophobia. In Canada, for example, instances of hate crimes against Muslims have risen 253 per cent in the past five years (Minsky, 2017).

shootings of black men in Canada sparked a chapter of the Black Lives Matter movement in Toronto, which quickly spread across Canada. The shootings of young black men at the hands of police have continued across North America, but the Black Lives Matter movement has remained strong and aimed at resisting anti-black racism in Canada and internationally (Black Lives Matter Toronto, 2019).

More recently, Muslim communities and their allies have rallied against Islamophobia across the globe. In 2017, rallies were sparked across Canada after people in a mosque were shot at in Quebec; six people were killed. The rallies denounced the US travel ban on people from Muslim countries as well as Canada's Zero Tolerance for Barbaric Cultural Practices Act, which critics say unnecessarily targets Muslim people (and makes them a target for law enforcement) (Draaisma, 2017). Canada continues to see acts of racism, as well as acts of resistance to racism, across the country.

> **Islamophobia** Prejudice or discrimination toward Muslim people.
>
> **genocide** The state-sanctioned murder of people who belong to a particular group based on any number of traits (race, ethnicity, religion, sexual orientation, ability, etc.) with the intention of eradicating that group.

Patterns of Intergroup Relations

Globalization and more open borders have resulted in many heterogeneous countries with a diversity of races, cultures, ethnicities, languages, religions, and media. Sociologists use four main categories to help classify the ways that dominant groups interact with minority groups: genocide (or expulsion), segregation, assimilation, and pluralism/multiculturalism.

Genocide

Genocide is the deliberate extermination of a large group of people, especially those of a particular ethnic group or nation. Genocide is most likely to occur when the dominant group is much larger than the minority and when the minority group is of little economic value to the dominant group (duPreez, 1994).

There are many horrible examples of genocide in human history, some of which were mentioned at the start of this chapter. The most infamous historical genocide, and the one for which the term was coined, is the Holocaust, where Hitler and his Nazi regime exterminated six million Jewish, homosexual, disabled, and Romani people during World War II. In the 1970s, the Khmer Rouge in Cambodia killed approximately two million of their own people in an attempt to halt Western influences. In 1994, the Hutu massacred 800,000 Tutsi in Rwanda in 100 days. This was due to the imposition of a colonialist system by the British whereby the government gave the minority population (Tutsi) various advantages over the Hutu, such as a Western-style education. And in Syria, since 2014, over 10,000 Syrians have been killed due to civil war.

Although Canada does not have as infamous a reputation as other countries, we too have taken part in genocides in our history. Germ warfare, starvation, malnutrition, and armed conflict were just some of the early tactics used against various First Nations and Inuit within what is now Canada, resulting in several genocides that continue through to today. The Beothuk, for example, lived in what is now known as Newfoundland with a population of approximately 1000 people prior to European settlers taking over their land. By 1829 no known living member of the Beothuk remained. Blankets contaminated with smallpox were proposed and possibly implemented in several areas across what is now Canada in a deliberate attempt at genocide; whether these were effective in spreading smallpox to Indigenous groups or whether the disease spread on its own, populations were devastated by the disease in the late 1700s and through the 1800s, even though vaccination was practised in North America starting in 1798, meaning that the spread of this disease could, in theory, have been stopped.

As mentioned at the beginning of the chapter, genocide of Indigenous Peoples continues in Canada today, largely through the accumulated atrocities of the past and the inaction of the present. For example, in 2016, 105 Indigenous communities did not have access to clean water—a commodity taken for granted by Canada's settler population (Government of Canada, 2017). This is largely the result of the purposeful placement of reserves by the Canadian government on undesirable land that is often near environmental hazards and expensive to maintain in terms of infrastructure (Assembly of First Nations Environmental Stewardship Unit, 2005). Again, the past discrimination combined with the present reluctance to invest in undoing our past wrongs has resulted in the deaths of Indigenous people at disproportionate rates compared to the Canadian population as a whole (see also Chapter 12).

Expulsion

Rather than kill the minority group, dominant groups may force a minority group to leave a region or may confine them to one particular location. In 1979, nearly a million ethnic Chinese were expelled from Vietnam, partly as a result of hostility between Vietnam and China. In a more recent example, since 2003 approximately 2.4 million people have been displaced from Sudan. A United Nations (2014) report states that today approximately 43 million people around the world are displaced as a result of conflict and/or persecution. Of these, many have fled their home countries; however, the majority are displaced within their own country. Canada's history also includes the expulsion of one group at the hands of another. In the mid to late 1700s, the British military's campaign against New France included the "Great Upheaval" of the Acadian population, in which the British government deported almost the entire population of Acadians from the Maritime provinces (Faragher, 2006).

More recently, the Canadian government forcibly expelled and confined Japanese citizens into internment camps during the Second World War (Nakana, 2012). During the war 22,000 Japanese Canadians were removed from the coastline of British Columbia, taken from their homes, separated from their families, and put into camps (McAllister, 1999).

Segregation

While often not as violent as genocide and expulsion, many places deal with intergroup relations through segregation. Segregation is the physical separation of groups of people in terms of residence, workplace, and other social structures. African Americans in the Southern United States lived under segregation laws for the first half of the twentieth century with separate schools, seating sections, washrooms, and even drinking fountains.

In another example, from 1948 until 1990 South Africa severely restricted the movement of blacks by means of segregation known as apartheid. During apartheid, blacks were expected to live in particular areas, work specific jobs, and not be seen in white areas. After decades of local resistance, combined with international pressure, apartheid was dismantled. In 1994, Nelson Mandela, one of the most prominent and vocal anti-apartheid activists, was elected the country's president. This was the first election that blacks—who are the majority of the population—were allowed to vote. Mandela had previously spent 28 years in prison for his anti-apartheid activities (Jones, 2019).

While it was not encoded in federal law, Canadian society also included racial segregation in all facets of social life. For example, some provinces had segregated black schools. The last Canadian segregated school closed in Nova Scotia in 1983 (Historca Canada, n.d.). Although segregation is no longer enforced in Canada, resources are still allocated along racial and ethnic lines, and metropolitan areas are often "unofficially" segregated by race and/or ethnicity (Fong, 2017).

Assimilation

Assimilation is the process by which one forgoes his or her own culture and traditions and assumes the traits of the dominant group. Usually it is a minority group that wants to conform to the standards of the dominant group that practises assimilation. One of the ways that white supremacy functions is by making others desire to be coded as white, encouraging assimilation. Assimilation is also often involuntary. Post-World War II (and post-internment), Japanese-Canadians were forced to assimilate into Canadian culture as much and as quickly as possible to avoid what the government called "repatriation" to Japan (though since most of the individuals being sent back to Japan were Canadian-born, this was more realistically a deportation). Canada passed orders in council that allowed the government to evaluate the loyalty of any Japanese-Canadian, and deport whomever they saw fit (CBC, n.d.). Japanese-Canadians felt pressure to 'prove' themselves as Canadian (and not a threat) by cooperating fully in resettlement programs, committing to getting Canadian educations, and through marrying outside their racial group (Stearns, 2010).

As another example of assimilation that still occurs today, sometimes people change their name in order to sound more British in order to avoid being discriminated against, such as in the job application studies discussed earlier in the chapter. Name changes are common practice in Hollywood and within the music industry. Stars such as Chloe Bennet (Chloe Wang), Bruno Mars (Peter Gene Hernandez), Nina Dobrev (Nikolina Konstantinova Dobreva), Nicky Jam (Nick Rivera Caminero), Alessia

> **segregation** The physical separation of groups of people in terms of residence, workplace, and other social structures.
>
> **apartheid** A policy of institutionalized racial segregation as well as political and economic racism. The term was first used in South Africa to describe the policies of South African and West South African (Namibian) governments from 1948 to 1994.
>
> **assimilation** The process by which members of a minority group adopt the cultural traits (including language, food, traditions, etc.) of the dominant culture; may be voluntary or forced.

Prior to rising to international stardom with his song "Just the Way You Are," Bruno Mars went by his given name Peter Gene Hernandez. Hernandez changed his name to Bruno Mars so that he would not be stereotyped as a Latin singer and would more easily assimilate into the mainstream American music industry.

Cara (Alessia Caracciolo), and Nicki Minaj (Onika Tanya Maraj) are just a few examples of those who have changed their names in order to improve their popularity.

Pluralism and Multiculturalism

Since its foundation as a colonial state, Canada has consisted of multiple different groups of people from different ethnic origins. These groups have mostly been eager to keep their distinct cultural features in order to preserve their identity and

> **pluralism** A philosophy that urges tolerance for racial/ethnic differences and protects the rights of minority individuals through provincial human rights codes and other legislation, while maintaining the dominance of the hegemonic group.

remain conscious of who they are and where they came from. For the most part, Canadian minorities have kept their cultures alive while living among members of other dominant and subordinate ethnic groups. This is referred to as **pluralism**, where minority ethnic groups are able to maintain their unique cultural practices and identities while a dominant culture is retained. A common metaphor to describe pluralism is the "melting pot," since even though distinct cultures are seen as valuable in pluralism, their value is seen in terms of what they add to the dominant culture (Mack, 1994).

Multiculturalism, in contrast, refers to a form of political thought that advocates for distinct and separate ethnicities and cultures and respect for all associated religions and customs, without the presence of a dominant culture. Multiculturalism is often likened to a "salad bowl," whereby all distinct ethnic groups live alongside one another without any group sitting on top.

The difference between these terms has consequences for policy implementation. Traditional pluralism has laws to protect minority individuals and, in that way, protects minority groups. Multiculturalism, however, works in the opposite way: it protects minority groups, with the expectation that this will also protect minority individuals. In practice, pluralism promotes assimilation while multiculturalism promotes ethnic distinctiveness and the maintenance of distinct groups. Contemporary Canada purports to be, or at least claims to aspire to be, multicultural, and since the 1970s Canadian policy mostly uses this word. However, in practice "Canadian multiculturalism" has been a kind of pluralism rather than multiculturalism in its purest form (Burnet & Driedger, 2014).

The four classifications above focus on the dominant group's approaches rather than on the actions of the subordinate groups. As we have seen, subordinate groups are anything but passive in their own histories. Their actions often involve resistance and can take many forms— from leaving entirely, to forming a new government, to changing the government from within, to building a groundswell that forces the government to change, to working within the current system to improve conditions for a particular group, to embracing assimilation as a survival strategy. All of these strategies have been employed at one time or another to counteract or otherwise influence the intergroup strategies discussed above.

Top 10 Takeaways

1 Race and ethnicity are social constructs. — pp. 168–170

2 Minority groups are those that have less power and control over their own lives than dominant groups. Visible minority in Canada refers to those Canadians who are neither white nor Indigenous. — pp. 170–171

3 Stereotypes are used to justify prejudice and discrimination. Prejudice involves thought while discrimination involves action. — pp. 171–172

4 Racism involves the process of othering, whereby we classify someone as not one of us. — pp. 172–177

5 Racial and ethnic discrimination are serious issues within Canada, including the Canadian labour market. — pp. 172–177

6 Functionalists argue that there are few practical consequences of ethnicity other than that it's a part of your identity. Racism is dysfunctional for society, so functionalists assume racism will resolve itself. — p. 177

7 Symbolic interactionists stress the link between ethnicity and identity. The contact hypothesis contends that the more interaction there is between people the less prejudice there will be. — p. 177

8 Conflict theorists use the exploitation theory to argue that racism is used to keep minority groups subordinate. Feminists argue that it's not just racism but also the intersection of race, gender, age, ability, and sexuality that maintain subordination in different ways. — pp. 177, 179

9 Indigenous and visible minority people have always existed within the country of Canada and have consistently pushed back against the discriminatory practices and racism in Canada throughout its history. — pp. 179–185

10 Societies deal with intergroup relations differently. The four most significant strategies of the dominant group are genocide or expulsion, assimilation, segregation, and pluralism or multiculturalism. — pp. 185–187

Questions for Critical Thinking

1. Explain what is meant when sociologists state that race is a social construction rather than a biological fact.

2. In South Africa, the majority of the population is black; however, blacks are seen as a minority in sociological terms. Explain how this is possible. How would a conflict theorist approach this explanation?

3. Choose any two stereotypes that you can think of that are related to race. Do research on the statistical significance of the stereotype, using at least one source by someone from the community that your stereotype was about. Is there evidence that the stereotype is a fact? If there is, can you think of any problems with how we gather data on topics such as this? How difficult was it to find a published scholar doing research on his or her own community?

4. Discuss some examples of "othering" that is occurring across North America. How have these particular groups been othered?

5. Explain any personal situations you may have encountered where you, or someone you were with, were the recipient of discrimination because of race. If you have not ever experienced this, reflect on why that might be.

6. Critique the functionalist perspective that race and ethnicity have few practical consequences.

7. Reflect on your upbringing with your family. Do you hold the same views as your parents/grandparents/caregivers regarding other races? How might symbolic interactionism account for generational differences in prejudice and racism?

8. Drawing upon Chapter 6 ("Class Inequality")," Chapter 7 (Gender"), and this chapter ("Race" and Racialization), explain disadvantage according to a feminist perspective. Explain why these three chapters are of particular concern to feminists.

9. Discuss the ways in which Canada specifically deals with intergroup conflicts.

10. How does disadvantage differ in Canadian society depending upon which ethnic group you belong to?

Recommended Readings

- **Fleras, A. (2016).** *Immigration Canada: Evolving Realities and Emerging Challenges in a Postnational World.* **Vancouver: UBC Press.** In this book, Fleras analyzes admission policies, refugee processing systems, the temporary foreign worker program, and the emergence of transnational identities.

- **Maynard, R. (2017).** *Policing Black Lives.* **Blackpoint, NS: Fernwood Publishing.** Maynard dispels myths about Canada as the land of racial equality by providing evidence of long-standing state practices that have restricted and continue to restrict black freedom.

- **Mills, S. (2016).** *A Place in the Sun: Haiti, Haitians and the Making of Quebec.* **Montreal/Kingston:** **McGill–Queen's University Press.** Mills explores the relationship between migration and politics in Quebec. He examines the ways that Haitian migrants both intervened in and shaped Quebec society. By drawing on the experiences of Haitian taxi drivers, exiled priests, aspiring authors, dissident intellectuals, and feminist activists, Mills challenges the view that migrants were peripheral to Quebec history.

- **Vowel, C. (2016).** *Indigenous Writes: A Guide to First Nations, Metis and Inuit Issues in Canada.* **Winnipeg, MB: Highwater Press.** In this book, Vowel discusses the fundamental issues of relationships; culture and identity; myth-busting; state violence; and land, learning, law, and treaties as experienced by Indigenous Peoples in Canada.

Recommended Websites

Diversity and Segregation in Canadian Cities
https://www.dshkol.com/2018/diversity-and-segregation-canadian-cities/
- This blog post by Dmitry Shkolnik uses heat maps to visually illustrate rates of segregation in cities across Canada.

The Black Experience Project
https://www.theblackexperienceproject.ca/
- The Black Experience Project was a study of lived experience of individuals who self-identify as black and/or of African heritage living in the Greater Toronto Area.

Whose Land
https://www.whose.land/en/
- This map illustrates the territories of various Indigenous groups across what is now Canada, providing background information about the treaties and agreements that cover the area, as well as information about Indigenous Peoples and their relationship to land.

Deadly Force
https://newsinteractives.cbc.ca/longform-custom/deadly-force
- A CBC Interactive website that summarizes the research done by CBC reporters to determine the extent to which black people are disproportionately killed by police in Canada.

Never Home
http://www.neverhome.ca/
- A website illustrating the systemic, racist barriers to immigration to Canada throughout its history.

Renew: Stories of Indigenous Innovation
http://indigenousreporting.com/
- This collection of stories gives a brief glimpse into how Indigenous people are fighting to improve the conditions in which they live.

Chapter 10

Deviance and Crime

As we learned in Chapter 6, education is an important tool for gaining access to decent jobs, income, and benefits. In March of 2019, it was revealed that over 50 people had taken part in a college admissions scheme where young people were accepted as students at prestigious colleges across the United States in return for a bribe. These students were often accepted under the premise of being a talented athlete, even in instances where the applicant had no athletic ability whatsoever. The families involved in the scandal were among America's most affluent, including famous actresses Lori Loughlin (*Full House*) and Felicity Huffman (*Desperate Housewives, When They See Us*). Because these wealthy families were not considered deviant, their crimes went viral soon after discovery.

Often people use the terms *deviance* and *crime* interchangeably. But just as *sex* and *gender* differ in their definitions, so too do crime and deviance. This chapter explores crime, deviance, and a sub-field of sociology known as criminology.

▲ Jassica Rinaldi/The Boston Globe via Getty Images

Learning Outcomes

1. Compare formal and informal modes of social control
2. Explain the difference between crime and deviance
3. Recognize that crime and deviance are relative
4. Describe the classical approaches to crime and deviance
5. Distinguish between early approaches and sociological approaches to crime

Key Terms

crime

criminology

dark figure of crime

deviance

folkways

formal social control

informal social control

labelling theory

mores

positivism

rational choice theory

social control

social disorganization

strain theory

stigma

victimless crime

white-collar crimes

Introduction

The study of crime and deviance, perhaps counterintuitively, helps us understand the behaviour of Canadians in their everyday lives: from getting dressed, to how and what they eat, to waiting in line to get into a club, to sexual relationships. All of these are driven by normative behaviours. But committing an assault with a deadly weapon is also driven by normative behaviours. *Norms* are social expectations that guide and control both human behaviour and human interactions in all social situations. For example, when you first meet someone, do you make eye contact? Do you smile? Do you shake hands, or do you kiss on one or both cheeks? Do you bow? These are all specific norms based on culture that guide even our most basic interactions. Sociologists divide norms into four categories: folkways, mores, deviance, and laws (or social control).

Folkways are the customs that people take part in every day. Because we have learned these behaviours since childhood, they are tied to expectations of normalized behaviour. For example, if you say, "How are you?" to someone you don't know well, there is an expectation they will reply, "Good, and you?" If you get to a club and there is a line, you know to go to the end of that line and wait your turn. When you are going to a job interview, you will dress very differently than when you go to a club (unless the job interview is at the club!). If you eat ice cream. you will you use a spoon rather than a fork. All of these seem intuitive to us, but they are learned behaviours that are specific to our culture, in both place and time.

People may look at us strangely or express displeasure if we break these folkways, but there are no serious consequences. Someone might yell at us or even shove us if we butt in line, but we are not going to get arrested. We may not get hired if we dress incorrectly for a job interview, but we won't be banished from town for doing so. And while we may get some strange stares for eating ice cream with a fork, we won't be fined for violating this norm.

Mores refer to social norms that are widely observed and are considered to have greater moral significance than others. The consequences of violating mores is far more severe than breaking a folkway and can result in sanctions. For example, mores include an aversion against taboos, such as incest, cannibalism, adultery, plagiarism, and sex before marriage. Depending on where you live, you may be arrested, banished, or fined for violating these mores.

folkways The customs that people take part in every day, such as holding open a door for someone walking behind you or not putting your elbows on the table while you eat.

mores Social norms that are widely observed and are considered to have greater moral significance than others.

deviance An action, behaviour, or state of being that leads to a negative reaction or response from a community or group.

Deviance and Social Control

Deviance is the violation of established social norms, actions, or behaviours. We must ask ourselves these questions: What are the accepted standards and social expectations around behaviours in a particular culture, and how are they defined as such? To what degree

Konstantin Kolosov/Shutterstock

more socially acceptable in Canada than in some other countries around the world.

When no one feels threatened by an action or activity—for example, by seeing someone with a beard—people are likely to view the behaviour as an expression of individuality: perhaps eccentric (depending on the beard) but not threatening and therefore not deviant. Reactions to uncommon, peculiar, and eye-catching behaviour depend largely on how the behaviour is viewed. For an act to be considered "deviant," other people have to respond to it in a particular way. They must try to control or eliminate the act and punish the actor. It is only through the response of the external social world that a behaviour becomes classified as deviant. This response is what sociologists call social control.

Social Control

Social control refers to all the institutions and procedures that force members of society to conform to rules of expected behaviour. The operation of social control is most obvious when it is *formal*, especially when the police and the courts enforce written laws. Formal social control gives specific people (such as police officers) the responsibility to enforce specific laws, using specific methods of enforcement. At the same time, ordinary people exercise another kind of social control that sociologists call informal social control. They do this through gossip, praise, or blame, among other things. In small communities, informal social controls are very effective at keeping social order.

Informal social controls are also effective in large, industrialized societies such as our own. This kind of control works because all humans seek the approval of others in order to obtain self-worth. Along with the threat of legal sanctions (e.g., fines or imprisonment), feelings of guilt and shame can be an important means of social control, even where crimes such as tax fraud, petty theft, and drunk driving are concerned. People may be more afraid of being publicly shamed for committing these actions than of the legal repercussions for doing so.

Most students will agree that having a tattoo is not deviant in our current society. Let's think through the idea that having a tattoo is not worthy of the label of deviance. Does your answer change if someone has 100 tattoos instead of 1? Does it matter where a tattoo is located? For example, if your tattoo is on your face, is that still socially acceptable? This thought experiment helps to illustrate that these rules can be complicated and can be difficult to articulate to people from other cultures.

does your notion of proper or acceptable conduct match those of your classmates or strangers? Is it possible that some of your behaviours would be considered unacceptable by others?

Deviance is socially constructed and is subjective: what is considered deviant in one place may not be considered deviant in another. Moreover, what is deviant during one time period may not be during another, even in the same location. Tattoos, for example, are more common in Canada now than they were 30 years ago and are

> **social control** All the institutions and procedures that influence members of society to conform to rules of expected behaviour. See also *formal social control* and *informal social control*.
>
> **formal social control** An authorized procedure that defines how specific people (such as police officers) will enforce the rules and laws of a society. See also *informal social control*.
>
> **informal social control** The maintenance of order through non-legal means, including gossip, praise, blame, and stigma. See also *formal social control*.

Identity as Deviance

Some people are deviant in our society just by existing. Deviance also applies to identities that differ from the cultural hegemony, such as being a woman in a school program mostly attended by men, being black in an area that comprises mostly

Informal social controls, such as gossip, can seem harmless when being committed but can have tragic consequences. After the suicides of three Ontario teenagers who had been bullied, Ontario high school students and sisters Anisa and Saba Hajizadeh organized a summit to warn teenagers of the harmful effects of gossip and to declare schools "gossip-free" zones" (Vyhnak, 2011). The summit took place in Ajax, Ontario, and highlighted how gossip has become so prevalent that many of us don't even recognize that we are taking part in it. Why do you think people gossip? Do you think gossip can be harmful?

white people, being Muslim in a predominantly Christian culture, being disabled in an able-bodied society, or being transgender among mostly cisgender people. In these cases, the person has no control over being "deviant," but the world treats that person as though he or she has done something "wrong." Social control can come in a spectrum of extremes, including the following:

- Genocide (as discussed in Chapter 9)
- Making a person's identity illegal (e.g., arresting gay men for having sex or policing black people as though they are acting suspiciously just because they are black)
- Infrasture that excludes groups of people (e.g., making bathrooms inaccessible to people with mobility issues or making them gender-specific with no non-binary option and creating rules around who "counts" as which gender)
- Street harassment

- The assumption of cultural hegemony when creating societal rules (such as making Christian holidays statutory holidays, but requiring people of other faiths to make special arrangements in order to accommodate their religious requirements, which might cause tension at work)
- More benign everyday stereotypes (such as assuming a female engineering student is in the wrong building and offering to help her find her way)

Deviance Is Relative

People hold widely different views about a wide variety of acts. In respect to some behaviours, we may even find a conflict between the formal and informal norms—for example, marijuana use was culturally normative (you were unlikely to face social consequences for admitting you had tried marijuana) long before it was legal in Canada. In other words, there is often widespread *dis*agreement with the written law. This is due to the social and cultural relativity of deviance. What is accepted in one group, community, or society might be rejected—even abhorred—in another. In North America, for example, we see kissing as an act of intimacy between two people, and we might have assumed that act to be a universal display of affection. However, Jankowiak, Volsche, and Garcia (2015) discovered that more than half of 168 cultures around the world do not use the romantic-sexual kiss and instead view it as "gross." In Canada, it is also a norm to use a toilet seat; however, in many countries around the world sitting on a toilet seat is considered unsanitary. What is deviant in one time or place may not be considered deviant in another. In other words, deviance is always relative.

Crime

A crime is any act formally banned by law, specifically, in Canada, by the Criminal Code of Canada. Defining certain acts as crimes gives the state the authority to seek, apprehend, try, convict, and punish offenders, and the Criminal Code specifies a suitable range of punishments for each crime. Criminology is the scientific approach to the study of the causes of crime, the ways to prevent crime, and the punishment and rehabilitation of those who break the law. It is a sub-field of sociology that also draws on psychology, political science, law, history, and anthropology. Criminology focuses on understanding causes, patterns, and trends of crime. Sociologists who study crime are interested in both the social context in which crime occurs, as well as the contexts within which laws are created and enforced. Taking a sociological approach to crime often means considering structural factors, such as poverty and racism, in explanations of what is considered a crime, how particular laws are enforced, and why particular people commit crimes.

Although crime and deviance are often conflated, the two are separate phenomena that can at times overlap. Crime is an action (or an omission to act) that has been designated as requiring formal social intervention. Deviance, on the other hand, involves actions or behaviours that violate social norms, which may or may not have formal interventions attached. Not all deviance is a crime, as you may have realized by now based on the chapter so far. Similarly, some actions or behaviours are criminal yet not viewed as deviant by the majority of society. For example, most drivers do not believe that driving 120 kilometres per hour in a 100 kilometre per hour zone on the highway is deviant, but it *is* technically against the law. Alternatively, some people believe

that a 40-year-old woman having a sexual relationship with a 20-year-old man is deviant; however, it is legal. Many actions and behaviours in society are both criminal and deviant: murder, sexual assault, kidnapping, and theft are just some examples. Of particular interest to sociologists is how certain behaviours become defined as deviant and/or criminal while others do not. For example, why did Canada legalize marijuana when it did? Why was 19 deemed as the lawful age to consume and purchase marijuana in most provinces and territories in Canada, when 18 is considered the age of majority where one can vote and is legally considered an adult? Why would this age restriction vary between provinces—for example, why do only Alberta and Quebec use 18 as the legal age for purchasing marijuana? Why does Manitoba have different age restrictions for marijuana (19) and alcohol (18)?

Criminologists, then, are concerned with these shifting and culturally relevant definitions of deviant behaviour and how they often influence our ideas about crime and criminality. In other words, criminologists study how crime becomes socially constructed. For example, 40 years ago it was common to see many people smoking cigarettes at parks, in banks, at doctor's offices, and even in some post-secondary classrooms. But, over the past 15 years, smoking has become increasingly deviant, and, as a result, many smoking laws have been put into effect to prevent this behaviour in public settings (and at times in private settings, even in one's own vehicle if children are present). In contrast, smoking marijuana has historically been viewed as deviant behaviour and thus has been controlled through sometimes strict laws. As the use of marijuana has become more normalized, the laws on its use have become more tolerant.

Within the bounds of the Criminal Code, we find many kinds of crime. Most offences have a victim or (as in the case of drunken driving) run a serious risk of causing someone else serious harm. There are, however, victimless crimes. No one suffers directly from these acts, except perhaps the people engaged in the behaviour and their families. Such victimless crimes include gambling, possessing drugs, and parking illegally. These are crimes because the Criminal Code defines them as such, making their perpetrators subject to legal action. These victimless crimes are more often debated and their criminal status more likely to change over time than, for example, robbery or arson.

We know a great deal about the prevalence of certain crimes, including murder and kidnapping. That's because occurrences of these crimes are often reported

> **crime** Any act formally prohibited by criminal law.
>
> **criminology** The interdisciplinary approach to the study of what gets defined as a crime, the causes of crime, the ways to prevent crime, and the punishment and rehabilitation of those who break the law.
>
> **victimless crime** A category of crime from which no one suffers directly except perhaps the persons engaging in the behaviour.

In the News

Marijuana Crackdowns and Pardons

On 20 April 2016, federal health minister Jane Philpott announced that the Liberal government would introduce legislation to legalize marijuana in the spring of 2017. Less than a month later, Toronto police conducted "Project Claudia," a large, coordinated series of raids on 43 marijuana dispensaries, where 90 people were arrested and 257 charges were laid (Westoll, 2017). On 17 October 2018, marijuana was officially legalized across Canada. However, those who had been charged with drug crimes prior to legalization were left with those charges on their record, some of whom were then unable to cross the border into the United States (Cain, 2019). The federal government passed legislation in the summer of 2019 to expedite the process for those with small possessions charges to be able to apply for pardons, which might otherwise have taken five to ten years (Harris, 2018). These pardons may or may not be considered at the border, but they will ensure that those with marijuana possessions charges will be able to state that they do not currently have a criminal record, which may previously have prevented them from being eligible for certain jobs. This brief summary of major events in criminal law and policy illustrates just how quickly and how significantly things can change, even in the same country.

---

to the police and recorded as official data. Of these reported crimes, a high percentage result in arrests and convictions. But people are much less willing to report some other crimes. Sexual assaults are an example: many women—most commonly the victims—fear the psychological, legal, and public humiliations that have often gone along with such reporting. In other words, being a *victim* of sexual assault is also treated by Canadian society as deviant. Movements such as the Me Too movement are intentional attempts to normalize sexual assault survival (see Chapter 7). Some studies suggest that only about 5 per cent of sexual assaults in Canada are brought to police attention (Perreault, 2015; Rotenberg & Cotter, 2018. Within this small 5 per cent, an even smaller percentage result in convictions (see Figure 10.1).

There are other crimes that are also likely to go unreported; these include robbery, break and enter, theft, selling drugs, and assault with a deadly weapon. Victims are often afraid to report attempts at extortion—demands for money coupled with a threat of physical violence—because they fear revenge by the person or people who committed the crime. Some crimes, such as successful cons, involve what Goffman called "cooling the mark out," which refers to hiding from a victimized person the fact that he or she has been conned at all. In other cases, these crimes are seen as too small or inconsequential to report, or victims do not expect anything to result from reporting the crime. Some of these crimes—in particular, theft of property that has lower value—are far less likely than violent crimes to be solved. For example, clearance rates for break-ins tend to hover around 30 per cent, while clearance rates for more serious physical assaults tend to hover around 70 per cent (Statistics Canada, 2015a).

Overall, only a small fraction of all law-breaking is reported to police, investigated, prosecuted, and charged as a crime. This

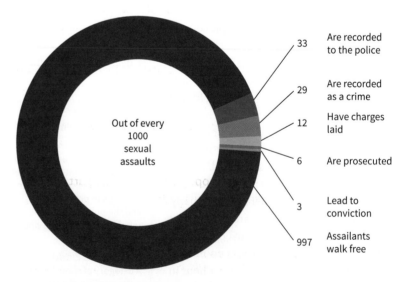

33	Are recorded to the police
29	Are recorded as a crime
12	Have charges laid
6	Are prosecuted
3	Lead to conviction
997	Assailants walk free

Out of every 1000 sexual assaults

Figure 10.1 Sexual Assaults in Canada

Source: See Winterdyk, *Canadian Criminology*, 3e, Figure 2.2, p. 42. Based on research by Dr Holly Johnson, copyright of YWCA Canada, used with permission.

Practising Sociology

What Is Deviant to You?

You have been hired to work as a social worker upon completion of your degree. Your very first job is with an adoption agency that requires you to assess potential homes for children. Every home you see is large; has a big, safe yard; and is financially secure. The only differences are those that you see listed below. Rank your choice of homes from 1 to 10, with 1 being your top choice of placement for the child.

When you are finished, get into groups of four with your classmates. Compare your top three choices with each other, as well as your last two choices. Reflect on the differences and similarities in choices. Why might your choices not be consistent across the class?

	This family has replaced their normal toilets with composting toilets. Their toilets are filled with sawdust, and after use, they remove the feces and place it in a compost bin in the backyard. Later, they use that compost on their plants.
	This family shares a bed with all of their children, infants through teenagers.
	This family belongs to an Indigenous community and practises a weekly ceremony that involves being in an extremely hot sweat lodge for about three hours at a time. They plan to include their new child in this practice.
	This family practises social nudity. They live in a "nudist colony" and do not wear clothing in their community.
	This family involves married parents who date and have sex with other people. They believe that they are in a stable marriage and that dating other people strengthens their relationship.
	This family includes a transgender parent. The parent was incorrectly assigned a female gender at birth but now identifies as a man, and will be the child's father.
	This family believes in opening their home to all. At any given time, they have various friends sleeping over, renting spaces, or otherwise living in their home. They also have about 15 animals (cats and dogs).
	This family adheres to extremely traditional gender roles. The wife does not speak unless spoken to, does not have access to family money, and prepares a separate meal for her husband, which he eats without her.
	This family are Scientologists. As part of their religion, they believe in restricting the use of medicine, particularly medicine for pain or fever.
	This family is openly racist and are part of a group trying to exclude African Americans from employment in Canada.

Source: This exercise was adapted from Ulrich, Monika J. 2010. "Deviance and a Social Construct: An In Class Activity." Class Activity published in *TRAILS: Teaching Resources and Innovations Library for Sociology*. Originally published 2003 in *Deviance and Social Control*, edited by B. Hoffman and A. Demyan. Washington DC: American Sociological Association. (http://trails.asanet.org)

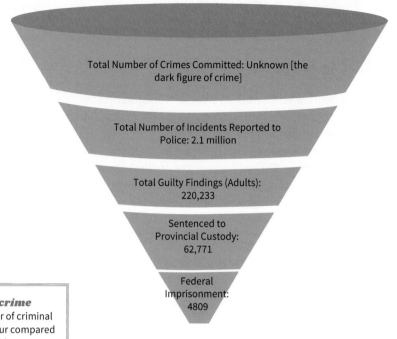

significant difference between the number of criminal incidents, reporting to police, and conviction is often called the **dark figure of crime**, or the crime funnel (see Figure 10.2).

Still, what we do know based on police-reported crime rates can tell us some things about the frequency and nature of crimes committed in Canada. For example, property crimes vastly outnumber violent crimes, and while crime

> **dark figure of crime**
> The actual number of criminal incidents that occur compared to the number of crimes reported to police, the number of crimes prosecuted, and the number of crimes that result in a conviction.

Figure 10.2 **The Crime Funnel**

Source: Adapted from Public Safety Canada (2018).

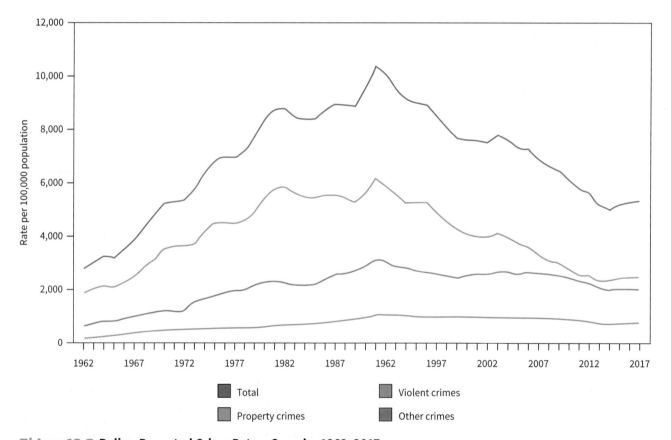

Figure 10.3 **Police-Reported Crime Rates, Canada, 1962–2017**

Source: https://www150.statcan.gc.ca/n1/daily-quotidien/180723/cg-b002-png-eng.htm

overall steadily decreased from 1992 to 2012, it has since started rising again in the past five years or so (see Figure 10.3). Criminologists look at these trends and investigate them to see what may be behind the change, and how these changes interrelate with what else is going on in society (for example: Do crime trends change when the economy changes?).

In earlier chapters, we have primarily provided an overview of the four main sociological theoretical approaches to the topic at hand. Because much of the discipline of criminology is focused on theorizing what causes people to commit crime, the process of how people become deviant or criminal, or how we might prevent crime, this chapter includes a much more in-depth theoretical section.

Major Perspectives on Crime and Deviance
Early Theories on Crime

During the Middle Ages, people in Europe believed that those who violated social norms were possessed. This approach to deviance and crime contended that demons, magic, and spirits worked together in mysterious ways to influence behaviour. The "presence" of these demons allowed for an easy explanation as to why a person would violate social norms. People believed to be witches and wizards were thought to possess the power to direct spirits or demons, so these individuals were held responsible for the deviant or criminal behaviour, rather than the perpetrators of the behaviour. It was during this time period that witch hunting emerged as a mechanism of social control. This approach had the effect of centralizing the control of deviance in the Catholic Church, but at this time the Church did not treat sinners with forgiveness or offer reconciliations; rather, punishment was usually physical and public.

In North America, the Salem witch trials occurred in Massachusetts between 1692 and 1693. The trials began after a couple of young girls in Salem Village, Massachusetts, claimed to be possessed by the devil and accused several local women of witchcraft. Hysteria spread throughout Massachusetts, resulting in a special court being convened for the more than 200 people who were accused of practising witchcraft (Blumberg, 2007). Twenty

Everett Historical/Shutterstock

This coloured woodcut from the sixteenth century depicts three women being executed as witches in Derneburg, Germany. Witch hunts in Europe often started in response to social strife, such as the frost that destroyed the harvest in the German region of Franconia in 1626 (Behringer, 2004). The hunt lasted four years and progressed from a hunt of poor, old women, to the city elite, including noblemen and -women (Behringer, 2004). Approximately 1500 executions were undertaken in this period alone.

people were hung as a result of the trials, although the spread of the hysteria resulted in even more deaths. Silvia Federici (2004) explains this phenomenon by pointing to the loss of labour power caused by the bubonic plague. According to Federici (2004), suspicions of witchcraft arose when the resulting lack of labour power caused state officials to criminalize women who practised medicine—particularly reproductive medicine—and grew herb gardens. Women used these herbs and medical knowledge to control their own fertility. For example, some herbs

The rational choice theory assumes that each person makes a calculated choice before entering into a criminal act. While this may be plausible for some crimes, is it likely for most?

grown by women during this time were known to induce abortion. Because this knowledge directly challenged the state's imperative to grow their decimated labour force, these women were demonized and accused of practising witchcraft as a means of social control.

By the mid-eighteenth century, there was a movement to revamp approaches to law making and punishment with a focus on balancing crime with its accompanying punishment (Seigel & McCormick, 2010). During this time period, Cesare Beccaria (1764), an Italian aristocrat, and Jeremy Bentham (1838), an English philosopher, argued that crime was not the result of supernatural forces but, rather, was purposeful. Beccaria and Bentham argued that committing crime produces a kind of pleasure for some; thus, pain is required in order to prevent criminal behaviour. This approach became known as the **rational choice theory** and is based on the position that crime is the result of a person's rational choice to commit it or not. This approach argues that if a crime requires little work for a large payout (think large drug deals) then people will be attracted to the unlawful behaviour. As a result, people must fear the punishment that they will receive if they are caught committing the crime more than they desire the reward from the crime. Similarly, criminal behaviour must be met with certain, swift, and severe punishment if society wants to control crime and criminal behaviour.

Biological Approaches

In the nineteenth century, theorists began to critique the classical approaches to criminal and deviant behaviour by arguing that the scientific method needed to be applied to the study of crime. This school of thought became known as **positivism** and focused on the level of the individual, specifically biology. Positivists believed that if we could identify the specific physical features distinguishing criminals from non-criminals, we would then be able to figure out how to prevent and control criminal behaviour. This view came to be known as *biological determinism*. Cesare Lombroso (1835–1909) was a major proponent of this approach. While a physician in the army, Lombroso performed a postmortem on a notorious criminal and found that the criminal shared skeletal characteristics most commonly associated with animals. In an attempt to apply the scientific method (positivism) to the study of criminals, Lombroso argued that some individuals were born to be criminals as a result of congenital factors that compelled them to a life of crime. Unsurprisingly, these physical characteristics closely approximated those associated with African Americans, because of the Eurocentrism and racism that influenced Lombroso's analysis (Rigby, 1996).

This line of work continued with William Sheldon in the 1940s, who argued that behaviours could be predicted by focusing on body types. Sheldon argued that there were three basic body types; *mesomorphs*, who are extroverted, aggressive, and muscular; *ectomorphs*, who are thin, fret a lot, and are introverted; and *endomorphs*, who are laid back, extroverted, and soft and limp. According to Sheldon, delinquents were most likely to be *mesomorphs*.

Biological approaches to crime are mostly disregarded by contemporary criminologists. However, some biological evidence is still presented in court today, such as evidence of connections between nutritional deficiencies and anti-social behaviour (Benton, 2007).

Sociological Approaches

As you have seen throughout this text, sociologists are most often concerned with the social environment in which people are located. As a result, sociologists critique early approaches to crime for being too individualist and for failing to understand that there are broader crime patterns. We have come a long way from assuming that we can pick out criminals simply by their facial structure and body mass. Sociologists also understand that not all individuals rationally weigh the benefits and risks of their criminal activity prior to committing a crime. For example, when two people engage in a fist fight, the intent is to hurt one another, but in the seconds prior to that fight breaking out, most people do not have a "rational" conversation in their head about what could happen if they hit the other person too hard.

Functionalism

One early functionalist approach to studying deviance was the **social disorganization** approach, developed in the 1930s and 1940s.

> ### *rational choice theory*
> The early criminological approach to crime that assumed people weigh the pros and cons of committing a crime and then make a logical decision to either commit a crime or not.
>
> ### *positivism* A philosophy
> that prizes reason, logic, and the scientific method (observation and analysis) over belief or faith.
>
> ### *social disorganization*
> A theory that believed the industrialization, urbanization, and immigration that accompanied modernization had shattered society's traditional order and values, making it difficult to maintain effective social control and, resulting in modern, industrial societies being more conducive to deviance than others.

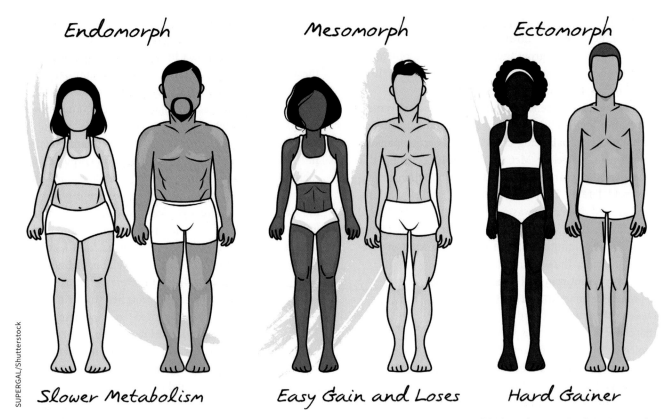

Endomorph   Mesomorph   Ectomorph

Slower Metabolism   Easy Gain and Loses   Hard Gainer

William Sheldon believed that extroverted, muscular, and aggressive men were most likely to be criminals. His conclusions began to be discredited almost as soon as they were proposed, although these body classifications are still used as a means of body classification.

Social disorganization theorists claimed that modern, industrial societies are more susceptible to deviance than others. They proposed that the industrialization, urbanization, and immigration that accompanied modernization had shattered society's traditional order and values, making it difficult to maintain effective social controls. This, in turn, spread social ills, crime and "vice," especially among the working class and the poor.

This view made a lot of sense to people a century ago, when people were struggling with coming to terms with the major changes that industrialization had caused, such as the move to city life, large-scale immigration, mass production, mass literacy, and the rise of the working class. The theory has since been modified to consider how tumultuous times affect social networks and to keep those relationships in mind as factors that influence whether people experiencing major change turn to crime (Bursik & Grasmick, 1996). Social disorganization theory still has some utility when considering people with low socio-economic status and relative uncertainty in their day-to-day existence.

> **strain theory** A theory that proposes that the cause of deviance lies in society's unequal opportunity structure—the strain between societal expectations and societal opportunities is what encourages criminal behaviour in some.

Another functionalist approach, **strain theory**, has particular relevance to the study of deviance and crime. According to Robert Merton (1957), the cause of deviance lies in society's unequal opportunity structure. In Merton's theory, deviance is driven by a basic conflict or paradox: a gap between culturally defined *goals* and socially approved *means* of achieving those goals.

Merton uses American society as his example. He proposes that one of the main goals of American society (in the 1950s) was success, especially in obtaining money, material goods, and "the good life." Most people have been taught to value success and to aspire to own a home, have a family, own material possessions (nice cars, good TVs, etc.), and go on vacation. For those of you who were brought up in middle- to upper-class families, the means to these goals is quite straightforward: go to school; get the credentials required; find employment; build credit through getting car loans, credit cards, and buying a home; get promotions; get married; have children; start saving for their educations, etc. The goals and means are very closely related

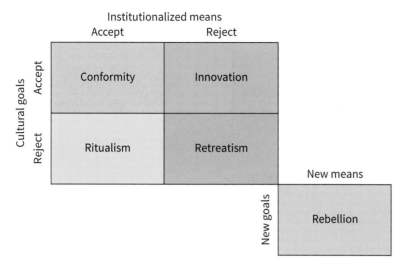

Figure 10.4 **Merton's Anomie Theory**

Source: https://en.wikipedia.org/wiki/Robert_K._Merton#/media/File:Mertons_social_strain_theory.svg

and easily accessible. Yet social inequality ensures that most people will fail because they will lack access to the socially approved means and resources that allow them to gain success, such as a university education or a white-collar job. Therefore, if they are serious about reaching their goal they may have to find other means.

Merton called this gap between goals and means *anomie*. (Recall Durkheim's theory of anomie in Chapter 2.) This state of anomie allows for various solutions, which Merton called *adaptations*. They include *conformity, ritualism, retreatism, rebellion,* and *innovation* (see Figure 10.4). People try one or more of these solutions to bridge the gap. Most people are conformists. Recognizing they will probably never "strike it rich," they live out their lives according to societal dictates as best they can, believing that if they follow the rules, they may one day be rewarded. Other people *seem* to conform, but they are just "going through the motions"; they no longer believe in the possibility of personal success. Merton called this adaptation *ritualism*. These ritualists, Merton suggested, are too well trained to give up entirely, but they no longer have any hopes for themselves. Other people, realizing they will never achieve their goals, just give up. They become *retreatists*—by drinking, doing drugs, or committing suicide, among other things. Still others *rebel* against inequality and reject the norms and values on which it is based. They may try to change the political order. The historic importance of youthful protest around the world, especially in places with high rates of youth unemployment, shows the social significance of this kind of adaptation to anomie.

A final adaptation to anomie is *innovation*. As Merton describes it, innovation occurs when a person has internalized the cultural goals but has not internalized a duty to the institutional norms—the legitimate "ways and means" of gaining these goals. In its simplest form, innovation is crime; the use of non–socially accepted means to gain wealth and success. In North American society, the many pressures on people to gain success

> **white-collar crimes**
> Crimes committed by high-status people, often in the course of their work; they include fraud, forgery, tax evasion, price-fixing, work-safety violations, and embezzlement.

often make other norms seem trivial. Far from being strange, criminal behaviour can seem like a perfectly logical response to a striking lack of options coupled with a passionate commitment to meeting social expectations Note that Merton's theory is used to explain crime primarily by those in the lower classes—for those who have the socially accepted means to achieving societal expectations, deviance and criminal behaviour must be explained another way.

Conflict Theory

Conflict theorists are interested in the strategy or mechanism by which one group comes to prevail over another. From a conflict perspective, the creation of "deviance" or "crime" is a way of imposing and justifying control by the powerful. Thus, the focus of this approach is to explain how laws get made and enforced, why certain social groups or subcultures dislike certain acts, and how they gain and wield control over other people's behaviour.

From the conflict standpoint, the study of deviance and control is the study of lawmaking: to determine why governments make certain laws at certain times and whom these laws favour. By this reasoning, social control serves one group in society—the powerful—at the expense of everyone else. Conflict theorists argue that governments are responsible for producing *criminogenic environments*— environments where laws privilege certain groups at the expense of less privileged groups. Conflict theorists challenge the idea that "justice is blind" and that the law is a neutral agent reflecting the interests of society as a whole. For example, these theorists argue that crimes committed by the wealthy, such as white-collar crimes, are punished more leniently than crimes

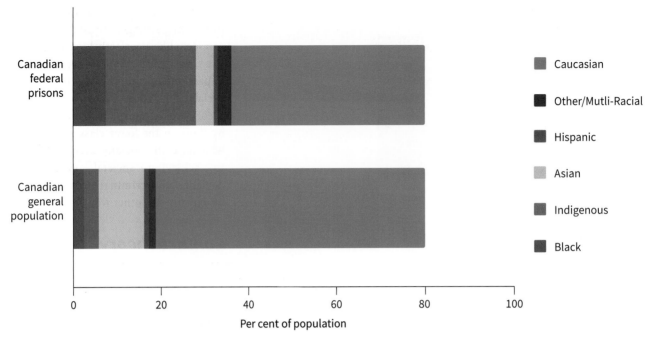

Figure 10.5 Proportion of Population vs. Rate of Incarceration, by Race, Canada, 2015–2016

Source: http://www.intersectionalanalyst.com/intersectional-analyst/2017/7/20/everything-you-were-never-taught-about-canadas-prison-systems

by the lower class. Similarly, they study the disproportionate incarceration of Indigenous people and black Canadians in Canada to see how and why Indigenous and black people are targeted by the state for incarceration (see Figure 10.5; also see Chapter 9).

In comparison to their proportion in the Canadian population, Caucasian and Asian offenders are underrepresented, while black and Indigenous offenders are disproportionately overrepresented. For example, while Indigenous people make up about 3 per cent of the entire population of Canada, they account for over 28 per cent of the male incarceration rate and 38 per cent of incarcerated females (Reitano, 2017).

Symbolic Interactionism

The interactionist approach examines the effect of social control on the people who are considered deviant. The most significant effort to understand deviance that emerged out of this approach is called **labelling theory**. Labelling theory argues that people come to identify and behave in ways that

> **labelling theory**
> A symbolic interactionist approach to deviance that believes people come to identify with and behave in ways that reflect how others label them.

reflect how others label them. Society and its members create definitions of deviance and then apply these labels to some members only. Take the example of unintended teenage pregnancy as evidence of labelling theory. While there are clearly two parties involved in creating a pregnancy, usually only the teenager who is pregnant is labelled deviant, not the other individual, who is equally responsible for causing the pregnancy! Howard Becker (1963) explains:

> Social groups create deviance by making the rules whose infraction constitutes deviance, and applying those rules to particular people and labeling them as outsiders. From this point of view, deviance is not a quality of the act the person commits, but rather a consequence of the application by others of rules and sanctions to an "offender." (p. 114)

From a labelling perspective, the question of interest is "secondary deviation"—that is, repeated deviance and, even, a deviant career. The goal is to explain why people who deviate from social norms a single time go on to deviate repeatedly (see Figure 10.6). Research has shown that a person labelled as deviant by others may come to see him- or herself as the labeller does (Bowers, 2000). The result is an internalized deviant identity, sometimes a decline in self-esteem, and even further deviant behaviour (or "secondary deviation") that fits in with the new self-image (Kaplan, & Johnson, 2001).

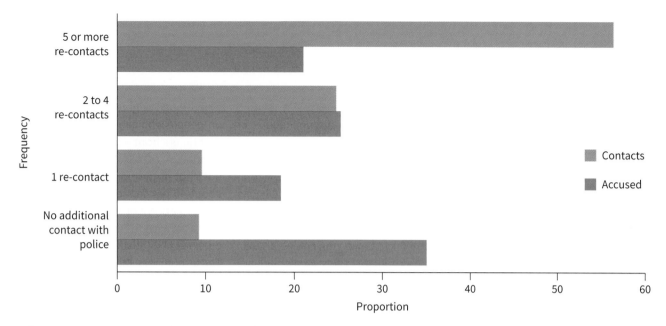

Figure 10.6 **Frequency of Re-contact with Police, Saskatchewan, 2009–2012**

A 2016 Statistics Canada study on repeat offenders in the Saskatchewan justice system found that, over a three-year period, the 37,054 individuals who came into contact with police in Saskatchewan in 2009/2010 were responsible for more than 143,000 criminal incidents. Of these people, 7800 (those with five or more re-contacts) were liable for 81,199 incidents, meaning that 21 per cent of accused were responsible for over half (57 per cent) of those incidents reported from 2009/2010 to 2011/2012) (Brennan & Matazzaro, 2016). In other words, a small number of individuals are responsible for a disproportionate number of repeated contacts with police.

Source: https://www150.statcan.gc.ca/n1/pub/85-002-x/2016001/article/14633-eng.htm

To understand repeated deviance, labelling theorists look for causes of deviant behaviour in labelling practices that make some acts especially shameful in some societies and not in others. Some sociologists, such as Edwin Lemert, ask how deviance becomes a "master status" that comes to define, more than any other personal feature, the way a person is viewed in his/her community—for example, if there was one kid in your high school who was thought to be "trouble," and you knew that even if you'd never had a conversation with that person. Others, such as Howard Becker, ask how labelling results in the exclusion of "outsiders." Finally, others still, such as Erving Goffman, ask how stigmatization (see below) damages people's identity and increases the chance a person will continue to deviate.

Labelling theorists remind us that no behaviour is innately deviant; deviance is always socially defined. Defining and treating other people as deviant is what sociologists mean by "labelling." So, the questions of interest for labelling theorists are these: "Are some people more likely to be singled out and accused of deviance than others? And if so, why?" Why, commonly, do the law, the press and public opinion stigmatize and punish powerless people? Further, why do some people have

> **stigma** A mark of shame or social disgrace that discredits an individual or a group.

more power than others in deciding what kinds of people are to be labelled and stigmatized?

It is sometimes hard to tell why some people are singled out for labelling—racial or class prejudice quickly come to mind—but easy to see the effects of labelling. One effect of applying a deviant label is stigmatization. A **stigma** is a mark of shame or social disgrace, and it discredits an individual or a group. The stigma of being labelled a deviant—for example, by having a criminal record—reminds others of what happens to people who violate social norms. In other words, stigmatization is a type of social control.

Stigmatization can include stereotyping and racial profiling (as discussed in Chapter 9). For example, newspapers may stigmatize people by the ways they report on race in crime stories. Reporting that a criminal is black is likely to strengthen stereotypes of black people as more likely to commit crimes. Reporting that a criminal is white (a fact that is rarely reported) is unlikely to have the opposite, positive effect on perceptions of black people. Stigmatization also occurs during the reporting of mass shootings. People of colour who commit these crimes are often demonized and portrayed as inherently

#Sociology

Stigmatizing the Body

In August 2014, dozens of women gathered in downtown Edmonton, Alberta, to rally against "mommy fat shaming" and body shaming in general, by employers and the mass media in general (CTV News, 2014). This was one of many rallies, protests, and conferences happening around the world surrounding the Fat Acceptance movement, which is trying to eliminate the stigmatization of overweight people—those labelled as "fat." This label carries a significantly discrediting value and is often associated with some type of anti-fat discrimination

Rudo film/Shutterstock

(Goffman, 1986). Plus-size people have reported discrimination in many aspects of life, including from airlines, potential employers, and even family doctors (Sabin, Marini, & Nosek, 2012; Majumder, 2008; Bias & Evans, 2016). This stigma not only harms overweight people but, as the Fat Acceptance movement argues, it perpetuates body ideals that are simply unrealistic and harmful to the self-esteem of all individuals in society, especially women. Indeed, people may engage in unhealthy eating habits in order to avoid acquiring this fat label.

Efforts have been made to eliminate this stigma, but some of them have been ill-founded, such as when the retail store Addition Elle fired one of its employees for using the word *fat* in her Facebook profile (Rieger, 2016). The store apologized for firing the employee after backlash from the public, who argued that overweight people are simply taking the "fat" identity back from those who stigmatize it. This conflict illustrates the complexity of destigmatizing the "fat" identity since some attempts to destigmatize overweight people, such as proudly calling oneself a fat supporter, may be perceived by some as destigmatizing the identity but by others as perpetuating stigma and discrimination.

Although stigma is often placed on people who carry a trait or label that differs from what is considered normal in society, the fat stigma does not fit this norm. For example, about 40 per cent of Canadian men and 27 per cent of Canadian women over the age of 18 are considered overweight (Statistics Canada, 2015). These numbers increase to almost 60 per cent and 45 per cent, respectively, when obese people—those who are severely overweight—are considered. Thus, it appears that being overweight—and potentially being stigmatized as fat—is the norm rather than something unusual. These statistics show that it is not always rare, criminal, or unusual traits that are stigmatized.

If being overweight is indeed the norm, why does it continue to be stigmatized? As mentioned, there have been movements in fashion and the modelling industry in particular to challenge the label and associated stigma. Here are just a few of the many hashtags that have taken off to celebrate bodies of all sizes:

- #Effyourbeautystandards
- #Honourmycurves
- #Celebratemysize
- #beautybeyondsize
- #Bodypositivity

evil, while white people who commit mass shootings often have long articles written about their backgrounds, families, mental health, and speculation regarding when the shooter began to stray "down the wrong path" (Park, Holody, & Zhang, 2012). Stigmatization can also lead to racial profiling when police officers use stereotypes to justify their behaviour. For example, in 2018 the Ontario Human Rights Commission (OHRC) obtained lengthy

evidence that the Toronto Police Service had been racially profiling black Torontonians, primarily through its "carding" program, which enables police officers to stop and record information on any individual as they see fit (OHRC, 2018). This is especially concerning considering that black individuals are estimated to be 19.5 times more likely than white people to be involved in a police shooting that results in death (OHRC, 2018).

And yet, despite all of the above, labelling and stigmatization do not invariably result in lowered self-esteem, a deviant identity, or a deviant career (or "secondary deviation"). That is perhaps the greatest weakness of labelling theory. Some people continue their deviant acts even though they have never been labelled. Others give up their deviant acts even though they *have* been labelled. Most important, labelling theory doesn't work well in explaining "major" crimes, including sexual assault, homicide, or robbery: crimes that most people agree are serious and deserve harsh penalties.

Feminism

As we already know from earlier chapters, most of the theorizing about women and girls has historically been androcentric—from a man's perspective. Feminist theorists seek to explore how women's experiences of deviance and

crime differ from those of men. Most important, feminist theorists examine how *definitions* of deviance and crime differ based on gender. Let's return to the teenaged pregnancy example from above and think about who is largely "blamed" for teenaged pregnancy. The person who is pregnant (usually a woman) is much more stigmatized and labelled as deviant compared to the person who contributed DNA (usually a man). Recall also the witch hunts at the beginning of this theory section, where societies blamed major ecological disasters on mostly women living in poverty.

Feminists also argue that the detection or "policing" of the behaviours of girls and boys or women and men differs dramatically. Think about how girls and boys are socialized or about the activities that girls are encouraged or discouraged to participate in (recall Chapter 7). Think about sexual relationships during high school. Boys who are promiscuous are referred to as players and at times freely discuss the number of "kills" they have, whereas girls who have sex with more than one person in high school or outside a relationship can easily be labelled "hoes" or a "thot" and socially ostracized.

Feminists are also at the forefront of efforts to change the laws around crimes that are primarily perpetrated against women. One area in which there has been much publicized progress is in reforming the law against sexual assault. Indeed, Canada now has robust laws against various forms of sexual assault. Feminists have focused on these crimes for many reasons. After all, sexual assault is a terrifying, violent, and humiliating experience that can have lasting consequences and that many women undergo and most women fear. It also comprises a set of crimes that have historically not been prioritized by the police or courts. Changing the laws related to sexual assault, providing help and other services to women who have been assaulted, changing attitudes toward these crimes in society and in police and court officials, and finding ways to prevent sexual assault are therefore important tasks facing society.

Finally, feminists are interested in how and why women commit crimes. Until relatively recently, almost all criminology was done exclusively on men. However, women have very different reasons for committing crimes than men, and the crimes they commit also vary from those of their male counterparts (Savage, 2019; Liddell & Martinovic, 2013). Feminists note that when we lump men and women together, important trends

In the News

The Burden of Proof in Rape and Sexual Assault Cases

Jian Ghomeshi, centre left, with his lawyer, arriving to court in 2016.

Prior to being charged with sexual assault, Jian Ghomeshi was a household name across Canada among those 40 years of age and older. Throughout the 1990s, he was a member of the band Moxy Früvous, and he became a television and radio broadcaster in the early 2000s. He held many positions at CBC, with his most prominent being *Q*, a talk show that featured interviews with prominent entertainment and cultural figures. The show, which ran from 2007 until his dismissal in 2014, was the highest rated show in CBC history (Zekas, 2010).

In 2014, an ex-girlfriend of Ghomeshi's made accusations that he had engaged in non-consensual rough sex—an accusation he denied. A few months later, CBC terminated Ghomeshi, stating that evidence had come to light that required CBC to discontinue its relationship with him. The evidence included private pictures and videos related to his sexual life. Less than a month later, Ghomeshi was charged with four counts of sexual assault and one count of overcoming resistance by choking. The charges were in relation to three separate women (CBC News, 2014). Three months later, Ghomeshi was charged with three additional counts of sexual assault related to three more women (Donovan & Hasham, 2015).

Ghomeshi's trial began on 1 February 2016 and lasted eight days. Despite six women sharing very similar stories of non-consensual sexual violence, Ghomeshi was found not guilty. In a number of the cases the women had engaged in what could be considered amicable, or even flirtatious, behaviour with Ghomeshi after the alleged attack occurred. The judge ruled that this behaviour problematized their accusations and went against what he deemed to be appropriate behaviour by a victim. Experts on victimization, however, argue that putting the victims' post-incident behaviour on trial is unfair as there is often much confusion following an assault, with some women at least partially blaming themselves for the incident (Donovan, 2016).

The Ghomeshi case draws our attention to the intersections of class, gender, and power in the criminal justice system—Ghomeshi was a well-known, wealthy man—but also to the difficulties associated with the burden of proof being on the female accuser. The criminal justice system's understanding of sexual assaults and the responses of (mostly) female victims is still gravely misunderstood.

---

can get missed. For example, while Indigenous offenders are disproportionally represented in the criminal justice system, the fastest-growing group of incarcerated people is Indigenous women (Savage, 2019). Feminists argue that if we are to successfully deter women from crime and rehabilitate women who commit crime, we must do criminological research on women.

Furthermore, there is almost no criminology on non-binary people, and because the criminal justice system is set up based on the gender binary, people (particularly transgender people, who are also overrepresented in prisons) can get misgendered within the criminal justice system, which can have negative impacts on their rehabilitation (Kirkup, 2016).

Top 10 Takeaways

1 Although crime and deviance are often used interchangeably, the two are separate phenomena that can at times overlap. Crime is an action (or an omission to act) in a way that is designated as requiring formal social intervention (whether or not that intervention always occurs). Deviance, on the other hand, involves actions, behaviours, or states of being that violate social norms and elicit either formal or informal social control responses. Crime can be deviant, and deviance can be a crime, but they can also be mutually exclusive. *pp. 192–195*

2 Formal social control gives specific people the responsibility to enforce formal social rules, using specific methods of enforcement. At the same time, ordinary people exercise another kind of social control that sociologists call informal social control. *p. 193*

3 Criminology is the interdisciplinary approach to the study of the definition of what is considered a crime, the causes of crime, the ways to prevent crime, and the punishment and rehabilitation of those who break the law. It is a sub-field of sociology that also draws on psychology, political science, law, history, and anthropology. *pp. 195–197*

4 Victimless crimes are crimes that no one suffers directly from, except perhaps the people engaged in the behaviour and their families. Such victimless crimes include gambling, the possession of drugs, and illegal parking. *pp. 196–197*

5 Only a small fraction of all law-breaking is reported to police, investigated, and eventually prosecuted. This decrease from criminal incidents to police reporting to actual prosecution is often called the dark figure of crime, or the crime funnel. *pp. 196, 198*

6 Early approaches to explaining criminal behaviour focused on possessions and witch hunts (the devil made me do it), rational choice theory (weigh the pros and cons of criminal behaviour before acting), and biological determinism (criminal behaviour is in-born and can be seen in particular facial features and body types). *pp. 199–201*

7 Functionalists use the social disorganization and strain theory to explain why some groups of people are more prone to commit crimes than others. *pp. 201–203*

8 Conflict theorists focus on the criminogenic environment that creates particular laws and ways of enforcing those laws, which disadvantage certain groups. *pp. 203–204*

9 Symbolic interactionists are interested in the ways that people become labelled as deviant or criminal, as well as the stigma associated with those labels. *pp. 204–207*

10 Feminists are interested in both crime perpetrated mostly against women, as well as female offenders. *pp. 207–208*

Questions for Critical Thinking

1. Research a different culture and find the ways in which its informal social controls are similar to or different from Canadian informal social controls.

2. Discuss why it is important for us to understand why people commit crime, how we make laws, and the ways in which we punish individuals. What are some of the implications or outcomes from having these types of understanding?

3. Provide an example of a crime that is not considered deviant by most. Research the history of the laws surrounding this crime. How did the laws come into effect?

4. Make a list of victimless crimes. Then, research the associated punishments for these crimes. Reflect on why we define these actions (or inactions) as crimes if there is not a victim.

5. Explain the dark figure of crime. What crimes do you think have the biggest discrepancies between the number of actual offences versus the ones reported? Why?

6. Research and discuss two current biological approaches to explaining crime; the so-called Twinkie defence and premenstrual dysphoric disorder. Are these plausible defenses? Why or why not?

7. Use a functionalist approach to explain the proportion of crimes committed by non-white and poor people in Canada. What are the positives and negatives of this approach?

8. Up until 2011 there was a mandatory sentence of a minimum of five years in jail for a crack cocaine charge, which was much more severe than the sentencing for a straight cocaine charge. Use the conflict perspective to explain this phenomenon.

9. Think of an example of a person you have known who was labelled by others (someone who has many tattoos, dyes their hair colour outside what is considered normal, has committed a crime, engaged in sexual behaviour, etc.). How and why was a label attached? Was there stigma attached to the label? How did this affect the individual's life?

10. Research five female and five male criminals. Discuss the rationale that is provided for their behaviour in the media, the types of crimes that they have committed, and the types of sentences they have received. Is there a gendered difference between the two groups?

Recommended Readings

- **Cullen, D. (2009).** *Columbine.* **New York: Hachette Book Group.** Author Dave Cullen delves into the minds and mountains of evidence surrounding the Columbine shooting.

- **Dostoevsky, F. (2002).** *Crime and punishment.* **New York: Penguin.** A classic story of the psychology of crime. Dostoevsky envelops the reader into the brilliant but tortured mind of Raskolnikov, a man who commits murder and then comes face to face with the most enduring questions of human nature.

- **Kerman, P. (2010).** *Orange is the new black.* **New York: Spiegel & Grau.** The book that inspired the hit series: Piper Kerman recounts the story of what led to her sentencing of 15 months at the federal correctional facility in Danbury, Connecticut.

- **Lamb, W. (2003).** *Couldn't keep it to myself: Testimonies from our imprisoned sisters.* **New York: HarperCollins.** After teaching a writing class to a group of women prisoners at the York Correctional Institute in Connecticut, acclaimed author Wally Lamb compiled their unforgettable stories in this collection. The prisoners write impassioned testimonies of how their lives led them to where they are now and, in the process, reclaim their lives.

- **Wright, R. (2005).** *Indigenous son.* **New York: Harper Perennial Modern Classics.** Wright writes a contemporary take of Dostoevsky's classic: he weaves us through the complex conscience of Bigger Thomas before, during, and after he murders a young woman. It explores themes of poverty and racism in 1930s America.

Recommended Websites

Statistics Canada: Crime and Justice Statistics
https://www.statcan.gc.ca/eng/subjects-start/crime_and_justice

- A comprehensive website providing data about crime in Canada. According to the website, these statistics come within the scope of the following five objectives: public order, safety, and national security through prevention and intervention; offender accountability, reintegration, and rehabilitation; public trust, confidence, and respect for the justice system; social equality and access to the justice system for all citizens; and, serving victims' needs.

Department of Justice
https://www.justice.gc.ca/eng/

- The Department of Justice website offers informal legal assistance and advice to the general public. It provides information about family law, criminal justice, funding, Canada's justice system, and Canadian laws.

Public Safety Canada
http://www.publicsafety.gc.ca

- The mandate of Public Safety Canada is "to keep Canadians safe from a range of risks such as natural disasters, crime and terrorism." You can find information on national security, border strategies, countering crime, emergency management, and more resources.

The Canadian Resource Centre for Victims of Crime (CRCVC)
https://crcvc.ca/about-us/

- Since 1993, the Canadian Resource Centre for Victims of Crime (CRCVC) has provided advocacy for victims and survivors of serious crime in Canada. Their services include helping victims obtain needed services and resources, assisting them in their judicial hearings, offering victims long-term emotional support, providing resources for victims, and more. (Information obtained from the Canadian Resources website.)

Canadian Crime Stoppers Association
http://www.canadiancrimestoppers.org/aboutus

- Crime Stoppers provides citizens with a vehicle to anonymously supply the police with information about a crime or potential crime.

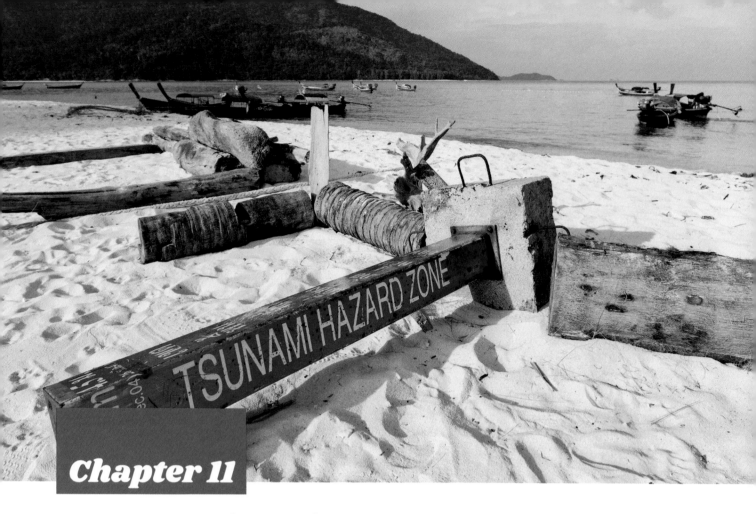

Chapter 11

Population and Environment

The Indian Ocean earthquake occurred on 26 December 2004. This earthquake was one of the deadliest natural disasters recorded in history. The 9.1–9.3 magnitude earthquake triggered a series of tsunamis along the coastlines bordering the Indian Ocean. Tsunamis are formed by a displacement of water—in this case, slippage of the boundary between two of the earth's tectonic plates. Waves up to 100 feet (30.5 metres) high pummeled the coastal communities of 14 countries, killing between 230,000 and 280,000 people. Indonesia, Sri Lanka, India, and Thailand were the hardest-hit countries. In total 1.7 million people were displaced as a result of the damage done to their hometowns.

Clearly, this natural disaster had a large impact on the environment and the populations living within these countries. Strong evidence suggests that climate change is a direct influencer on the number and magnitude of natural disasters that occur worldwide (Harvey, 2018). Furthermore, climate change has been linked to the consumption patterns of the world's population.

This chapter explores population changes and influences, as well as the environmental impacts of having to sustain us as consumers of natural resources.

Learning Outcomes

1. Explain the importance of demography in understanding world issues

2. Review and critique theories of population growth/decline

3. Understand the effects of population growth worldwide

4. Clarify all that is included in our natural environment

5. Review the theoretical approaches to the environment

6. Describe the relationship between population and the environment

Key Terms

baby boom

cohort

demography

demographic transition

ecofeminism

ecological footprint

environmental racism

fertility rate

growth rate

internal migration

Malthus theory

migration

mortality rate

negative population growth

net migration rate

pull factors

push factors

social demography

treadmill of production

Introduction

We have noted several times that social institutions are inherently conservative (lower case *c*), meaning there is a tendency for social order to persist from one day to the next. That is because of individual and collective investment in the existing social order. People's beliefs, commitments, promises, and obligations lock them into place. They expect to be rewarded for their effort by society if they stay the course. As well, the dominant social classes impose penalties to prevent significant change: they force us to co-operate at school, at work, at church, and as citizens, in order to maintain their dominance.

Still, societies change all the time. As we have seen in earlier chapters, identities, roles, and institutions are in constant flux. The social order struggles continuously with social change and conflict, because of at least in part inequality and people's work to dismantle social inequalities. As well, as we will see in this chapter, society transforms because of fluctuations in the natural environment. Change in our human connection with the environment is best seen over decades, generations, and centuries. Yet, every now and then, humans are forced to take inventory of their prospects: in effect, to choose the collective future of the species.

In previous chapters, we have explored the impacts that the Industrial Revolution had on Western society. After the Industrial Revolution, the social world was no longer seen as a product of natural "forces" or supernatural "design" but as a human product. The results of this change in thinking were dramatic. People realized that if *we* had made society the way it is, we could also remake it. We could reshape society to fit our needs and values. And new theories about what form society could or should take led to the development of sociology.

Today, we are in the midst of another revolution just as profound. Many of the conditions historically connected to industrial development and capitalism—for example, worker health and safety—have been improved, even if all of the problems have not been completely solved. New organizations—labour unions, social democratic political parties, feminist movements, and a welfare state—have made important contributions to people's well-being.

However, there are new concerns about the future course of world history and many of these have to do with the environment and ecology. The depletion of the ozone layer and the atmospheric "greenhouse effect" are making it hazardous to be out in the sun. The destruction of the Amazon rainforest and the emission of industrial pollutants threaten air quality. Oil spills, the dumping of industrial waste, and plastic garbage threaten life in the rivers, lakes, and oceans, destabilizing food resources. These new social problems face us *all*, regardless of class or political system, though they disproportionately affect marginalized communities—in Canada, particularly Indigenous communities (Smith, 2016). The developing world suffers more than the developed world from these so-called natural hazards and disasters, although their frequency, extremity, and cost are all affected by sociological forces.

Even in the short term, the depletion of Canada's and the world's natural resources means a loss of jobs and the end of traditional ways of life (e.g., the cod fishery in Newfoundland). In the longer run, it may mean global disaster. Awareness of these issues has been slowly growing

In Canada, the amount of land burned by wildfires every year has approximately doubled since the 1970s because of climate change and is expected to double again as climate change continues (CBC, 2019). Indigenous people are disproportionately at risk of these fires, and evacuations can have greater negative impact on Indigenous people because of their history of forced displacement, risk of experiencing racism, and lack of resources required to rebuild (Blake, 2019).

around the world, and it is within this context that we see green parties arise in multiple countries (Grant & Tilly, 2019).

Let's begin our discussion of the environment and ecology by looking at population issues. To a large extent the ecological problem is "us"—people. Most problems are aggravated by the sheer number of people in the world—7.6 billion people as of August 2018. Solving problems of poverty, inequality, intolerance, war, environmental damage, and a falling quality of life is difficult when the population is growing rapidly. For ecological and other reasons, we must come to terms with the world's population problem—understand it, then solve it. The social science that provides materials for the study of population is demography.

Demography

Sociology and demography are two separate disciplines, but they are intimately linked. **Demography** is the scientific study

> **demography** The study of the size, structure, distribution, and growth of the world's population.
>
> **social demography** The effects of population changes on the organization of societies, and vice versa.

of the size, structure, distribution, and growth of the world's population. **Social demography**, the topic of this chapter, is concerned with the effects of population on the organization of societies, and vice versa. Demographers play a central role in collecting and analyzing population data, such as census data. And sociologists rely on demographers for this information to help us understand social problems in the context of social populations.

Demography and sociology are also linked because they complement each other. Population analysis is typically macro in scope, because it looks at large numbers of people over long periods of time. Yet the patterns it uncovers are often a result of millions of people making individual decisions, such as when to marry and how many children to have. For example, right now in India and China men outnumber women by 70 million, which has researchers concerned about the effects of this trend, such as how it relates to health, housing prices, trafficking, or prostitution and public safety (Denyer & Gowen, 2018). It is sociology that has the theoretical and methodological tools to examine how and why people make the individual decisions that lead to these macro-level trends, to consider their effects, and to suggest social policy to mitigate their effects and influence these decisions in the future.

One of the traditional concerns of demography is measuring and predicting population growth. Changes in the size and structure of a population have continuing and important effects on our personal lives. For example, information on the size and age structure of society influences the demand for, and availability of, housing, education, health care, and employment. No wonder, then, people were concerned when researchers concluded that the earth's *optimum* population size is one or two billion, but its *expected* population size is approximately 9 billion to 10 billion by 2050 and could be as high as 12.5 billion (Vidal, 2012; Cohen, 1995).

Still, this conclusion makes some assumptions. It bases the optimum (or ideal) population on the earth's known resources and our own consumption patterns. It also implies that we can accurately predict how the world's population will change over the next 30 years. The "population problem" also takes a different shape in different parts of the globe. In 1990, the Canadian government decided to raise the ceiling on the number of immigrants allowed into the country. That decision was based on a projection of current demographic trends. These trends suggested that unless we increase the immigration rate, Canada's population by the year 2025 would be *smaller* than it is today. In Africa, by contrast, the population is projected to grow to over 1.3 billion people without any substantial immigration (Vidal, 2012). However, as we will discuss later in the chapter, population numbers alone do not account for the whole picture when it comes to use of the earth's resources. First, we will discuss theoretical approaches to the topic of population and demographic prediction.

Theoretical Perspectives on Population
Functionalism

Functionalists believe that birth and death rates work together as self-regulating, opposing forces to keep the

population stable and within a range that the planet can sustain. For this reason, Thomas Malthus (1766–1834) argued that rapid growth in population was dangerous for society and a sign of impending doom. In 1798, he wrote *An Essay on the Principle of Population*, where he proposed what is now known as the **Malthus theory**.

Malthus argued that food supplies grow at a much slower rate than population; thus, the population of the world will inevitably outgrow its food supply. He believed that war and widespread famine would be the result—in other words, that the planet would self-correct through massive death—unless birth rates were regulated.

While we have not hit the point of worldwide famine, the population has indeed continued to grow. The world's population did not hit its first billion until around 1800. It took approximately 130 years for it to double to 2 billion. However, the time between billions keeps shrinking. In 1960 the population hit 3 billion and in 1975 it hit 4 billion. In just over 40 years that number has nearly doubled, to 7.6 billion in 2018 (https://www.census.gov/popclock/).

However, other demographers—whom we will call anti-Malthusians here—take a different approach to population growth. The anti-Malthusians disagree that food production will always be outpaced by population growth and believe instead that the **demographic transition** approach provides a more accurate analysis of the future. This approach, diagrammed in Figure 11.1 and based on Europe's population changes, argues that society moves through four different stages of population change. In Stage 1—pre-industrialization—both birth rates and death rates were high. Life expectancy in the western world was only between 30 and 40 years of age during this phase (Glover, 2014). In the Stage 2, death rates started to slow while births remained high. In Stage 3, birth rates slowed to match death rates (Glover, 2014). Stage 4 was

> **Malthus theory** Thomas Malthus's theory that population will increase at a faster rate than its means of subsistence (i.e., food production). Malthus proposed that unless population growth is stopped through moral or legal restraint, it will inevitably be stopped by disease, famine, war, widespread poverty, and degradation.
>
> **demographic transition** The transition from high birth and death rates to lower birth and death rates as a country or region develops from a pre-industrial to an industrialized economic system.

> **GrowthBusters: Hooked on Growth**
>
> Dir. Dave Gardner (2011). A documentary exploring how beliefs about economic consumption and population growth impact responses to evidence that we are outgrowing our planet.

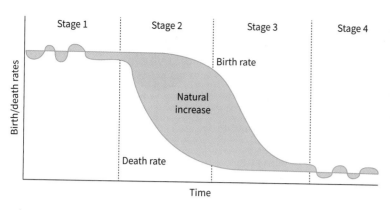

Figure 11.1 **Demographic Transition Model**
Source: Tepperman, L. (2014). *Starting points*. Don Mills, ON: OUP Canada, p. 75.

Overpopulated

By Hans Rosling (2014). A BBC documentary that showcases statistician Hans Rosling using state-of-the-art 3D graphics to illustrate how rapidly the world is changing.

Symbolic Interactionism

Symbolic interactionists also have a role to play in anti-Malthusian demographic transition theory, as they study how these different stages play out in individual lives and how the lives and choices of individuals leads to these larger, systemic trends. Population growth and change take place within a political, economic, and social context, with cultural beliefs and practices also affecting the changes in a population's size and structure.

Such beliefs include views on preferred family size, on the use of birth control, and on the importance of a child's gender, among other things. Equally, the size and structure of a population affects cultural practices. For example, as the proportion of the population made up of people who are over age 65 increases, there is a greater acceptance of aging as a natural, even desirable, part of life. With the aging of the large baby boom generation, we may even see aspects of old age glorified.

added relatively recently and is the stage where both birth rates and death rates are low and balance each other out. Anti-Malthusians now argue that there will be a natural population shrinkage. They predict that as women become more educated and marriages continue to be postponed, there will be a drastic reduction in the number of births in most of the world and that the world population will slowly self-correct through natural birth-rate decreases. There is some evidence of the anti-Malthusian approach reflecting worldwide demographics, as the global fertility rate (the number of births per woman of child-bearing age in the population) has declined steadily since 1964 (World Bank, 2017).

> **fertility rate** The number of children born per child-bearer in a given society.
>
> **baby boom** Marks a significant increase in the number of births post–World War II.

Feminism

This is where feminists join the anti-Malthusian theorists, as they propose furthering the rights of women as vital to population control worldwide. They argue that we do not need to have policies in place to forcefully limit population growth. In fact, feminists argue that any type of policy to control population is in fact a policy to control  women's reproductive rights. For feminists, population control is simply a matter of providing women with equal access to education and economic opportunities, especially education about and access to birth control.

Women who work for pay tend to produce fewer children by choice. Also, women who are better educated are often better able to provide medical care for themselves and their children, leading to lower infant mortality rates (Shapiro & Teniku, 2017). Thus, for feminists, the way to ensure the world does not become overpopulated is to empower women.

Conflict Theory

At the same time as population dynamics change, there is also a shift in resource use and inequality around the world. There are countries that produce and consume an abundance of food while others continue to experience famine. Some countries produce more food than their people can consume while others make less than is required for the survival of their population. The global food system also means that the food-producing countries are not always the countries whose populations have access to food. Thus, widespread inequality between countries makes it hard to truly assess if the Malthusian theory is at play.

As with many categories discussed in this text, age categories such as "seniors" are socially constructed. Do you think the definition of "senior" will change if medical technology continues to advance, and the average life expectancy in Canada continues to increase?

Rawpixel.com/Shutterstock

Sustainable

Dir. Matt Wechsler (2016). A documentary that focuses on our relationship with the planet and our food system. It sheds light on the implications of agricultural issues, such as soil loss, pesticide use, and water depletion, on our health.

Conflict theorists highlight these global inequalities as major forces in worldwide demography and propose that these resource stresses and global inequalities will lead to both local and global disruptions. These theorists sometimes fall under what is called neo-Malthusian theory, which echoes Malthus's concerns that population growth will result in major global conflict and catastrophe; these theorists, however, take the production abilities of industrial agriculture into account in their calculations. They have noted that at some periods in history, where land scarcity and population growth intersect, there is a higher ratio of armed conflicts (Ursdal, 2005). Overall, evidence for neo-Malthusian theory is uncertain.

Population Growth in Canada

Changes in the size and structure of a given population are caused by variations in the birth rate (births divided by total

> **growth rate** The rate at which population size increases each year.
>
> **negative population growth** The rate at which population size declines.

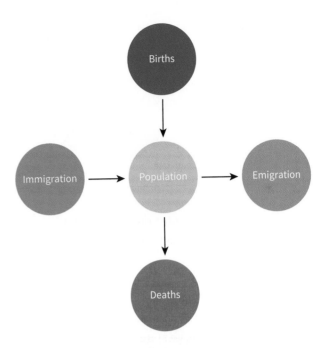

Figure 11.2 **Population Change**
The four factors that affect population change. Births and immigration increase population while deaths and emigration decrease total population.

population), the death rate (deaths divided by total population), and the net migration rate (the difference between the number of people immigrating to, and people emigrating from, a given country). The **growth rate** is the rate at which population size increases each year. In the case of **negative population growth**, it is the rate at which population size declines. We calculate the growth rate by subtracting the number of deaths and out-migrations (people leaving) from the number of births and in-migrations (people arriving), and we express the result as a proportion of the mid-year population. Since about 1980, the growth rate in Canada has levelled off at a level just below zero (Barbieri & Ouellete, 2012). To understand why, we must understand changes in the four factors that influence population size: fertility, mortality, immigration, and emigration (see Figure 11.2).

Fertility

In the past, high fertility played a critical part in Canada's population growth (see Figure 11.3). Contrary to what many think, immigration did not play a decisive role in twentieth-century Canada before about 1970. The net migration of 4.0 million persons from 1901 to 1981 composed 21.2 per cent of Canada's population growth over this period (Barbieri & Ouellette, 2012). The

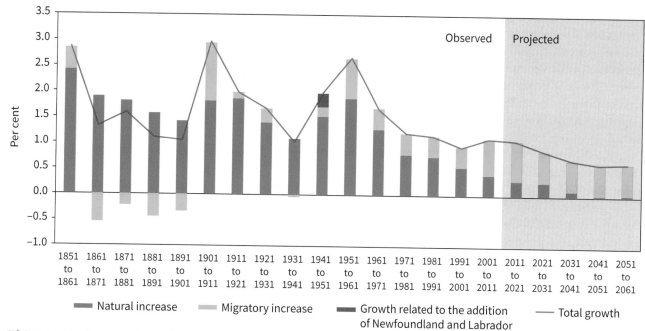

Figure 11.3 Average Annual Growth Rate, Natural Increase and Migratory Increase, Canada, 1951 to 2061

Source: https://www150.statcan.gc.ca/n1/pub/11-630-x/11-630-x2014001-eng.htm, Chart 1.

other 80 per cent occurred through natural increase (i.e., births). Immigration had such relatively little impact because, often, there were as many or more people leaving the country as there were entering it and because rates of fertility were so high (Barbieri & Ouellete, 2012).

There are many factors that influence a society's fertility rate (see Figure 11.4). Since the Second World War, the biggest population change in Canada was caused by the baby boom. This was a sudden and considerable rise in the birth rate in the 1950s and early 1960s. The baby boom was a response to the end of restraints on marriage and child-bearing caused by the Depression and then the war, as well as to the rapid increase in economic prosperity after the war. The birth rate reached its peak and began to decline again around the end of the 1950s.

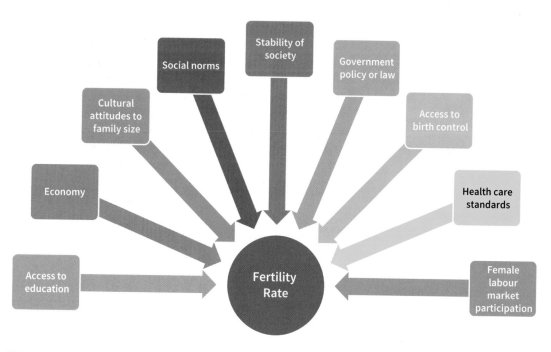

Figure 11.4 Factors Affecting Fertility Rate

A **cohort** is a group of people who share similar life experiences at the same point in time. For example, all the people who were born in the same year form a birth cohort. The baby boom of the 1950s had (and continues to have) a large impact on Canadian society, by changing the relative advantage of one cohort compared with the others by virtue of its size. Almost one-third of people in Canada fall under this cohort (see Table 11.1).

As members of this cohort have moved through their lives, the structure of Canadian policies and programs has had to be responsive to their needs in education, consumption, housing, recreation, and so on. Now, the most significant challenge is that the baby boomers are aging, and society needs to meet their needs, including access to pensions and greater need for medical attention. Younger age groups are too small to be able to support the baby boomers through contributions to pension and social security funds, and the situation is projected to just get worse (see Figure 11.5). In fact, there is some increasing hostility toward baby boomers for taking up a disproportionately large share of Canadian social funding. New solutions for supporting elder adults will be needed early

> **cohort** A group of people who were born within a certain time frame and, as a result, share similar life experiences.
>
> **mortality rate** The measurement of the number of deaths in a particular population divided by the population as a whole, per unit of time (usually per year).

in the next century; and this is the case around the world. For example, despite our own demographic issues, Canada actually has a higher proportion of its population between 15 and 65 years of age (i.e., working age) than the rest of the G7 countries, thanks to our relatively open immigration policies (Statistics Canada, 2017). Even in high-fertility countries, the proportion of people over age 65 is increasing (He, Goodkind, & Kowal, 2016).

In short, that unusual burst of high fertility—the baby boom generation—has reshaped Canada's society and culture forever. Normally, the younger siblings and children of the baby boomers—variously called the "baby bust" generation and generations X and Y—would benefit from their small cohort size. They are, demographically, in shorter supply, and that ought to make them more valuable in the job market. However, this expected advantage has, so far, failed to materialize, because of a worldwide recession from the early 2000s to late 2010s that has kept unemployment rates high and wages low, has sent young people back to school for more and different kinds of education, and has kept older individuals attached to the labour market for longer periods of time.

Mortality

Like birth, death has a profound effect on population growth. Demographers calculate a **mortality rate**. From this, they can then calculate life expectancies at each age. The most commonly used indicator is life expectancy at birth. According to the World Health Organization's (2008) indicators, a Canadian woman's life expectancy

Generation Squeeze

https://www.gensqueeze.ca/ A website that aims to amplify the voice of younger Canadians (under 45 years old) by highlighting social inequalities between younger and older cohorts and mobilizing political involvement.

Table 11.1 Canadian Cohorts

Cohort	Birth Years	Age in 2018	# as of 2011
Baby boomers	1944–1965	53–74	9.6 million
Baby busters (generation X)	1966–1971	47–52	2.8 million
Children of baby boomers (generation Y, or millennials*)	1972–1992	26–46	9.1 million
Generation Z or the Internet generation	1993–2011	7–25	7.3 million

*Note that these terms are flexible, and broadly speaking the "children of baby boomers" category includes what many people would categorize as the tail end of generation X as well as millennials. The millennial category is regularly said to start in 1981.)

Source: Generations in Canada, Age & Sex. Statistics Canada. https://www12.statcan.gc.ca/census-recensement/2011/as-sa/98-311-x/98-311-x2011003_2-eng.cfm

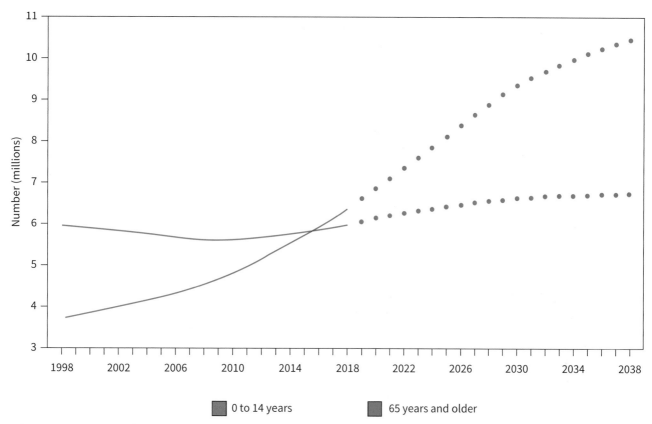

Figure 11.5 Population Aged 0 to 14 years and 65 Years and Older, 1998 to 2018 (Estimates) and 2019 to 2038 (Projections), Canada

Source: https://www150.statcan.gc.ca/n1/daily-quotidien/190125/cg-a001-eng.htm

is approximately 85 years (84.7), and a Canadian man's is 81 years (80.9). Canadian mortality began to fall in the early nineteenth century and continued falling through the early twentieth century. It declined more slowly in the north, on reserves, and in isolated parts of the Maritimes. In other parts of the country, mortality rates levelled off around mid-century.

Overall, mortality rates have been declining, yet women continue to enjoy a lower mortality rate than men at every age. This is the case in all industrial countries, including Canada, and there are various reasons for it. Males have higher mortality rates as infants, and this, along with other evidence, suggests that women are biologically hardier than men. Tobacco and alcohol use,

#Sociology

#HowToConfuseAMillennial

In September 2016, the hashtag #HowToConfuseAMillennial began trending on Twitter. Baby boomers used social media to make fun of members of Generation Y, also known as "millennials." Members of the older generation often say that millennials are lazy and spoiled. Examples of Tweets include "*What do you mean there's no Wi-Fi?*"

and "*Tell them your number is in the book*" (Parry, 2016). However, millennials fought back using the same hashtag: "*Destroy the environment, destroy the economy, destroy the housing market and then call Millennials lazy*"; "*Tell us education is important, continually raise the cost of tuition, then wonder why we're broke*" (Lynch, 2016). These tweets

insinuate that millennials are trying their best, but it is the impact of the recession that has caused social and economic disadvantages. Do you think it is fair that previous cohorts blame current ones for the problems of society? How about vice-versa, such as the #okboomer trend of November 2019?

more frequent among men, also has an effect (McCartney, Mahmood, Leyland, Batty, & Hunt, 2011). As well, men typically die in larger numbers as casualties of war, from automobile accidents, and from stress-related illnesses (see Chapter 12).

As we saw in Chapter 6, socio-economic status remains an important factor in mortality risks. In most countries, people with high socio-economic status have the lowest mortality rates. Lower-status people are more exposed to occupational hazards. They have a lower standard of living that includes less and lower-quality food, more daily stress, worse sanitation, and often less access to medical care.

Because mortality is related to the level of economic well-being, there is a long-term relationship between unemployment rates and mortality rates. In particular, the incidence of heart disease and heart attacks increases during periods of high unemployment (Zagożdżon, Parszuto, Wrotkowska, & Dydjow-Bendek, 2014). It remains to be seen whether public health measures can reduce these effects, or whether job creation can do so more efficiently.

There are also correlations between different mortality rates and race. For example, Indigenous people in Canada have a lower life expectancy and higher rates of disability than other Canadians: the reasons include poverty and poor access to health care (Statistics Canada, 2015; see also Chapter 12). Mortality differences may not be as great as in the past, but the differences that persist are caused by differences in average income, nutrition, and education among some groups. They also reflect regional variations in environmental quality (and environmental racism, as discussed later in this chapter), stress, and differences in standards of living. As shown in Chapter 12, Indigenous people are affected dramatically by a number of other social health factors, such as poor health-care delivery, a high smoking rate, and exposure to harsh climates (Patterson, Finn, & Barker, 2018).

Mortality rates, then, are at least partially a reflection of social inequalities. Interestingly, social inequality does not only negatively affect those at the bottom of the hierarchy. Epidemiological research shows that high levels of inequality negatively affect the health of even the wealthiest as a result of a reduction in social cohesion leading to more stress, fear of backlash, and insecurity for everyone (Institute for Policy Studies, n.d.). We know, however, that people do live longer, healthier lives in rich regions of rich countries. And one of the social benefits unequally distributed in any stratified society will be access to life-saving medical technology in desperate situations.

Two-thirds of the world's childhood deaths could be avoided by improving health care, education, and nutrition availability worldwide. This is supported by evidence from China and Sri Lanka, both of which have had rapidly reduced infant mortality levels as they have developed. What's more, violence decreases as education increases, as poverty declines, and as the state becomes more developed. While the United States may be an exception to this given that its firearm homicide rate is 24 times that of other high-income countries, in general, going to school and having a reliable, livable income helps you live longer (Grinshteyn & Hemenway, 2019).

Migration: Immigration and Emigration

The last major part of population growth is **migration**, which encompasses both immigration and emigration. By itself, migration neither increases nor decreases the world's population: it merely redistributes it. Yet such redistribution can have a profound impact on particular locations. In Canada, migration has played a significant role in national development. Understanding the factors promoting or inhibiting immigration, emigration, and internal migration is important for understanding the Canadian national character.

The **net migration rate** is the number of immigrants minus the number of emigrants in a given year, per 1000 inhabitants, at mid-year. **Internal migration** refers to people moving from one region of a country to another. Patterns of internal migration are useful when studying changing circumstances in various regions of a country. All migration, whether internal or external, is affected by push and pull factors. **Pull factors** in migration are all those factors that encourage people to move to a particular area; they are what make that particular location more desirable. Pull factors include better job opportunities, more tolerance for ethnic or religious minorities, and greater freedoms. They promise people a better life. **Push factors** are all those factors that encourage people to leave an area. These factors include famine, a lack of job opportunities, discrimination, and fear of oppression. Migration out of an area may reflect changes in the job opportunities available around the country, a rising cost of living, a lack of affordable housing, or

migration The number of people moving in and out of a region.

net migration rate The number of immigrants, minus the number of emigrants, per year per 1000 inhabitants.

internal migration People moving from one region of a country to another. Patterns of internal migration are useful indexes of changing circumstances in various regions.

pull factors All those factors that encourage people to move to a particular area (in relation to migration).

push factors All those factors that encourage people to leave an area (in relation to migration).

Current Research

Death Anxiety

Are you afraid of death? Do you think about death often? Those were the questions that inspired a 2017 study by Henry P.H. Chow. He studied the causes of death anxiety in university students in western Canada. Death anxiety is "the emotional distress and insecurity heightened by encounters with death or thoughts of death" (Kastenbaum, 2000, as cited in Chow, 2017). Chow asked a sample of 501 students to fill out a survey, which was analyzed to identify the main factors that cause high levels of death anxiety.

The study found that all students displayed a moderate level of death anxiety. Chow found that females experienced higher levels of

Syda Productions/Shutterstock

death anxiety than males, possibly because they tend to be more open about their emotions. Students who were not very religious were also more afraid of death, perhaps because they had more uncertainty about what would happen after death. Students who were unclear about their life's purpose also had more death anxiety. As well, loneliness was linked to death anxiety. Students who were unhappy with their self-image and the way they viewed themselves were also more anxious about death. Bad psychological health can affect one's outlook on life, which might explain these results. Non-white students suffered from higher levels of death anxiety than their white peers, which could be related to differences in cultural attitudes toward death. Surprisingly, Chow found that students from higher socio-economic backgrounds were more afraid of death than those from lower ones (Chow, 2017).

Do these findings resonate with you? What sociological factors contribute to your feelings about death and dying?

feared discrimination against a given ethnic, religious, or cultural group.

The importance of geographic pushes and pulls is shown in a study that analyzed migration out of First Nations reserves in Canada. It reports that involvement in mainstream employment and education "stimulates out-migration" (Gerber, 1984, p. 158). On the other hand, distance from major urban centres and institutional completeness inhibit migration (see https://munkschool.utoronto.ca/ethnicstudies/2013/08/qa-with-raymond-breton-the-role-of-religion-in-the-integration-of-minorities-in-canada/). Current studies find that these two factors remain central in Indigenous decisions to migrate—the need for employment and access to resources act as pushes, while the fear of acculturation and assimilation pull some First Nations youth to

stay on their reserves (Amorevieta-Gentil, Bourbeau, & Robaitaille, 2015). In addition, greater distance makes the move off-reserve more costly by making it harder to stay in touch with the reserve community.

The same can be said of ethnic and racial communities in large Canadian cities. People with more education and job skills are more likely to leave these communities for other neighbourhoods and work settings. But the greater the *social distance* between an ethnic group and the outside world, the less likely people are to make that trip. If their own community is institutionally complete, they are more likely to stay within it. Canada has seen a rise in ethnic communities referred to as enclaves. Statistics Canada defines ethnic enclaves as "residential areas where minority groups, composed mainly of recent immigrants, settle upon arrival in some neighbourhoods because of

Since the earth belongs to all of us, it should be everyone's right to move around freely (Velasco, 2016). That is the argument put forward by those who support the "open borders" approach to migration. People should have the freedom to choose to move and live somewhere without any problems. But those who do not agree with unrestricted migration say that it is the responsibility of the migrants' home countries to take care of them.

Part of the fear around immigration concerns the safety of citizens. With the growing numbers of terrorist attacks recently, security has become an obsession (Velasco, 2016). However, in reality, immigrants are not a threat to security. In fact, "even as the number of illegal immigrants in the U.S. tripled between 1990 and 2013," the crime rate fell (Bregman, 2016). Another concern about immigration is that immigrants will take jobs, force down wages, and take advantage of social assistance. However, as Bregman points out (2016), more people in a country help to develop the economy by increasing the demand for goods and services, thereby creating jobs. There is also no evidence that immigrants abuse government programs. Finally, as discussed, our demographic situation is such that we, particularly in Canada, *need* immigrants in order to sustain our economy and the needs of the baby boomers as they continue to age.

We need new models for thinking about the way migration is regulated. With Trump's "build a wall" rhetoric, and the injustices faced by refugees around the world, including in Canada, it seems we are far from adopting an "open borders" perspective.

limited economic resources and the existence of affordable housing and a certain 'cultural comfort'" (Statistics Canada, 2019). In 1981, Toronto, Montreal and Vancouver had six known ethnic enclaves. By 2001, Statistics Canada reported that that number had increased to 254 (Jimenez, 2017). These enclaves provide some comfort to the marginalization that people in ethnic communities may feel; however, they can also serve to further isolate these communities from the larger community.

Environmental Challenges

There are universal challenges to the environment as a result of human behaviour and consumption patterns. Environmental sociologists study the interrelationship between society and environmental concerns that will be discussed in the following sections of this chapter.

Long after Malthus, researchers are still trying to answer the question of how many people the earth can sustain. Wackernagel and Rees (1996) developed the concept of the **ecological footprint** as a tool to measure our growing population's needs relative to the earth's capacity to support those needs. An ecological footprint measures the total area of land and water a population needs in order to provide the resources to sustain that population's lifestyle and to absorb the wastes that the population generates. One unit of productive land space is known as one global hectare. According to the Canadian Index of Well-being (2018), in 2016 Canada's ecological footprint measure was 7.7. This means that Canadians required 7.7 global hectares per person—approximately 16 football fields each—in order to meet their demand for resources and to absorb their ecological waste (see Table 11.2 for a comparison of the top 10). On average the resources used in one year take 1.5 years to regenerate (Canadian Index of Well-being, 2018). While the planet has yet to grow beyond its carrying capacity—largely because of technological advances in agriculture—academics and scientists today continue to be concerned about sustained population growth and consumption habits, and their impact on the environment.

> **ecological footprint** The impact of human activities measured in terms of the area of biologically productive land and water required to produce the goods consumed and to assimilate the wastes generated.

The Natural Environment

Today, compared to a generation or two ago, we are all much more aware of the natural environment. This is due in large part to the rise of the environmental movement

Table 11.2 Ecological Footprint, Top 10 Countries, 2016

Rank	Country	Ecological Footprint (gha/person)
1	Quatar	14.4
2	Luxembourg	12.9
3	United Arab Emirates	8.9
4	Bahrain	8.6
5	Kuwait	8.6
6	Trinidad and Tobago	8.4
7	United States of America	8.1
8	Canada	7.7
9	Mongolia	7.7
10	Bermuda	7.5

Source: Global Footprint Network, 2019, http://data.footprint network.org/#/?

as expressed in the important work of environmental and climate scientists, such as Rachel Carson, David Suzuki, and Ulrich Beck. Equally, organizations including Greenpeace and movements such as Idle No More have raised our awareness of deeply problematic issues, from Alberta's oil sands projects to the accumulation of plastic in our oceans.

By *natural environment*, we mean all living and non-living things that occur without human intervention. This includes animals, plants, minerals, sunlight, as well as processes such as weather, water cycles, etc. Humans need an adequate amount of nutritious food and clean water in order to survive. This is why Thomas Malthus was interested in the relationship between food supply and population growth—the planet itself is a limited resource that in theory could cap human population growth.

Effects of Consumption

To survive in the natural environment—to produce enough food and shelter, for example—and to develop the tools we need for protection against other species, we harvest and process natural resources. Modern medicine depends on modern pharmaceuticals, but these rely, in turn, on natural minerals and plants as well as fossil fuels and clean water. The same is true of modern agriculture, which relies on mineral and chemical fertilizers in addition to water. To heat our homes and transport our food, we depend on petroleum-based fuels. The plastics we use for food transport and storage also rely on petroleum. To build our homes and cities, we need wood from trees; granite, limestone, and sand for concrete and bricks; iron ore and bauxite for steel; and other materials.

And, of course, we crave luxuries, too, from televisions to mobile phones to cars to home furnishings. These are all derived from natural resources, all requiring energy to extract and manufacture. Finally, the resource extraction and manufacturing processes themselves usually take large amounts of water and energy.

Water is a resource of particular concern. Global water consumption has been made possible by the building of dams and reservoirs, which affect over 50 per cent of the river basins in the world. However, the water available to humanity is not equally distributed. Currently, 2.3 billion people live in areas that lack an adequate water supply, and by 2050, 3.5 billion people will be in this situation (Population Reference Bureau, 2009). A report by the United Nations World Water Assessment Programme points out the following:

As demand for water increases across the globe, the availability of fresh water in many regions is likely to decrease because of climate change, warns the latest edition of the United Nations' World Water Development Report (WWDR4). It predicts that these pressures will exacerbate economic disparities between certain countries, as well as between sectors or regions within countries. Much of the burden, it says, is likely to fall on the poor. (UNESCO, 2017)

The same report notes that four main sources drive the demand for water: namely, agriculture, production of

Practising Sociology

What Is Your Footprint?

First, look up your ecological footprint on http://www .footprintcalculator.org/. Then brainstorm some ways that you could, in theory, change your footprint, and reflect on the barriers that might prevent you from making that change as well as the benefits of making that change.

My current ecological footprint: _____ global hectares

Ways to Reduce Your Footprint	Barriers to Implementing This Change (Financial, Sociological, Structural, etc.)	Benefits
Bike to school	Would take an extra 2 hrs/day to commute; would lose social status by giving up car; uncomfortable in inclement weather; part of my route is illegal to bike on; bike theft is common in my area; I'm not in great shape	Save money on gas; get in shape

Reflection: How many of the barriers that get in the way of you reducing your footprint are within your control? How many are socially constructed? What can you do despite these barriers?

There's a 24-pack of water in the garage. Don't worry. We won't be running out anytime soon!

Kayden Chan

Because of the abundance of resources in Canada, and the time scales at which resource depletion is occurring, it can be difficult to see that we are running out of precious resources, such as water, when we look around our environment. And keep in mind that over 100 Indigenous communities in Canada do not have access to clean water (see Chapter 9). Inequality can also hide the scarcity of certain resources.

energy, industrial uses, and human consumption. Most agricultural production is water intensive, and "agriculture alone accounts for 70% of all water withdrawn by the combined agriculture, municipal and industrial (including energy) sectors" (ENESCO, 2017). Thus, as the global population continues to grow, and the demand for food continues to grow, the demand for water will grow accordingly.

Like water, most of the natural resources we need are non-renewable: there is only so much petroleum, aluminum, iron, etc., on (or in) the earth. Once we have used it all . . . well, no one knows how to finish that sentence yet. One strategy is recycling these materials to get more use out of them. Another is to invent alternatives (for example, synthetic rubber to replace rubber extracted from a rubber tree) or find natural alternatives (for example, wind or solar power to replace petroleum). A third strategy is to look for new resources in currently inaccessible places (for instance, under the sea, at the centre of the earth, or on asteroids). A fourth is to reduce the rate at which we use these resources; however, this is only a short-term answer as it only slows down the inevitable disappearance of these finite resources.

Cowspiracy: The Sustainability Secret

Dir. Kip Andersen and Keegan Kuhn (2014). A documentary exploring the effects on the planet of large-scale farming. This documentary argues that these large-scale farming operations are the leading cause of global warming, water depletion, species extinction, deforestation, and ocean dead zones.

Before the Flood

Dir. Fisher Stevens (2016). A documentary featuring actor and environmental activist Leonardo DiCaprio. The film discusses all of the opposition to climate change. DiCaprio critiques the level of fossil fuels emitted by the US.

Theoretical Approaches to the Environment

With global temperatures and sea levels rising, we have begun to see new issues developing that we may not be entirely prepared for. While sociology has generally kept its distance from natural sciences, the effects of climate change are generating problems that need to be understood from a sociological perspective as much as a scientific one. We need to not only understand the effects of climate change on the population but also the causes that can be traced back to how our society is organized, functions, and is reproduced. Furthermore, each of the sociological theories has a part to play in understanding these issues.

Functionalism

Functionalists, concerned especially with the proper and effective functioning of society and how that can be reproduced, are concerned with how climate change will disrupt our social systems and infrastructure. For example, higher than average summer temperatures mean there is more demand on power systems as people try to shelter themselves from the heat, while more intense and frequent storms can cause damage resulting in even more outages (Dominianni et al., 2018). This can

World Events

Companies such as Apple (as an example) are always competing to release a newer and faster model. During the writing of this textbook, for example, Apple released the iPhone X, the iPhone XR, and the iPhone XS, with an expectation that the iPhone 11 would be released before this book publishes. Apple sold an estimated 30 million of these new iPhones in the first few months. What happened to those phones that most of those 30 million people already had prior to obtaining the newest release?

According to a recent United Nations report, China is the largest e-waste—electronic waste consisting of computers and cellphones, among other items—dumping site in the world (Watson, 2013). Many of these products were initially manufactured in China and are returned to China when no longer in use. Indeed, the United Nations data suggests that about 70 per cent of global electronic waste ends up there (Watson, 2013).

For the past decade, Guiyu, a town located in China's main manufacturing zone, has been the largest hub for disposal of e-waste (Watson, 2013). The United Nations report indicates that Guiyu is experiencing an "environmental calamity" as a result of this disposal industry. Toxic pollutions are released during the recycling processes, contaminating workers and the environment with heavy metals—such as lead, beryllium, and cadmium—while simultaneously releasing hydrocarbon ashes into the air, water, and soil (Wason, 2013). In 2018, however, Beijing officially stopped accepting garbage from other countries and China has embarked on a mission to rid the country of toxic waste (Petric, 2018).

Canada produces more solid waste per capita than any other country in the world, and recently our attempts to dump this waste in other countries (such as the Philippines and Malaysia) have been denied (Ferreras & Drolet, 2019). We will need to find new strategies for processing our own waste (and, ideally, producing less of it in the first place) if we want to avoid further international incidents.

Poravute/iStock.com

How many smart phones have you gone through in your lifetime? Have you ever thought about the environmental impact of discarding your old smart phone for a new model?

have a cascading effect as power outages could affect health-care systems, food supplies, transit, communication, and public safety—all of which need to be taken into consideration for a society to properly function.

Conflict Theory

On an even larger scale, we are starting to see the first climate change refugees, as people are being forced to leave their homes and even their countries because of severe climate effects and in order to survive (Berchin, Valduga, Garcia, & de Andrade Guerra, 2017). With deforestation and desertification, the rising ocean levels and temperatures, and the resulting economic issues, some estimates predict there will be nearly 150 million climate

change refugees by 2050 (Berchin et al., 2017). Conflict theory is interested not only in how this will predominantly affect the poor and vulnerable but also how capitalism, with its need for significant economic and population growth, is a driving force of climate change and violently unsustainable economic and industrial practices.

The Treadmill of Production

In Canada, we live in a capitalist economy that is driven by profits and increasing inequalities (see Chapter 6). Part of this mindset includes a strong desire for economic expansion that is at odds with protecting the environment. American sociologist Allan Schnaiberg (1980) argues that a dangerous contradiction exists between capitalist pursuits and environmental well-being. Capitalism requires continued and unchecked growth, while the earth's ability to provide raw materials is limited. Schnaiberg refers to this quest to increase production and profit as the **treadmill of production**. Similar to a conflict perspective, this approach argues that the economy is the driver of decision-making. Schnaiberg (1980) argues that having the economy at the forefront of decision-making leads to two major environmental concerns: (1) the high extraction of natural resources and (2) the high accumulation of waste. The short-term benefits of economic expansion to quality of life overshadow the long-term consequences of resource depletion and dumping of waste.

Some conflict theorists have argued that there is in fact a treadmill of accumulation rather than a treadmill of production. Regardless of any efforts to manage environmental concerns, the argument goes, the swiftness of irreversible climate change suggests that the only real solution is to overthrow capitalism altogether. Capitalists, of course, argue that in fact these pitfalls of capitalism (called "externalities" by economists) can be mitigated through government policy—but this requires political will.

Environmental Racism

One of the key conflict theory approaches to our environmental challenges is the study of how these challenges affect—and will continue to disproportionately affect— poor, Indigenous, and racialized people, both within Canada and globally. This is called **environmental racism**. Sociologists underscore that while natural disasters are,

by their definition, natural, the *impacts* of environmental disasters, such as wildfires, floods, earthquakes, etc., are socially constructed (Pulido, 2017). Conflict theorists who study the environment examine the distribution of both resources and environmental hazards (Pulido, 2017). In other words, they explore the inequality between those who are using the majority of resources and those who are most feeling the negative effects of that resources use.

Think for a moment about a flood. Who had to buy a house on a flood plain because it was all they could afford? Who influenced city council to build or not build a dyke or dam to protect one area over another? Which regions of the country or world could and could not afford to implement preventative measures? How do a person's circumstances make that person more able to evacuate when asked and more able to recover and rebuild after a disaster? Which victims of disasters receive relief first?

This thought experiment helps to illustrate how sociological inequalities are exacerbated by climate change: as natural disasters become more frequent and more severe, marginalized people will be disproportionately affected (SAMHSA, 2017; Bradley, 2017).

Feminism

Similarly, feminism observes how climate change will negatively affect women, especially those in the developing world. Researchers in Bangladesh  found that women face unique challenges associated with income, household assets, health and food security, education, and many other factors that contribute to decent living conditions, all of which are associated with climate change impacts (Momtaz & Asaduzzaman, 2018). Women in these communities had to survive cyclones, floods, and droughts and still had to find a way to make a living and find adequate resources (Momtaz & Asaduzzaman, 2018).

Emerging in the 1970s but gaining real attention in the 1980s and 1990s, **ecofeminism** is an approach that sees critical connections between the domination of nature and the exploitation of women. Central to this activist approach is the belief that, historically, men have dominated and exploited both women

> **treadmill of production**
> A theory that argues the economy (and capitalism's demand for continual growth) drives the decision-making of society, without regard for the physical limitations to growth, such as finite resources, or the environmental impact of growth.
>
> **environmental racism**
> The inequality between those who are using the majority of resources and those who are most feeling the negative effects of that resource use, as well as the policies and structures that maintain those inequalities on the basis of race, both within a country and between countries.
>
> **ecofeminism** A feminist analysis of environmental impacts that draws parallels between the historical exploitation of women and the historical exploitation of the planet.

and nature and that this is because men have "feminized nature."

Interestingly, there is a duality of feminist approaches to the environment. On one hand, many feminists have long been fighting against the stereotypes that women are inherently more emotional and in touch with nature (Banerjee & Bell, 2007). On the other hand, some ecofeminists argue that women do have a deeper connection to the world around them and therefore are the ideal activists, stewards, and advocates for environmental change (Sutton, 2007).

Symbolic Interactionism

Symbolic interactionists are interested in how we as a society perceive climate change and the resulting effects, and why this is important. Researchers from the University of Cambridge investigated how news sources portrayed "America's first climate change refugees" and how these individuals are represented in a way that distances them socially from the rest of Americans—as a problem that's "over there and doesn't affect me" (Herrmann, 2017). This deliberate attempt to "other" these people affected by climate change makes it more difficult to empathize with them, but it also overshadows their resilience in surviving these changes, as well as the strategies they used to persist in difficult conditions (Herrmann, 2017). This example illustrates how the way a problem is constructed by the media can deeply affect our thoughts about and emotions around the problem and can ultimately sway our actions in response.

The Population/ Environment Connection

What we have seen in Western societies in the past 50 years is a dramatic and justifiable growth in concern about the environment. More and more people feel strongly about the need for improvements in water purity, air quality, and higher waste disposal standards—including improved monitoring of landfills, recycling, packaging, and toxic chemical disposal. People want assurances that consumer products are environmentally friendly. Increasingly, people support the conservation of energy, the reduction of acid rain, and safer use of pesticides. However, people also want improved standards of living, which—at least so far—come with increased infrastructure needs and, as a result, increased resource consumption and higher costs to the environment (Schandi & Dodds, 2008).

Environmental concern is as economically significant as it is socially significant. Protecting the environment requires changes in consumer behaviour, among other things. It also requires more state regulation and higher production costs, which, in turn, create a higher risk of job losses because a company that cannot afford to make the changes a state demands may relocate to a country with lower environmental standards.

Yet these costs, risks, and changes are inevitable. Humans have dramatically transformed the environment, mainly through industrialization, so much that natural scientists have taken to calling our current global era the Anthropocene—an era where human impact is the defining feature of our planet (Martin et al., 2019). The entire global ecology is affected, especially the equilibrium of the biosphere and the interdependence between living systems. This raises concerns about survival of humanity as a species. Indeed, the ultimate source of concern for environmental change is its potential effect on the "livability" of the globe and its ability to support the variety and complexity of ongoing human activities. Moreover, urban-industrial civilization threatens human self-regulating systems as well as natural ecosystems. For instance, many respiratory and cardiovascular health problems are related to environmental pollution. The future of humanity depends on a better understanding of natural ecosystems and their relation to human populations.

Throughout the world, international bodies (like ENESCO), governments at every level, including local movements, are responding. They are developing plans for research, education, legislation, and regulation of the environment. For example, in 2018 the government of Ontario released its Made-in-Ontario Environment Plan to better protect the air, land, and water; address litter and reduce waste; support Ontarians to continuing doing their share to reduce greenhouse gas emissions; and help communities and families prepare for climate change (Ministry of the Environment, 2018).

A failure to take preventive steps may lead to the positive checks Malthus associated with overpopulation: massive death and dislocation. Yet, unlike what Malthus predicted, these checks are not a result of overpopulation *per se*. They are social, not demographic, in their nature. That's why human societies will have to change dramatically: the earth is unable to support our current standards of human life. But in order to deal with global problems such as the greenhouse effect, governments will have to build international consensus, and sacrifices will be

From My Perspective

Emily Eaton

There is no greater threat to the future of life on earth than global climate change. In order to rescue a habitable earth, climate science tell us we need to transition away from fossil fuels, and we need to start that transition now. Yet the Canadian Association of Petroleum Producers (2019) forecasts growing Canada's tar sands industry by 30 per cent over current levels by 2030. In Canada, which has some of highest greenhouse gas emissions per capita in all of the world (The Conference Board of Canada, 2013), there has thus far been little talk about a just transition away from fossil fuels. Those who are calling for such a transition have been painted as extreme environmentalists, out of touch with resource-dependent communities and threats to prosperity.

Emily Eaton, PhD, Associate Professor

My research investigates the corporate power and influence of the fossil fuel industries in Canada and the ways in which these industries have blocked a transition to a green economy. We need the tools of sociology to understand why we face the existential threat of climate change and how we can undermine the power and influence of fossil fuel companies in order to move toward economies that are good for workers, marginalized communities, and the earth. It is the oil and gas industry and its reach into civil society that has blocked progress on climate change for the past 40 years. Their message has been that, as consumers, it is up to each one of us, individually, to change our consumption and that we cannot be critical of fossil fuel industries if we rely on their products (plastics, fuels, etc.) in our daily lives. Yet 40 years of focusing on individual choice to reduce fossil fuel consumption has only led to rising levels of energy consumption in Canada and across the world. Sociology's emphasis on structures of power and patterns of influence allows us to see through the messaging of individual consumption and identify the fossil fuel companies and their influence on politicians and everyday institutions as the actors blocking a just transition.

In reality, it is fossil fuel corporations that are sitting at the table when governments are discussing climate change: they are pressuring politicians to delay action, approve expanded extraction, and loosen regulations. These same companies are behind social media groups that mobilize workers to parrot the industry's messaging that implementing climate change policies will sell out workers and destroy good jobs, even though those calling for transition have focused on centring social justice through managed decline, job re-training, and supports for affected communities. It is also these companies that are sponsoring community events, sportsplexes, shelters, and other good works to shore up their image. And it is the same companies that are providing bias-balanced educational resources that suggest the industry will save the environment through innovation. Sociology allows us to see through these discourses and to plan for another world—a managed phase-out of fossil fuels with the view of ensuring justice for workers and marginalized communities.

Source: Provided by Emily Eaton, used by permission.

needed. Privileged countries around the world have been the beneficiaries of overconsumption for a long period of time. At the same time many countries have lived far lower standards of life with far less access to capitalistic pursuits that tend to lead to overconsumption.

The poor are, unfortunately, more likely to suffer the effects of climate change (Berchin et al., 2017). Environmental problems such as unsafe water, overcrowding, poorly maintained and insufficient infrastructure, air pollution, and hazardous work conditions all affect the poor more than anyone else. Yet aid agencies and governments pay little attention to urban infrastructure. To get the developing world's co-operation in addressing global problems, the developed world must help it address the environmental problems that affect its poorest citizens.

In short, environmental problems result from an interaction of technological, social and economic factors. By itself, population plays only a small but concerning part. However, population planning can play a part in solving these problems or making them worse. Throughout the world, international bodies (such as ENESCO) and governments at every level (including local movements) are responding. They are developing plans for research, education, legislation, and regulation of the environment. Meanwhile, remembering that "natural disasters" are influenced by many sociological factors that we can control, sociology can help to keep the focus on what we *can* do, rather than what we can't, to prevent and mitigate such disasters.

Top 10 Takeaways

1 Demography is the study of the size, structure, distribution, and change in the world's population. Social demography, the topic of this chapter, is concerned with the effects of population dynamics on the organization of societies, and vice versa. — p. 215

2 One of the traditional concerns of demography is measuring and predicting population growth. Changes in the size and structure of a population have continuing and important effects on our personal lives and on a society's ability to function. — p. 216

3 Thomas Malthus argued that population and food supplies do not grow at the same rate. Food supplies grow at a much slower rate; thus, if birth rates go unchecked the population of the world will quickly outgrow its food supply. The anti-Malthusians believe that the demographic transition approach provides a more accurate analysis of the future. For feminists, population control is simply a matter of providing women with equal access to education and economic opportunities, especially education about and access to birth control. — pp. 216–217

4 Changes in the size and structure of a given population are caused by variations in the birth rate, the death rate, and the net migration rate. — pp. 218–224

5 An ecological footprint measures the total area of land and water a population needs in order to provide the resources being used and to absorb the wastes that the population generates. — p. 224

6 Humans are over-consuming the planet's natural resources and are producing an excess of waste. — pp. 224–228

7 Functionalists are concerned with the disruption that climate change will inflict on our existing social structures. Symbolic interactionists are interested in how we perceive and discuss climate change and its resulting effects. — pp. 227, 230

8 Conflict theorists look at how climate change exacerbates inequalities. The treadmill of production theory argues that rapid economic growth and pursuit of profits led to demands for natural resources and new technologies requiring more and more energy. *Environmental racism* refers to the disproportionate use of resources on the planet and how the people who use the least resources are the most vulnerable to climate change and its effects. — pp. 228–229

Feminists focus on how climate change disproportionately affects women. Ecofeminism is an approach that sees critical connections between the domination of nature and the exploitation of women. pp. 229–230

 Environmental problems result from an interaction of technological, social, and economic factors. Population planning can play a part in solving these problems or making them worse. pp. 230–232

Questions for Critical Thinking

1. Many nations are currently experiencing population declines (for example, Bosnia, Croatia, Germany, Greece, Hungary, and Ukraine). Their birth rates are low and emigration rates are high. How does this relate to the demographic model? Does this pattern suggest that the model needs a new stage?

2. Demography is an approach that helps us understand population change. From the perspective of Canada and Canadian cities, what are some demographic trends that Canadians will be responding to in the future? What are some strategies for dealing with these trends?

3. What are the implications of negative population growth for industrialized nations?

4. Has your own community changed over your lifetime? Have there been economic changes? Social changes? Are there more or fewer social problems (poverty, addiction, crime, etc.)? What might the results of shifts in a community be over time?

5. What are the strengths and weaknesses of the treadmill of production theory?

6. Explain the connection between feminism and the environment.

7. What theoretical approach do you believe has the best approach to understanding our population changes? Explain your answer.

8. How might we get people to shift their thinking to live in more sustainable ways?

9. Look up a recent natural disaster in your area. In what ways was this disaster socially constructed?

10. Do you think that environmental problems are mainly the result of overpopulation or from issues of structural inequality? Explain your answer.

Recommended Readings

- Batool, Z., & Morgan, S.P. (2017). **The second demographic transition: A review and appraisal.** *Annual Review of Sociology,* **43.** The authors examine the emergence of the second demographic transition and critique the way it applies to real-life occurrences.

- Rosling, H. (2013). *Don't panic: The truth about population.* **Wingspan Productions. https://www.gapminder.org/videos/dont-panic-the-facts-about-population/** Rosling, a statistician, uses data to explain how the future of the world population is not as bleak as you may think.

- Mayhew, R.J. (2016). *New perspectives on Malthus.* **Cambridge: Cambridge University Press.** This book is a collection of essays by various Malthus experts looking at his work from several different subject areas. It explores how Malthus's ideas can be applied to the current world.

- Walker, R.J. (2016). **Population growth and its implications for global security.** *American Journal of Econometrics and Sociology,* **75**(4), **980–1004.** Walker discusses the effects of global population growth on economic development, political conflict, environmental degradation, and numbers of refugees in the world's developing countries.

- Faist, T. (2016). **Cross-border migration and social inequalities.** *Annual Review of Sociology,* **42**(1), **323–346.** This review article examines how migration results in upward social mobility but also reinforces deep social inequalities.

- Butler, T. (2015). *Overdevelopment, overpopulation, overshoot.* **New York, NY: Goff Books.** This book is a series of photo essays showing how overpopulation has created the world's most serious environmental problems.

Recommended Websites

Statistics Canada Population and Demographics
https://www150.statcan.gc.ca/n1/en/subjects/population_and_demography

- Statistics Canada has extensive population and demographic data by province and territory and by city. Many of these data sets are interactive. They also perform all kinds of projections.

David Suzuki Foundation
https://davidsuzuki.org/

- The David Suzuki Foundation works with governments and businesses to improve the environmental impact of people in Canada and around the world. The website contains information on its latest projects, including what you can do to help.

350.org
https://350.org/

- This is an organization dedicated to reducing carbon emissions around the planet, with an emphasis on environmental justice.

The Climate Reality Project
https://www.climaterealityproject.org/

- Created by Al Gore, this organization focuses on analyzing and debunking the spin placed on climate change in the media in order to help make clear what is going on in the world and to inform us about how we can make changes to help.

https://paulbeckwith.net/

- Paul Beckwith (University of Ottawa) is one of the world's leading climate systems scientists. He creates videos discussing current and potential future outcomes of climate change.

Chapter 12

Health and Illness

Health may seem at first glance to be a purely scientific field: a disease is identified, understood, and a cure is administered. However, we have to keep in mind that science is performed by, for, and within society and is significantly affected by social factors. One illustrative example is in regard to vaccines.

Since the 1998 publication of a (since discredited) study regarding a possible link between the measles, mumps, and rubella vaccine and autism, the "anti-vax" movement has tirelessly campaigned to spread the idea that the government and companies are lying about vaccines for profit and control (Jolley & Douglas, 2014). This movement has had a material effect on whether people will get themselves or their children vaccinated, leading to a reduction in herd immunity and the resurgence of previously controlled diseases (Jolley & Douglas, 2014).

As sociologists we need to ask the following questions about health that medical science alone cannot answer: How do social movements affect public health practices? How can we use social influence to affect health choices? These sociological questions could quite literally be the difference between life and death.

Introduction

Over the past decade we have continued to hear of outbreaks of illnesses throughout North America that are preventable with immunization. In 2011, there were 776 reported cases of measles in Canada, and 118 in the United States (MSS, 2012; Roos, 2011). In 2018, there were 29 cases reported in Canada in contrast to 292 cases reported in the United States (CDC, 2018a; Government of Canada, 2018b). Similarly, in 2018 there were also 261 cases of the mumps reported in Canada and 2106 reported in the United States (Government of Canada, 2018b; CDC, 2018b). While these numbers may be medical data, as sociologists we can investigate why there has been a decrease in Canada and an upsurge in the United States. Did the "anti-vax" movement have a material effect? Did different health care systems limit access to vaccinations? Did geographical and population differences come into play?

Some of the mumps cases that have occurred over the last decade are well known since Canada's own Sidney Crosby, captain of the Pittsburgh Penguins, contracted mumps in 2014—one of 14 NHL players who fell ill with the virus. Although these outbreaks are quite low in comparison to other countries around the world, medical professionals advise getting booster vaccines to ensure that the strength of our childhood vaccines stay intact.

It is fabulous that we live in an era where doctors can quickly manufacture antibodies that protect us against infectious diseases—especially considering that just over 60 years ago there were more than 100,000 measles cases per year in the United States, with measles-associated deaths occurring each year (CDC, 1999). However, what about countries that don't have vaccines readily available? According to the World Health Organization, there were just over 100,000 cases of measles-associated deaths outside of Canada and the United States and over 500,000 cases of the mumps

Canadian hockey player Sidney Crosby of the Pittsburgh Penguins contracted mumps in 2014.

© Jerry Coli | Dreamstime.com

in 2017 (WHO, 2018a). Moreover, while vaccinations have eliminated diseases that have previously killed millions of people—e.g., smallpox and polio—and have weakened the effects of others—e.g., chickenpox and meningitis—some people are concerned with the potential for negative side effects. Two apprehensions are that (1) the vaccination could potentially cause the illness it is supposed to be protecting us from, and (2) that the measles, mumps, and rubella (MMR) vaccination may be linked to autism in children, as mentioned at the start of the chapter.

Most of the fear is born out of a study published in 1998 by Andrew Wakefield and colleagues, in which it was suggested that the MMR vaccine *may* predispose children to pervasive development disorder. The study had a very small sample size of 12 and methodology that was not seen as rigorous; however, the paper received wide publicity and vaccination rates began to drop (Rao & Andrade, 2011). The study was refuted in 2010 and Wakefield and his colleagues were found guilty of ethical violations and scientific misrepresentation (Rao & Andrade, 2011). For the past 20 years epidemiological studies have been conducted and published that completely refute any link between the vaccination and autism (CDC, 2018), yet the anti-vaccination (or "anti-vax") movement still exists.

In particular, there has been resurgence against the MMR vaccination, with celebrities such as Jenny McCarthy, Jim Carrey, Charlie Sheen, Alicia Silverstone, and Rob Schneider at the forefront. Believing that her son's autism was directly correlated with receiving the MMR vaccination, Jenny McCarthy specifically began a media campaign touting herself as an "autism expert." She was given air time on shows such as *Oprah Winfrey*, thereby giving credence to her campaign (Hussain, Ali, Ahmed, & Hussain, 2018).

The president of the United States has even tweeted, before becoming president, about the potential ill-effects of vaccinating children. Tweets like the screen capture above infer a correlation between vaccinations and autism.

There are also other sociological reasons why some people do not have their children vaccinated, such as for religious beliefs around medical interventions. As a direct correlation to the spread of anti-vaccination sentiment, some countries have seen a drop in vaccination rates, leading to recent outbreaks in diseases that were practically eliminated, such as measles (Hussain et al., 2018).

Whatever the cause, what we do know is that drops in immunization rates poses a global threat, as vaccinations protect not only the individual vaccinated but also prevent the person vaccinated from being a carrier of disease, thereby protecting those who cannot be vaccinated because of advanced age, illness, immune system issues, or severe allergies. Our world is more connected than it ever has been, with people easily travelling between countries daily, which translates to a higher probability of the transmission of diseases that had previously been eradicated in one part of the world (Hussain et al., 2018).

Vaccination trends draw our attention to some important issues in the sociology of health and illness: Who is the least likely to vaccinate and why? In what ways do social factors, such as wealth, politics, and location, affect who is and is not vaccinated, and how does this affect us as a society? Should parents be forced to immunize their children?

Sociology can help answer these questions and place them in context. For example, sociologists have studied whether the choice not to vaccinate is related to affluence. Studies show that families who choose not to vaccinate tend to be from the highest and lowest income regions (see Sakai, 2018). One explanation for this is policy-related. In Canada, for example, since it is the law that all children attend primary or secondary school and that all those attending public school must be vaccinated, an unvaccinated child must attend a private school (Government of Ontario, 2019). This policy allows the most affluent members of Canadian society to make decisions that put everyone, including the most vulnerable, at risk. In contrast, while parental attitudes and knowledge account for some (22 per cent) of the under-vaccination rates of low- and middle-income countries, approximately half (45 per cent) of under-vaccination was found to be the result of immunization systems failures, such as being under-supplied with vaccines or not having trained staff (Rainey et al., 2011).

What Is Health and Illness?

Health is one of those words that we all use but that is actually a difficult concept to describe. In 1948 the World

Health Organization (WHO) defined **health** as a "state of complete physical, mental, and social well-being and not merely the absence of disease or infirmity" (WHO, 1948, p. 100). **Illness**, in contrast, is a period of impaired or abnormal functioning of the body or mind not caused by physical trauma. Health and illness are often viewed as personal responsibilities: if we follow healthy lifestyles, such as exercising, eating according to a food guide, and not smoking or drinking alcohol, and we are good patients who listen to our physicians and keep our appointments (including getting vaccinated), we will be rewarded by experiencing good health. While these behaviours may certainly play a role in health at the micro-level, at the macro-level there are also broader socio-cultural factors that impact our health. In addition, such factors influence these micro-level behaviours and lifestyle choices themselves, such as our culture, socialization, and social class.

The **sociology of health and illness**, then, studies the interaction between social forces and health. Sociologists examine how our social life impacts rates of disease and death in different population segments, and in turn how those rates compare to society as a whole. The sociology of health and illness also seeks to understand how illness is defined and understood, as our understanding of what is healthy, and what is an illness, changes over time and place (consider how being gay used to be defined as an illness). In addition, this discipline investigates the ways that social institutions, such as the family, work, government, school, and religion, may influence health and illness, as well as the rationale for seeking particular types of care. For example, midwifery, the profession of caring for a person during pregnancy, labour, birth, and the postpartum period, declined drastically in the early 1900s to the point of being practically unavailable by the beginning of World War II because of competition from doctors and urbanization (Beth, 1991; CAM, 2019). However, recent research shows us that the practice has been regaining popularity since the 1970s; it was legislated and regulated in the 1990s, and in 2010 there were 943 practising midwives across Canada (Canada Midwifery Regulators Council, 2017). In response, sociologists are interested in questions such as these: What movements are driving the change in midwife use in Canada? How does legislation affect this practice? Are midwives an option for only certain people? What drives people's choices for one form of health care over another? Sociology is, in short, interested in

how our health care system defines, affects, and addresses health and illness, and how social systems both respond to and drive individual health outcomes.

Social Determinants of Health

The **social determinants of health** are the conditions under which people are born, grow, live, work, and age. A broad range of factors that determine individual and population health are influenced by a society's distribution of wealth, power, and social resources (Wanless, Mitchell, & Wister, 2010). These social determinants of health are mostly responsible for the health inequalities we see in society—the unfair and avoidable differences in health status within and between countries (WHO, 2019). Figure 12.1 lists the social determinants of health according to the Public Health Agency of Canada. In this chapter, we will discuss four conditions whereby we continue to see major health inequalities: income inequality, Indigeneity, immigrant status, and gender.

Income Inequality and Health

Poverty and income inequality have long been known to influence an individual's health (Raphael, 2002). Low-income Canadians are more likely to die earlier and to suffer more illnesses than Canadians with higher incomes, regardless of age, sex, or race (Public Health Agency of Canada, 2013). When exploring self-rated health outcomes, 73 per cent of Canadians in the highest income group rate their health as very good or excellent compared to only 47 per cent of those in the lowest income bracket (Public Health Agency of Canada, 2013). Furthermore, Canadians with lower socio-economic status are less likely to visit a physician than those of higher socio-economic status (Public Health Agency of Canada, 2013).

It has been argued that one of the most obvious indicators of poverty is oral health. Consider that when we converse with anyone face-to-face—teachers, potential employers, customers, and/or potential dates—often the first thing people notice is our teeth. Oral health is not covered by public health care in Canada in the same ways that our physical health care is, resulting in most dental

health A state of complete physical, mental, and social well-being and not merely the absence of disease or infirmity.

illness A period of impaired or abnormal functioning of the body or mind not caused by physical trauma.

sociology of health and illness The interaction between society and health: how our social life impacts rates of disease and death in different population segments, and in turn how those rates compare to society as a whole.

social determinants of health The many sociological conditions of a person's life that influence their health, including income, social status, employment, working conditions, education, literacy, childhood, physical location, social supports, health behaviours, access to health care, genetic endowments, gender, race, and culture.

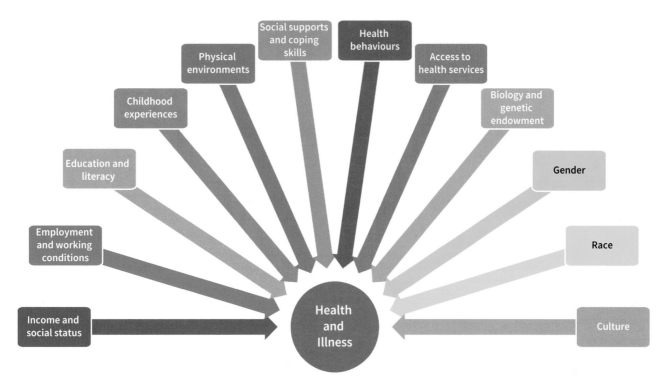

Figure 12.1 **Social Determinants of Health**

Source: Adapted from Public Health Agency of Canada, 2013.

procedures requiring either private insurance through employment or personal payment. While over 80 per cent of Canadians access a dentist annually, 32 per cent have no dental insurance—50 per cent of whom are from the lower income brackets (Canada Dental Association, 2018). Individuals living in areas where there are greater levels of income inequality are more likely to report their oral health as poor/fair and to report a prolonged absence from visiting a dentist (Moeller & Quinonez, 2016). Furthermore, Canadians who were so poor that they had issues with food security scored lower on nearly every oral health indicator compared to those who were not food insecure (Muirhead, Quiñonez, Figueiredo, & Locker, 2009). This indicates that poor oral health is tied not only to general inequality but also to living in poverty.

Some of our most vulnerable citizens are those that rely on social assistance—the government system designed to provide those in poverty with income support. However, data from national government surveys in Canada, the United States, and the United Kingdom illustrate that social assistance is not protecting people's health (Siddiqi & Sod-Erdene, 2018a). There are several explanations for why this is occurring. First, the amount of social assistance that individuals receive is insufficient (Siddiqi & Sod-Erdene, 2018b). In the mid-1990s, income support programs across Canada experienced drastic cuts to programs; these cuts were most drastic

in Ontario and British Columbia, leaving many families living on less than $500 per month for all basic needs (Cumming & Caragata, 2011). Second, social assistance receipt in Canada and in the United States requires work-related activities in exchange for benefits (Cumming & Caragata, 2011; Siddiqi & Sod-Erdene, 2018b). Many of these work experiences expose people in poverty to precarious job conditions and unstable jobs with no benefits (Siddiqi & Sod-Erdene, 2018b). Research suggests that precarious work—part-time, irregular hours, insecure, poorly paid, and without vacation—can actually be more harmful to health than unemployment (Siddiqi & Sod-Erdene, 2018).

Poverty has a direct impact on the health of those with low incomes, as described above. Income inequality, in contrast, affects the health of all Canadians by weakening our social infrastructure (Raphael, 2002). Indeed, even the affluent are affected by inequality because of reductions in social cohesion, causing stress and insecurity (Inequality.org, n.d.). We can see this in Figure 12.2: as the mini coefficient of conditional longevity decreases (a measurement from 0 to 1, where 0 is absolute equality and 1 is complete inequality), we see an increase in the inequality of life expectancy. Essentially, this means that the more inequality in a country, the higher the risk of premature death for everyone within that country (Neumayer & Plümper, 2016).

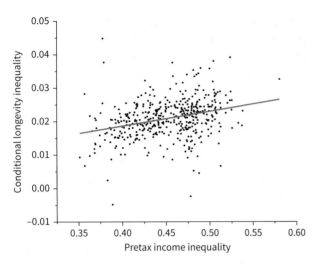

Figure 12.2 **Longevity Inequality vs. Income Inequality in 28 Countries, 1974–2011**

Source: Neumayer & Plümper, 2016. Copyright © American Public Health Association 2016.

The Canadian Institute for Health Information (CIHI, 2015) released a report called *The Trends in Income-Related Health Inequalities in Canada* examining whether the health gaps between lower- and higher-income individuals had changed from 2005 to 2015. The report indicated that inequalities persist in Canada with little to no progress being made in reducing inequalities in health by income level (CIHI, 2015). Since the early 2000s, inequalities have widened for 3 out of 16 health indicators in particular. The incidence of smoking, chronic obstructive pulmonary disease (COPD), and mental health–related illnesses have lowered in higher income groups while increasing in lower income groups (CIHI, 2015). While the gap between low- and high-income Canadians did not widen for 11 out of 16 indicators, they remained steady for 9 of them, with the lower income group experiencing worse health. For example, obesity, especially among women, remains higher among the lower classes

Current Research

The Relationship between Housing and Health

Housing and income are two of the most important social determinants of health (SDOH). Research shows that being unhoused can lead to poor mental and physical health. Conversely, experiences of poor mental and physical health place people at greater risk of experiencing housing loss. Most people who experience homelessness in Canada do so on a short-term basis. However, health outcomes are much worse for the small proportion of individuals who are homeless for long periods of time.

A recent study conducted by Julia Woodhall-Melnik et al. (Woodhall-Melnik, Dunn, Svenson, Patterson, & Matheson, 2018) investigated the journeys of 25 men into chronic or long-term homelessness. Dr Woodhall-Melnik and her team conducted a thematic analysis of transcripts from semi-structured interviews with men who had been homeless for 30 days or longer in 2014. They found that all of the men interviewed had experienced trauma or adversity in youth. Examples of this trauma or adversity included living in severe poverty; having interactions with the youth justice and child protection systems; experiencing physical injury; having early onset mental illness; experiencing early substance use; witnessing parental or caregiver substance use; being abandoned by a caregiver; and undergoing physical, sexual, or emotional abuse.

Woodhall-Melnik et al. (2018) theorize that the men who experienced youth trauma and long-term homelessness followed one of three paths:

1. *Entry into homelessness during youth.* The men in this pathway described leaving their caregivers' homes, couch surfing, and living in other unstable conditions before the age of 18. They left high school and ultimately ending up on the streets or in emergency shelters.

2. *Entry into homelessness during adulthood.* The men in this pathway lived with their caregivers until they were able to move into rented accommodations. This was often done with friends or romantic partners. These men held jobs and many experienced layoffs, job loss, or workplace injuries, which were followed by problematic substance use and relationship loss. For many of these men, their entry into homelessness corresponded with the loss of their relationships.

3. *Entry into homelessness during later adulthood.* The men in this pathway experienced mental illness or developmental delays and remained with their parents or caregivers until they passed away. These men were then left without the means to care for themselves and subsequently entered homelessness.

These pathways indicate a need to provide youth who experience trauma or adversity with targeted services to improve health, housing, and social outcomes in later life.

Source: Provided by Dr Julia Woodhall-Melnik.

(CIHI, 2015). Inequalities that did narrow, for two of the indicators studied, were the result of worsening health among the richest class; at the same time there was no change among the lowest income group for those same indicators (CIHI, 2015).

Indigeneity and Health

When we look at health across Canada, we see that certain groups of people continue to experience disadvantages. For example, when looking at Indigenous people in Canada, we see a 10- to 15-year gap in life expectancy when contrasted with non-Indigenous people, as well as differences between First Nations, Métis, and Inuit populations (see Figure 12.3).

Indigenous people are affected by major health problems at much higher rates than non-Indigenous populations in Canada. They have higher infant and young child mortality; higher maternal morbidity (i.e., illness) and mortality; higher rates of infectious diseases; higher rates of malnutrition; higher rates of death and diseases associated with smoking, alcohol, and other drugs; higher rates of obesity, diabetes, and hypertension; and higher rates of diseases caused by environmental contamination (Gracey & King, 2009; King, Smith, & Gracey, 2009). Most of these issues are directly related to poverty, including factors related to

poor living conditions, environmental contaminants, and inadequate food supply. These conditions are often the result of environmental racism, a byproduct of colonialism in which Canadian government policies and regulations have led to racialized groups, particularly Indigenous people, living in areas where they have to endure harsh conditions, limited supplies and services, and potential exposure to toxic chemicals (Hanrahan, 2017; also, see Chapter 11).

One instance in which we can see the social production of health issues in relation to Indigeneity is the prevalence of tuberculosis in Indigenous people in Canada compared to non-Indigenous Canadians. The difference in the rates of tuberculosis is quite significant—the rate is 290 times higher for Inuit peoples (Patterson, Finn, & Barker, 2018). There are a number of sociological factors at play here that contribute to this inequality, such as poor and often crowded living conditions, a 60 per cent smoking rate, issues with isolation and health care delivery, harsh climates, and inadequate education around tuberculosis treatment and prevention (Patterson, Finn, & Barker, 2018). While this issue is still ongoing, some progress has been made due to changes in treatment and diagnosis, improved technology, and increased resources (Patterson, Finn, & Barker, 2018)—although nowhere near the progress that has been made on tuberculosis in the non-Indigenous Canadian population.

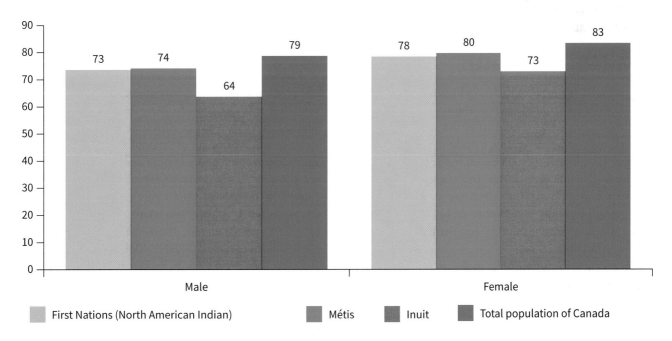

Figure 12.3 **Life Expectancy at Birth by Indigenous Status, 2017**

Indigenous peoples in Canada continue to have lower life expectancies than non-Indigenous Canadians.

Source: Statistics Canada, Projections of the Aboriginal Populations, Canada, Provinces and Territories, 2001 to 2017 (catalogue number 91-547-XIE).

Immigrant Status and Health

While the health trends of Indigenous peoples have shown some signs of improvements—albeit very slowly—there remains little to no change for immigrants to Canada, especially those who have lived in Canada for less than 10 years (Keung, 2017). Some researchers have called attention to the so-called healthy immigrant effect, which refers to a trend where newcomers, upon arrival to Canada, are healthier than the average Canadian mostly because of the requirements of entry (Keung, 2017). However, over time and over successive generations their health as well as that of their children and grandchildren declines (Keung, 2017). Immigrant and refugee youth are also more likely than non-immigrants to end up in the emergency room for mental health issues. Research finds that this is most likely due to the fact that the ER is the only accessible medical care for most immigrants and refugees in Canada (Saunders et al., 2018). And while not all immigrants are racialized, and not all racialized people are immigrants, the effects of racism that negatively impact the health of visible minority Canadians also have an effect on those immigrants who are also visible minorities (Nestel, 2012).

Immigrants continue to experience a lower life expectancy than non-immigrant Canadians, with the average age at death approximately six years younger than that of long-term Canadian residents (Keung, 2017).

healthy immigrant effect Refers to a trend where newcomers to Canada are healthier than the overall Canadian population (on average) due mostly to the requirements of entry as an immigrant.

Gender and Health

As mentioned, life expectancies vary by gender—and this difference seems to hold true in almost every modern population around the globe. Part of this seems to be biological: male infant mortality, outside of social factors, is higher than female mortality, even in the most extreme conditions (Zarulli, et al., 2018). This suggests that there may be a biological survival advantage to being female, which is still not fully understood but has become more apparent over time as health care, and particularly obstetrics, have improved.

There are also significant social factors that adversely affect men's health. Research shows that women are generally more health conscious and are proactive with their health care (Assari, 2017). As one example, although women are roughly as likely as men to describe their mental health as very good or excellent, they are more likely to turn to a health specialist when they are experiencing a mood disorder (Statistics Canada, 2015b).

As a result, nearly two-thirds of diagnosed mood disorders are reported by women (Statistics Canada, 2015b). It is unclear whether diagnosis results in better health outcomes for these illnesses, but these diagnosis gaps are likely at least related to the differences in suicide rates, which are approximately three times higher for men than for women in Canada (Navaneelan, 2012). Men are also more likely to be employed in an occupation that involves physical danger (Assari, 2017); for example, 97 per cent of people who died in a job-related death in 2017 were men (AWCBC, 2019).

Other health service gaps in the system remain, however, many times leaving women underserved (Amin, 2018). For example, because women are expected to live longer than men, they are more likely to develop chronic health problems that often appear with age (Statistics Canada, 2015a). Experts at Women's College Hospital in Toronto, Ontario, argue that although women are more likely to report severe and long-lasting pain, they are less likely to have their pain treated as aggressively as men (Amin, 2018). In addition, women are often overlooked in health studies even though they have different risk factors and respond differently to treatments (Amin, 2018), and medical journals neglect to publish articles that pay attention to sex and gender (Gahagan, Gray, & Whynacht, 2015). Historically, research—including diagnostic techniques—have only been studied in men and male animals; thus, effects that vary by sex and gender are often unknown, and treatments that address women specifically are nowhere near as advanced as treatments that specifically address men (Amin, 2018).

Women also experience disproportionate rates of sexual and physical violence and have an increased risk of death as a result of family violence. More than one-quarter of all violent crimes reported in 2016 were related to domestic violence, and 79 per cent of that violence was perpetuated against women (Government of Canada, 2018e). Women are also twice as likely to be sexually assaulted, beaten, choked, or threatened with a gun; more likely to report injury caused by abuse; and more likely to experience long-term post-traumatic-stress-like effects than men (Government of Canada, 2018e). Violence against women can cause long-term physical and mental health problems that are not always understood by the health care system (OWH, 2018). These effects include harm to an individual's health; possible long-term harm to children; and harm to communities, such as lost work and homelessness (OWH, 2018). (See Chapter 7 for a more in-depth discussion.)

So far, this section has discussed gender as a binary, which is how it was understood by Canadian society

In the News

Why Is Alcoholism on the Rise for Women?

Darling! This is no time for housework, it's wine o'clock!

memphisslim/Shutterstock

Canada's chief public health officer, Dr Theresa Tam, argues that the rise in heavy drinking among Canadian women is a serious cause for concern. The number of alcohol-related deaths in women rose more than 26 per cent from 2001 to 2017 while the rate for men increased by only 5 per cent during the same period (Canadian Institute for Health Information, 2018a). The most popular alcoholic drink in 2018 was wine—which could easily be deduced from any of the hundreds of memes and advertisements proclaiming that "It's wine time" (Statista, 2018a).

Gabrielle Glaser's (2013) book *Her Best-Kept Secret: Why Women Drink—and How They Can Regain Control* engages with some of the research on women's alcohol consumption, finding that nearly two-thirds of American women drink "regularly." In addition, female alcohol consumption has moved beyond the binge-drinking university student to include many more women in their forties who are drinking to get drunk (Glaser, 2013). Glaser argues that wine has become a culturally sanctioned de-stressor to help women contend with their overextended lives. While some studies have suggested that female drinkers in early mid-life may use alcohol as a route to assert their identity away from traditionally female responsibilities, such as caring for others, and to "return temporarily to a younger, carefree version of themselves" (Emslie, Hunt, & Lyons, 2015, p. 437), Glaser (2013) contends that women over 30 are much more likely to drink alone at home to escape stress. Tam also believes that drinking is in part used as a mechanism to deal with stress that has become glorified in the media (Canadian Institute for Health Information, 2018a).

Regardless of why women are drinking so much more, it is a serious health concern. The economic cost of alcohol-related harm across Canada has been calculated at $14.6 billion per year (Hensley, 2018). Frequent alcohol consumers are much more likely to experience short-term consequences, such as car accidents, violent episodes, alcohol poisoning and injury, as well as long-term consequences such as cirrhosis, diabetes, hypertension, and stroke (GBD, 2016; Alcohol Collaborators, 2018). In addition, alcohol consumption has been linked to both breast and colon cancer (Educalcool, 2018).

for many years and how the majority of studies are still organized. However, research has begun on the health outcomes of transgender and non-binary people. Their health outcomes are significantly affected by such social factors as the following: medical personnel's lack of training in how to treat transgender patients, a medical system not set up to serve individuals with non-binary gender identities, and treatments that have not been designed for intersex bodies. In addition, transgender and non-binary people experience higher rates of bullying, social isolation, and being victims of violence (Aparicio-García, Díaz-Ramiro, Rubio-Valdehita, López-Núñez, & García-Nieto, 2018). In short, social factors affect the health outcomes of men, women, and other genders in complex ways that are still being understood.

On Hold

By Vice Canada (2015). A documentary that explores the difficulties obtaining access to health care within Canada for transgender patients.

Social Epidemiology

Epidemiology is the study of the distribution and determinants of health and illness, and the application of this study to the control of health problems (WHO, 2018b). Social epidemiology is a branch of epidemiology that focuses particularly on the effects of social-structural factors on health distribution. Social epidemiology assumes that the distribution of advantages and disadvantages in a society will also reflect the distribution of health and disease (Honjo, 2004). This approach is concerned with this central question: What effect do social factors have on individual and population health (Honjo, 2004)?

Researchers in social epidemiology commonly use two concepts: incidence and prevalence. Incidence refers to the occurrence or rate at which new cases of a specific illness occur within a given population during a specific period of time—usually in a given year. For example, the incidence of cancer in Canada in 2015 was 141,000 (Statistics Canada, 2018a). The prevalence of specific illness refers to the total number of cases that exist at a specific period of time. The prevalence of cancer in 2015 was estimated at 2.1 million Canadians living with cancer (Statistics Canada, 2018b). These two concepts are closely related to morbidity—the prevalence and patterns of disease in a population—and mortality—the incidence and patterns of death in a population. Approximately 78,000 people died of cancer in 2015 in Canada. It is predicted that one in two Canadians will be diagnosed with cancer in their lifetime and that one in four adults will die from cancer or a cancer-related illness (Canadian Cancer Society's Advisory Committee on Cancer Statistics, 2015). This sounds quite depressing! However, we are extraordinarily lucky to be alive today when disease and death is no longer concentrated mostly in the young and is now primarily concentrated in the older population. Even with cancer, 90 per cent of diagnoses are in those over the age of 50 (which may seem very old to most of you, but not to me!) (Canadian Cancer Society's Advisory Committee on Cancer Statistics, 2018).

Sociologists may also use life expectancy of the average citizen to gauge healthfulness. Life expectancy is the average number of years that a person is expected to live. Life expectancy rates can fall because of disease, war,

social epidemiology A branch of the study of the distribution and determinants of health and illness that focuses particularly on the effects of social-structural factors on health.

incidence Refers to the occurrence or rate at which new cases of a specific illness occur within a given population during a specific period of time (usually a year).

prevalence The total number of cases of a particular illness that exist in a specific geography at a specific period of time.

morbidity The prevalence (total number) and patterns of disease in a population.

mortality The incidence and patterns of death in a population.

life expectancy The number of years that a person is expected to live based on the average number of years lived by a particular population.

sick role A social role that defines the behaviour that is appropriate for and expected of those who are sick.

famine, lack of education, and overall poor health and can rise according to scientific breakthroughs, health care, and social programs and policies implemented at any given time. In general, the higher the life expectancy, the healthier the population is assumed to be. As discussed, in Canada life expectancy is generally high: the average Canadian man will live to 79 years of age while the average Canadian woman will live to 83 years (Statistics Canada, 2018c). This is rather incredible considering that in the 1900s, life expectancy was 47 years for men and 50 years of age for women, representing a 60 per cent increase (Norris & Williams, 2000).

Theoretical Perspectives on Health and Illness

Functionalism

Recall that functionalists believe that we all have a role to play in society in order for society to function properly. In most cases, having an illness at least temporarily prevents us from performing all of our daily tasks at the same capacity as when we are healthy. Thus, functionalists believe that sickness is something that must be controlled so that too many people aren't prevented from fulfilling their roles simultaneously.

Sickness is controlled in two ways: through a system of medical care and through societal rules that keep too many people from being or becoming sick. Some of these rules are at the macro level and are formal—for example, as mentioned you cannot attend public school in Canada unless you have received your vaccinations. Others happen more at the micro level and are informal. When we find out we are unwell, we are officially labelled as "sick" and as a result take on the sick role, which functions as a micro-level method of social control.

Talcott Parsons (1953) first analyzed the sick role and highlighted four major elements of this particular role:

1. Sick people in the "sick role" are not held responsible for being sick.

Practising Sociology

The Sick Role

Think for a moment about your own sick role. This can be affected by your upbringing, your school, the media you consume, and a variety of other social forces. Here are some questions to consider:

How do you act when you are sick? What do you "do"?	
How would your parents expect you to act when sick?	
What actions should you take when you are sick? What should you consume?	
What would others suggest for you? How would your sick role change if you were in poor or severely in debt? If you made over $100,000 per year?	
How do people act when sick in media that you enjoy?	
What would someone have to do to convince you that they were sick?	
Should a sick employee stay at home or "tough it out"? Why?	
Should a doctor's orders be followed to the letter, or do you know what works for you? Do you go to a doctor at all when you're sick?	

2. Sick people are exempt from regular responsibilities (work, family, and social obligations).
3. The sick person must dislike being sick and actively do his or her best to get better (and must not stay sick permanently).
4. The sick person must seek help from appropriate medical professionals so that he or she can safely return to normal routines.

Parsons argued that our medical doctors act as gatekeepers for the sick role, either verifying our condition as an "illness" or

> **gatekeeper** Talcott Parson's term for medical professionals who are charged with either verifying our condition as an "illness" or determining that we are "recovered."

determining that we are "recovered." In Parson's time, this often meant that people were dependent on doctors to excuse them from school/work for illness, and to provide a remedy so they could be fully functional again. This is no longer always the case as many people with certain illnesses are expected and even desire to work unless they need hospitalization. This theory does not, then, account for those living with disabilities, chronic illness, or mental health issues. Recent research suggests that, today, being labelled with a mental illness may come with two distinct and opposing reactions from society: people with a mental illness diagnosis tend to have stronger core networks of support while also experiencing higher rates of rejection and discrimination from acquaintances and strangers (Perry, 2011).

Conflict Theory

Conflict theorists, in contrast to functionalists, point out that our dependence on the medical profession has moved far beyond doctors' ability to prescribe the proper medication to overcome an illness or even to excuse our absences. Rather, conflict theorists argue  that medicine has become a major institution of social control (Conrad, 2007), a process that is called the "medicalization" of society.

Sociologist Peter Conrad defined medicalization as the "process whereby non-medical problems become defined and treated as medical problems, usually in terms of illnesses and disorders" (Conrad, 1992, p. 210).

Examples of "medicalized" conditions include low sex drive, erectile dysfunction, infertility, menopause, alcoholism and substance-related disorders, expansion of depression, post-traumatic stress disorder, eating disorders, sleep disorders, excessive hair growth, lack of hair growth, social phobias, hyperactivity disorders, and chronic fatigue syndrome, among others.

Conflict theorists also discuss the ways in which health has become a commodity for the wealthy, who pursue health through gym memberships, a plethora

medicalization The process by which conditions, experiences, and issues become defined and treated as illness or disease and, therefore, as something to be studied, diagnosed, and treated.

of vitamins and supplements, health coaches, nutritionists, chefs and meal services, personal trainers, and self-help books. The global health industry is reportedly a $4.2 trillion industry with a number of billion-dollar sectors. Health has become about convincing people to take on healthier behaviours (having the right memberships and using the right products) rather than changing the structural conditions that contribute to health and illness.

Symbolic Interactionism

Symbolic interactionists are interested in the meanings that people associate with health and illness and the ways in which these concepts have been defined as opposites. In fact, what is considered to be "healthy" or "ill" falls within a wide spectrum and differs sub-  stantially based upon the resiliency and expectations of some people over others. These labels have real consequences for an individual's life. Often a label of some type of illness—such as having cancer, being HIV positive, having bipolar disorder—becomes an individual's "master status," overshadowing all other aspects of their lives. Symbolic interactionists, such as Goffman, also observe the ways in which the structure around us, as well as social categories such as class, gender, and age, can support or conflict with our understandings of health and how we define it (Goffman, 1983).

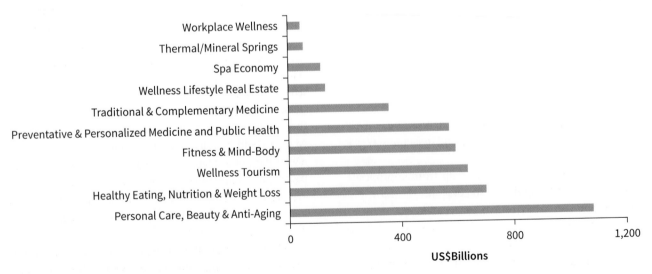

Figure 12.4 **Global Health Industry Profits**
Source: Global Wellness Institute, Global Wellness Economy Monitor, 2018.

In addition, interactionists focus on the roles played by both health care professionals and patients. They would say that patients are not just passive in their health care; rather, they are active in seeking out medical advice (and at times Internet advice by entering their symptoms into a search bar), reading about prevention, and seeking out medical assistance.

Patients may also actively choose not to listen to their doctor's recommendations or follow their pharmacist's directions for medical intervention. For example, how many of you know the correct dosage for your choice of medication for headache? Are you supposed to take two pills every four hours? Two pills every eight hours? One pill every twelve hours? Despite the correct dosage being clearly labelled on the medication, many people actively choose to ignore the instructions. This non-compliance could in part be due to the prevalence of self-medication in our society (Sado et al., 2017).

Feminism

Feminist research is concerned with how gender acts as a social determinant of health in concert with other social factors, and it uses an intersectional framework —developed by black feminist sociologist Kimberlé Crenshaw (1991) and defined in Chapter 2— in order to move beyond a single-axis analysis (such as looking at class or gender or race all on its own) (Keane, 2014).

At the macro level, many feminists have also focused attention on the medicalization of women's bodies and lives. A whole host of medication has been developed to deal with women's hormonal shifts during premenstrual syndrome (PMS) and menopause, although these are typical to the functioning of female bodies (and in fact their absence is *also* considered to be an illness to be treated by medication). Furthermore, when women seek medical attention because of feeling unwell the very first question that they are most often asked is "Could you be pregnant?" Feminists argue that this focus on women's reproductive capacity and their potential role as mothers needs to stop overshadowing a diversity of concerns related to health and illness (see, for example, Inhorn & Whittle, 2001).

A Brief History of the Canadian Health Care System

Any conversation about health and illness must also include a discussion of health care systems. These systems directly influence the main questions about public health: who receives what treatment (and who does not). Health care systems are easy to take for granted, but these complex networks are defined by policy decisions, funding choices, political ideologies, specific implementation of health strategies, the behaviour of all individuals within that system, and the physical locations where they exist. These factors all converge in the health care system to affect the health outcomes of those who are covered by a given system (and to define who is and is not covered) and are constructed by political and historical forces.

Up until the 1950s, people in Canada (with exceptions for some Inuit and First Nations peoples who were and are covered under federal treaties) were responsible for paying for their own health care. In 1957, governments

#*Sociology*

"Freebirth" versus Hospital Birth

Doctors and midwives warn that although giving birth is a natural process, many unknowns can happen, putting the baby and mother at risk (Hollander et al., 2017). Despite this warning by medical professionals, Canada is seeing an increase in "freebirth"—women delivering children at home without the help of doctors, midwives, or other medical professionals (Perrier, 2019). Women in New Brunswick who were interviewed as part of a 2015 study by the University of British Columbia reported choosing freebirth because their needs or fears hadn't been addressed by doctors (Perrier, 2019). In the UK, mothers reported the following as some of the reasons they opted for freebirth: control and autonomy of their bodies, negative experiences with the medical system, and a view of the biomedical model as being inadequate (Feely, Burns, Adams, & Thomson, 2015). A survey of Ontario women found that those who choose to have their births in hospital, in contrast, have a desire for pain relief and a fear that something might go wrong (Murray-Davis, McDonald, Rietsma, Coubrough, & Hutton, 2014).

While freebirth can be dangerous, it is also compelling. One woman, Simone Thurber, gave birth in a river in the remote Daintree Rainforest in northeast Australia, with her husband and other children nearby; a video of the birth has been viewed more than 77 million times on YouTube (Perrier, 2019). Such worldwide interest is something that, in turn, captures the interest of sociologists.

This information is vital as a means of understanding why people make the choices they make, and how those choices can be influenced. Sociologists argue that if we, as a society, want people to choose to have their births where medical intervention can occur if it is necessary, then we need to adjust the biomedical model of childbirth and medical care so that pregnant people feel dignified, supported, and participatory in the birthing process (Feely et al., 2015).

noBorders - Brayden Howie/Shutterstock

followed the example set by Saskatchewan and officially took on responsibility for the health care of Canadian citizens. The Hospital Insurance and Diagnostic Services Act of 1957 provided for medically necessary care and services in hospital settings with half of the funding coming from the federal government and half from the provincial government. The Medical Care Act was then passed in 1966, which provided for one-half of provincial and territorial costs for medical services provided by a doctor outside of hospitals. Finally, the Canada Health Act was passed in 1984, replacing the federal hospital and medical insurance acts and consolidating their principles. This act enshrined five universal principles of health care into Canadian law. According to the act, health care in Canada must be as follows (Government of Canada, 2018c):

- *Universal*: The system must cover all Canadians.
- *Accessible*: The system must provide access for everyone without financial or other barriers so that no one can be discriminated against on the basis of age, income, or health status.
- *Comprehensive*: The system must cover all medically necessary services.
- *Portable*: The system must provide coverage between provinces should a person move.
- Publicly administered: The system must be operated by a public body on a not-for-profit basis.

Brenda

I was born in St Catharines, Ontario, Canada in 1958. The Medical Care Act took effect in 1966. This is an important fact as my life has been plagued by health issues. As long as I can remember, if I needed or wanted to see a doctor, whether or not I had money had no bearing on whether or not I saw one.

Brenda Arndt

Brenda, 60-year-old retired cancer survivor and dragon boat enthusiast.

Because of a car accident, I was on long-term disability from 1993 until I was forced to retire in 1999 at 41 years old. My health has caused me a lot of financial difficulties, because of inability to work, but still I have never had to worry about paying for health care. Fortunately, I had a pension plan that included disability.

In 2006, two years after completing treatment for breast cancer, I was diagnosed with chronic myeloid leukemia (CML). The standard treatment for CML is a daily dose of a very expensive chemotherapy drug known as a tyrosine kinase inhibitor. These drugs are not paid for by our health care system. I am fortunate that my benefits do pay them, and I have been taking them daily for 12 years. With them I remain in a drug-induced remission; without them, I will die. Depending on the dosage, they range from $4,000 to $8,000 per month.

Shortly after being diagnosed with CML, I joined an online support group. There are members from all over the world in the group. I have come to be very close to a man who lives in Nepal, where poverty is rampant and there are no drug plans. This gentleman had to sell most of his land, which he used to feed his family and as a means of income in order to get medication. When that money ran out, he was forced to rely on the kindness of strangers sending him unused medication. He has since been able to secure false paperwork giving him access to a drug plan in India. He lives in fear every day that he may be found out.

Our health care system continues to save my life every day.

Source: Provided by Brenda Arndt, used by permission.

Current Issues in Health Care

If you ask Canadians to differentiate themselves from Americans, you will generally hear a couple of answers: we say "sorry" more often, and we have free health care. Our universal health care system is a point of Canadian pride and is often held up as a model for other countries to follow. While highly regarded, Canada's health care system is expensive and faces several challenges (Simpson et al., 2018). The American-based Commonwealth Fund ranks 11 nations' health care systems annually, and Canada has

finished either ninth or tenth for several years now. The system is found to be underperforming despite its high cost (Simpson, Walker, Drummond, Sinclair, & Wilson, 2018). The two major issues we will discuss next are its high and increasing cost and wait times. Both issues result in a need for alternative provisions of care beyond acute, emergency services as the main health care access point.

Rising Costs

Given its single-payer (often called "socialized"), universal health care, Canada has significant costs to take into consideration, with many costs growing each year—hospitals and medications account for a large part of this. According to the Canadian Institute for Health Information, hospitals account for 28.3 per cent of health-care spending in Canada, at a per capita cost of $1871 per Canadian. Drugs cost $1086 per Canadian when averaged across the population, making up 16.4 per cent of total health costs. Physician costs round out the top three spending drivers, at 15.4 per cent per Canadian, or $1014 per person (CIHI, 2018).

Part of the rise in cost for Canadian health care has been attributed to our aging population (see Figure 11.5 in the previous chapter). In 2012, almost one in seven Canadians was a senior, and by 2030 that number is expected to jump to nearly one in four (Government of Canada, 2014). This extraordinary change in our demographics presents new challenges for our health care system.

As people age, they are more likely to develop chronic health conditions (Nicolli & Partridge, 2012). The two most common chronic conditions for seniors are high blood pressure and arthritis. While the fact that more Canadians are living longer and healthier than ever is an amazing achievement for our society, it means that there are more people requiring health care for longer periods of time (Simpson et al., 2017).

Wait Times

While Canadians have access to care for urgent problems—such as heart attacks and strokes—and emergent problems—including cancer and diabetes care—less urgent problems require extremely long wait times (Simpson et al., 2017). In data from the Commonwealth Fund, Canada was rated the worst in our ability to get a same- or next-day appointment when sick, in wait times

Have you had to go to an emergency room for something that was not an emergency? What factors other than an aging population and increased overall volume might be contributing to wait times in hospitals?

to get treatment in emergency departments, and in wait times to see a specialist or for elective surgery. In addition, we were rated second-worst in getting after-hours care without resorting to visiting an emergency department (Barua, 2017). In 2016–17, 90 per cent of those in hospital were assessed within 3.1 hours (a 1.6 per cent increase over 2015–16), while it took 24.5 hours for 90 per cent of those who needed a bed to receive one (up 12.6 per cent from 2015–16) (Canadian Institute for Health Information, 2019). The Canadian Institute for Health Information identifies the wait time for an overnight bed as the key challenge over the past 10 years, and it continues to get worse rather than better.

Recall that health care is provided at the provincial level but is partially funded at the federal level for most Canadians (although it is delivered federally for First Nations and Inuit). This has led to a complex system that is inefficiently run with the bulk of its focus on acute care. As we have seen in this chapter, improved health care overall and changing populations have resulted in more chronic issues. As a result, chronic patients take up space in acute care centres, such as emergency rooms, because they have nowhere else to go. Wait times are further increased by the ongoing shortage of doctors in Canada—the country ranked twenty-sixth out of 34 developed countries in 2012 with a ratio of only 2.4 doctors for every 1000 citizens (Islam, 2014).

By studying these issues, sociologists can help clarify what the issues are and compare similar data with other countries to see how they have solved or are solving these issues. In this way, sociologists can make informed policy recommendations and determine how best to influence social opinion so that the most effective policies are supported on a national scale.

Recent Shifts in Health and Health Policy

In Canada, we have recently witnessed some major social shifts in how we understand, define, and perceive what is "ill" and what is "healthy" from the legalization and growth of marijuana for medical purposes to the changes in attitudes toward medical assistance in dying. We are also experiencing an increase in mental health and

Prescription Thugs

Dir. Christopher Bell (2015). A documentary that questions the practices of pharmaceutical companies and their relationship to drug addiction.

trauma needs, and an alarming rate of drug overdoses because of opioids. We will briefly outline these emerging and ongoing changes here.

Mental Health and Trauma

One area of health that has gained increasing recognition over the years is our mental health—our emotional and cognitive well-being. A person's mental health can affect and be affected by family and home life, employment or lack thereof, intimate relationships, financial situation, and many other factors. Research shows that those living in poverty are more at risk of developing mental health issues stemming from instability and stress and that even the risk of losing one's job can lead to detrimental and in some cases debilitating mental health states (Watson & Osberg, 2018). Furthermore, depression and other conditions cost the public health care system a lot of money ($651 million in 2013). Thus, mental health is an issue that must be understood both medically and sociologically in order to address it scientifically and socially (Chiu, Lebenbaum, Cheng, de Oliveira, & Kurdyak, 2017).

As mentioned, our relationships with others are affected by our mental health and, in turn, impact our mental health as well. Interpersonal violence (IPV), or domestic violence, has been strongly connected with mental health issues in both the victim and the perpetrator. Anxiety disorder and post-traumatic stress disorder (PTSD) are linked to victimization, while anti-social personality disorder is linked with perpetrating IPV (Kimmes, Beck, & Stith, 2019). Factors such as insecure housing and financial need are a contributor to both mental health issues and IPV because they leave people more vulnerable to violence and lessen their control over their lives and autonomy (Osuji & Hirst, 2015). Researchers recommended three approaches to improve this issue: (1) community-based prevention programs, (2) stable housing strategies with significant mental health services, and (3) reintegration (Osuji & Hirst, 2015). What is important to understand is that these factors—mental health, abuse, trauma, social and financial stability, housing, and health care—all affect and are affected by each other, thus weaving a complex web of interactions and factors that sociology seeks to understand and explain.

Marijuana for Medical Purposes

Recreational cannabis was not legalized until 17 October 2018; however, Canada has provided access to marijuana for medical purposes since 1999. The laws and regulations surrounding medical marijuana have continued to develop since that time, with the latest set of regulations established on 24 August 2016. Access to Cannabis for Medical Purposes Regulations (ACMPR) allow licensed producers to grow and sell cannabis products for medical use and allow individuals to grow their own cannabis for medical purposes (Statista, 2018b).

Marijuana has been shown to help some people with a number of pain, mood, and memory ailments by supplementing naturally produced chemicals in our body (Manzanares, Julian, & Carrascosa, 2006). As of June 2018 there were more than 330,000 marijuana clients registered in Canada. The total market size of marijuana for medical purposes in Canada in 2015 was approximately $40 million and is projected to grow to over $2 billion by 2020 (Statista, 2018b). Studies continue to show that physicians are divided on the benefits of marijuana for medical purposes (Penner, 2018). As a result, not all doctors will prescribe marijuana despite patient request.

Think back to the "sick role" that was discussed earlier in the chapter. Normally, doing recreational drugs would violate the sick role because these are understood to make you sick, which goes against the sick role's duty to do everything you can to get better. Does marijuana being legalized and deemed by some as a "medicine" (i.e., legitimized by the medical industry) change how it interacts with the sick role? This is further complicated when the lines between

medication and recreation are blurred, which has led some professionals to be suspicious of the motivations of patients asking for this drug (Pedersen & Sandberg, 2013). Here we can see that our understanding of a substance is constructed through the intersecting forces of research, media, legal discourse, and social institutions, all of which are sociological forces that shape our views.

madsci/iStock.com

Has your opinion on marijuana, for use as medication and/or recreation, changed? What about the opinion of your parents? Can you pinpoint what influences have informed your opinions?

Medically Assisted Death

Although medically assisted dying has drawn much media attention in the past couple of years, people have been fighting for the right to choose to die with dignity for decades. In the early 1990s, a woman named Sue Rodriguez, suffering from amyotrophic lateral sclerosis (ALS), fought the courts for the legal right to have a physician help in ending her life (Fenton, 2013). Rodriguez lost her court cases in three separate courts, including the Supreme Court of Canada. Despite the court ruling, Rodriguez committed suicide in 1994 with the help of an anonymous doctor. It would take two decades for the Supreme Court to reconsider its stance on medically assisted dying.

In 2015 the Supreme Court of Canada ruled in *Carter v. Canada* that the parts of the Criminal Code that prohibited medical assistance in dying would no longer be valid. *Carter v. Canada* is a landmark decision where the laws against assisted suicide were challenged as contrary to the Canadian Charter of Rights and Freedoms by several parties, including the families of those suffering from fatal diseases. In a unanimous decision, the court struck down the provisions against assisted suicide in the Criminal Code, thereby giving Canadian adults who are mentally competent and suffering intolerably from fatal diseases the right to a doctor's assistance in dying. In June 2016, the Parliament of Canada passed federal legislation known as Bill C-14 that allows eligible Canadians to request medical assistance in dying.

The Medical Assistance in Dying (MAID) Statute Law Amendment Act outlines the procedural safeguards and eligibility criteria for medically assisted suicide. Between 10 December 2015 and 31 December 2017, there were 3,714 medically assisted deaths in Canada; this accounted for 1.07 per cent of all deaths during the reporting time (Health Canada, 2018). Cancer was cited as the most frequent underlying medical condition associated with an assisted death, representing approximately 65 per cent of all deaths. The majority of Canadians who have received assistance in dying are between 56 and 90 years old, with the average age being approximately 73 years old (Health Canada, 2018).

Many faith-based hospitals and long-term care homes, however, continue to refuse to allow medically assisted death on their premises (Martin, 2018). When calling an ambulance, most patients are taken to the nearest hospital regardless of its religious affiliation. In theory, then, patients could be denied their legal right to this publicly funded medical intervention because of circumstances beyond their control. Thus, despite *Carter v. Canada*, we

are still working toward reconciling the rights of doctors to practise medicine in a way that aligns with their beliefs with the rights of patients to receive treatments wherever they live (Martin, 2018).

The legal battle over the right to die is a deeply sociological issue. Consider how Durkheim, first mentioned in Chapter 1, did research specifically concerned with suicide and the different social forces that might lead a person to consider it. Consider how our legal frameworks can concern themselves even with people's right to their own life, and also how our social and legal outlook on these issues has changed over time and across social contexts. And lastly, notice how groups organize and mobilize to generate social and structural change, which can have significant material effect on people's options. These are all sociological issues that accompany the philosophical ones that arise when we consider a person's right to death.

Opioid Crisis

The Government of Canada (2018d) frames the opioid crisis as a serious and complex public health issue. Opioids are medications that have traditionally been used to relieve pain. In 2017, approximately 11 lives were lost in Canada *each day* to an opioid overdose, the majority of which were unintentional. The situation seems to only be getting worse: 3,017 opioid-related deaths occurred in 2016, and that number increased to 4,100 in 2017 and increased again to 4,460 in 2018. The crisis is believed to be due to a combination of high rates of opioid prescribing by physicians as well as the emergence of strong synthetic opioids, such as fentanyl and carfentanil, in the illegal drug supply (Government of Canada, 2018d). Indeed, one study noted that one-third of the people who had died from overdose had an active prescription for opioids at the time of death, and 38 per cent of those had non-prescription drugs in their system (Gomes et al., 2018). Moreover, the most common non-prescription opioid used was fentanyl (41 per cent), demonstrating the link between these two issues and the need for further research and action (Gomes et al., 2018).

Opioid overdoses are not just happening among the young and poor, which is often the myth surrounding drug use. Rather, opioid overdose is most rampant among those over the age of 30, and opioid-related fatalities were predicted to be the leading cause of death among Canadians aged 30 to 39 in 2017 (Government of Canada, 2018d; see also Figure 12.5). Celebrities such as Heath Ledger, Prince, Tom Petty, and Mac Miller have all died due, at least in some part, to an opioid overdose. On a personal note, two men in their early forties that I went to school with as well as two of my daughters' schoolmates died of accidental opioid overdoses in 2018.

Crackdownpod

Prod. Garth Mullins. A podcast hosted and produced by documentarian and organizer Garth Mullins and led by drug use activists. This program explores issues surrounding drugs, drug policy, and the drug war in order to provide a media alternative that reports on the ongoing overdose crisis in BC. https://crackdownpod.com/

World Events

Climate Change Is Bad for Your Health

A report that came out in October 2018 from the United Nations Intergovernmental Panel on Climate Change warns of catastrophic consequences if there are not "rapid, far-reaching, and unprecedented changes in all aspects of society" to slow global warming (Miller & Croft, 2018; also see Chapter 11). The consequences are not just to our environment; researchers warn that our health is also in danger (Azad, 2018; World Health Organization, n.d.).

Indeed, scientists have found evidence of multiple health risks associated with climate change:

- Changes in air pollution and aeroallergen levels
- Altered transmission of other infectious diseases

- Effects on food production via climatic influences on plant pests and diseases
- Drought and famine
- Population displacement due to natural disasters, crop failure, water shortages
- Destruction of health infrastructure in natural disasters
- Conflict over natural resources
- Direct impacts of heat and cold. (WHO, n.d.)

Think about how these hazards are linked to infrastructure and social issues. Who will be more adversely affected by extreme weather? What could increases in certain diseases mean for those without health insurance?

Think also about the impacts on your own life. On the first few sunny, warm days of spring, how many of you put down your car windows, crank the tunes, and drive much faster than when the weather is cooler? How many of you consume more alcohol when it's warmer outside? Can you think of ways that the warming planet has changed your behaviours over your lifetime? Do those changes have an impact on your health—positive or negative?

99Art/Shutterstock

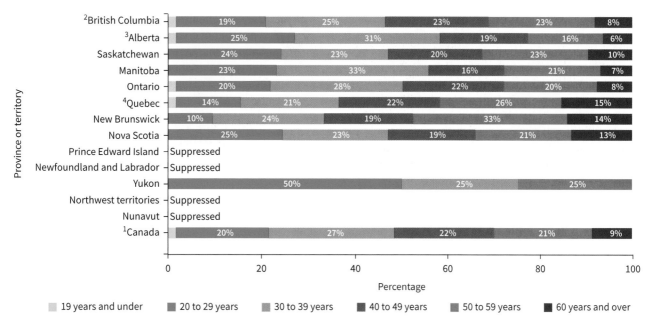

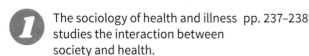

Figure 12.5 Age Group Distribution of Accidental Apparent Opioid-Related Deaths by Province or Territory, 2018

1. Data reported by some provinces and territories do not include all stages of investigation (ongoing, completed) or time periods. Because of rounding, percentages may not add to 100%.

2. Data from British Columbia include deaths related to all illicit drugs including, but not limited to, opioids.

3. For Alberta, 2018 data on age group were only available from January to September.

4. Data for 2016 and 2017 from Quebec include deaths with completed investigations only. Available 2018 data from Quebec include unintentional deaths with ongoing investigations related to all illicit drugs including, but not limited to, opioids.

Source: https://health-infobase.canada.ca/datalab/national-surveillance-opioid-mortality.html#AORD, Figure 2 (by age). © All rights reserved. National report: Apparent opioid-related deaths in Canada. Public Health Agency of Canada, 2018. Adapted and reproduced with permission from the Minister of Health, 2019.

Top 10 Takeaways

1 The sociology of health and illness pp. 237–238 studies the interaction between society and health.

2 The social determinants of health pp. 238–243 are the sociological, rather than individual, factors that affect health. These are income and social status, employment and working conditions, education and literacy, childhood experiences, physical environments, social supports and coping skills, healthy behaviours, access to health services, biology and genetic endowment, gender and culture.

3 The major inequalities in health pp. 283–243 in Canada are based upon sociological differences, such as income, Indigeneity, immigration status, and gender.

4 Functionalists argue that there pp. 245–246 are four elements to the sick role: people are very rarely held responsible for being sick, they are exempt from regular responsibilities, they dislike the sick role, and they seek help from professionals so that they can return to their normal routines. Doctors act as the gatekeepers to the sick role.

5 Conflict theorists argue that the medicalization of society has occurred whereby medicine has become an institution of social control. p. 246

9 Universal health care is facing a number of challenges in Canada: increased wait times, demographic shifts, and the associated rising costs. pp. 249–251

6 Symbolic interactionists are interested in how people and states of being become labelled as sick or healthy. pp. 246–247

10 While the use of opioids, marijuana, and medically assisted suicide have been occurring for some time in Canada, the drastic increase in deaths related to opioid use and the legalization of marijuana and medically assisted suicide make them emerging issues in the Canada health care system. pp. 251–254

7 Feminists draw our attention to the medicalization of women's bodies. p. 247

8 The Canada Health Act follows five principles: it is universal, accessible, comprehensive, portable, publicly administered. p. 248

Questions for Critical Thinking

1. In what ways can health be understood as a sociological concept, as opposed to exclusively a scientific one?

2. What are some of the social determinants of health, and which do you feel affect you the most personally?

3. How can income, immigration status, or gender come into play in regard to health?

4. What are some ways the "sick role" has changed for you since childhood, and in what ways has it stayed the same?

5. Should dental care be covered by the Canadian health care system?

6. How is mental illness engaged with medically, and how does that differ from how someone would be treated for a cold?

7. Should menopause be considered an illness?

8. Why are each of the five components of the Canada Health Act significant?

9. What are some health care challenges that you or others in your life have had to engage with, and what could be done to overcome them?

10. Safe injection sites are one of the ways that community activists have been trying to reduce the number of opioid-related deaths in Canada. If safe injection sites prevent deaths and the spread of disease, why are they so controversial?

Recommended Readings

• Germov, J. (2019). *Second opinion: Introduction to health sociology* (6th ed.). Don Mills, ON: Oxford University Press. Germov discusses all of the important history and concepts required to understand the social origins of health and illness. The author covers the major sociological theories and perspectives relevant to health, including the social patterns in the distribution of health and illness, the social construction of health and illness, and the social organization of health care.

• Strohschein, L., & Weitz, R. (2013). *The sociology of health, illness and health care in Canada: A critical approach.* Toronto: Nelson College Indigenous. Stohschein and Weitz (2013) review the social patterning of health and illness, the social construction of health and illness, and the social organization of health care. The authors evaluate and interpret the most current available research findings, Canadian statistics, and trends in health. The text's authors contextualize the sociology of health, illness, and health care in Canada's political, historical, and cultural landscape.

- **Geddes, G. (2017). *Medicine unbundled: A journey through the minefield of Indigenous health.* Victoria, BC: Heritage House.** This book uncovers the dark legacy of segregated Indigenous health care in Canada. Based on interviews with Indigenous elders, Geddes discovers the Indigenous peoples' experiences of segregated health care and "Indian hospitals" that existed across Canada. The elders tell of drug and surgical experiments and electroshock treatments to destroy the memory of sexual abuse.

- **Armstrong, P., & Pederson, A. (2015). *Women's health: Intersection of policy, research and practice* (2nd ed.). Toronto: Women's Press.** Armstrong and Pederson provide a comprehensive picture of women's health in Canada, exploring women's health in different social and geographical locations, the gendering of care work, and the ways in which research can influence health policy. Drawing on gender-based analysis and highlighting the diversity among women, this book calls for a renewed commitment to advocating for women's health.

Recommended Websites

Health Canada
https://www.canada.ca/en/health-canada.html
- Health Canada is a department under the federal government of Canada that provides information on maintaining and improving health. It works to reduce health risks of Canadians and to ensure that high-quality health services are accessible.

Public Health Agency of Canada
https://www.canada.ca/en/public-health.html
- The Public Health Agency of Canada helps Canadians to improve their health. The agency focuses on preventing disease and injuries, promoting good physical and mental health, and providing information to support informed decision making.

Canada Public Health Association
https://www.cpha.ca
- Canada Public Health Association is a national, not-for-profit association that advocates for universal and equitable access to the basic conditions necessary for optimal health. The association promotes the public health perspective and research to government leaders and policy makers.

Office of Women's Health
https://www.womenshealth.gov
- Although American based, the Office of Women's Health provides information on critical women's health issues by informing and advancing policies and educating health care professionals and consumers.

Glossary

absolute poverty A way of defining poverty based on an individual's ability to afford the basic necessities (food, shelter, and medicine, for example) for physical survival. See also *relative poverty*.

achieved status Attributes that individuals gain throughout their life based on effort.

affinal A family relationship by marriage.

agency The ability of individuals to make free, independent decisions.

agents of socialization Institutions and other structured relationships within which socialization takes place.

anomie Instability resulting from a breakdown of standards and values or from a lack of purpose or ideals.

apartheid A policy of institutionalized racial segregation as well as political and economic racism. The term was first used in South Africa to describe the policies of South African and West South African (Namibian) governments from 1948 to 1994.

ascribed status Advantages and disadvantages assigned at birth.

assimilation The process by which members of a minority group adopt the cultural traits (including language, food, traditions, etc.) of the dominant culture; may be voluntary or forced.

baby boom Marks a significant increase in the number of births post–World War II.

backstage interactions Interactions where people are free of the expectations and norms that dictate front stage behaviour.

bilateral descent A system of family lineage in which the relatives on the mother's side and on the father's side are equally important for emotional ties and for transfer of property or wealth.

binary construction The classification of a concept (in this case, gender or sex) into one of two mutually exclusive groups.

biological determinism The idea that our behaviour is determined solely by our genetic makeup or other biological attributes.

blaming the system A perspective that views environmental factors and systemic discrimination as responsible for an individual's circumstances.

blaming the victim A perspective that holds individuals accountable for their circumstances.

bourgeoisie The owners of the means of production; the capitalists.

bureaucracy Formal organizations that thrive in both the public and private sector.

caste system A hierarchy of groups separated from each other by rules of ritual purity and prevented from intermarrying, changing status through social mobility, or carrying out particular jobs (as determined by one's status).

charter groups Canadians of British and French ancestry; so-named because settlers from England and France first came to what is now Canada with royal permission to trade and settle (i.e., royal charters).

clan system Where every individual is connected to a large network of relatives.

class A social hierarchy based on the unequal distribution of material resources.

class consciousness Occurs when members of an oppressed group come together in recognition of their domination and oppression and collectively act to change it.

class system A hierarchy of groups with different market conditions, work situations, and life chances. In Marxist theory, classes stand in different relations to the means of production.

classism Prejudice against people of a certain standing in the social hierarchy based on their material wealth and power.

coalition The aligning of groups toward a common goal.

cognitive theory of development A theory by psychologist Jean Piaget that describes the development of abilities to think, believe, remember, perceive, and reason.

cohabitation Two or more adults who live together, share expenses, and have a sexual and/or romantic relationship without being legally married.

cohort A group of people who were born within a certain time frame and, as a result, share similar life experiences.

common sense The knowledge we get from our life experiences, through conversations with others and from what we have heard our parents say, what we read, what we see on television, and what we hear on streaming services.

conflict theory A sociological approach that assumes that social behaviour is best understood in terms of conflict between competing groups over scarce resources.

conformity When individuals or members of a group seek to be similar in terms of dress and behaviour.

conspicuous consumption The purchasing of expensive goods and services primarily for the purpose of putting one's wealth on display.

contact hypothesis A symbolic interactionist theory that contends that contact between people who are from different racial or ethnic groups but who are otherwise of equal status will result in a reduction in prejudice.

content analysis A research method for studying documents and communications, which might be texts of various formats, pictures, audio, or video.

convenience sampling A method of narrowing down potential respondents in a population by asking only those people who pass a particular place.

counterculture A subculture with values and norms that oppose the dominant culture.

crime Any act formally prohibited by criminal law.

criminology The interdisciplinary approach to the study of what gets defined as a crime, the causes of crime, the ways to prevent crime, and the punishment and rehabilitation of those who break the law.

cultural relativism An appreciation that all cultures have their own norms and values and thus should be understood on their terms rather than according to one's own cultural standards.

cultural universals Common cultural features found in all societies.

culture A collection of beliefs, values, norms, behaviours, language, and material objects that are passed on from one generation to the next.

culture shock The feelings of disorientation and uncertainty that people experience when they encounter unfamiliar cultural practices.

dark figure of crime The actual number of criminal incidents that occur compared to the number of crimes reported to police, the number of crimes prosecuted, and the number of crimes that result in a conviction.

Davis-Moore hypothesis The belief that inequality is a functional and essential part of society.

degradation ceremony The process by which people are stripped of their former selves (i.e., depersonalized).

demographic transition The transition from high birth and death rates to lower birth and death rates as a country or region develops from a pre-industrial to an industrialized economic system.

demography The study of the size, structure, distribution, and growth of the world's population.

dependent variable The variable that is being tested and measured in a scientific experiment.

deviance An action, a behaviour, or a state of being that leads to a negative reaction or response from a community or group.

diffusion The spread of invention or discovery from one area to another.

discrimination Unjust actions taken as a result of prejudice that favour one group over another group.

divorce The legal ending of a marriage by a court of law.

"doing drag" Performing (in public or on a stage) while embodying a gender identity that does not align with the sex that the performer was assigned at birth.

double-consciousness Feeling as though your identity is divided into several parts, making it impossible to have one unified identity.

dysfunction An element or a process of society that may lead to a decrease in stability.

ecofeminism A feminist analysis of environmental impacts that draws parallels between the historical exploitation of women and the historical exploitation of the planet.

ecological footprint The impact of human activities measured in terms of the area of biologically productive land and water required to produce the goods consumed and to assimilate the wastes generated.

egalitarian family A family where both partners are equal and, as a result, contribute equally to decision making.

elite A small group that has power or influence over others and that is regarded as being superior in some way.

emphasized femininity The idealized or most highly regarded traits associated with being a woman; in our current Canadian culture, this includes being attractive, compliant, caring, and available to men.

endogamy The practice of marrying *within* one's own group (class, caste, ethnic group, religion, etc.).

environmental racism The inequality between those who are using the majority of resources and those who are most feeling the negative effects of that resource use, as well as the policies and structures that maintain those inequalities on the basis of race, both within a country and between countries.

ethnicity A shared set of cultural traits—such as language, religion, national origin, traditions, and historical heritage—leading to a sense of collective existence or belonging.

ethnocentrism The tendency to assume that one's own culture and way of life represents the norm or is superior to all others.

exception fallacy A flawed principle of logic in which an observer makes conclusions about an entire group based on observed behaviour of a non-representative sample of individuals (e.g., one or two people's actions being used to form stereotypes about an entire group).

exogamy The practice of marrying *outside* one's own group (class, caste, ethnic group, religion, etc.).

experiment A method designed to study a possible cause-and-effect relationship under well-controlled, carefully regulated laboratory conditions.

exploitation theory A conflict theory that contends that racism keeps minority group members in low-paying jobs, supplying the capitalists with a cheap reserve of labour.

expressive exchanges Exchanges of emotional services between spouses, including emotional support, love, affection, friendship, and companionship.

extended family A broad social group that includes everyone with whom one has kinship; this can include multiple generations (e.g., grandparents, great-grandparents) as well as more tenuous kinship links (e.g., cousins, second cousins).

fake news Misinformation that is presented as being authentic.

false consciousness Marx's term for when the working class mistakenly identifies with the capitalist class.

family A social group containing two or more people who function as a unit for the purposes of economic co-operation, socialization, procreation (in some cases), companionship, and emotional support; may refer to one household or to a wider group of people related by blood.

femininity The sets of traits (including behaviours, roles, attributes, personality, physical appearance, and values) that are associated with being a woman in any given culture; these change over time and place.

feminist theory A sociological approach that attempts to understand, explain, and change the ways in which the construction of gender creates inequality.

feral children Human children who have lived in isolation from human contact from a very young age, some of whom are believed to have been raised by animals.

fertility rate The number of children born per child-bearer in a given society.

folkways The customs that people take part in every day, such as holding open a door for someone walking behind you or not putting your elbows on the table while you eat.

formal organizations Deliberately planned groups that coordinate people, capital, and tools through formalized roles, statuses, and relationships to efficiently achieve a specific set of goals.

formal social control An authorized procedure that defines how specific people (such as police officers) will enforce the rules and laws of a society. See also *informal social control*.

front stage interactions Interactions where people's behaviour reflects internalized norms and expectations.

functionalist theory A sociological approach that assumes social behaviour is best understood in terms of parts working together to maintain the larger society as a whole.

gatekeeper Talcott Parson's term for medical professionals who are charged with either verifying our condition as an "illness" or determining that we are "recovered."

Gemeinschaft Past society as defined by a shared past and communal networks, such as family and religious institutions.

gender Human traits (including behaviours, roles, attributes, personality, physical appearance, and values) that a culture associates with a particular sex.

gender roles The attitudes and activities that members of a culture typically expect, or desire, of other members of that culture based on their perceived sex.

gender socialization The process of learning "appropriate" sex specific behaviour.

gender stratification A hierarchical system of categorization based on gender. Traits associated with masculinity are considered positive, while traits associated with femininity are considered negative. Any deviations from these categories are understood as not just negative but dangerous. These classifications and associated power imbalances apply to all different aspects of social life.

gendered division of labour The cultural categorization of work (whether inside the home or in public) by gender.

gendered wage gap The difference in the amount of money that is earned by different genders. See also *pink ghettos*.

genocide The state-sanctioned murder of people who belong to a particular group based on any number of traits (race, ethnicity, religion, sexual orientation, ability, etc.) with the intention of eradicating that group.

Gesellschaft Present society as defined by market relations, business contracts, individuality, and competition.

glass ceiling Invisible barriers to advancement that women face in the labour market. These can be related to unconscious bias as well as to reduced qualifications because of gendered expectations (such as which school program to complete or expectations of labour at home).

glass escalator The invisible benefits granted to men in the labour market, especially white heterosexual men who embody hegemonic masculinity.

globalization The worldwide integration of government policies, cultures, social movements, and financial markets.

growth rate The rate at which population size increases each year.

health A state of complete physical, mental, and social well-being and not merely the absence of disease or infirmity.

healthy immigrant effect Refers to a trend where newcomers to Canada are healthier than the overall Canadian population (on average) due mostly to the requirements of entry as an immigrant.

hegemonic masculinity The idealized or most highly regarded traits associated with being a man; in our current Canadian culture, this includes being strong, capable, financially successful, and heterosexual.

homogamy The tendency of people with similar characteristics to marry each other.

hypothesis A proposition or tentative statement about the relationship between two or more variables that we can test through research.

I Mead's term for the element of the self that is spontaneous, creative, and impulsive.

ideology of gender A set of widespread social beliefs that gender is a binary and that there are "natural" differences between men and women (i.e., hegemonic masculinity and emphasized femininity). This ideology is entirely socially constructed and is harmful to everyone.

illness A period of impaired or abnormal functioning of the body or mind not caused by physical trauma.

incest Sexual activity between closely related members of the same kin group.

instrumental exchanges Exchanges of practical or technical services between spouses that do not include emotions but do include money and labour.

incidence Refers to the occurrence or rate at which new cases of a specific illness occur within a given population during a specific period of time (usually a year).

independent variable The variable that is changed or controlled in a scientific experiment to test the effects of the dependent variable.

informal social control The maintenance of order through non-legal means, including gossip, praise, blame, and stigma. See also *formal social control*.

in-group A group or category to which people feel they belong.

innovation Occurs when existing cultural items are manipulated or modified to produce something new and socially valuable.

internal migration People moving from one region of a country to another. Patterns of internal migration are useful indexes of changing circumstances in various regions.

intersectionality The interrelationships among various systems of discrimination and disadvantage as they apply to an individual or group, resulting in unique experiences of inequality based on the individual or group's overlapping circumstances (e.g., race, class, gender, and ability).

intersex An umbrella term that applies to someone who is born with one of several possible variations in sex characteristics from the discrete gender binary categories; these differences can be chromosomal, gonadal, hormonal, or related to visible genitalia.

Islamophobia Prejudice or discrimination toward Muslim people.

kin group A group of people related by blood or marriage.

labelling theory A symbolic interactionist approach to deviance that believes people come to identify with and behave in ways that reflect how others label them.

language A shared system of communication that includes both verbal and nonverbal gestures to convey meaning.

latent functions The unintended and often hidden ways in which an institution or social phenomenon operates.

life expectancy The number of years that a person is expected to live based on the average number of years lived by a particular population.

looking-glass self A sense of oneself formed through interaction with others by assessing how they view us.

low income cut-off (LICO) A method of defining poverty that identifies income thresholds of families who are likely to spend a larger proportion of their income on necessities than an average family of similar size.

low income measure (LIM) A method of defining poverty that calculates the low-income threshold of a household as one-half of the median income of a household of the same size in a similar-sized community.

macrosociology The study of society, social institutions, and large social groups.

Malthus theory Thomas Malthus's theory that population will increase at a faster rate than its means of subsistence (i.e., food production). Malthus proposed that unless population growth is stopped through moral or legal restraint, it will inevitably be stopped by disease, famine, war, widespread poverty, and degradation.

manifest functions The intended and easily recognized ways in which an institution or social phenomenon operates.

market basket measure (MBM) A method of defining poverty that calculates how much income a household requires to meet its needs. This includes subsistence needs, such as basic food and shelter. It also includes the needs to satisfy community norms.

masculinity The sets of traits (including behaviours, roles, attributes, personality, physical appearance, and values) that are associated with being a man in any given culture; these change over time and place.

master status A status that dominates all others.

material culture The physical artifacts and objects found in a culture.

matriarchy Systematic gender inequality in favour of women. Women are favoured or exclusively granted power, such as political decision-making authority, control of resources, and ability to inherit wealth.

matrix of domination The ways that race, sexuality, and class (among other inequalities) intersect with gender, making inequality not just more pronounced but unique for each individual based on their circumstances; coined by Patricia Hill Collins.

matrilineal descent A system of passing down wealth and power that counts only kin relationships through female family members.

McDonaldization The process by which the principles of the fast-food industry have come to dominate organizations.

Me Mead's term for the socialized element of the self.

mechanical solidarity Characteristic of societies with a minimal division of labour and group solidarity.

medicalization The process by which conditions, experiences, and issues become defined and treated as illness or disease and, therefore, as something to be studied, diagnosed, and treated.

meritocracy A system of rewards based purely on demonstrated ability.

microsociology The study of small social groups and individual social interaction.

migration The number of people moving in and out of a region.

minority groups Those groups that have less power and control over their own lives than the dominant group in a society.

mixed methods A way of conducting research that involves both quantitative and qualitative data.

mode of production A way of producing the material things we need to survive.

moral order Unwritten social norms and conventions that serve to maintain societal order.

morbidity The prevalence (total number) and patterns of disease in a population.

mores Social norms that are widely observed and are considered to have greater moral significance than others.

mortality The incidence and patterns of death in a population.

mortality rate The measurement of the number of deaths in a particular population divided by the population as a whole, per unit of time (usually per year).

multiculturalism The freedom of individuals of all origins to preserve, enhance, and share their cultural heritage and to participate in society fully and equally.

negative population growth The rate at which population size declines.

net migration rate The number of immigrants, minus the number of emigrants, per year per thousand inhabitants.

nonmaterial culture/symbolic culture The intangible and abstract components of a society, including a society's values and norms and religious beliefs.

norms The rules and expectations by which a society guides the behaviour of its members.

nuclear family A kinship structure consisting solely of two parents and their children.

obedience The notion that an individual will adhere to a set of rules or social codes.

objectivity A lack of bias, prejudice, or judgment.

operant conditioning A method of training that rewards compliant behaviours and punishes deviant behaviours.

organic solidarity Characteristic of societies with a large division of labour and group interdependence.

organizations Large groups that have a collective goal or purpose.

othering The classification of a group of people as "not one of us," i.e., different and therefore lesser; intentionally used on a political level to dehumanize a group of people in order to make it morally acceptable to discriminate against them.

out-group A group to which people do not feel they belong.

participant observation A method for gathering information by participating in the social group being studied.

patriarchy The cultural system in which men hold power and authority; the father is the authority in the family and descent is reckoned in the male line.

patrilineal descent A system of passing down wealth and power that counts only kin relationships through male family members.

peer group A group of companions with whom one interacts, particularly from late childhood through adolescence and into early adulthood, and who relate to one another as equals.

pink ghettos Employment areas dominated by women, characterized by lower average wages, more precarious work (e.g., part-time, high turnover), and being undervalued in society.

pluralism A philosophy that urges tolerance for racial/ethnic differences and protects the rights of minority individuals through provincial human rights codes and other legislation, while maintaining the dominance of the hegemonic group.

population In research, the set of all individuals who share some specific characteristic of interest to the researcher.

positivism A philosophy that prizes reason, logic, and the scientific method (observation and analysis) over belief or faith.

poverty The state of lacking sufficient material resources to live a life that is considered normal or comfortable in a society. See also *absolute poverty* and *relative poverty*.

prejudice A negative or hostile attitude toward members of a particular group simply because they belong to that group, based on assumptions and stereotypes about their characteristics.

prestige Honour and respect; a type of stratification that is separate from income, authority, or class position.

prevalence The total number of cases of a particular illness that exist in a specific geography at a specific period of time.

primary group A small group characterized by intimate face-to-face interactions.

primary socialization The early socialization of children, much of which takes place in a family setting.

proletariat The workers; those who produce for the bourgeoisie.

pull factors All those factors that encourage people to move to a particular area (in relation to migration).

push factors All those factors that encourage people to leave an area (in relation to migration).

qualitative research Using the scientific method to gather non-numerical data; usually uses smaller sample sizes and is interested in detailed analysis of motivations and personal interpretations.

quantitative research Using the scientific method to gather numerical data; usually used for larger sample sizes, quantitative research is interested in broader analysis of behaviours and trends that can be applied to populations as a whole.

questionnaires A set of questions with a choice of predetermined answers devised for the purpose of a survey.

race A group whose members are defined as sharing the same physical characteristics, especially skin tone. Personality and cultural attributes have been assigned to these different racial categories in ways that justify and perpetuate white supremacy.

racism Systemic prejudice and discrimination by the dominant racial group against subordinate racial groups in a society.

rational choice theory The early criminological approach to crime that assumed people weigh the pros and cons of committing a crime and then make a logical decision to either commit a crime or not.

reference group Any group that individuals use as a standard for evaluating themselves.

relative poverty A way to define poverty that compares an individual's circumstances against the general living standards of the society or group in which they live; a low standard of living compared to most. See also *absolute poverty*.

reliability Refers to the extent to which a measure produces consistent results.

research ethics Governing principles that dictate standards of behaviour for the collection, analysis, and interpretation of data in order to ensure that undertaking these tasks does not do harm.

reserve A section of land set aside for a particular Indigenous band or nation by the Canadian government. Rules about reserves are set by the Canadian government, despite Indigenous Peoples' demands for sovereignty.

resocialization A learning process that reshapes the individual's personality by teaching radically different values, norms, and role expectations, often within a total institution.

response bias The tendency of people to answer questions untruthfully or in ways that may be misleading.

role conflict A situation that occurs when incompatible expectations arise when one individual holds two or more social positions.

role exit The process of disengaging from a role that is central to one's self-identity in order to establish a new role.

role strain The difficulty that arises when the same social position imposes conflicting demands and expectations.

sample A relatively small number of people drawn from the population of interest.

sanctions Rewards for adhering to a norm and punishments for violating a norm.

Sapir-Whorf hypothesis The theory that language shapes reality.

scientific method An investigative process that involves the creation and testing of hypotheses through systematic observation and measurement.

second shift The double burden of work and housework experienced by women; coined by Arlie Hochschild.

secondary data analysis Examines and interprets data gathered by another researcher or by the government.

secondary group A formal impersonal group with little social intimacy.

secondary socialization The ongoing and lifelong process of socialization, including accumulated learning in adolescence and adulthood.

segregation The physical separation of groups of people in terms of residence, workplace, and other social structures.

sex The social construction of categories based on physical and biological characteristics; in the hegemonic Canadian society, these categories are male and female.

sexual harassment Any behaviour that is of a sexual nature (this can be conduct, comment, gesture, or touching) and that is likely to cause offence or humiliation or that might be perceived as demanding something sexual of a person in order to receive an opportunity or advancement. Note that this definition relies on perceptions and expectations of the person being harassed, as well as on how the behaviour will be seen by the wider social audience (i.e., what might cause humiliation); therefore, which behaviours fall under this term have changed over time.

sick role A social role that defines the behaviour that is appropriate for and expected of those who are sick.

significant others Those people who play a major role in shaping a person's self.

single-parent (or lone-parent) family A family in which only one parent lives with dependent children.

snowball sampling A method of narrowing down potential respondents in a population by starting with one respondent and asking that person to recommend the next person to talk to.

social control All the institutions and procedures that influence members of society to conform to rules of expected behaviour. See also *formal social control* and *informal social control*.

social demography The effects of population changes on the organization of societies, and vice versa.

social determinants of health The many sociological conditions of a person's life that influence their health, including income, social status, employment, working conditions, education, literacy, childhood, physical location, social supports, health behaviours, access to health care, genetic endowments, gender, race, and culture.

social disorganization A theory that believed the industrialization, urbanization, and immigration that accompanied modernization had shattered society's traditional order and values, making it difficult to maintain effective social controls and resulting in modern, industrial societies being more conducive to deviance than others.

social epidemiology A branch of the study of the distribution and determinants of health and illness that focuses particularly on the effects of social-structural factors on health.

social institution A social structure made up of two or more relationships (i.e., stable patterns of meaningful orientations to one another.

social integration The internalization of norms and values that allow us to function well as a group.

social mobility The movement of individuals among different levels of the occupational hierarchy. Movement may be vertical or horizontal, across generations or within a generation.

social network A network of individuals (such as friends, acquaintances, and co-workers) connected by interpersonal relationships.

social reproduction The process by which a society reproduces itself from one generation to another and also within generations.

social science A major category of academic discipline, concerned with society and the relationships among individuals within a society—included in this are sociology, anthropology, political science, and social geography, among others.

social scripts The culturally constructed, socially enforced practices that we are all expected to follow when we interact in social situations.

social structure Any enduring, predictable pattern of social relations among people in society.

social stratification A system of inequality that integrates class, status, and domination with other forms of differentiation, such as gender, race, ethnicity, ability, religion, and sexual orientation.

socialization The learning process through which an individual becomes a capable member of society.

society The largest-scale social structure, whose members interact with one another, share a common geographic territory, and share common institutions.

socio-economic status (SES) A method of ranking people that combines measures of wealth, authority (or power), and prestige.

sociological imagination The ability to place and understand the personal experiences of individuals within the societal context in which these experiences occur.

sociological perspective The ability to see the general in the particular and the strange in the familiar.

sociology The systematic study of human and social behaviour; including culture, social structures, relationships, social interactions, and the study of society as a whole.

sociology of health and illness The interaction between society and health: how our social life impacts rates of disease and death in different population segments, and in turn how those rates compare to society as a whole.

standpoint theory A feminist political position that argues that knowledge stems from social position.

status A socially defined position within society.

stereotype A broadly believed idea or trait about a particular group, in which the trait is assumed to apply to all members of that group.

stigma A mark of shame or social disgrace that discredits an individual or group.

strain theory A theory that proposes that the cause of deviance lies in society's unequal opportunity structure—the strain between societal expectations and societal opportunities is what encourages criminal behaviour in some.

structure The identifiable elements of society that produce relatively stable opportunities and constraints in people's lives.

structured interview An interaction where respondents are asked a standard set of questions in the same form and the same order.

subculture A segment of a culture that has characteristics that distinguish it from the broader culture.

subjectivity An interpretation of reality through our own experiences, opinions, values, feelings, and beliefs.

symbol An object, image, or event used to represent a particular concept.

symbolic interactionism A sociological perspective asserting that people create meaning through interactions.

systematic random sampling A method of narrowing down potential respondents in a population by taking a complete list of all members of the population, choosing a random starting point, and selecting people on a set interval.

systemic discrimination Biases against subordinate groups that are so deeply embedded in a society's institutions and customs that they are hard to see but are enforced across the society and create perpetual disadvantages for the subordinate group.

theory A set of propositions intended to explain a fact or social phenomenon.

total institutions Institutions in which people are monitored 24 hours a day, seven days a week, as they are in prisons, mental hospitals, and military barracks.

transgender An umbrella term for people whose gender identity does not align with the sex that they were assigned at birth.

treadmill of production A theory that argues the economy (and capitalism's demand for continual growth) drives the decision-making of society, without regard for the physical limitations to growth, such as finite resources, or the environmental impact of growth.

two-spirit A modern umbrella term used by some Indigenous peoples within North America to describe people within their communities who fulfill one of many traditional non-conforming roles that transgress the hegemonic gender binary (including a third gender, multiple genders, and transgender identities); as with all identities related to gender, the identity of two-spirit is distinct from sexual orientation.

unobtrusive measures Measures that don't require the researcher to intrude in the research context.

unstructured interview An interaction where respondents are asked flexible and open-ended questions.

validity Refers to accurately measuring a concept.

values Beliefs about ideal goals and behaviour that serve as standards for social life.

variable Any trait, quality, or characteristic that can vary in size over time or across individuals or groups.

victimless crime A category of crime from which no one suffers directly except perhaps the persons engaging in the behaviour.

visible minority Racial groups that have less power and control over their own lives than the dominant group in a society. In Canada, this refers to anyone who is not white and who is non-Indigenous (not because Indigenous Peoples are a dominant group but because Indigenous Peoples have enough unique traits to be considered separately within the sociological study of Canada).

white-collar crimes Crimes committed by high-status people, often in the course of their work; they include fraud, forgery, tax evasion, price-fixing, work-safety violations, and embezzlement.

xenocentrism The preference for a culture other than one's own.

xenophobia The fear and/or distrust of people and traits that are perceived to be foreign or strange.

References

Chapter 1

Amnesty International Canada. (2018). *Final written submission: National Inquiry on Missing and Murdered Indigenous Women and Girls.* Retrieved from https://www.amnesty.ca/sites/amnesty/files/Amnesty%20International%20Canada%20National%20Inquiry%20MMIWG%20Final%20Written%20Submission.pdf

Berger, P. (1963). *Invitation to sociology: A humanistic perspective.* New York: Garden City.

Brown, S., Souto-Manning, M., & Laman, T. (2010). Seeing the strange in the familiar: Unpacking racialized practices in early childhood settings. *Race Ethnicity and Education 13*(4), 513–532.

Clement, W. (2001). Legacy for a new millennium, edited by Harry H. Hiller. *Canadian Journal of Sociology, 26*(3), 405–420.

Cumming, S. J. (2014). *Lone mothers exiting social assistance: Gender, social exclusions and social capital.* Waterloo: University of Waterloo.

Delanty G. (2007). Sociology. In G. Ritzer (Ed.), *Blackwell Encyclopedia of Sociology.* Hoboken, NJ: John Wiley & Sons.

Denzin, N.K. (1992). *Symbolic interactionism and cultural studies: The politics of interpretation.* Hoboken, NJ: Blackwell.

Edmiston D. (2018). The poor "sociological imagination" of the rich: Explaining attitudinal divergence towards welfare, inequality and redistribution. *Social Policy & Administration, 52*(5), 983–997.

Étile, F. (2007). Social norms, ideal body weight, and food attitudes. *Health Economics, 16*(9). https://doi.org/10.1002/hec.1251

Granovetter, M. (1974). *Getting a job: A study of contacts and careers.* Cambridge, MA.: Harvard University.

Mills, C.W. (1955). *The sociological imagination.* Oxford, England: Oxford University Press.

Ravelli, B., & Webber, M. (2016). *Exploring sociology* (3rd ed.). Toronto: Pearson Publishing.

Chapter 2

Aikenhead, G., & Dyke, L. (2013). Unethical experiments highlight need for aboriginal scientists. *The Vancouver Sun.* Retrieved from http://www.vancouversun.com/life/Unethical+experiments+highlight+need+aboriginal+scientists/8924801/story.html

Barr, N. (2015). The end of thinking. *Quartz.* Retrieved from https://qz.com/572269/most-of-the-information-we-spread-online-is-quantifiably-bullshit/

Bell Hooks Biography. (2017). In *Notable biographies.com.* Retrieved from http://www.notablebiographies.com/He-Ho/Hooks-Bell.html

Cassino, D. (2016, September 26). How today's political polling works. *Harvard Business Review.* Retrieved from https://hbr.org/2016/08/how-todays-political-polling-works

Cillizza, C. (2017, January 21). Sean Spicer held a press conference. He didn't take questions. Or tell the whole truth. *The Washington Post.*

Fandos, N. (2017, January 22). Fact-checking the White House "alternative facts." *The Seattle Times.*

Harrison, D., & Albanese, P. (2017). *Growing up in Armyville: Canada's military families during the Afghanistan mission.* Waterloo, ON: Wilfrid Laurier University Press.

hooks, b. (1981). *Ain't I a woman* (1st ed.). Boston, Mass: South End Press.

Humphreys, L. (1970). *Tearoom grade: Impersonal sex in public places.* Chicago: Aldine

Humphreys, L., Gill, P., Krishnamurthy, B., & Newbury, E. (2013). Historicizing new media: A content analysis of Twitter. *Journal of Communication, 3,* 413. Retrieved from https://proxy.library.brocku.ca/login?url=http://search.ebscohost.com/login.aspx?direct=true&db=edsgao&AN=edsgcl.332311364&site=eds-live&scope=site

Kesslar, G. (2017, January 22). Spicer earns four Pinocchios for false claims on inauguration crowd size. *Washington Post.* Retrieved from https://www.washingtonpost.com/news/fact-checker/wp/2017/01/22/spicer-earns-four-pinocchios-for-a-series-of-false-claims-on-inauguration-crowd-size/

Kidder, D., & Oppenheim, N. (2010). *The intellectual devotional biographies: Revive your mind, complete your education, and acquaint yourself with the world's greatest personalities.* Gordonsville: Rodale.

Mehler Paperney, A. (2015). No Canada does not spend more on refugees than on pensioners. *Global News.* Retrieved from https://globalnews.ca/news/2349786/no-canada-doesnt-spend-more-on-refugees-than-pensioners/

Morris, A. (2015). *The scholar denied: W.E.B. Du Bois and the birth of modern sociology.* Oakland, CA: University of California Press.

Mosby I. (2013). Administering colonial science: Nutrition research and human biomedical experimentation in Aboriginal communities and residential schools, 1942–1952. *Social History, 46,* 145–172.

Most Asked Questions on Google. (2017). Retrieved 28 October 2017 from https://www.mondovo.com/keywords/most-asked-questions-on-google

Ogan, C., & Varol, O. (2017). What is gained and what is left to be done when content analysis is added to network analysis in the study of a social movement: Twitter use during Gezi Park. *Information, Communication & Society, 20*(8), 1220–1238. https://doi.org/10.1080/1369118X.2016.1229006

Parsons, T. (1951). *The social systems.* London: Routledge: Taylor and Francis Group.

Patterson, J. (2002). Understanding family resilience. *Journal of clinical psychology, 58,* 233–246. https://doi.org/10.1002/jclp.10019

Ramp, W., & Harrison, T.W. (2012). Libertarian populism, neoliberal rationality, and the mandatory long-form census: Implications for sociology. *Canadian Journal of Sociology/Cahiers Canadiens de Sociologie, 37*(3), 273. Retrieved from https://proxy.library.brocku.ca/login?url=http://search.ebscohost.com/login.aspx?direct=true&db=edsjsr&AN=edsjsr.canajsocicahican.37.3.273&site=eds-live&scope=site

Raywat S. D. (2011). The mandatory census: Tension between individual rights and the public good. *Canadian Journal of Public Health/Revue Canadienne de Sante'e Publique, 102*(6), 414. Retrieved from https://proxy.library.brocku.ca/login?url=http://search.ebscohost.com/login.aspx?direct=true&db=edsjsr&AN=edsjsr.41995647&site=eds-live&scope=site

Sanderson, B. (2017, February 13). Statistics Canada says response rate to 2016 census is highest yet. CBC *News*. Retrieved from https://www.cbc.ca/news/canada/statistics-canada-census-lockheed-martin-1.3975666

Statistics Canada. (2015). Social assistance receipt amongst refugees claimants in Canada. *Statistics Canada*. Retrieved from http://www.statcan.gc.ca/pub/11–626–x/11–626–x2015051–eng.htm

Tyszkiewicz, M. (2017). Putting sex worker rights front and centre at SlutWalk Toronto. *Torontoist*. Retrieved from https://torontoist.com/2017/08/putting-sex-worker-rights-front-centre-slutwalk-toronto/

Webb, E., Campbell, D., Schwartz, R., & Sechrest, L. (1966) *Unobtrusive measures: Nonreactive research in the social sciences*. Chicago: Rand McNally.

W.E.B. Du Bois. (2017). In *Biography.com*. Retrieved from https://www.biography.com/people/web-du-bois-9279924

Wilson, R.T., Hasanali, S.H., Sheikh, M., Cramer, S., Weinberg, G., Firth, A., . . . Soskolne, C.L. (2017). Review paper: Challenges to the census: International trends and a need to consider public health benefits. *Public Health, 151*, 87–97. https://doi-org.proxy.library.brocku.ca/10.1016/j.puhe.2017.05.015

Zimbardo, P. (2008). How good people turn evil, from Stanford to Abu Ghraib. *TED Talk*. Retrieved from https://www.ted.com/talks/philip_zimbardo_on_the_psychology_of_evil?language=en

Chapter 3

Abolfotouh, E., & Abolfotouh. (2015). Awareness and predictors of female genital mutilation/cutting among young health advocates. *International Journal of Women's Health, 7*, 259–269. Retrieved from https://www.ncbi.nlm.nih.gov/pmc/articles/PMC4346006/

Althaus, F. (1997). Female circumcision: Rite of passage or violation of rights? *International Perspectives and Sexual and Reproductive Health, 23*(3), 130.

Assunção, C., Brown, M., & Workman, R. (2017). Pokémon is evolving! An investigation into the development of the Pokémon community and expectations for the future of the franchise. *Press Start, 4*(1), 17–35. Retrieved from https://proxy.library.brocku.ca/login?url=http://search.ebscohost.com/login.aspx?direct=true&db=a9h&AN=123972609&site=eds-live&scope=site

Bourdieu, P. (1986). The forms of capital. In J.E. Richardson (Ed.), *Handbook of theory of research in education* (pp. 241–258). Santa Barbara, CA: Greenwood Press.

Clare, R. (2016). Black lives matter: The Black Lives Matter Movement in the National Museum of African American History and Culture. *Transfers, 1*, 122. https://doi-org.proxy.library.brocku.ca/10.3167/TRANS.2016.060112

Cox, A. (2014, 5 August). I stood firm on my hair and won self-respect. *The Toronto Star*. Retrieved from https://www.thestar.com/life/2014/08/05/i_stood_firm_on_my_hair_and_won_selfrespect.html

Da Silva, M. (2015, 4 December). Black hair discrimination prompts protest. *Now Toronto*. Retrieved from https://nowtoronto.com/news/black-hair-discrimination-prompts-protest

Davis, P.E. (2003). Good hair and bad hair: What this seems to say about us. *Multicultural Education, 10*(4), 39–41. Retrieved from https://proxy.library.brocku.ca/login?url=http://search.ebscohost.com/login.aspx?direct=true&db=eue&AN=507842408&site=eds-live&scope=site

Dominion Institute. (2015). Defining Canada: A nation chooses the 101 things that best define their country. Retrieved from https://www.historicacanada.ca/sites/default/files/PDF/polls/canada101_part3_en.pdf

Field, J. (2008). *Social capital* (2nd ed.). New York: Routledge.

Jankowiak, W.R., Volsche, S.L., & Garcia, J.R. (2015). Is the romantic-sexual kiss a near human universal? *American Anthropologist, 117*(3), 535–539.

Keating, S. (2010, 28 January). Hockey is more than a Canadian game. *Reuters*. Retrieved from https://www.reuters.com/article/us-olympics-ice-hockey-canada/hockey-is-more-than-a-game-to-canadians-idUSTRE60S00G20100129

Kiwanuka, N. (2017, 3 August). The politics of natural hair. tvo. Retrieved from https://tvo.org/article/current-affairs/the-politics-of-natural-hair

Kubota, R. (2015). Race and language learning in multicultural Canada: Towards critical antiracism. *Journal of Multilingual & Multicultural Development, 36*(1), 3–12. https://doi-org.proxy.library.brocku.ca/10.1080/01434632.2014.892497

Lehmann, W., & Trwoer, H. (2018). Forms of capital and habitus in the decision to go on academic exchange. *Canadian Review of Sociology, 55*(1). https://doi.org/10.1111/cars.12182

Lorenz, S.L. (2015). Media, culture, and the meanings of hockey. *International Journal of the History of Sport, 32*(17), 1973–1986. https://doi-org.proxy.library.brocku.ca/10.1080/09523367.2015.1124863

Murdock, G.P. (1945). *Social structure*. New York: The MacMillan Company.

Newton, S. (2018). The excessive use of force against blacks in the United States of America. *International Journal of Human Rights, 22*(8), 1067. Retrieved from https://proxy.library.brocku.ca/login?url=http://search.ebscohost.com/login.aspx?direct=true&db=edb&AN=132160205&site=eds-live&scope=site

Oreopoulos, P. (2011). Why do skilled immigrants struggle in the labour market? A field experiment with thirteen thousand resumes. *American Economic Journal: Economic Policy, 3*(4), 148–171.

Perception Institute. (2016). The good hair study. Retrieved from https://perception.org/goodhair/results/

Pogue, G. (2017). Flag & football in America. *Diverse Issues in Higher Education, 21*, 32. Retrieved from https://proxy.library.brocku.ca/login?url=http://search.ebscohost.com/login.aspx?direct=true&db=edsgao&AN=edsgcl.516664391&site=eds-live&scope=site

Smith, T.W. (2015). Buzz words. *New Scientist, 227*(3039), 41–43.

Statistics Canada. (2017). Police reported hate crimes. *The Daily*. Retrieved from https://www150.statcan.gc.ca/n1/daily-quotidien/170613/dq170613b-eng.htm?HPA=1

Tasker, J.P. (2018, 31 January). Canada passes bill to make O Canada lyrics gender neutral. *CBC News*. Retrieved from http://www.cbc.ca/news/politics/anthem-bill-passes-senate-1.4513317

Tickner, J.A. (2002). Feminist perspectives on 9/11. *International Studies Perspectives, 3*(4), 333–350.

Chapter 4

Andreassen, C.S., Pallesen, S., & M. Griffiths. (2017). The relationship between addictive use of social media, narcissism, and self-esteem: Findings from a large national survey. *Addictive Behaviours, 64,* 287–283.

Beach, C. (2008). Canada's aging workforce: Participation, productivity and living standards. *Bank of Canada.* Retrieved from https://www.bankofcanada.ca/wp-content/uploads/2010/09/beach.pdf

Bentley, C.S. (2008). The great information equalizer. *New American, 24*(8).

Berndt, T.J., & Keefe, K. (1995). Friends' influence on adolescents' adjustment to school. *Child development, 66*(5), 1312–1329.

Boyd, D. (2015). *It's complicated: The social lives of networked teens.* New Haven: Yale University Press.

Center for Research on Globalization. (2013). Non-Muslims carried out more than 90% of all terrorist attacks in America. Centre for Research on Globalization. Retrieved from https://www.globalresearch.ca/non-muslims-carried-out-more-than-90-of-all-terrorist-attacks-in-america/5333619

Davis, J.N. (1997, September). Birth order sibship size and status in modern Canada. *Human Nature, 8*(3), 205–230.

Delroy, P., & Trapnell. (1999). Birth order effects on personality and achievement within families. *Psychological Science 10*(6).

Denton, F., & Spencer, B. (2010). Chronic health conditions: Changing prevalence in an aging population and some implications for the delivery of health care services. *Canadian Journal on Aging, 29*(1), 11–21.

Dombrowski, S.C. (2011). Feral children. In *Assessing and treating low incidence/high severity psychological disorders of childhood* (pp. 81–93). New York: Springer.

Donnelly, M.K. (2013). Drinking with derby girls: Exploring the hidden ethnography in research of women's flat track roller derby. *International Review for the Sociology of Sport, 49*(3/4), 346–366.

Downey, A. (2015). Proceedings from 14th Python in Science Conference: *Will Millennials ever get married?* Retrieved from http://conference.scipy.org/proceedings/scipy2015/pdfs/allen_downey.pdf

Dunbar, L. (2017). *Youth gangs in Canada: A review of current topics and issues.* Public Safety Canada. Retrieved from https://www.publicsafety.gc.ca/cnt/rsrcs/pblctns/2017-r001/2017-r001-en.pdf

Government of Canada. (2011). *Family violence: How big is the problem in Canada?* Retrieved from https://www.canada.ca/en/public-health/services/health-promotion/stop-family-violence/problem-canada.html

Harlow, H.F., Dodsworth, R.O., & Harlow, M.K. (1965). Total social isolation in monkeys. *Proceedings of the National Academy of Sciences of the United States of America, 54*(1), 90–97.

Harris, A. (2016). Transition and the art of engagement, nuts and bolts. Student Services Department, Australian College of Applied Psychology (ACAP). Retrieved from http://fyhe.com.au/past_papers/papers11/FYHE-2011/content/pdf/5A.pdf

Hernandez, D., McCarthy, T., & McGown, M. (2017). Mandalee Bay attack: At least 59 killed in deadliest US shooting. *The Guardian.* Retrieved from https://www.theguardian.com/us-news/2017/oct/02/las-vegas-active-shooter-harvest-country-music-festival

hooks, b. (2004). Understanding patriarchy. In *The will to change: Men, masculinity, and love* (pp. 17–34). New York: Atria Books.

Hopton, J. L., & Huta, V. (2013). Evaluation of an intervention designed for men who were abused in childhood and are experiencing symptoms of posttraumatic stress disorder. *Psychology of Men & Masculinity, 14*(3), 300–313. Retrieved from https://doi-org.proxy.library.brocku.ca/10.1037/a0029705

Hutton, J., Horowitz-Kraus, T., Mendelsohn, A., DeWitt, T., & Holland, S. (2015). Home reading environment and brain activation in preschool children listening to stories. *Pediatrics, 136*(3). Retrieved from https://pediatrics.aappublications.org/content/136/3/466

Indian, M., & Grieve, R. (2014). When Facebook is easier than face-to-face: Social support derived from Facebook in socially anxious individuals. *Personality and Individual Differences, 59,* 102–106.

Internet World Stats. (2019). *Canada.* Retrieved from https://www.internetworldstats.com/stats14.htm#north

Irwin, M.D. (2015). Mourning 2.0: Continuing bonds between the living and the dead on Facebook. OMEGA—*Journal of Death and Dying, 72*(2), 119–150.

Itard, J.M.G. (1962). *The wild boy of Aveyron.* New York: Meredith Company.

Kelly, D., Pomerantz, S., & Currie, D. (2005). Skater girlhood and emphasized femininity: "You can't land an ollie properly in heels." *Gender & Education, 17*(3), 129–148.

Mannheim, K. (1952). The problem of generations. In P. Kecskemeti (Ed.), *Essays on the sociology of knowledge: Collected works* (Vol. 5, pp. 276–322). New York: Routledge.

Marshall, V., & Mueller, M. (2002). Rethinking social policy for an aging workforce and society: Insights from the life course perspective. *Canadian Policy Research Networks.* Retrieved from https://www.voced.edu.au/content/ngv:39646

Matthews, R.J. (2005). The body beautiful: Adolescent girls and images of beauty. In B. Ravelli (Ed.), *Exploring Canadian sociology: A reader* (pp. 39–50). Toronto, ON: Pearson Education Canada.

Metzl, J. (2017). When the shooter is white. *The Washington Post.* Retrieved from https://www.washingtonpost.com/news/made-by-history/wp/2017/10/06/when-the-shooter-is-white/?utm_term=.b4c4bc8411b8

Mitchell, B., & Lovegreen, L. (2009). The empty nest syndrome in midlife families: A multimethod exploration of parental gender differences and cultural dynamics. *Journal of Family Issues, 30,* 1651–1670.

Newton, M. (2004). *Savage girls and wild boys: A history of feral children.* USA: Picador.

Ng, E., Lyons, S., & Schweitzer, L. (2016). Millennials in Canada: Young workers in a challenging labour market. In E. Parry & J. McCarthy (Eds.), *The Palgrave handbook of age diversity and work.* London: Palgrave Macmillian.

Nielsen Music Canada. (2015). *Canadian music year end report.* Retrieved from https://www.nielsen.com/ca/en/insights/reports/2016/2015-music-canada-year-end-report.html

Piaget, J. (1952). *The origins of intelligence in children.* New York: W.W. Norton & Co. https://doi.org/10.1037/11494-000

Ruiz-Grossman, S. (2017). The double standard in how the media is portraying the Las Vegas shooter. *Huffington Post.* Retrieved from http://www.huffingtonpost.ca/entry/double-standard-white-privilege-media-las-vegas-shooting_us_59d-3da15e4b04b9f92058316

Salmon, C., & Daly, M. (1998). Birth order and familial sentiment: Middleborns are different. *Evolution and Human Behavior, 19*, 299–312.

Schrag, C. (1954). Leadership among prison inmates. *American Sociological Review, 19*(1), 37–42.

Television Bureau of Canada. (2014). TV basics 2013–2014. Retrieved from http://www.tvb.ca

Thuo, M., & Madhanit, E. (2017). Transition to university life: Insights from high school and university female students in Wolaita Zone, Ethiopia. *Journal of Education and Practice, 8*(4).

Truth and Reconciliation Commission of Canada. (2008). About us. Retrieved from http://www.trc.ca/about-us.html

Vogel, E., Roberts, L., Rose, J., & Eckles, K. (2014). Social comparison, social media, and self-esteem. *Psychology of Popular Media Culture, 3*(4), 206–222.

Wallace, M. (1999). *Birth order blues*. New York: Henry Holt and Co.

Wilkins-Laflamme, S. (2018). Islamophobia in Canada: Measuring the realities of negative attitudes toward Muslims and religious discrimination. *Canadian Review of Sociology, 55*(1), 86–110.

Wister, A., & Mitchell, B. (2015). Midlife challenge or welcome departure? Cultural and family-related expectations of empty nest transitions. *The Journal of Aging and Human Development, 81*(4), 260–280.

Wortley, S. (2010). *Identifying street gangs: Definitional dilemmas and their policy implications*. Ottawa, ON: Public Safety Canada.

Wu, H., Guzman, N., & Garza, E. (2015). International student's challenge and adjustment to college. *Hindawi Publishing Corporation*. Retrieved from https://www.researchgate.net/publication/276350988_International_Student's_Challenge_and_Adjustment_to_College

Wyrich, A. (2017). The striking difference between Trump's response to Pulse and Las Vegas shootings. *The Daily Dot*. Retrieved from https://www.dailydot.com/layer8/trump-las-vegas-pulse-response/

Chapter 5

Bloch, F. (2011, March). Social networks, employment, and insurance. *CESifo Economic Studies, CESifo, 57*(1), 183–202.

Bond, N. (2011). Gemeinschaft and Gesellschaft. In J. Marjanen, J. Ifversen, M. Pernau, & M. Planck (Eds.), *Contributions to the history of concepts*. New York/Oxford: Berghahn Independent Publishing.

Bonesteel. M. (2017, 17 May). New Baylor lawsuit alleges football team uses gang rape as a bonding experience. *The Washington Post*.

Byrne, E., Vessey, J.A., & Pfeifer, L. (2018, February). Cyberbullying and social media: Information and interventions for school nurses working with victims, students, and families. *Journal of School Nursing, 34*(1), 38–50.

Collins, P.H. (1990). *Black feminist thought: Knowledge, consciousness, and the politics of empowerment*. Boston: Unwin Hyman.

Creed, P.A., French, J., & Hood, M. (2015). Working while studying at university: The relationship between work benefits and demands and engagement and well-being. *Journal of Vocational Behavior, 86*, 48–57. http://dx.doi.org/10.1016/j.jvb.2014.11.002

Cumming, S. (2014). *Lone mothers exiting social assistance: gender, social exclusion and social capital*. Waterloo, ON: University of Waterloo.

Devlin, R., & Pothier, D. (2006). Introduction: Towards a critical theory of dis-citizenship. In D. Pothier & R. Devlin (Eds.), *Critical disability theory: Essays in philosophy, politics, policy, and law*. Vancouver, BC: UBC Press.

Durkheim, E. (1933). *Division of labor in society*. New York, Macmillan.

Ebaugh, H. (1988). *Becoming an ex: The process of role exit*. Chicago: University of Chicago Press.

Feldman, D. (2019). According to Netflix, we all have 6 shows in common. *Forbes*. Retrieved from https://www.forbes.com/sites/danafeldman/2019/02/13/according-to-netflix-we-all-have-6-shows-in-common/#59a2856463d0

Goffman, E. (1959). *The presentation of self in everyday life*. New York: Anchor.

Hamilton, R., Scott, D., O'Sullivan, L.F., & LaChapelle, D.L. (2013). *An examination of the rookie hazing experiences of university athletes in Canada. Canadian Journal for Social Research, 3*(1), 35–48

Hughes, E. (1945). Dilemmas and contradictions of status. *American Journal of Sociology, 50*(5), 350–359.

Johnson, J., & Holman, M. (2004). *Making the team: Inside the world of sports initiations and hazing*. Toronto: Canadian Scholars' Press Inc.

Kerrigan, F., & Hart, A. (2016). Theorising digital personhood: A dramaturgical approach. *Journal of Marketing Management, 32*, 17–18.

Lewchuk, W., Laflèche, M., Procyk, S., Cook, C., Dyson, D., Goldring, L., . . . Viducis, P. (2015). The precarity penalty: The impact of employment precarity on individuals, households and communities. *Poverty and Employment Precarity in Southern Ontario*. Retrieved from https://pepsouwt.files.wordpress.com/2012/12/precarity-penalty-report_final-hires_trimmed.pdf

McDonald, M. M., Navarrete, C. D., & Van Vugt, M. (2012). Evolution and the psychology of intergroup conflict: The male warrior hypothesis. *Philosophical Transaction of the Royal Society B, 367*(1589), 670–679. https://doi.org/10.1098/rstb.2011.0301

Merton, R. (1957). *Social theory and social structure*. New York Free Press.

Milgram, S. (1967). Small world problem. *Psychology Today, 2*, 60–67.

Montag, A. (2018). Ellen DeGeneres grew up poor but says, "You shouldn't live your life in fear of money." *CNBC.com*. Retrieved from https://www.cnbc.com/2018/05/02/ellen-degeneres-explains-her-attitude-about-money.html

Nuwer, H. (2000). *High school hazing: When rights become wrongs (social studies, teen issues)*. New York: Franklin Watts.

OWN. (2010). Oprah opens up about her abusive childhood. *Oprah Women's Network*. Retrieved from http://www.oprah.com/own-oprahshow/oprah-opens-up-about-her-abusive-childhood-video

Pew Institute. (2018). *Social media use in 2018*. Pew Institute. Retrieved from https://www.pewinternet.org/2018/03/01/social-media-use-in-2018/

Ritzer, G. (2015). *The McDonaldization of society*. Los Angeles: Sage.

Scott, J., & Marshall, G. (2015). *Oxford dictionary of sociology*. Oxford University Press

Seidman, S. (2008). *Contested knowledge: Social theory today* (4th ed.). Oxford: Blackwell.

Smith, Ainsley. (2018, January). U of T research shows the middle class is disappearing. *Urbanized.* Retrieved from http://dailyhive.com/toronto/uoft-reasearch-toronto-middle-class-disappearing-2018

Statista. (2018). Most popular social networks worldwide as of July 2019, ranked by number of active users (in millions). Retrieved from https://www.statista.com/statistics/272014/global-social-networks-ranked-by-number-of-users/

Waters, T., & Waters, D. (2010). The new zeppelin university translation of Weber's class, status, party. *Journal of Classical Sociology, 10*(2), 153–158.

Weber, M. (1946). *Essays in sociology.* New York: Oxford University Press.

Weber, M. ([1908] 1978). *Economy and society.* Berkeley/Los Angeles, CA: University of California Press.

Chapter 6

Arriagada, P. (2017). Insights on Canadian society: Food insecurity among Inuit living in Inuit Nunangat. *Statistics Canada.* Retrieved from https://www150.statcan.gc.ca/n1/pub/75–006–x/2017001/article/14774–eng.htm

Berlin, I. (2003), Race: The power of an illusion interview. *California Newsreel.* Retrieved from http://www.pbs.org/race/000_About/002_04–background-02–08.htm

Biswas, A. (2018). How government policies in India and China are widening income inequality. *Quartz India.* Retrieved from https://qz.com/1250756/how-government-policies-in-india-and-china-are-widening-income-inequality/

Block, S. (2017). Canada's population is changing but inequality remains a problem. *Behind the Numbers.* Retrieved from http://behindthenumbers.ca/2017/10/27/population-changing-income-inequality-remains/

Brownlee, J. (2005). *Ruling Canada: Corporate cohesion and democracy.* Halifax, NS: Fernwood Publishing.

Canadian Council on Social Development. (2001). *Defining and re-defining poverty: A CCSD perspective.* Retrieved from http://www.ccsd.ca/index.php/component/content/article?id=112

Carroll, W. (2004; 2010). *Corporate power in a globalizing world.* Toronto: Oxford University Press.

Citizens for Public Justice. (2017). Poverty trends 2017. *Citizens for Public Justice.* Retrieved from https://www.cpj.ca/poverty-trends-2017

Clement, W. (1975). *The Canadian corporate elite.* Toronto: McClelland and Stewart

Crawford, C. (2013). Understanding the poverty and exclusion of Canadians with disabilities. Council of Canadians with Disabilities. Retrieved from http://www.ccdonline.ca/en/socialpolicy/socialpolicy/demographic-profile/poverty-and-exclusion-of-canadians-with-disabilities

Davies, S., Maldonado, V., & Zarifa, D. (2014). Effectively maintaining inequality in Toronto: Predicting student destinations in Ontario universities. *Canadian Review of Sociology/Revue Canadienne de Sociologie, 51*(1), 22–53.

Davis, K., & Moore, W. (1945). Some principles of stratification. *American Sociological Review, 10*(2), 242–249.

Ebaugh, H. (1988). *Becoming an ex: The process of role exit.* Chicago: University of Chicago Press.

deGroot-Magetti, G. (2002). *A measure of poverty in Canada: A guide to the debate about poverty lines.* Citizens for Public Justice. Retrieved from http://action.web.ca/home/cpj/attach/A_measure_of_poverty.pdf

Erlichman, J. (2018). One in 100: Canada's "embarrassing" lack of female CEOs among top TSX companies. *BNN Bloomberg.* Retrieved from https://www.bnnbloomberg.ca/female-ceos-noticeably-absent-from-canada-s-c-suite-1.1103584

Evans, P. (2017, 7 December). Median family net worth was $295.1K last year, Statistics Canada says. *CBC News.*

Finnie R., Mueller R.E. (2008). The backgrounds of Canadian youth and access to post-secondary education: New evidence from the Youth in Transition Survey. In R. Finnie, R.E. Mueller, A. Sweetman, & A. Usher (Eds.), *Who goes? Who stays? What matters? Accessing and persisting in post-secondary education in Canada.* Montreal and Kingston: McGill-Queen's University Press and School of Policy Studies, Queen's University.

Forsythe, P. (2018). Protocol targets grim practice of human trafficking in Niagara. *Niagara this Week.* Retrieved from https://www.niagarathisweek.com/news-story/8290252–protocol-targets-grim-practice-of-human-trafficking-in-niagara/

Frenette, M. (2017). *Economic insights: Postsecondary enrolment by parental income: Recent national and provincial trends.* Ottawa: Statistics Canada.

Gaetz, S., Gulliver, T., & Richter, T. (2014). The state of homelessness in Canada 2014. *The Homeless Hub.* Retrieved from https://www.homelesshub.ca/SOHC2014

Global Slavery Index. (2018). *2018 global findings.* Retrieved from https://www.globalslaveryindex.org/2018/findings/global-findings/

Government of Nova Scotia. (2008). Poverty backgrounder. Retrieved from https://novascotia.ca/coms/department/backgrounders/poverty/index.html

Greenstone, M., Looney, A., Patashnik, J., & Yu, J. (2013). *Thirteen economic facts about social mobility and the role of education* (Policy memo). Retrieved from https://www.brookings.edu/wp-content/uploads/2016/06/THP_13EconFacts_FINAL.pdf

Harris, L., Janmaat, J., Evans, M., & Carlaw, K. (2018). Negotiating the frame for a living wage in Revelstoke, British Columbia: An econ-anthropological approach. *Human Organization, 77*(3), 202–213. https://doi-org.proxy.library.brocku.ca/10.17730/0018–7259.77.3.202

Henry, N. (2019). Black enslavement in Canada. *The Canadian Encyclopedia.* Retrieved from https://www.thecanadianencyclopedia.ca/en/article/black-enslavement

Healthcare of Ontario Pension Plan (HOOP). (2017, August). Women at greatest risk of poverty in senior years. Retrieved from https://hoopp.com/docs/default-source/newsroom-library/research/hoopp-research-article-women-at-greatest-risk-of-poverty-in-senior-years.pdf?sfvrsn=aabc1621_2

Howard, L. (2006). Untouchable citizens: Dalit movements and democratization in Tamil Nadu. *Contemporary Sociology, 35*(5), 521.

Knox, S. (2018). Human trafficking remains a key issue in Niagara. *Iheartradio.ca.* Retrieved from http://www.iheartradio.ca/610cktb/news/human-trafficking-remains-a-key-issue-in-niagara-1.3700727

Levitas, R. (1998). *The inclusive society? Social exclusion and New Labour.* Basingstoke: Macmillan.

Lawrence, B. (2016). Enslavement of Indigenous People in Canada. *The Canadian Encyclopedia.* Retrieved from https://www.thecanadianencyclopedia.ca/en/article/slavery-of-indigenous-people-in-canada

Lewis, O. (1966, October). The culture of poverty. *Scientific American, 215*(4), 19–25.

Livingstone, D.W., & Watts, B. (2018). The changing class structure and pivotal role of professional employees in an advanced capitalist "knowledge economy": Canada 1982–2016. *Studies in Political Economy: A Sociologist Review, 99*(1), 79–96.

McInturff, K., & Lambert, B. (2016, March). Making women count. *Canadian Centre for Policy Alternatives.* Retrieved from https://www.policyalternatives.ca/publications/reports/making-women-count-0

McQuaig, L., & Brooks, N. (2010). *The trouble with billionaires.* New York: Penguin Random House.

Mills, C.W. (1956). *The power elite.* New York: Oxford University Press.

Mitchell, A and Shillington, R. (2002). *Poverty, inequality and social inclusion.* Laidlaw Foundation.

Morissette, R., & Galarneau, D. (2016). *Labour market participation of immigrant and Canadian-born wives, 2006–2014.* Catalogue 11–626–X–No.055. Ottawa, ON: Statistics Canada.

Moss, W., & Gardner-O'Toole, W. (1991). *Aboriginal people: History of discriminatory laws.* Retrieved from http://publications.gc.ca/Collection-R/LoPBdP/BP/bp175–e.htm

Murphy, B., Zhang, X., & Dionne, C. (2012). Low income in Canada: A multi-line and multi-index perspective. *Government of Canada.* Retrieved from http://publications.gc.ca/site/eng/411612/publication.html

Niño, Z. M., Roope, L., & Tarp, F. (2017). Global inequality: Relatively lower, absolutely higher. *Review of Income & Wealth, 63*(4), 661–684. https://doi-org.proxy.library.brocku.ca/10.1111/roiw.12240

Noakes, S. (2017, 17 January). Rich man, poor man: A closer look at Oxfam's inequality figures. *CBC News.* Retrieved from https://www.cbc.ca/news/business/oxfam-inequity-statistics-1.3937943

Ontario Ministry of Finance. (2017). 2016 Census highlights. Retrieved from https://www.fin.gov.on.ca/en/economy/demographics/census/cenhi16–7.html

Osberg, L. (2018). *The age of increasing inequality: The astonishing rise of Canada's 1%.* Toronto: Lorimer.

Porter, J. (1965). *The vertical mosaic.* Toronto: University of Toronto Press.

QS Top Universities. (2018) *University of Toronto ranking.* Retrieved from https://www.topuniversities.com/universities/university-toronto#wurs?awc=10032_1550960193_a143b0deb2020a0d6f89bdcc2084e722&utm_source=awin_affiliate_marketing&utm_medium=other_Affiliate&utm_campaign=WGST_F17_USA-Canada&partnerid=10866

Restoule, J., Mashford-Pringle, A., Chacaby, M., Smillie, C., Brunette, C., & Russel, G. (2013). Supporting successful transitions to post-secondary education for Indigenous students: Lessons from an institutional ethnography in Ontario, Canada. *International Indigenous Policy Journal, 4*(4). https://doi.org/10.18584/iipj.2013.4.4.4

Roberman, S. (2015). Not to be hungry is not enough: An insight into contours of inclusion and exclusion in affluent western societies. *Sociological Forum, 30*(3).

Ross, D., & Shillington, R. (1994, July 1). *The Canadian fact book on poverty.* Ottawa: Canadian Council on Social Development.

Ryan, W. (1971). *Blaming the victim.* New York: Penguin Random House.

Sarlo, C. (1996). *Poverty in Canada.* Vancouver: Fraser Institute.

Seabrook, J. (2014). Culture as a cause of poverty has been widely misinterpreted. *The Guardian.* Retrieved from https://www.theguardian.com/commentisfree/2014/aug/14/culture-poverty-poor-power-welfare-sanctions-cuts

Statistics Canada. (2013). Low income definitions. Retrieved from https://www150.statcan.gc.ca/n1/pub/75f0011x/2012001/notes/low-faible-eng.htm

Statistics Canada. (2015a). Fifty years of families in Canada: 1961 to 2011.

Statistics Canada. (2015b). Income of Canadians, 2000–2013. *The Daily.* Retrieved from https://www150.statcan.gc.ca/n1/daily-quotidien/151217/dq151217c-eng.htm

Statistics Canada. (2016a, 15 October). The surge of women in the workforce.

Statistics Canada. (2016b). Education indicators in Canada: An international perspective. *The Daily.* Retrieved from https://www150.statcan.gc.ca/n1/daily-quotidien/161215/dq161215b-eng.htm

Statistics Canada. (2017a). High income trends amongst Canadian tax filers. *The Daily.* Retrieved from https://www150.statcan.gc.ca/n1/daily-quotidien/171115/dq171115a-eng.htm

Statistics Canada. (2017b). Household income in Canada 2016 Census. *The Daily.* Retrieved from https://www150.statcan.gc.ca/n1/daily-quotidien/170913/dq170913a-eng.htm

Statistics Canada. (2017c, 2 August). Census in brief: Portrait of children's family life in Canada in 2016. Retrieved from https://www12.statcan.gc.ca/census-recensement/2016/as-sa/98–200–x/2016006/98–200–x2016006–eng.cfm

Statistics Canada. (2017d). Aboriginal fact sheet. Cat 89–656–X. Retrieved from https://www150.statcan.gc.ca/n1/pub/89–656–x/89–656–x2015001–eng.htm

Statistics Canada. (2019). Measuring low income and Canada's official poverty line. Retrieved from https://www.statcan.gc.ca/eng/consultation/mbm

Swanson, J. (2001). *Poor-bashing: The politics of exclusion.* Toronto: Between the Lines.

Torjman, S., & Makhoul, A. (2016). *Disability supports and employment policy.* Caledon Institute of Social Policy.

University of Toronto. Fees/future students. Retrieved from https://future.utoronto.ca/finances/fees/

Veblen, T. (1899). *Theory of the leisure class.* Penguin Random House.

Wall, K. (2017). Insights into persons living with a disability in Canada. Catalogue no. 75–006–X. Retrieved from https://www150.statcan.gc.ca/n1/en/pub/75–006–x/2017001/article/54854–eng.pdf?st=Le93AjgM

Wang, F. (2013). Educational equity in the access to post-secondary education: A comparison of ethnic minorities in China with Aboriginals in Canada. *Interchange, 44*(1–2), 45–62.

White, G. (2017). There are currently 4 black CEOs in the Fortune 500. *The Atlantic.* Retrieved from https://www.theatlantic.com/business/archive/2017/10/black-ceos-fortune-500/543960/

Wood, P. H. (2003). *Strange new land: Africans in Colonial America.* Oxford: Oxford University Press.

Chapter 7

Armstrong, P. (2004). Gender relations. In L. Tepperman & J. Curtis (Eds.), *Sociology.* Toronto: Oxford University Press.

Beasley, M., & Fischer, M. (2012). Why they leave: The impact of stereotype threat on the attrition of women and minorities from science, math and engineering majors. *Social Psychology of Education, 15*(4), 427–448.

Bezanson, K., & Luxton, M. (2006). *Social reproduction: Feminist political economy challenges neo-liberalism*. Montreal: McGill-Queen's University Press.

Bianchi, S.M., Sayer, L., Milkie, M., & Robinson, J.P. (2012). Housework: Who did, does or will do it and how much does it matter? *Social Forces, 91*(1), 55–63.

Bittman, M., England, P., Sayer, L., Folbre, N., & Matheson, G. (2003). When does gender trump money? Bargaining and time in household work. *American Journal of Sociology, 109*, 186–214.

Blackless, M., Charuvastra, A., Derryck, A., Fausto-Sterling, A., Lauzanne, K., & Lee, E. (2000). How sexually dimorphic are we? Review and synthesis. *American Journal of Human Biology, 12*(151), 151–166.

Bradley, L. (2018). "I was terrified, and I was humiliated": #MeToo's male accusers, one year later. *Vanity Fair*. Retrieved from https://www.vanityfair.com/hollywood/2018/10/metoo-male-accusers-terry-crews-alex-winter-michael-gaston-interview

Brewster, M. (2017). Lesbian women and household division of labour. *Journal of Lesbian Studies, 21*(1), 47–67.

Brines, J. (2006). Economic dependency, gender and the division of labor at home. *The American Journal of Sociology, 100*(3), 652–688.

Budig, M. (2002, May). Male advantage and the gender composition of jobs: Who rides the glass escalator? *Social Problems, 49*(2), 258–277.

Budig, M., & Hodges, M. (2010). Differences in disadvantage: Variations in motherhood penalty across white women's earning distribution. *American Sociological Review, 75*(5), 795–728.

Butler, J. (1990). *Gender trouble: Feminism and the subversion of identity*. New York: Routledge.

Canadian Institute for Health Information. (2017). *Physicians in Canada Summary Report, 2016*. Ottawa, ON: CIHI.

Casey, L. (2018, 26 April). Van attack suspect Alek Minassian was searching for job, set to graduate. *Global News*. Retrieved from https://globalnews.ca/news/4170290/toronto-van-attack-alek-minassian-background/

Catalyst. (2018). Women in science, technology, engineering and math (STEM). Retrieved from http://www.catalyst.org/knowledge/women-science-technology-engineering-and-mathematics-stem

Chamberlain, A., Zhao, D., & Stansell, A. (2019). *Progress on the gender pay gap: 2019*. Retrieved from https://www.glassdoor.com/research/studies/gender-pay-gap-2019/

Collins, P.H. (2000). *Intersecting oppressions*. Thousand Oaks, CA: Sage Publications.

Connell, R.W. (1987). *Gender and power*. Stanford: Stanford University Press.

Cognard-Black, A. (2004). Will they stay or will they go? Sex-typed work among token men who teach. *The Sociology Quarterly, 45*(1), 113–139.

Cohen, J. (2007). Professionalism in medical education, an American perspective: From evidence to accountability. *Medical Education, 40*(7), 607–617.

D'Ambrozia, G. (2017). Because of modern feminism Disney princess gender roles are changing. *Odyssey*. Retrieved from https://www.theodysseyonline.com/eligible-princes

De Welde, K., & Laursen, S. (2011). The glass obstacle course: Informal and formal barriers for women PhD students in STEM fields. *International Journal of Gender, Science and Technology, 3*(3), 571–595.

Department of Justice. (2017). *Victimization of Indigenous women and girls*. Federal Government of Canada. Retrieved from https://www.justice.gc.ca/eng/rp-pr/jr/jf-pf/2017/july05.html

Doucet, A. (2007). Stay-at-home fathering. *Community, Work and Family, 10*(4), 455–473.

Drolet, M., Uppal, S., & LaRochelle-Cote, T. (2016). Insights on Canadian society: The Canada-US gap in women's labour market participation. *Statistics Canada*. Retrieved from https://www150.statcan.gc.ca/n1/pub/75-006-x/2016001/article/14651-eng.htm

Easterly, D.M., & Ricard, C.S. (2011). Conscious efforts to end unconscious bias: Why women leave academic research. *Journal of Research Administration, 42*(1), 1–73.

Engels, F. ([1884] 1962). The origin of the family: Private property and the state. In K. Marx & F. Engels, *Selected Works* (Vol. 2). Moscow: Foreign Languages Publishing House.

Fortin, N.M., & Huberman, M. (2002). Occupational gender segregation and women's wages in Canada: An historical perspective. *Canadian Public Policy, 27*, 11–39.

Francis, B. (2010). Gender, toys and learning. *Oxford Review of Education, 36*(3), 325–344.

Galabuzi, G. (2006). *Canada's economic apartheid: The social exclusion of racialized groups in the new century*. Toronto: Canadian Scholar's Press Inc.

Goldberg, A., Smith, J., & Perry-Jenkins, M. (2012). The division of labour in lesbian, gay and heterosexual new adoptive parents. *Journal of Marriage and Family, 74*(4), 812–828.

Greenstein, T.N. (2009). National context, family satisfaction and fairness in the division of household labour. *Journal of Marriage and Family, 71*, 1039–1051.

Heisz, A., Jackson, A., & Picot, G. (2002). *Winners and losers in the labour market of the 1990s*. Ottawa: Analytical Studies Branch, Statistics Canada.

Hochschild, A. (1989). *The second shift*. New York: Viking Penguin.

Izenberg, D., Oriuwa, C., & Taylor, M. (2018). Why is there a gender wage gap in Canadian medicine? *Healthydebate.ca*. Retrieved from https://healthydebate.ca/2018/10/topic/gender-wage-gap-medicine

Janzen v. Platy Enterprises Ltd., [1989] 1 SCR. 1252.

Harper, J., Lima, G., Kolliari-Turner, A., Rossell Malinsky, F., Wang, G., Jose Martinez-Patino, M. . . . Pitsiladis, Y.P. (2018). The fluidity of gender and implications for the biology of inclusion for transgender and intersex athletes. *Current Sports Medicine Reports, 17*(12), 467–473.

Kilbourne, J. (2010). *Killing us softly 4: Advertising images of women*. Cambridge Documentary Films.

Kimmel, M. (2004). *The gendered society* (2nd ed.). New York: Oxford University Press.

Kassam, A. (2018, 19 April). Legal discrimination is alive and well: Canada's Indigenous women fight for equality. *The Guardian*. Retrieved from https://www.theguardian.com/world/2018/apr/19/canada-indigenous-women-fight-for-equality-discrimination-first-nations

Knudsen, K., & Waerness, K. (2008). National context and spouse's housework in 34 countries. *European Sociological Review, 24*, 97–113.

Korkki, P. (2011, 21 May). Talk about pay today, or suffer tomorrow. *New York Times*. Retrieved from https://www.nytimes.com/2011/05/22/jobs/22search.html

Kurdek, L. (2007. The allocation of household labour by partners in gay and lesbian couples. *Journal of Family Issues, 28*(1), 132–148.

Koivunen, J., Rothaupt, J., & Wolfgram, S. (2009). Gender dynamics and role adjustment during the transition to parenthood: Current perspectives. *The Family Journal: Counselling and Therapy for Couples and Families, 17*(4), 323–328.

Kullberg, K. (2013, December). From glass escalator to glass travelator: On the proportion of men in managerial positions in social work in Sweden. *The British Journal of Social Work, 43*(8), 1492–1509.

Lachance-Grzela, M., & Bouchard, G. (2010). Why do women do the lion's share of housework? A decade of research. *Sex Roles, 63*, 767–780.

Laframboise, S., & Anhorn, M. (2008). The way of two spirited people. *Dancing to Eagle Spirit Society*. Retrieved from http://www.dancingtoeaglespiritsociety.org/twospirit.php

Mannino, C.A., & Deutsch, F.M. (2007). Changing the division of household labour: A negotiated process between partners. *Sex Roles, 56*, 309–324.

Man-Hsin, L., & Tso, E. (2014). Evolution of Disney princess' gender roles over time. Retrieved from http://homes.lmc.gatech.edu/~mlin73/ticahere/image/Disney%20Essay.pdf

McInturff, K., & Tulloch, P. (2014). *Narrowing the gap: The difference that public sector wages make.* Canadian Centre for Policy Alternatives. Retrieved from https://policyalternatives.ca/wage-gap

McNamara, B. (2017). Model Hanne Gaby Odie says she is intersex. *Teen Vogue*. Retrieved from https://www.teenvogue.com/story/hanne-gaby-odiele-is-intersex

Nakhaie, M.R. (2002). Class, breadwinner ideology, and housework among Canadian husbands. *Review of Radical Political Economics, 34*, 137–157.

National Inquiry into Missing and Murdered Indigenous Women and Girls. (2019). *Executive Summary*. Retrieved from https://www.mmiwg-ffada.ca/final-report/

Native Women's Association of Canada. (2016). Fact sheet: Missing and murdered Aboriginal women and girls. NWAC. Retrieved from https://www.nwac.ca/wp-content/uploads/2015/05/Fact_Sheet_Missing_and_Murdered_Aboriginal_Women_and_Girls.pdf

Nelson, A. (2009). *Gender in Canada* (4th ed.). Toronto: Pearson.

Newbould, M. (2016). When parents choose gender: Intersex, children, and the law. *Medical Law Review, 24*(4), 474–496.

Ohlheiser, A. (2017, 19 October). The woman behind "Me Too" knew the power of the phrase when she created it—10 years ago. *The Washington Post*. Archived from the original.

Park, A. (2017). #MeToo reaches 85 countries with 1.7 million Tweets. *CBC News*. Retrieved from https://www.cbsnews.com/news/metoo-reaches-85-countries-with-1-7-million-tweets/

Pascoe, C.J. (2007). *Dude, you're a fag: Masculinity and sexuality in high school.* California: University of California Press.

Peterson, J. (n.d.). The gender scandal: Part one (Scandinavia) and part two (Canada). [blog]. Retrieved from https://jordanbpeterson.com/political-correctness/the-gender-scandal-part-one-scandinavia-and-part-two-canada/

Poisson, J. (2011, 21 May). Parents keep child's gender secret. *The Star*. Retrieved from https://www.thestar.com/life/parent/2011/05/21/parents_keep_childs_gender_secret.html

Registered Nurses' Association of Ontario. (2019). Nursing pay. *Careers in Nursing: A World of Opportunities*. Retrieved from http://careersinnursing.ca/why-nursing/work-expectations/nursing-pay

Renzetti, C., & Curran, D. (1999). *Women and society* (4th ed.). Boston: Allyn and Bacon.

Roen, K. (2018). Shaping parents, shaping penises: How medical teams frame parents' decisions in response to hypospadias. *British Journal of Health Psychology, 23*(4), 967–982.

RuPaul. (1995). *Lettin' it all hang out: An autobiography.* New York: Hyperion Books.

Samotin, P., & Dancygor, L. (2018, 26 April). Incels: Breaking down the disturbing thriving online community. *Glamour*. Retrieved from https://www.glamour.com/story/what-is-incel-breaking-down-online-community-celibate-men

Statistics Canada. (2015). *Women and education.* Cat 89–503–X. Retrieved from https://www150.statcan.gc.ca/n1/pub/89-503-x/2010001/article/11542-eng.htm#a9

Statistics Canada. (2017). *Daily average time spent in hours on various activities by age group and sex, 15 years and over, Canada and provinces.* Retrieved from https://www150.statcan.gc.ca/t1/tbl1/en/tv.action?pid=4510001401

Statistics Canada. (2018). Labour force characteristics by province, age group and sex, seasonally adjusted (Quebec, Ontario, Manitoba, Saskatchewan, Alberta, and British Columbia). *The Daily*. Retrieved from https://www150.statcan.gc.ca/n1/daily-quotidien/180608/t005a-eng.htm

Wallis, M., & Kwok, S. (2008). *Daily struggles: The deepening racialization and feminization of poverty in Canada.* Toronto: Canadian Scholar's Press.

Williams, C., Muller, C., & Kilanski, K. (2012). Gendered organizations in the new economy. *Gender & Society, 26*(4), 549–573.

West, C., & Zimmerman, D. (1987). Doing gender. *Gender and Society, 1*(2), 125–151.

Youngjoo, C., & Weeden, K. (2014, April). Overwork and the slow convergence in the gender gap in wages. *American Sociological Review.* https://doi.org/1177/0003122414528936

Chapter 8

Abedi, M. (2018, 22 January). 5 Ontario women have allegedly been killed by men in their lives in 2018—and it's only January. *Global New.*

Abott, K. (2003). Urban Aboriginal women in BC and the impact of the matrimonial real property regime. Indigenous and Northern Affairs Canada. Government of Canada. Retrieved from http://www.aadnc-aandc.gc.ca/eng/1100100032669/1100100032761

Arends-Tóth, J.V., & Van de Vijver, F.J.R. (2007). Cultural and gender differences in gender-role beliefs, sharing household-task and child-care responsibilities, and well-being among immigrants and majority members in the Netherlands. *Sex Roles, 57*, 813–824. https://doi.org/10.1007/s11199-007-9316-z

Amato, P.R. (2000). The consequences of divorce for adults and children. *Journal of Marriage and the Family, 62*, 1269–1687.

American Society for Reproductive Medicine. (2019). Assisted reproductive technologies. Retrieved from https://www.asrm.org/topics/topics-index/assisted-reproductive-technologies/

Baumrind D. (1991). The influence of parenting style on adolescent competence and substance use. *Journal of Early Adolescence, 11*(1): 56–95.

BBC. (2017, 11 August). Polygamous couple from Bountiful, BC, jailed for luring child bride. *BBC News*. Retrieved from https://www.bbc.com/news/world-us-canada-40903974

Beatie, T. (2008). *Labor of love: The story of one man's extraordinary pregnancy by Thomas Beatie.* New York: Seal Press.

Bezanson, K., & Luxton, M. (2002). *Social reproduction: Feminist political economy challenges neo-liberalism.* Montreal/Kingston: McGill-Queens University Press.

Bradby, H. (1999). Negotiating marriage: Young Punjabi's women's assessment of their individual and family interests. In R. Barot, H. Bradley, & S. Fenton (Eds.), *Ethnicity, gender and social change.* London: Palgrave Macmillan.

Bushnik, T., Cook, J., Hughes, E., & Tough, S. (2010). Seeking medical help to conceive. *Statistics Canada.* Retrieved from https://www150.statcan.gc.ca/n1/pub/82–003–x/2012004/article/11719–eng.htm

CBC News. (2017, July). Winston Blackmore and James Older found guilty of polygamy by BC judge. Retrieved from https://www.cbc.ca/news/canada/british-columbia/bc-polygamy-trial-1.4218735

Georgas, J. (2003). Family: Variations and changes across cultures. *Online Readings in Psychology and Culture, 6*(3). https://doi.org/10.9707/2307–0919.1061

Goode, W.J. (1970). *World revolution and family patterns.* New York: Free Press.

Haselschwerdt, M., & Hardesty, J. (2016). Managing secrecy and disclosure of domestic violence in affluent communities. *Journal of Marriage and Family, 79*(2), 556–570.

Hyman, I., Guruge, S., & Mason, R. (2008). The impact of post-migration changes on marital relationships: A study of Ethiopian immigrant couples in Toronto. *Journal of Comparative Family Studies, 39*(2), 149–164.

Infante, D., Sabourin, T C., Rudd. J.E., & Shannon, E.A. (2009). Verbal aggression in violent and nonviolent marital disputes. *Communication Quarterly, 38*(4), 361–371.

Kane, L. (2018, 28 June). BC polygamy sentence will be a "wake up call" some experts say, but others disagree. *The Vancouver Star.* Retrieved from https://www.thestar.com/vancouver/2018/06/28/bc-polygamy-sentence-will-be-a-wake-up-call-some-experts-say-but-others-disagree.html

Keshavarz, S., & Baharudin, R. (2009). Parenting style in a collectivist culture of Malaysia. *European Journal of Social Science, 10*(1), 66–73.

Lawrence, E., Cobb, F., Rothman, A., Rothman, M., & Bradbury, T. (2018). Marital satisfaction across transition to parenthood. *Journal of Family Psychology, 22*(1), 41–58.

Livingston, G., & Cohn, D. (2010). Birth rate decline linked to recession. Pew Research Center. Retrieved from http://www.pewsocialtrends.org/2010/04/06/us-birth-rate-decline-linked-to-recession/

Luxton, J., & Corman, J. (2001). *Getting by in hard times: Gendered labour at home and on the job.* Toronto: University of Toronto Press, Scholarly Publishing Division

Miszkurka, M., Steensma, C., & Phillips, S.P. (2016). Correlates of partner and family violence among older Canadians: A lifecourse approach. *Health Promotion and Chronic Disease Prevention Canada, 36*(3), 48–53.

Nomaguchi, K., & Milkie, M.A. (2017). Sociological perspectives on parenting stress: How social structure and culture shape parental strain and the well-being of parents and children. In K. Deater-Deckard, & R. Panneton (Eds.), *Parental stress and early child development.* New York: Springer.

Ogburn, W. (1933). *The family and its functions: Recent social trends.* New York: McGraw.

Perrin, D., & Palmer, D. (2004). *Keep sweet: Children of polygamy.* Dave's Press Inc.

Pinquart M., & Kauser, R. (2017, 10 April). Do the associations of parenting styles with behavior problems and academic achievement vary by culture? Results from a meta-analysis. *Culture Diversity Ethnic Minority Psychology.* https://doi.org/10.1037/cdp0000149

Popenoe, D. (1993, August). American family decline, 1960–1990: A review and appraisal. *Journal of Marriage and Family, 55*(3), 527–542.

Reed, J. (2014). *The birth control movement and American society: From private vice to public virtue.* Princeton: Princeton University Press.

Reese, L., Parker, E., & Peek-Asa, C. (2015). Financial stress and intimate partner violence perpetration among young men and women. *Injury Prevention, 2*(2).

Remennick, L. (2007). Being a woman is different here: Changing attitudes towards femininity, sexuality, and gender roles among former Soviet women living in Greater Boston. *Women's Studies International Forum, 30,* 326–341.

Ruggles, S. (1997). The rise of divorce and separation in the United States, 1880–1990. *Demography, 34*(4), 455–466.

Sanday, P.R. (2002). *Women at the centre: Life in a modern matriarchy.* New York: Cornell University Press.

Sinha, M. (2012). Violence against intimate partners. *Statistics Canada.* Cat # 85–002–X.

Stark, E., & Filtcraft, A. (1988). Women and children at risk: A feminist perspective on child abuse. *International Journal of Health Services, 18*(1), 91–118.

Statistics Canada. (2016). The rise of the dual-earner family with children. Retrieved from https://www150.statcan.gc.ca/n1/pub/11–630–x/11–630–x2016005–eng.htm

Statistics Canada. (2017a). Census in brief: Portrait of children's family life in 2016. Retrieved from http://www12.statcan.gc.ca/census-recensement/2016/as-sa/98–200–x/2016006/98–200–x2016006–eng.cfm

Statistics Canada. (2017b). Number and proportion of couples in mixed unions in census metropolitan areas, 2011. Retrieved from http://www12.statcan.gc.ca/nhs-enm/2011/as-sa/99–010–x/2011003/tbl/tbl3–eng.cfm

Statistics Canada. (2017c). Family household and marital status key results. *The Daily.* Retrieved from https://www150.statcan.gc.ca/n1/daily-quotidien/170802/dq170802a-eng.htm

Steinberg L. (2001). We know some things: Parent-adolescent relationships in retrospect and prospect. *Journal of research on adolescence, 11*(1): 1–19.

Thomas, L. (2018, June). Gender differences in the consequences of divorce: A study of multiple outcomes. *Demography, 55*(3).

Toledo, M. (2009). First comes marriage, then comes love. *ABC News.* Retrieved from https://abcnews.go.com/2020/story?id=6762309&page=1

Tremblay, G. (2008, 22 June). He's pregnant. you're speechless. *NY Times.* Retrieved from https://www.nytimes.com/2008/06/22/fashion/22pregnant.html

Twenge, J., Campbell, K., & Foster, C. (2003). Parenthood and marital satisfaction: A meta analytic review. *Journal of Marriage and Family, 65*(3), 574–583.

Umberson, D., Pudrovksi, T., & Reczek, C. (2010). Parenthood, childlessness and well-being: A lifecourse perspective. *Journal of Marriage and Family, 72*(3), 612–629.

Weatherburn, D. (2011). Personal stress, financial stress and violence against women. *Contemporary Issues in Crime and Justice Bulletin Number 151.*

Winegar, J. (2016). Not so far away: Why US domestic violence is akin to honour crimes. *Women's News.* Retrieved from https://womensenews.org/2016/04/not-so-far-away-why-u-s-domestic-violence-is-akin-to-honor-crimes/

Witheridge, A. (2016, 2 June). We would love to have a baby together. *Daily Mail.* Retrieved from http://www.dailymail.co.uk/news/article-3613121/World-s-pregnant-man-weds-children-s-preschool-director-dramatic-divorce-wife-took-FOUR-YEARS.html

Wu, R., & Schimmele, C.H. (2005). Repartnering after the first union disruption. *Journal of Marriage and Family, 67,* 27–36.

Yavorsky, J., Dash, C., & Schoppe-Sullivan, S. (2015). The production of inequality: The gender division of labour across the transition to parenthood. *Journal of Marriage and Family, 77*(3), 662–679.

Chapter 9

Assembly of First Nations Environmental Stewardship Unit. (2005). Overview of environmental issues facing First Nations. Report submitted to the Nuclear Waste Management Organization. Retrieved from https://www.nwmo.ca/en/~/media/Site/Files/PDFs/2015/11/04/17/30/406_11–AFN-10.ashx

Bartlett, G. (2017). Tearful Justin Trudeau apologizes to N.L. residential school survivors. *CBC News.* Retrieved from https://www.cbc.ca/news/canada/newfoundland-labrador/justin-trudeau-labrador-residential-schools-apology-1.4417443

Black Lives Matter Toronto. (2019). BLMTO Freedom School. Retrieved from http://freedomschool.ca/

Bradshaw, J., & McCarthy, S. (2012, 1 January). Idle No More protests beyond control of chiefs. *The Globe and Mail.*

Bundale, B. (2018, 28 May). A part of daily life: Racial profiling and shopping while black in Canada. *Global News.* Retrieved from https://globalnews.ca/news/4236922/shop-while-black-in-canada-racial-profiling/

Burnet, J., & Driedger, L. (2014). Multiculturalism. *The Canadian Encyclopedia.* Retrieved from https://www.thecanadianencyclopedia.ca/en/article/multiculturalism

CBC (n.d.). The case against Japanese Canadians, the "enemy aliens." *CBC Archives.* Retrieved from https://www.cbc.ca/archives/entry/japanese-canadians-the-case-against-the-enemy-aliens

Center for Research on Globalization. (2013). Non-Muslims carried out more than 90% of all terrorist attacks in America. Retrieved from https://www.globalresearch.ca/non-muslims-carried-out-more-than-90-of-all-terrorist-attacks-in-america/5333619

Conference Board of Canada. (2017). *Racial wage gap.* Retrieved from http://www.conferenceboard.ca/hcp/provincial/society/racial-gap.aspx

Dechief, D., & Oreopoulos, P. (2012). *Why do some employers prefer to interview Matthew but not Samir? New evidence from Toronto, Montreal and Vancouver.* CLSSRN working papers.

Dickason, O.P., & Newbigging, B. (2019). *Indigenous peoples within Canada: A concise history* (4th ed.). Toronto: OUP Canada.

Draaisma, M. (2017). Thousands gather across the country to protest against Islamophobia. *CBC News.* Retrieved from https://www.cbc.ca/news/canada/toronto/protest-us-consulate-islamophobia-white-supremacy-1.3967434

duPreez, P. (1994). *Genocide: The psychology of mass murder.* London: Boyers and Bowerdean.

Elliott, J.K. (2019). Nearly 50% of Canadians think racist thoughts are normal: Ipsos poll. *Global News.* Retrieved from https://globalnews.ca/news/5262461/canadian-racism-ipsos-poll/

Europol. (2015). About Europol. Retrieved from https://www.europol.europa.eu/about-europol/european-counter-terrorism-centre-ectc

Faragher, J. M. (2006). "A great and noble scheme": Thoughts on the expulsion of Acadians. *Acadiensis, 36*(1), 82–92.

Fleras, A. (2010). *Unequal relations: An introduction to race, ethnic and Aboriginal dynamics in Canada.* Toronto: Pearson

Fong, E. (2017). Residential segregation of visible minority groups in Toronto. In E.S. Coloma, & G. Pon (Eds.), *Asian Canadian studies reader* (pp. 260–275). Toronto: University of Toronto Press.

Galabuzi, G.E. (2011). *Canada's colour-coded labour market.* Ottawa: Canadian Centre for Policy Alternatives.

Gayle, D. (2018, 16 April). Arrest of 2 black men at Starbucks for trespassing sparks protests. *The Guardian.* Retrieved from https://www.theguardian.com/us-news/2018/apr/16/arrest-of-two-black-men-at-starbucks-for-trespassing-sparks-protests

Government of Canada (2011). *What is Indian status?* Retrieved from https://www.aadnc-aandc.gc.ca/eng/1100100032463/1100100032464

Government of Canada. (2017). *Welcome to First Nations profiles.* Indigenous and Northern Affairs Canada. Retrieved from http://fnp-ppn.aandc-aadnc.gc.ca/fnp/Main/index.aspx?lang=eng

Hanniman, W. (2008). Canadian Muslims, Islamophobia and national security. *International Journal of Law, Crime and Justice, 36*(4), 271–285.

Heart Research Institute (HRI). (2016). First Nation people's heart health. Retrieved from http://www.hricanada.org/about-heart-disease/first-nations-people-and-heart-disease

Henry, F., & Ginzberg, E. (1985). *Who gets the work? A test of racial discrimination in employment.* Toronto: Social Planning Council of Metropolitan Toronto.

Historica Canada. (n.d.). End of segregation in Canada. *Historica Canada.* Retrieved from http://www.blackhistorycanada.ca/events.php?themeid=7&id=9

Indigenous and Northern Affairs Canada. (2014). Indian residential schools. Retrieved from https://www.aadnc-aandc.gc.ca/eng/1100100015576/1100100015577

Johnson, J., Bottorff, J., Browne, S.G., Hilton, A., & Clarke, H. (2009). Othering and being othered in the context of health care services. *Health Communication, 16*(2), 255–271.

Jones, R. (2019). Apartheid ended 29 years ago. how has South Africa changed? *National Geographic.* Retrieved from https://www.nationalgeographic.com/culture/2019/04/how-south-africa-changed-since-apartheid-born-free-generation/

Kahle, S., Yu, S., & Whiteside, E. (2007). Another disaster: An examination of portrayals of race in Hurricane Katrina coverage. *Visual Communication Quarterly, 14*(2), 75–89.

King, T. (2012). *The inconvenient Indian.* Toronto: Doubleday Canada.

Kolbert, E. (2018). There's no scientific basis for race—It's a made-up label. *National Geographic.* Retrieved from https://www.nationalgeographic.com/magazine/2018/04/race-genetics-science-africa/

Laing, L. (2015). The twins that everyone can tell apart. *The Daily Mail*. Retrieved from http://www.dailymail.co.uk/news/article-2974869/The-twins-tell-apart-Striking-sisters-couldn-t-different-quirk-mixed-raced-parentage.html

Leonardo, Z. (2004). The unhappy marriage between Marxism and race critique: Political economy and the production of racialized knowledge. *Policy Futures in Education, 2*(3&4), 483–493.

Luciuk, L. (2018). Ukrainian internment in Canada. *The Canadian Encyclopedia*. Retrieved from https://www.thecanadianencyclopedia.ca/en/article/ukrainian-internment-in-canada

Mack, J.B. (1994). Cultural pluralism and multiculturalism: E Pluribus Unum or Ex Uno Plura? *Hitotsubashi Journal of Social Studies, 26*(2), 63–72. Retrieved from https://www.jstor.org/stable/43294357?seq=1#page_scan_tab_contents

Mandell, N., Lam, L., Borras, J., & Phonepraseuth, J. (2018). Living on the margins: Economic security amongst senior immigrants in Canada. In *Social Inequality and Spectre of Social Justice* (pp. 38–64). Retrieved from http://web.b.ebscohost.com.library.sheridanc.on.ca/ehost/pdfviewer/pdfviewer?vid=6&sid=89c-1ccd7–5868–49ad-a333–657cea4ecc74%40pdc-v-sessmgr01

Marcotte, R. (2010). Muslim women in Canada: Autonomy and empowerment. *Journal of Muslim Minority Affairs, 30*(3), 358–369.

Marshall, T. (2013). Oka crisis. *The Canadian Encyclopedia*. Retrieved from https://www.thecanadianencyclopedia.ca/en/article/oka-crisis

McAllister, K. (1999). Narrating Japanese Canadians in and out of the Canadian nation: A critique of realist forms of representation. *Canadian Journal of Communication, 24*(1).

McIntosh, P. (1989, July/August). White privilege: Unpacking the invisible knapsack. *Peace and Freedom Magazine*, 10–12.

McGettigan, T., & Smith, E. (2015). *A formula for eradicating racism: Debunking white supremacy*. New York: Palgrave Macmillan.

McRae, M. (2017). The Chinese head tax and the Chinese Exclusion Act. Canadian Museum for Human Rights. Retrieved from https://humanrights.ca/blog/chinese-head-tax-and-chinese-exclusion-act

Minsky, A. (2017, 13 June). Hate crimes against Muslims rise 253% in four years. *Global News*. Retrieved from https://globalnews.ca/news/3523535/hate-crimes-canada-muslim/

Nakana, T.U. (2012). *Within the barbed wire fence: A Japanese man's account of his internment in Canada*. New York: Lorimer.

Oreopoulos, P. (2011, November). Why do skilled immigrants struggle in the labor market? A field experiment with thirteen thousand resumes. *American Economic Journal: Economic Policy 3*, 148–171.

Parsons, T. (1975). *The social system*. London: Routledge Taylor and Francis.

Roy, P. (2008). The triumph of citizenship: The Japanese and Chinese in Canada, 1941–67. Vancouver: UBC Press.

The Sentencing Project. (2014). *Race and punishment: Racial perceptions of crime and support for punitive policies*. The Sentencing Project Website. Retrieved from https://www.sentencingproject.org/wp-content/uploads/2015/11/Race-and-Punishment.pdf

Skelton, O.D. (1965). *Life and letters of Sir Wilfrid Laurier*. Toronto: Institute for Research on Public Policy.

Smith, B. (2000). *The truth that never hurts: Writings on race, gender and freedom*. New Jersey: Rutgers University Press.

Statistics Canada. (2012). *The evolution of English–French bilingualism in Canada from 1961 to 2011*. Retrieved from https://www150.statcan.gc.ca/n1/pub/75–006–x/2013001/article/11795–eng.htm

Statistics Canada. (2016a). Immigration and ethnocultural diversity in Canada. Statistics Canada Cat 99–010–X. Retrieved from https://www12.statcan.gc.ca/nhs-enm/2011/as-sa/99–010–x/99–010–x2011001–eng.cfm

Statistics Canada. (2016b). Aboriginal Peoples Survey, 2012: Lifetime suicidal thoughts among First Nations living off reserve, Métis and Inuit aged 26 to 59: Prevalence and associated characteristics. Statistics Canada Cat 89–653–X. Retrieved from https://www150.statcan.gc.ca/n1/pub/89–653–x/89–653–x2016008–eng.htm

Statistics Canada. (2016c). 150 years of immigration in Canada. *The Daily*. Retrieved from https://www150.statcan.gc.ca/n1/pub/11–630–x/11–630–x2016006–eng.htm

Statistics Canada. (2017a). Aboriginal Peoples-Key Insights from 2016 Census. Statistics Canada. *The Daily*. Retrieved from https://www150.statcan.gc.ca/n1/daily-quotidien/171025/dq171025a-eng.htm

Statistics Canada. (2017b). Ethnic and cultural origins of Canadians: Portrait of a rich heritage. Retrieved from https://www12.statcan.gc.ca/census-recensement/2016/as-sa/98–200–x/2016016/98–200–x2016016–eng.cfm

Strong-Boag, V. (2016). Women's suffrage. *The Canadian Encyclopedia*. Retrieved from https://www.thecanadianencyclopedia.ca/en/article/womens-suffrage

Sweet, F. (2013). *Legal history of the color line: The rise and triumph of the one-drop rule*. New York: Backintyme.

Waters, M., & Eschbach, K. (1995). Immigration and ethnic and racial inequality in the United States. *Annual Review of Sociology, 22*, 419–446.

Yedlin, D. (2018). To some, it's the infamous five. *The Globe and Mail*. Retrieved from https://www.theglobeandmail.com/opinion/to-some-its-the-infamous-five/article746377/

Zenou, Y., & Boccard, H.. (1999). Racial discrimination and redlining in cities. *Journal of Urban Economics, 48*(2), 260–285.

Chapter 10

Beccaria C. ([1764] 1963). *On crimes and punishments*. Indianapolis, IN: Bobbs-Merrill.

Becker, H. (1963). *Outsiders: Studies in the sociology of deviance*. London: Free Press of Glencoe.

Behringer, W. (2004). *Witches and witch-hunts. A global history*. Malden, MA: Polity.

Bentham, J. ([1838] 1962). In John Bowring (Ed), *The works of Jeremy Bentham*. New York: Russel and Russel.

Benton, D. (2007). The impact of diet on anti-social, violent and criminal behaviour. *Neuroscience and Biobehavioral Reviews, 31*(5), 752–744.

Bias, S., & Evans, B. (2016, 7 November). Equality in the air? What happens if we view fat people as passengers with rights? *Huffington Post*. Retrieved from http://www.huffingtonpost.co.uk/stacy-bias/equality-in-the-air-what-_b_12838692.htm

Blumberg, J. (2007). Brief history of the Salem witch trials: One town's strange journey from paranoia to pardon. *Smithsonian.com*.

Bowers, L. (2000). *Social nature of mental illness*. UK: Routledge.

Bursik, R.J., & Grasmick, H.G. (1996). Neighbourhood-based networks and the control of crime and delinquency.

In H. Barlow (Ed.), *Crime and public policy* (pp. 107–130). Boulder: Westview Press.

Cain, P. (2019). How a weed conviction at 18 got a man banned at the U.S. border—37 years later. *Global News*. Retrieved from https://globalnews.ca/news/5381096/marijuana-conviction-banned-crossing-us-border/

CBC News. (2014, 26 November). Jian Ghomeshi to plead not guilty to sex assault, choking charges. Retrieved from https://www.cbc.ca/news/canada/jian-ghomeshi-to-plead-not-guilty-to-sex-assault-choking-charges-1.2850661

CTV News. (2014, 6 August). Bikini-clad women rally in Edmonton after woman taunted at beach. Retrieved from http://www.ctvnews.ca/health/bikini-clad-women-rally-in-edmonton-after-woman-taunted-at-beach-1.1948640

Donovan K. (2016, 26 October). CBC fires Jian Ghomeshi over sex allegations. *Toronto Star*. Retrieved from https://www.thestar.com/news/canada/2014/10/26/cbc_fires_jian_ghomeshi_over_sex_allegations.html

Donovan, K., & Hashem, A. (2015, 8 January). Jian Ghomeshi now charged with sexually assaulting 6 women. *Toronto Star*. Retrieved from https://www.thestar.com/news/crime/2015/01/08/jian_ghomeshi_trial_date_to_be_set_today.html#

Federici, S. (2004). *Caliban and the witch: Women, the body and primitive accumulation*. New York: Autonomedia.

Goffman, E. (1986). *Stigma notes on the management of spoiled identity*. United States: Prentice Hall.

Harris, K. (2018, 17 October). Liberal government to waive fee, waiting time for pot pardons. CBC News. Retrieved from https://www.cbc.ca/news/politics/pardon-pot-possession-goodale-1.4866175

Jankowiak, W., Volsche, S., & Garcia, J. (2015). Is the romantic-sexual kiss a near human universal? *American Anthropologist, 117*(3).

Kaplan, H., & Johnson, R. (2001). *Social deviance: Testing a general theory*. Berlin: Springer Science & Business Media

Kirkup, K. (2016, 26 January) How Ontario's prisons pioneered sensitivity to transgender inmates. TVO. Retrieved from http://tvo.org/article/current-affairs/shared-values/how-ontarios-prisons-pioneered-sensitivity-to-transgender-inmates

Liddell, M., & Martinovic, M. (2013). Women's offending: Trends, issues and theoretical explanations. *International Journal of Social Inquiry, 6*(1), 127–142.

Majumder, S. (2008). India grounds "fat" air hostesses. *BBC News*. Retrieved from http://news.bbc.co.uk/2/hi/south_asia/7439894.stm

Merton, R. (1957). *Social theory and social structure*. New York: Free Press.

Ontario Human Rights Commission (OHRC). (2018). *A collective impact: Interim report on the inquiry into racial profiling and racial discrimination of black persons by the Toronto Police Service*. Retrieved from http://www.ohrc.on.ca/en/public-interest-inquiry-racial-profiling-and-discrimination-toronto-police-service/collective-impact-interim-report-inquiry-racial-profiling-and-racial-discrimination-black#IV.%20Findings

Park, S., Holody, K., & Zhang, X. (2012). Race in media coverage of school shootings: A parallel application of framing theory and attribute agenda setting. *Journalism & Mass Communication Quarterly, 89*(3), 475–494

Perreault, S. (2015). Criminal victimization in Canada, 2014. *Juristat*. Statistics Canada Catalogue no. 85–002–X.

Reitano, J. (2017). Adult correctional statistics in Canada, 2015/2016. Statistics Canada Cat 85–002–x. Retrieved from https://www150.statcan.gc.ca/n1/pub/85–002–x/2017001/article/14700–eng.htm

Rigby, Peter. (1996). *African images: Racism and the end of anthropology*. Global Issues.

Rotenberg, C., & Cotter, A. (2018). Police-reported sexual assaults in Canada before and after #MeToo, 2016 and 2017. *Statistics Canada*. Retrieved from https://www150.statcan.gc.ca/n1/pub/85–002–x/2018001/article/54979–eng.htm?HPA=1

Sabin, J.A., Marini, M., & Nosek, B.A. (2012). Implicit and explicit anti-fat bias among a large sample of medical doctors by BMI, race/ethnicity and gender. *PLoS ONE, 7*(11), e48448. https://doi.org/10.1371/journal.pone.0048448

Savage, L. (2019). Female offenders in Canada, 2017. *Statistics Canada*. Retrieved from https://www150.statcan.gc.ca/n1/pub/85–002–x/2019001/article/00001–eng.htm#r10

Seigal, L., & McCormick, C. (2010). *Criminology in Canada: Theories, patterns and typologies* (3rd ed.). Toronto: Thomson Nelson

Sheldon, W. (1954). *Atlas of men: A guide for somatotyping the adult male at all ages*. New York: Harper.

Statistics Canada. (2015). Overweight and obese adults, 2014. Retrieved from https://www150.statcan.gc.ca/n1/pub/82–625–x/2015001/article/14185–eng.htm

Zekas, R. (2010, 1 May). Minding his peace and Q's artist in residence Jian Ghomeshi. Host of CBC Radio Q. *Toronto Star*. Retrieved from https://www.thestar.com/life/health_wellness/2010/04/29/jian_ghomeshi_minding_his_peace_and_qs.html

Ulrich, M.J. ([2003] 2010). Deviance and a social construct: An in class activity. trails: *Teaching Resources and Innovations Library for Sociology*. Originally published in B. Hoffman & A. Demyan (Eds.), *Deviance and social control*. Washington, DC: American Sociological Association.

Vyhnak, C. (2011, 30 November). Students put a gag on gossip. *Toronto Star*.

Westoll, N. (2017, 7 March). Canadian marijuana legislation timeline. *Global News*. Retrieved from https://globalnews.ca/news/3299980/canadian-marijuana-legalization-timeline/

Chapter 11

Amorevieta-Gentil, M., Bourbeau, R., & Robitaille, N. (2015). Migration among the First Nations. *Population Challenge and Life Course Strategic Knowledge Cluster Discussion Series, 3*(1).

Banerjee, D., & Bell, M.M. (2007). Ecogender: Locating gender in environmental social science. *Society & Natural Resources, 20*(1).

Barbieri, M., & Oullette, N. (2012). The demography of Canada and the United States from 1980s to the 2000s. *Population, 67*(2), 177–180.

Berchin, I.I., Valduga, I.B., Garcia, J., & de Andrade Guerra, J.B.S.O. (2017). Critical review: Climate change and forced migrations: An effort towards recognizing climate refugees. *Geoforum, 84*, 147–150. https://doi-org.proxy.library.brocku.ca/10.1016/j.geoforum.2017.06.022

Blake, E. (2019). Study says culturally-appropriate response vital for Indigenous evacuees. *CBC News*. Retrieved from https://www.cbc.ca/news/canada/north/indigenous-wildfire-evacuation-study-1.4993997

Bradley. (2017). More than misfortune: Recognizing natural disasters as a concern for transnational justice. *International*

Journal of Transnational Justice. Retrieved from https://academic.oup.com/ijtj/article/11/3/400/4161434

Bregman, R. (2016). The surprisingly compelling argument for open borders. *Fortune*. Retrieved from http://fortune.com/2016/04/17/immigration-open-borders/

Canadian Association of Petroleum Producers. (2019). *Crude oil forecast, markets and transportation*. Retrieved from https://www.capp.ca/publications-and-statistics/crude-oil-forecast

Canadian Index of Well-Being. (2018). *Ecological footprint*. Retrieved from https://uwaterloo.ca/canadian-index-wellbeing/what-we-do/domains-and-indicators/ecological-footprint

CBC Radio. (2019). We have to learn to live with fire: How wildfires are changing Canadian summers. Retrieved from https://www.cbc.ca/radio/we-have-to-learn-to-live-with-fire-how-wildfires-are-changing-canadian-summers-1.5135539

Chow, H.D.H. (2017). A time to be born and a time to die: Exploring the determinants of death anxiety among university students in a western Canadian city. *Death Studies, 41*(6), 345–352.

Cohen, J. (1995). Population growth and Earth's human carrying capacity. *Science, 269*(5222), 341. Retrieved from https://proxy.library.brocku.ca/login?url=http://search.ebscohost.com/login.aspx?direct=true&db=edsjsr&AN=edsjsr.2888267&site=eds-live&scope=site

Denyer & Gowen. (2018). Too many men. *The Washington Post*. Retrieved from https://www.washingtonpost.com/graphics/2018/world/too-many-men/?utm_term=.f189c245633b

Dominianni, C., Ahmed, M., Johnson, S., Blum, M., Ito, K., & Lane, K. (2018). Power outage preparedness and concern among vulnerable New York City residents. *Journal of Urban Health, 95*(5), 716–726. https://doi-org.proxy.library.brocku.ca/10.1007/s11524-018-0296-9

Ferreras, J., & Drolet, M. (2019). Canada can expect more nations to send trash back: Expert. *Global News*. Retrieved from https://globalnews.ca/news/5327533/canada-waste-recycling-asian-countries/

Gerber, L. (1984). Community characteristics and out-migration from Canadian Indian reserves: Path analysis. *Canadian Review of Sociology and Anthropology, 22*(2), 145–165.

Glover, D. (2014). Demographic transition model. *Population Education*. Retrieved from https://populationeducation.org/what-demographic-transition-model/

Grant, Z. P., & Tilley, J. (2019). Fertile soil: Explaining variation in the success of Green parties. *West European Politics, 42*(3), 495–516. https://doi-org.proxy.library.brocku.ca/10.1080/01402382.2018.1521673

Grinshteyn, E., & Hemenway, D. (2019). Violent death rates in the US compared to those of the other high-income countries, 2015. *Preventive Medicine, 123*, 20–26. https://doi-org.proxy.library.brocku.ca/10.1016/j.ypmed.2019.02.026

He, W., Goodkind, D., & Kowal, P. (2016). *An Aging World: 2015 International Population Reports*. Washington, DC: U.S. Government Printing Office.

Harvey, C. (2018, 2 January). Scientists can now blame individual natural disasters on climate change. *Scientific American*.

Herrmann, V. (2017). America's first climate change refugees: Victimization, distancing, and disempowerment in journalistic storytelling. *Energy Research & Social Science, 205*. https://doi-org.proxy.library.brocku.ca/10.1016/j.erss.2017.05.033

Institute for Policy Studies. (n.d.) *Facts: Inequality and Health*.

Jimenez, M. (2107, 8 February). Do ethnic enclaves impede integration? *Globe and Mail*.

Lynch, A. (2016). That how to confuse a millennial hashtag went down well then. *Metro*. Retrieved from http://metro.co.uk/2016/09/05/that-how-to-confuse-a-millennial-hashtag-went-down-well-then-6110078/

Martin, A.R., Cadotte, M.W., Isaac, M.E., Milla, R., Vile, D., & Violle, C. (2019). Regional and global shifts in crop diversity through the Anthropocene. *PLoS ONE, 14*(2), 1–18. https://doi-org.proxy.library.brocku.ca/10.1371/journal.pone.0209788

McCartney, G., Mahmood, L., Leyland, A., Batty, D., & Hunt, K. (2011). Contribution of smoking-related and alcohol-related deaths to the gender gap in mortality: Evidence from 30 European countries. *Tobacco Control, 20*(2), 166. Retrieved from https://proxy.library.brocku.ca/login?url=http://search.ebscohost.com/login.aspx?direct=true&db=edsjsr&AN=edsjsr.41320213&site=eds-live&scope=site

Ministry of the Environment. (2018). Made-in-Ontario environment plan. *Government of Ontario*. Retrieved from https://prod-environmental-registry.s3.amazonaws.com/2018-11/EnvironmentPlan.pdf

Momtaz, S., & Asaduzzaman, M. (2018). Climate change impacts and women's livelihood: Vulnerability in developing countries. New York: Routledge. Retrieved from https://proxy.library.brocku.ca/login?url=http://search.ebscohost.com/login.aspx?direct=true&db=cat00778a&AN=bu.b3149802&site=eds-live&scope=site

Parry, H. (2016). War on millennials! Baby boomers take to Twitter to point out the flaws of the younger generation with #HowToConfuseAMillenial hashtag. *Daily Mail*. Retrieved from http://www.dailymail.co.uk/news/article-3774839/War-Millennials-Baby-Boomers-Twitter-point-flaws-younger-generation-HowToConfuseAMillenial-hashtag.html

Patterson, M., Finn S., & Barker K. (2018). Addressing tuberculosis among Inuit in Canada. Canada *Communicable Disease Report, 44*(3/4), 82–5. https://doi.org/10.14745/ccdr.v44i34a02

Petric, S. (2018, 28 March). China is no longer world's dumping ground, but cleaning up its own backyard is proving to be a challenge. *CBC*.

Population Reference Bureau. (2009). 2018 world population data sheet with focus on changing age structures. Retrieved from https://www.prb.org/2018-world-population-data-sheet-with-focus-on-changing-age-structures/

Pulido, L. (2017). Environmental racism. *International Encyclopedia of Geography: People, the Earth, Environment, and Technology*. Retrieved from https://onlinelibrary.wiley.com/doi/abs/10.1002/9781118786352.wbieg0453

SAMHSA. (2017). *Greater impact: How disasters affect people of low socioeconomic status*. Retrieved from https://www.samhsa.gov/sites/default/files/dtac/srb-low-ses_2.pdf

Schandi, Hl, & Dodds, S. (2008). Balancing lives standards and environmental pressure. *Science Alert*.

Schnaiberg, A. (1980). *The environment: From surplus to scarcity*. New York: Oxford University Press.

Shapiro, D., & Tenikue, M. (2017). Women's education, infant and child mortality, and fertility decline in urban and rural sub-Saharan Africa. *Demographic Research, 37*, 21. https://doi-org.proxy.library.brocku.ca/10.4054/DemRes.2017.37.21

Smith, M.D. (2016, 2 June). First Nations communities suffering "more intense" impact of climate change, secret briefings. *National Post*.

Statistics Canada. (2015). *Life expectancy.*

Statistics Canada. (2017). Recent trends for the population aged 15 to 64 in Canada. *Statistics Canada Census Brief.* Retrieved from https://www150.statcan.gc.ca/n1/pub/89–645–x/2010001/life-expectancy-esperance-vie-eng.htm

Statistics Canada. (2019). *Settlement patterns and social integration of the population with an immigrant background in the Montréal, Toronto and Vancouver metropolitan areas.* Retrieved from https://www150.statcan.gc.ca/n1/en/pub/89–657–x/89–657–x2016002–eng.pdf?st=Q_AhvSxM

Sutton, P. (2007). *Environment: A sociological introduction.* Cambridge: Polity Press.

The Conference Board of Canada. (2013). Greenhouse gas (GHG) emissions. *How Canada Performs.* Retrieved from https://www.conferenceboard.ca/hcp/Details/Environment/greenhouse-gas-emissions.aspx

UNESCO. (2017). Background information brief. *United Nations World Water Assessment Programme.* Retrieved from http://www.unesco.org/new/fileadmin/MULTIMEDIA/HQ/SC/pdf/WWDR4%20Background%20Briefing%20Note_ENG.pdf

Ursdal, H. (2005). People vs. Malthus; Population pressure, environmental degradation and armed conflict. *Journal of Peace and Research, 42*(4), 417–436.

Velasco, J. (2016). *Open-border immigration policy: A step towards global justice. Migraciones Internacionales, 8*(4), 41–72.

Vidal, J. (2012, 26 April). Cut world population and redistribute resources, experts say. *The Guardian.*

Wackernagel, M., & Rees, W. (1996). Our ecological footprint: Reducing human impact on the earth. Philadelphia, PA: New Society Publishers.

World Health Organization. (2008). *Top 10 causes of death; Fact Sheet No 310.*

World Bank. (2017). *Fertility Rate 2017.*

Zagożdżon, P., Parszuto, J., Wrotkowska, M., Dydjow-Bendek, D. (2014, September). Effect of unemployment on cardiovascular risk factors and mental health. *Occupational Medicine, 64*(6), 436–441.

Chapter 12

Alcohol Collaborators. (2018). Alcohol use and burden for 195 countries and territories, 1990–2016: A systematic analysis for the Global Burden of Disease Study 2016. *The Lancet.* Retrieved from https://www.thelancet.com/journals/lancet/article/PIIS0140–6736(18)31310–2/fulltext

Amin, F. (2018, 1 February). Women short changed by health care gender gap: Women's College Hospital. *City News.* Retrieved from https://toronto.citynews.ca/2018/02/01/women-short-changed-health-care-gender-gap-womens-college-hospital/

Aparicio-García, M.E., Díaz-Ramiro, E.M., Rubio-Valdehita, S., López-Núñez, M.I., & García-Nieto, I. (2018). Health and Wellbeing of cisgender, transgender, and non-binary young people. *International Journal of Environmental Research and Public Health, 15*(10), 2133. https://doi.org/10.3390/ijerph15102133

Assari, S. (2017). Why do women live longer than men? *World Forum.* Retrieved from https://www.weforum.org/agenda/2017/03/why-do-women-live-longer-than-men

Association of Workers Compensation Boards of Canada. (AWCBC). (2019). *2017 fatalities in Canada by gender.* Retrieved from http://awcbc.org/?page_id=14

Azzad, A. (2018, 12 October). How climate change will affect your health. *CNN.* Retrieved from https://www.cnn.com/2018/10/12/health/climate-change-health-effects/index.html

Barua, B. (2017). When compared to similar countries, Canada's wait times are the worst. *Fraser Institute.* Retrieved from https://www.fraserinstitute.org/article/when-compared-to-similar-countries-canadas-health-care-wait-times-are-the-worst

Canadian Association of Midwives (CAM). (2019). What is a midwife? Retrieved from https://canadianmidwives.org/what-midwife/

Canadian Cancer Society's Advisory Committee on Cancer Statistics. (2015). *Canadian Cancer Statistics 2015.* Toronto, ON: Canadian Cancer Society..

Canadian Dental Association. (2017). The state of oral health in Canada. Retrieved from https://www.cda-adc.ca/stateoforalhealth/_files/thestateoforalhealthincanada.pdf

Canadian Institute for Health Information. (2015). *Trends in income related health inequalities.* Retrieved from https://www.cihi.ca/en/summary_report_inequalities_2015_en.pdf

Canadian Institute for Health Information (CIHI). (2018a). Alcohol harm on the rise for Canadian women. Retrieved from https://www.cihi.ca/en/alcohol-harm-on-the-rise-for-canadian-women

Canadian Institute for Health Information. (2018b). National health expenditure trends, 1975 to 2018. Retrieved from https://www.cihi.ca/en/health-spending/2018/national-health-expenditure-trends

Canadian Institute for Health Information. (2019). Emergency department wait times in Canada continue to rise. Retrieved from https://www.cihi.ca/en/emergency-department-wait-times-in-canada-continuing-to-rise

Canada Midwifery Regulators Council. (2017). Midwifery in Canada. Retrieved from https://cmrc-ccosf.ca/midwifery-canada

Centre for Disease Control and Prevention (CDC). (1999). *Achievements in public health 1900–1999.* Retrieved from https://www.cdc.gov/mmwr/preview/mmwrhtml/00056803.htm

Centre for Disease Control and Prevention (CDC). (2018a). Measles cases and outbreaks. Retrieved from https://www.cdc.gov/measles/cases-outbreaks.html

Centre for Disease Control and Prevention (CDC). (2018b). Mumps cases and outbreaks. Retrieved from https://www.cdc.gov/mumps/outbreaks.html

Chiu, M., Lebenbaum, M., Cheng, J., de Oliveira, C., & Kurdyak, P. (2017). The direct healthcare costs associated with psychological distress and major depression: A population-based cohort study in Ontario, Canada. *PLoS ONE, 12*(9), 1–13. https://doi-org.proxy.library.brocku.ca/10.1371/journal.pone.0184268

Conrad, P. (1992). Medicalization and social control. *Annual Review of Sociology, 18*(1), 209–232.

Conrad, P. (2007). *The medicalization of society.* Baltimore, MD: John Hopkins University Press.

Crenshaw, K. (1991). Mapping the margins: Intersectionality, identity politics, and violence against women of color. *Stanford Law Review, 43*(6), 1241. https://doi-org.proxy.library.brocku.ca/10.2307/1229039

Cumming, S., & Caragata, L. (2011). Rationing "rights": Supplementary welfare benefits and lone moms. *Critical Social Work, 12*(1), 66–85.

Educalcool. (2018). Alcohol and cancer risk. Retrieved from https://fqc.qc.ca/images/files/Alcohol%20and%20Risk%20of%20Cancer_VF.pdf

Emslie C., Hunt K., & Lyons, A. (2015). Transformation and time-out: The role of alcohol in identity construction among Scottish women in early midlife. *International Journal of Drug Policy, 26*(5), 437–445.

Feely, C., Burns, E., Adams, E., & Thomson, G. (2015). Why do some women choose to freebirth? A meta-thematic synthesis, part one. *Evidence-Based Midwifery, Royal College of Midwives,* 1, 4. Retrieved from http://search.ebscohost.com.proxy.library.brocku.ca/login.aspx?direct=true&db=edsgao&AN=edsgcl.452474444&site=eds-live&scope=site

Fenton, D. (2013). Who owns my life; Sue Rodriguez changed the way we think. *Windsor Star.* Retrieved from https://windsorstar.com/life/who-owns-my-life-sue-rodriguez-changed-how-we-think

GBD 2016 Alcohol Collaborators. (2018). Alcohol use and burden for 195 countries and territories, 1990–2016: A systematic analysis for the Global Burden of Disease Study 2016. *The Lancet.* Retrieved from https://www.thelancet.com/journals/lancet/article/PIIS0140–6736(18)31310–2/fulltext

Glaser, G. (2013). *Her best kept secret: Why women drink and how they can regain control.* New York: Simon & Schuster.

Goffman, E. (1983). The interaction order: American Sociological Association, 1982 presidential address. *American Sociological Review, 48*(1), 1–17.

Gomes, T., Khuu, W., Martins, D., Tadrous, M., Mamdani, M.M., Paterson, J.M., & Juurlink, D.N. (2018). Contributions of prescribed and non-prescribed opioids to opioid related deaths: Population based cohort study in Ontario, Canada. *British Medical Journal,* 1. Retrieved from https://proxy.library.brocku.ca/login?url=http://search.ebscohost.com/login.aspx?direct=true&db=edb&AN=131558401&site=eds-live&scope=site

Government of Canada. (2014). *Action for seniors.* Retrieved from https://www.canada.ca/en/employment-social-development/programs/seniors-action-report.html

Government of Canada. (2017). Health care in Canada. Retrieved from https://www.canada.ca/en/immigration-refugees-citizenship/services/new-immigrants/new-life-canada/health-care-card.html

Government of Canada. (2018a). Public health notice. Retrieved from https://www.canada.ca/en/public-health/services/public-health-notices/2018/outbreak-ecoli-infections-linked-romaine-lettuce.html

Government of Canada. (2018b). *Weekly measles and rubella report.* Retrieved from https://www.canada.ca/en/public-health/services/diseases/measles/surveillance-measles/measles-rubella-weekly-monitoring-reports.html

Government of Canada. (2018c). Canada's health care system. Retrieved from https://www.canada.ca/en/health-canada/services/health-care-system/reports-publications/health-care-system/canada.html

Government of Canada. (2018d). *National report: Apparent opioid-related deaths in Canada.* Retrieved from https://health-infobase.canada.ca/datalab/national-surveillance-opioid-mortality.html#ageSexAccidental

Government of Canada. (2018e). Family violence: How big is the problem? Retrieved from https://www.canada.ca/en/public-health/services/health-promotion/stop-family-violence/problem-canada.html

Government of Ontario. (2019). Vaccines for children at school. Retrieved from https://www.ontario.ca/page/vaccines-children-school#section-3

Gracey, M., & King, M. (2009). Indigenous health part 1: Determinants and disease patterns. *The Lancet, 374,* 65–75.

Gahagan, J., Gray, K., & Whynacht, A. (2015). Sex and gender matter in health research: Addressing health inequities in health research reporting. *International Journal for Equity in Health, 14*(12). Retrieved from https://equityhealthj.biomedcentral.com/articles/10.1186/s12939-015-0144-4

Hanrahan, M. (2017). Water (in)security in Canada: National identity and the exclusion of Indigenous peoples/L'(in)securite de l'eau au Canada: l'identite nationale et l'exclusion des peuples indigenes. *British Journal of Canadian Studies, 1,* 69. https://doi.org/10.3828/bjcs.2017.4

Health Canada. (2018). *Third interim report on medical assistance in dying.* Retrieved from https://www.canada.ca/content/dam/hc-sc/documents/services/publications/health-system-services/medical-assistance-dying-interim-report-june-2018/medical-assistance-dying-interim-report-june-2018–eng.pdf

Hensley, L. (2018). Alcohol is killing Canadians, So why are we still drinking? *Global News.* Retrieved from https://globalnews.ca/news/4634194/harms-of-drinking-alcohol/

Hollander, M., de Miranda, E., van Dillen, J., de Graaf, I., Vandenbussche, F., & Holten, L. (2017). Women's motivations for choosing a high risk birth setting against medical advice in the Netherlands: A qualitative analysis. *BMC Pregnancy and Childbirth,* 1, 1. https://doi-org.proxy.library.brocku.ca/10.1186/s12884–017–1621–0

Honjo, K. (2004). Social epidemiology: Definition, history and research examples. *Environmental Health and Preventive Medicine, 9*(5), 193–199. Retrieved from https://www.researchgate.net/publication/50833604_Social_Epidemiology_Definition_History_and_Research_Examples

Hussain, A., Ali, S., Ahmed, M., & Hussain, S. (2018). The anti-vaccination movement: A regression in modern medicine. *Cureus, 10*(7), e2919.

Inequality.org. (n.d.) Inequality and health. *Inquality.org.* Retrieved from https://inequality.org/facts/inequality-and-health/

Inhorn, M.C., & Whittle, K.L. (2001). Feminism meets the "new" epidemiologies: Toward an appraisal of antifeminist biases in epidemiological research on women's health. *Social Science & Medicine, 53*(5), 553–567. https://doi.org/10.1016/S0277-9536(00)00360-9

Islam, N. (2014). The dilemma of physician shortage and international recruitment in Canada. *International Journal of Health Policy & Management, 3*(1), 29–32. https://doi-org.proxy.library.brocku.ca/10.15171/ijhpm.2014.53

Jolley, D., & Douglas, K.M. (2013). The effects of anti-vaccine conspiracy theories on vaccination intentions. *PLoS ONE, 9*(2), 1–9. https://doi-org.proxy.library.brocku.ca/10.1371/journal.pone.0089177

Keane, H. (2014). Feminism and the complexities of gender and health. *Australian Feminist Studies, 29*(80), 180–188. https://doi-org.proxy.library.brocku.ca/10.1080/08164649.2014.928192

Keung, N. (2017, 15 March). Newcomers to Canada benefit from "healthy immigrant effect," Toronto study finds. *Toronto Star.* Retrieved from https://www.thestar.com/news/immigration/2017/03/15/immigrants-have-60–lower-mortality-rate-than-non-immigrants-toronto-study-finds.html

Kimmes, J.G., Beck, A.R., & Stith, S.M. (2019). Mental health factors and intimate partner violence perpetration and victimization: A meta-analysis. *Psychology of Violence, 9*(1), 1–17. https://doi-org.proxy.library.brocku.ca/10.1037/vio0000156.supp

King, M., Smith, A., & Gracey, M. (2009). Indigenous health part 2: The underlying causes of the health gap. *The Lancet, 374*(9683), 76–85.

Manzanares, J., Julian, M., & Carrascosa, A. (2006). Role of the cannabinoid system in pain control and therapeutic implications for the management of acute and chronic pain episodes. *Current Neuropharmacology, 4*(3), 239–257. Retrieved from https://www.ncbi.nlm.nih.gov/pmc/articles/PMC2430692/

Martin, S. (2018, 28 January). Fight to death: Why Canada's physician assisted dying debate has just begun. *Globe and Mail.* Retrieved from https://www.theglobeandmail.com/opinion/sandra-martin-physician-assisted-death-debate/article37742446/

Miller, B., & Croft, J. (2018, 8 October). Planet only has until 2030 to stem catastrophic climate change, experts warn. *CNN.* Retrieved from https://edition.cnn.com/2018/10/07/world/climate-change-new-ipcc-report-wxc/index.html

Ministere de la Sante et des Services Sociaux (MSS). (2012). Final report on the provincial outbreak of measles in 2011.

Moeller, J., & Quinonez, C. (2016). The association between income inequality and oral health in Canada: A cross-sectional study. *International Journal of Health Services.* Retrieved from https://journals-sagepub-com.library.sheridanc.on.ca/doi/full/10.1177/0020731416635078

Muirhead V, Quiñonez C., Figueiredo R., & Locker, D. (2009). Oral health disparities and food insecurity in working poor Canadians. *Community Dentistry & Oral Epidemiology, 37*(4), 294–304. https://doi-org.proxy.library.brocku.ca/10.1111/j.1600-0528.2009.00479.x

Murray-Davis, B., McDonald, H., Rietsma, A., Coubrough, M., & Hutton, E. (2014). Deciding on home or hospital birth: Results of the Ontario choice of birthplace survey. *Midwifery, 30*(7), 869–876. https://doi.org/10.1016/j.midw.2014.01.008

Navaneelan, T. (2012). Suicide rates: An overview. *Health at a Glance.* Statistics Canada Catalogue no. 82–624–X. Retrieved from https://www150.statcan.gc.ca/n1/pub/82–624-x/2012001/article/11696–eng.htm

Nestel, S. (2012). Colour coded health care: The impact of race and racism on Canadians' health. *Wellesley Institute.* Retrieved from http://nccdh.ca/resources/entry/colour-coded-health-care

Neumayer, E., & Plümper, T. (2016). Inequalities of income and inequalities of longevity: A cross-country study. *American Journal of Public Health, 106*(1), 160–165. https://doi.org/10.2105/AJPH.2015.302849

Nicolli, T., & Partridge, L. (2012). Ageing as *A Risk Factor. Current Biology, 22*(17), 741–752. Retrieved from https://www.science-direct.com/science/article/pii/S0960982212008159

Norris, S., & Williams, T. (2000). *Healthy aging, adding years to life and life to years.* Science and Technology Division. Retrieved from http://publications.gc.ca/Collection-R/LoPBdP/BP/prb0023–e.htm

Office of Women's Health (OWH). (2018). Effects of violence against women. Retrieved from https://www.womenshealth.gov/relationships-and-safety/effects-violence-against-women

Osuji, J., & Hirst, S. (2015). History of abuse and the experience of homelessness: A framework for assisting women overcome housing instability. *Housing, Care & Support, 18*(3/4), 89–100. https://doi-org.proxy.library.brocku.ca/10.1108/HCS-03–2015-0004

Palacois, M., & Barua, B. (2018). Price of public health insurance 2018. Fraser Institute. Retrieved from https://www.fraserinstitute.org/studies/price-of-public-health-care-insurance-2018–edition

Patterson, M., Finn, S., & Barker, K. (2018). Addressing tuberculosis among Inuit in Canada. *Canada Communicable Disease Report, 44*(3/4), 82. Retrieved from https://proxy.library.brocku.ca/login?url=http://search.ebscohost.com/login.aspx?direct=true&db=edb&AN=129377709&site=eds-live&scope=site

Pedersen, W., & Sandberg, S. (2013). The medicalisation of revolt: A sociological analysis of medical cannabis users. *Sociology of Health & Illness, 17.* Retrieved from https://proxy.library.brocku.ca/login?url=http://search.ebscohost.com/login.aspx?direct=true&db=edsgao&AN=edsgcl.315985620&site=eds-live&scope=site

Penner, D. (2018, 20 Augst). Doctors divided over cannabis legalization as deadline nears. *Vancouver Sun.* Retrieved from https://vancouversun.com/news/local-news/doctors-divided-over-cannabis-legalization-as-deadline-nears

Perrier, C. (2019, 3 January). Why some people are choosing freebirth over hospital births. *CBC Radio.* Retrieved from https://www.cbc.ca/radio/thecurrent/the-current-for-january-2-2019-1.4954395/why-some-women-are-choosing-freebirth-over-hospital-delivery-rooms-1.4963063

Perry, B.L. (2011). The labelling paradox: Stigma, the sick role, and social networks in mental illness. *Journal of Health and Social Behavior, 52*(4), 460–77. https://doi.org/10.1177/0022146511408913

Public Healthy Agency of Canada. (2013). What makes Canadians healthy or unhealthy? Retrieved from https://www.canada.ca/en/public-health/services/health-promotion/population-health/what-determines-health/what-makes-canadians-healthy-unhealthy.html

Rainey, J., Watkins, M., Ryman, T., Sandhu, P., Bo, A., & Banerjee, K. (2011). Reasons related to non-vaccination and under-vaccination of children in low and middle income countries: Findings from a systemic review of the published literature, 1999–2009. *Vaccine, 29*(46), 8215–8221. https://doi.org/10.1016/j.vaccine.2011.08.096

Rao, S., & Andrade, C. (2011). The MMR vaccine and autism: Sensation, refutation, retraction and fraud. *Indian Journal of Psychiatry, 53*(2), 95–96. Retrieved from https://www.ncbi.nlm.nih.gov/pmc/articles/PMC3136032/

Raphael, D. (2002). *Poverty, income inequality, and health in Canada.* Toronto: The CSJ Foundation For Research and Education.

Rocketto, L. (2018). The 10 health questions everyone was Googling in 2018—answered. *The Insider.* Retrieved from https://www.thisisinsider.com/most-searched-health-questions-of-2018–answers-2018–12

Roos, R. (2011, 24 May). US measles surge this year is biggest since 1996. *CIDRAP News.*

Sado, E., Kassahun, E., Bayisa, G., Gebre, M., Tadesses, A., & Mosisa, B. (2017). Epidemiology of self-medication with modern medicines among health care professionals in Nekemte town, Western Europe. *BioMed Central, 10,* 533. Retrieved from https://www.ncbi.nlm.nih.gov/pmc/articles/PMC5663131/

Sakai, Y. (2018). The vaccination kuznets curve: Do vaccination rates rise and fall with income? *Journal of Health Economics, 57*, 195–205. https://doi.org/10.1016/j.jhealeco.2017.12.002

Saunders, N.R., Gill, P.J., Holder, L., Vigod, S., Kurdyak, P., Gandhi, S., & Guttmann, A. (2018). Use of the emergency department as a first point of contact for mental health care by immigrant youth in Canada: A population based study. *Canadian Medical Association Journal, 190*(40). Retrieved from http://www.cmaj.ca/content/190/40/E1183

Siddiqi, S., & Sod-Erdene, O. (2018a). Income support recipients are in worse or no better health than their peers. Why is social assistance failing at this important objective? *Policy Options.* Retrieved from http://policyoptions.irpp.org/magazines/july-2018/social-assistance-is-not-improving-health/

Siddiqi, S., & Sod-Erdene, O. (2018b). Social assistance programs in Canada falling behind. Making evidence matter. Retrieved from https://evidencenetwork.ca/social-assistance-programs-in-canada-falling-behind/

Simpson, C., Walker, C., Drummond, D., Sinclair, D., & Wilson, R. (2017). How healthy is the Canadian health care system. *Queen's Gazette.* Queen's University. Retrieved from https://www.queensu.ca/gazette/stories/how-healthy-canadian-health-care-system

Statista Canada. (2018a). Alcohol consumption in Canada—statistics and facts. Retrieved from https://www.statista.com/topics/2998/alcohol-consumption-in-canada/

Statista Canada. (2018b). Medical marijuana in Canada—statistics and facts. Retrieved from https://www.statista.com/topics/3194/medical-marijuana-in-canada/

Statistics Canada. (2015a). Life expectancy. Retrieved from https://www150.statcan.gc.ca/n1/pub/89-645-x/2010001/life-expectancy-esperance-vie-eng.htm

Statistics Canada. (2015b). Women and health. Retrieved from https://www150.statcan.gc.ca/n1/pub/89-503-x/2010001/article/11543-eng.htm

Statistics Canada. (2018a). Cancer incidence in Canada 2015. Retrieved from https://www150.statcan.gc.ca/n1/daily-quotidien/180129/dq180129a-eng.htm

Statistics Canada. (2018b). Fact sheet cancer in Canada. Retrieved from https://www.canada.ca/en/public-health/services/publications/diseases-conditions/fact-sheet-cancer-canada.html?fbclid=IwAR21EUf324LjFM7jMWozI4g_0XyLCd0FXxHF8rGIbbKcv6b7gJrES7wuLII

Statistics Canada. (2018c). Life expectancy. Retrieved from https://www150.statcan.gc.ca/n1/pub/89-645-x/2010001/life-expectancy-esperance-vie-eng.htm

Wakefield, A.J., Murch, S.H., Anthony, A., Linnell, J., Casson, D.M., Malik, M. . . . Walker-Smith, J.A. (1998, 28 February). Ileal-lymphoid-nodular hyperplasia, non-specific colitis, and pervasive developmental disorder in children. *The Lancet, 351*(9103), P637–641.

Watson, B., & Osberg, L. (2018). Job insecurity and mental health in Canada. *Applied Economics, 50*(38), 4137–4152. https://doi-org.proxy.library.brocku.ca/http://www.tandfonline.com/loi/raec20

Wanless, D. M., Mitchell, B.A., & Wister, A.V. (2010). Social determinants of health for older women in Canada. Does rural-urban residency matter? *Canadian Journal on Aging/La Revue Canadienne du Vieillissement, 29*(2), 233–247.

Woodhall-Melnik, J., Dunn, J.R., Svenson, S., Patterson, C., & Matheson, F.I. (2018). Men's experiences of early life trauma and pathways into long-term homelessness. *Child Abuse & Neglect, 80*, 216–225.

World Health Organization. (n.d.). Climate change and human health—risks and responses. Retrieved from https://www.who.int/globalchange/summary/en/index6.html

World Health Organization. (2018a). *WHO vaccine preventable diseases: Monitoring system. Global Summary.* Retrieved from http://apps.who.int/immunization_monitoring/globalsummary/incidences?c=CHN

World Health Organization. (2018b). Epidemiology. Retrieved from https://www.who.int/topics/epidemiology/en/

World Health Organization. (2019). Social determinants of health. Retrieved from https://www.who.int/social_determinants/sdh_definition/en/

Zarulli, V., Barthold Jones, J.A., Oksuzyan, A., Lindahl-Jacobsen, R., Christensen, K., & Vaupel, J.W. (2018). Women live longer than men even during severe famines and epidemics. *Proceedings of the National Academy of Sciences of the United States of America.* https://doi.org/10.1073/pnas.1701535115

Index

Note: Page numbers in **bold** indicate definitions, and page numbers in *italics* indicate figures.

Wakefield, Andrew, 237
Walcott, Rinaldo, 14
Walker, R.J., 233
WALL-E (dir. Stanton), 225
Wang, F., 119
Ward, M. and M. Belanger, 165
waste, 228
water: demand for and consumption of, 225–7
Way, Maclain and Chapman Way, 45
wealth, 113; in Canada, 114–16, 117; global inequality and, 109; sociological imagination and, 5; super-rich people, 107; *see also* income inequality; poverty
Webb, E., D. Campbell, R. Schwartz, and L. Sechrest, 33–4
Weber, Max, 11, 98, 99–100, 113
Wechsler, Matt, 218
weight: as personal trouble and public issue, 4–6
Weinstein, Harvey, 141
welfare state, 24
Wells, John, 120
West, Candace and Don Zimmerman, 142
Weston, Galen, Sr., 107
"When I Grow Up" (Pussycat Dolls), *65*, 65
white privilege, 173–4, 178
Whorf, Benjamin, 47
Who Rules America, 124

Whose Land, 189
Wilcher, Deanie, 150
Wild Child, The (dir. Truffaut), 68
Wild Child: The Story of Feral Children (TLC), 68
Wild Country (dir. Way and Way), 45
wildfires, *215*
Winfrey, Oprah, 89
witches, 199–201, 207
Wollstonecraft, Mary, 26
women: advertising and, 134; alcoholism and, 243; contributions to sociology, 26–7; crime and, 207–8; divorce and, 159; elderly, 118; employment and work, 137; environment and, 229–30; gender inequality and, 27; gender roles and, 141; health and, 242; immigrant, 118, 161–2; Indigenous, 5, 118, 140; life expectancy and, 220–1; medicalization and, 247; Muslim, 90; in post-secondary education, 132; poverty and, 117–18; racialized, 119; reproductive choice and, 217; right to vote and, 179; in Saudi Arabia, 137; sexual assault and, 196; socialization and, 71; violence and, 139–40, 242; as witches, 199–201; work–family balance and, 161–2
Women's College Hospital, 242

Women's health: Intersection of policy, research and practice (Armstrong and Pederson), 257
Woodhall-Melnik, Julia et al., 240
words: cultural differences and meanings of, 47; untranslatable, 47
work. *See* employment and work
work–family balance, 160–2
workplaces, 92; family benefits and, 151; gender inequality in, 137–9; sexual harassment in, 140
World Health Organization (WHO), 220, 236, 237–8
World Inequality Report, 109
World Values Survey Database, 62
Wretched of the Earth, The (Fanon), 26
Wright, E.O., 124
Wright, R., 210

xenocentrism, **58**, **265**
xenophobia, **43**, *45*, 60, **265**
youth gangs, 78

Zenko, M., 104
Zero Tolerance for barbaric Cultural Practices Act, 185
Zimbardo, Philip, 38
Zimmerman, George, 184